Victorian Culture and the Origin of Disciplines

Current studies in disciplinarity range widely across philosophical and literary contexts, producing heated debate and entrenched divergences. Yet, despite their manifest significance for us today, seldom have those studies engaged with the Victorian origins of modern disciplinarity. *Victorian Culture and the Origin of Disciplines* adds a crucial missing link in that history by asking and answering a series of deceptively simple questions: how did Victorians define a discipline, what factors impinged upon that definition, and how did they respond to disciplinary understanding? Structured around sections on professionalization, university curriculums, society journals, literary genres, and interdisciplinarity, *Victorian Culture and the Origin of Disciplines* addresses the tangled bank of disciplinarity in the arts, humanities, social sciences, and natural sciences, including musicology, dance, literature, and art history; classics, history, archaeology, and theology; anthropology and psychology; and biology, mathematics, and physics. Chapters examine the generative forces driving disciplinary formation and gauge its success or failure against social, cultural, political, and economic environmental pressures. No other volume has focussed specifically on the origin of Victorian disciplines in order to track the birth, death, and growth of the units into which knowledge was divided in this period, and no other volume has placed such a wide array of Victorian disciplines in their cultural context.

Bennett Zon is Professor of Music at Durham University, where he is founding director of the Centre for Nineteenth-Century Studies. He is a founding co-director of the International Network for Music Theology, founding co-owner of Nineteenth-Century JISCmail, and founding general editor of *Nineteenth-Century Music Review* and the book series Music in Nineteenth-Century Britain. He received his DPhil in Music History from Oxford University. Recent publications include *Evolution and Victorian Musical Culture* and *Evolution and Victorian Culture* (co-edited with Bernard Lightman).

Bernard Lightman is Distinguished Research Professor of Humanities at York University, Toronto. He is a Fellow of the Royal Society of Canada and is currently President of the History of Science Society. Lightman received his PhD in the History of Ideas from Brandeis University. His research focusses on the cultural history of Victorian science. Among his most recent publications are the edited collections *Global Spencerism*, *A Companion to the History of Science*, and *Science Museums in Transition* (co-edited with Carin Berkowitz).

The Nineteenth Century Series

Series editors: Joanne Shattock and Julian North

The series focuses primarily upon major authors and subjects within Romantic and Victorian literature. It also includes studies of other nineteenth-century British writers and issues, where these are matters of current debate: for example, biography and autobiography; journalism; periodical literature; travel writing; book production; gender; non-canonical writing.

Recent in this series:

South Seas Encounters
Nineteenth-Century Oceania, Britain, and America
Edited by Richard Fulton, Stephen Hancock, Peter Hoffenberg, and Allison Paynter

Male Adolescence in Mid-Victorian Fiction
George Meredith, W. M. Thackeray, and Anthony Trollope
Alice Crossley

Wordsworth and Evolution in Victorian Literature
Entangled Influence
Trenton B. Olsen

Edward Lloyd and His World
Popular Fiction, Politics and the Press in Victorian Britain
Edited by Sarah Louise Lill and Rohan McWilliam

Science, Language, and Reform in Victorian Poetry
Political Dialects
Barbara Barrow

Victorian Culture and the Origin of Disciplines
Edited by Bernard Lightman and Bennett Zon

For more information about this series, please visit: https://www.routledge.com

Victorian Culture and the Origin of Disciplines

Edited by
Bernard Lightman and
Bennett Zon

Routledge
Taylor & Francis Group
NEW YORK AND LONDON

First published 2020
by Routledge
605 Third Avenue, New York, NY 10017

and by Routledge
2 Park Square, Milton Park, Abingdon, Oxon, OX14 4RN

First issued in paperback 2021

Routledge is an imprint of the Taylor & Francis Group, an informa business

Library of Congress Cataloging-in-Publication Data
A catalog record for this title has been requested

ISBN 13: 978-1-03-224093-0 (pbk)
ISBN 13: 978-0-367-22842-2 (hbk)

Typeset in Sabon
by codeMantra

Contents

List of Figures

List of Contributors

Rachel Bryant Davies is Lecturer in Comparative Literature at the Queen Mary University of London.

Theresa Jill Buckland is Professor of Dance History and Ethnography in the Department of Dance, University of Roehampton, London.

Simon Goldhill is Professor of Greek, University of Cambridge.

H. S. Jones is Professor of Intellectual History at the University of Manchester.

Roisín Laing is Leverhulme Early Career Fellow at Durham University.

Barbara Larson is Professor and Chair, Department of Art, University of West Florida.

Bernard Lightman is Distinguished Research Professor in the Humanities Department at York University, Toronto, Canada.

David Lowther is Leverhulme Early Career Fellow (Modern British History) in the Department of History, Durham University.

Renata Kobetts Miller is Professor of English and Deputy Dean of Humanities and the Arts at the City College of New York.

Joan Richards is Professor of History at Brown University.

Efram Sera-Shriar is Research Grants Manager and Museum Research Fellow at the Science Museum Group in London, United Kingdom.

Bennett Zon is Founding Director of the Centre for Nineteenth-Century Studies at Durham University.

Acknowledgements

Victorian Culture and the Origin of Disciplines is the result of an eponymous conference held in March 2016 at Durham University. The conference was one of many outcomes made possible through a very generously funded Christopherson-Knott Fellowship that Bennett Zon held at Durham in 2016. The fellowship was complemented by strong financial and administrative support of Durham's Institute of Advanced Study. We would also like to thank the Taylor & Francis Group of Routledge, in particular Bryony Reece, for their help in guiding the volume through the publication process as well as two anonymous referees for their useful suggestions, enabling us to strengthen the collection.

Introduction

Bernard Lightman and Bennett Zon

Currents in Disciplinarity

The Victorian biologist Thomas Henry Huxley once asserted, 'Neither the discipline nor the subject-matter of classical education is of such direct value to the student of physical science as to justify the expenditure of valuable time upon either'.[1] Read as a declaration of disciplinary warfare against the oppressive hegemony of classics, Huxley's denunciation could not be more clearly stated. Not only does he seem to denigrate the subject and discipline of classics; he also claims that an exclusively scientific education can produce culture just as well as a classical one: 'for the purpose of attaining real culture', he opines, 'an exclusively scientific education is at least as effectual as an exclusively literary education'.[2] Despairing categorical chauvinisms like this give the impression of arch disciplinary specializationism, and in many respects Huxley may well conform to type, but his disciplinary antagonism masques a deeper epistemic and educational concern. Far from arguing *against* classics and *for* science Huxley contends that science is just as indispensable a component in modern culture, and hence education, as classics.[3] He, it is often forgotten, was not arguing for the elimination of literature from education; rather he was claiming that modern literature, as well as science, should be added to a curriculum overly focussed on classical literatures and languages.[4] Huxley's disciplinary concerns are prescient because they directly imbricate anxieties over socio-educational organization and the power politics of knowledge.[5] Not only do they register a broad complaint against entrenched (often class-based) asymmetries in attitude towards the disciplines of science and classics; they also signal a deep and abiding engagement with the realities of disciplinarity and the lived cultural environment – with what we might characterize today as a distinction between disciplines as practice and disciplinarity as theory.

Current distinctions between practice and theory, disciplines and disciplinarity, begin in an etymological tension at the root of the word 'discipline' itself. According to Sugimoto and Weingart the *Oxford English Dictionary* describes discipline as the 'antithesis' of disciplinarity: 'Discipline pertains to practice or experience in the context of disciples or scholars, whereas doctrine (the property of the doctor or teacher) is more concerned with abstract theory'.[6] 'Antithesis' may be too strong a word for some, however, especially amongst theorists who make claims about the inextricable mutuality of theory and practice, and the dynamic instability of any disciplinary ontology. Citing Bourdieu, Luhmann, and Foucault, James Chandler, for instance, uses the terminology of 'system' to describe how disciplines intrinsically problematize the interactive, power-based relationship of theory and practice; disciplines 'compose a system' – 'as a network of relatively autonomous practices in asymmetrical relation to each other'.[7] Ronald Schleifer makes similar claims when he characterizes a discipline as a form of collaboration between theory and practice. For Schleifer disciplinary knowledge describes a subject 'that can be conceived as *collective* rather than individual and as *multi-modal* in its articulations'.[8] Christina Nadler advocates a not-dissimilar epistemic reading by using Deleuze and Guattari to explain a discipline as 'a plane of immanence', a deterritorialized 'boundless space without structure, only consisting of relations, movement, and affects'. In Nadler's terms, as an area of study and knowledge production, theory, and practice, a discipline is preconditioned as 'always already deterritorialized'.[9]

Inconclusive as it is, recent research proves that the entanglement of theory and practice need not discourage attempts at defining a discipline and disciplinarity. According to sociologist Sarah Burton a discipline is a discipline because it provides a sense of 'home': 'to adhere to a discipline is to be part of something'.[10] Ken Hyland articulates much the same sentiment by connecting disciplines to concepts of identity, community, and ultimately academic discourses: a discipline, he suggests,

> is a common enough label, used to describe and distinguish topics, knowledge, institutional structures, and individuals in the world of scholarship. While emergent multi-focused and practitioner-based fields may challenge conventional notions of academic disciplines, students and academics themselves typically have little trouble in identifying their allegiances.[11]

More negative appellations include terms like 'silos',[12] or Donald Campbell's epithet, 'the ethnocentrism of disciplines',[13] while more neutral terminology describes a discipline as a 'recognized community of researchers',[14] 'communities of practice',[15] an 'organized social grouping',[16] or even 'academic tribes'.[17] Incontestably, a home, community, group, or tribe can also be a site of discipline as control, however. Foucault, inevitably, looms large in disciplinary studies precisely for his assertion that discipline congenitally exerts mechanisms of control over traditional academic formations:[18] by necessity disciplines institutionalize knowledge.[19] Yet disciplinary 'home' is also constituted by a latticework of intersecting, self-regulatory factors designed to control control. Sugimoto and Weingart identify several factors corroborated for the nineteenth century by findings in *Victorian Culture and the Origin of Disciplines*, including the creation and triangulation of (1) theoretical conceptualizations about the discipline's understanding of cognition, society, communication, identity and separateness, tradition, and institutions; (2) historical and current narratives concerning its great men, societies and conferences, governmental funding and recognition, social need, institutional recognition, publications, and relationships to other disciplines; and (3) measurements of its quality and influence through citation, individual esteem, and the dissemination of ideas.[20]

Perhaps, unsurprisingly, the same taxonomy appears elsewhere in the literature, not least in textbooks on conducting interdisciplinary research. Repko and Szostak put it succinctly and maintain that established disciplines (1) claim a body of knowledge about certain subjects or objects; (2) have methods of acquiring knowledge and theories to order that knowledge; (3) seek to produce new knowledge, concepts, and theories within or related to their domains; (4) possess a recognized core of courses; (5) have their own community of experts; (6) are self-contained and seek to control their respective domains as they relate to each other; and (7) train future experts in their discipline-specific master's and doctoral programmes.[21] Definitions like this may give the impression that by their very nature disciplines always exist in a constant state of self-reification, but current trends in interdisciplinarity problematize that impression, and some of the chapters in *Victorian Culture and the Origin of Disciplines* positively disprove it from an historical perspective. A common feature of all disciplinary definitions, no matter how inveterately specialist, is the soluble or porous nature of disciplinary identity – even Repko and Szostak define a discipline as seeking 'to produce new knowledge, concepts, and theories within or *related to* [author's italics] their domains'.[22] Today the language of disciplinary relationality is ubiquitous: there is inter-, multi-, trans-, anti-, post-, de-, hegemonic, meta-, re-,[23] and even neo-disciplinarity,[24] each with its own theoretical and practical claims. But is prefixity-disciplinarity (to coin another neologism) so very different from Huxley's? Are we not arguing much the same thing in updated terminology?

Currents in Victorian Disciplinarity

Current theories of disciplinarity can only take us so far since they use as their starting point the contemporary state of the disciplines. How have scholars understood the condition of the disciplines during the Victorian period? The most extensive study of the Victorian disciplines can be found in Martin Daunton's edited collection *The Organisation of Knowledge in Victorian Britain* (2005). Daunton's book is thorough. It covers the natural sciences, mathematics, the social sciences, political economy, classics, history, English literature, universities and colleges, publishing, libraries, and the formation of the British Academy. Daunton states that the 'main concern in this collection of essays is with academic, official and legitimate knowledge'; the transmission of this type of knowledge into 'popular knowledge' is put to the side. Since the emphasis is on official knowledge and its organization, Daunton characterizes the 'prime aim' of the collection as the consideration of 'the epistemological sites of Victorian Britain and how they were ordered'. The book, then, concentrates on privileged sites of knowledge, such as clubs or societies; national bodies such as the Royal Geographical Society; the exclusive Royal Society and British Academy; institutions of higher learning; and state institutions such as Kew Gardens, the Royal Observatory, and the British Museum. *The Organisation of Knowledge in Victorian Britain* explores how each of these bodies had their own distinctive structure of power and authority.[25]

Surprisingly, the chapters have relatively little to say about the state and development of the disciplines, even though half of the chapters are organized around a specific discipline. The index contains only four references under the heading of 'disciplines'. The decision to pursue a line of analysis that emphasizes individual sites of knowledge does not always highlight how disciplines cut across space and time. When contributors to the collection explicitly take up the theme of disciplines, two major points emerge. First, as Daunton asserts, 'disciplines formed a hierarchy, determined by the status of their practitioners, the social cachet provided by different forms of knowledge, and the intellectual standing of their epistemology'. Those disciplines with the highest intellectual standing from 1820 to 1860 were ones that adopted analytical procedures. After the 1860s the experimental method reigned supreme.[26] Here Daunton draws on the chapter by John Pickstone, where he discusses his important notion of different ways of knowing, with its obvious debts to Foucault.[27]

Second, as John Gibbins declares in the Daunton collection, the nineteenth century was a particularly important period for the development of new disciplines in the arts and social sciences, many of which are recognizable today: 'Sociology, psychology, philosophy, politics, economics, history, anthropology, geography, languages, literature, philology, and education', Gibbins states, 'became mature or *sui generis* in this period'. Since, according to Gibbins, very few new disciplines have emerged since 1900 in the arts, humanities, and social sciences, the two generations of scholars that 'pioneered' the organization of knowledge in Britain from 1830 really 'constructed the architecture of knowledge' that we now work with. But how did the new disciplines originate? Gibbins maintains that the new disciplines formed from the old ones 'like offshoots of old stars'.[28] They formed, as Carol Atherton submits, due to the related 'processes of professionalisation and specialisation'. Over the course of the century the Victorian 'man of letters' who wrote for a broad and general audience was replaced by professional academics who wrote for specialist audiences, primarily their fellow professionals.[29] Daunton's important collection, and the prominence it gives to the role of epistemological sites, disciplinary hierarchies, and the processes of professionalization and specialization, provides an excellent springboard for the more forensic investigation of causalities defining the methodology underpinning *Victorian Culture and the Origin of Disciplines.*

Apart from Daunton, Victorian disciplines are usually studied piecemeal, often as a part of larger, more disciplinary focussed studies. In his *Cultural Boundaries of Science* (1999), for example, Thomas Gieryn has explored another concept of relevance to understanding the disciplines arising out of relatively recent scholarship. Reinterpreting Bourdieu's understanding of cultural reproduction and Giddens's concept of social structuration, and broadly reflecting theoretical currents in Romanticism and concepts of disciplinary boundary,[30] Gieryn discusses how sociologists treat the boundaries of science as 'episodically established, sustained, enlarged, policed, breached, and sometimes erased in the defense, pursuit, or denial of epistemic authority'. The ever-changing arrangement of boundaries and territories is always 'contingent upon immediate circumstances'. Gieryn applies this dynamic picture of the relationship between science and 'non-science' to an analysis of nineteenth-century British physicist John Tyndall's boundary work. In order to create an autonomous cultural space for science Tyndall had to redraw the boundaries of the Victorian cultural landscape so that beliefs about religion or mechanics could not be used to frustrate the professional needs of scientists. As Gieryn asserts, Tyndall had not only to demonstrate what science is 'but why and how science is not-religion and not-mechanics'. This complicated '"double" boundary-work' – for Tyndall was building different boundaries on two fronts – was intended to place science in a powerful position in the competition for cultural authority and occupational resources.[31] But for Gieryn, as for many sociologists and historians of science, science is a product of culture. Therefore Gieryn's observations about the boundary work undertaken by scientists like Tyndall are not just valid for the scientific disciplines. All disciplines are created through boundary work contingent on the specific context at that particular point in time. Disciplines are constantly changing protean bodies of knowledge because their practitioners are continuously shoring up old boundaries or erecting new ones in light of changing social, political, economic, and cultural circumstances. If this can be said about science, usually looked upon as one of the most stable forms of knowledge, then it can be said about any discipline. As Max Schoenfield suggests,

> Modern European humanism was an interdisciplinary project—a merger of economic, cultural, technological, and political formations.

> It involved . . . the interlocked transformations of boundaries, permeable boundaries among disciplines, and the organization of those disciplines as professional and intellectual categories.[32]

However, against the concept of ever-changing boundaries between disciplines in the nineteenth century, we must also recognize the insights coming out of scholarly work that emphasizes the continuities in Victorian intellectual life. Back in the early seventies the neo-Marxist scholar Robert Young argued that natural theology formed a common context for Victorian knowledge in the first half of the nineteenth century and that evolution filled the same role in the second half of the century.[33] Although Young's notion of a common context has been heavily criticized in recent decades, there is yet an important insight to be gleaned from his work. Demarcation disputes leading to a realignment of boundaries between disciplines throughout the century have to be seen against the backdrop of the notion of a larger unity of knowledge. Despite realizing that in 1834 science was endlessly subdividing into new, seemingly disconnected, disciplines the polymathic William Whewell, Master of Trinity College, Cambridge, believed that there were general principles that united the disintegrating empire of science.[34] Although figures from the second half of the century might have disagreed with the theological principles that sustained Whewell's belief in a fundamental unity underlying the sciences, they would have shared his enthusiasm for some conception of oneness connecting all knowledge. Whether it was an evolutionary unity or something else, it was a unity nonetheless. Writing in *A New History of the Humanities* (2013), for example, Rens Bod makes a not dissimilar claim of disciplinary history more largely. For Bod the history of the humanities is a study in finding 'metapatterns', i.e. ascertaining principles and patterns that allow us 'to discern new patterns not found by humanities scholars themselves'.[35] Contesting Dilthey's division between the concern of sciences (explaining) and humanities (understanding), Bod describes disciplinary boundaries collapsed by methodological mutuality: 'the quest for principles and patterns in the humanities is a continuous tradition', he avers.[36]

Disciplinarity in *Victorian Culture and the Origin of Disciplines*

Insofar as possible this volume eschews the trappings of using preconceived theoretical templates in favour of a simpler, perhaps rhetorical device by posing, and then seeking, an answer to a series of deceptively simple questions which have never previously been asked together: how did Victorians define a discipline? What factors impinged upon that definition? How did they respond to disciplinary understanding? We aim to address these questions by focussing on Victorian culture and its creation, maintenance, and promulgation of disciplines, covering the period of the long nineteenth century. We gather as evidence those aspects of culture we consider to be essential to the formation of a discipline, including an examination of professionalization, university curriculums, society journals, literary genres, and interdisciplinarity, and we use those aspects to organize our volume's structure. To provide as much breadth as possible *Victorian Culture and the Origin of Disciplines* addresses disciplinarity from the arts, humanities, social sciences, and sciences: for example musicology, dance, literature, and art history; classics, history, archaeology, and theology; anthropology and psychology; and biology, mathematics, and physics. Many of the chapters examine either the origins and birth of a new discipline or the radical re-definition of an older, already-established discipline. By locating the creation and evolution of a discipline within its cultural context, however, we can go further. We can discover the generative forces driving disciplinary formation and gauge its success or failure against social, cultural, political, and economic environmental pressures. Failure to protect, or expand, the territory of a discipline could, for example, lead to amalgamation with another discipline, and possibly even its complete extinction. The volatile environment also produced conditions favourable for creating new disciplines, however.

No other volume has focussed specifically on the origin of Victorian disciplines in order to track the birth, death, and growth of the units into which knowledge was divided in this period, and no other volume has placed such a wide array of Victorian disciplines in their cultural – and arguably organic – context. The importance of the Victorian age for the development of the disciplines is undeniable. However, instead of conceiving of disciplines as being formed from old ones like offshoots of old stars, as Gibbins put it in the Daunton volume, perhaps it is more compelling to adopt a genuinely organic metaphor. For understanding Victorian disciplines through an examination of such issues as professionalization, university curriculums, society journals, literary genres, boundary making, and interdisciplinarity has revealed the existence of a complex 'tangled bank' of disciplinary roots and plants, to draw on Darwin's vivid metaphor from the final paragraph of the *Origin of Species*. Some of the growths are healthy, while others are in a state of decay or even death. The intertwined roots and plants are sometimes hard to separate, even if the tools of specialization and professionalization are used in the attempt to tease them apart. A simple story of specialization and professionalization cannot fully encompass the lush disciplinary vegetation that thrived in the Victorian period. This volume is an attempt to offer a more complex and culturally organic account. Inevitably, however, with a book of this size it is impossible to cover all disciplines, or their cultural contexts. The findings in our representative sampling are, however, indicative of research which could benefit from being tested by digital methodologies underpinning collaborative projects, like those linking the University of Virginia's Networked Infrastructure for Nineteenth-Century Electronic Scholarship and Springer's recent series The Digital Nineteenth Century.[37]

Chapters

The volume is divided into six thematic sections, each containing two chapters. The first section, 'Professional Validation', deals with the relationship between professional validation and disciplinary development in natural science and the study of dance. Bernard Lightman's chapter tracks the emergence of the new scientific disciplines during the nineteenth century. Behind the move away from natural history and natural philosophy towards the modern scientific disciplines that we are familiar with lies a complex story of institutional, as well as social, generational, and cultural transformation. He explores one crucial aspect of this process: the interplay between the creation of new disciplines and the enduring desire to unify science. In the first half of the century religious concepts provided the glue that integrated natural philosophy and natural history into a coherent whole. John Herschel's *A Preliminary Discourse on the Study of Natural Philosophy* (1830) and William Swainson's *A Preliminary Discourse on the Study of Natural History* (1834) are his representative texts. During the second half of the century some Victorian scientists continued to cultivate a similar vision of unity, though against the backdrop of the decline of natural history and natural philosophy as disciplinary categories. Here Lightman's central figures are Francis Orpen Morris, Lord Kelvin, and James Clerk Maxwell. But at the same time another group of Victorian scientists, which included John Tyndall and T. H. Huxley, pushed for a more thoroughgoing redefinition of science that grounded unity in more secular, professional principles. Their goal, Lightman argues, was to transform the disciplinary landscape, which required that they challenge the institutions that supported the old vision of unity.

Since the study of dance did not become a university discipline until the twentieth century, Theresa Buckland's chapter in the section on professional validation focusses on the earlier, tentative moves towards disciplinary status during the nineteenth century. She discusses how dance professionals in Victorian Britain looked towards France as a model, which since the mid-seventeenth century boasted a nationally organized body of experts, and provided the Eurocentric world with the best of its teachers and dancers. Purveying a codified system of deportment and movement that signalled social status, the British dancing master himself (or occasionally herself) was often ridiculed and criticized as socially pretentious and inconsequential. Unregulated in their practice and without nationally recognized credentials, leading dancing teachers in the

Victorian period made several unsustained attempts to professionalize their occupation. It was not until the later nineteenth century, however, that there appeared long-standing professional organization among instructors, a few dedicated journals by and for dance professionals, a limited number of monographs, and scientific interest from outside the subject's ranks. A specialist society on the subject (focussed on folk dance) was only established in 1911.

The second section, 'University Education', focusses on the development of art history and history as disciplines in the universities. As Daunton points out, the universities did not move to the centre of the organization of knowledge until the end of the century, after the University of Cambridge redefined itself as a major research university on the German model and the provincial institutions in England followed a similar path.[38] Barbara Larson's chapter examines the agenda of the first art historians who were appointed as chairs within universities or art institutions in Europe. Within the span of twenty years Germany, Austria, France, and Britain witnessed the establishment of chairships in art history, marking the academic institutionalization of a nascent discipline formerly attached to history, aesthetics, and nationalist antiquarianism. Larson argues that consolidation of this field within the academy and its validation as a discipline through the appointment of chairships are aligned with a scientific, positivist outlook held by early chairs that eschewed the notion that art was in essence subjective and its history ultimately unmoored from a rational trajectory. Britain's first art history chair (University of Edinburgh, 1880), Gerard Baldwin Brown, was a follower of Spencer. Brown believed that social and evolutionary forces lie behind the historical creation of art. Artistic products were the result of communal celebrations with roots in animal instincts. Art making had only become possible when, through evolutionary history, humans no longer had to expend all of their energy in the act of survival. Effervescent energy could be applied to the creation of art. In sum, positivist thinking by early art history chairs in Germany, France, and England at a critical moment in discipline formation helped to build the field's credibility through alignment of its methodologies with those of medicine and the natural sciences.

While Larson deals with art history and university education, H. S. Jones draws our attention to the development of history as a discipline within the universities, focussing on the figure of Thomas Tout at the University of Manchester. In the early twentieth century, the Manchester History department, shaped by Tout, was hugely influential in the British historical profession. Tout is usually seen as one of the leading historians who aimed to displace the Whiggish pieties of William Stubbs and Edward Augustus Freeman in the name of a professionalism that laid claim to a scientific authority founded on specialization. Tout's department invented the undergraduate thesis in the United Kingdom;

Tout was an early advocate of graduate studies; and he wrote of the importance of creating 'historical laboratories'. This makes Tout sound like an unalloyed modernist. But Jones argues that the significance of Tout for the discipline is more complex than this narrative implies. Jones reminds us that Tout was a pupil of Stubbs, wrote a reverential obituary of Freeman, and was not inclined to disparage the previous generation of historians. Jones's chapter sets out a new account of the Victorian roots of the conception of historical practice espoused by Tout. It emphasizes the formative influence of the struggle for an independent University of Manchester – launched before Tout's arrival, and finally achieved in 1903–1904 – in shaping the professional identity of Tout and his peers. There was a structural connection between a federal university in which the examining function was separate from the teaching and an approach to historical education which focussed on the communication of the results of historical research. The dissolution of the federal structure released Tout and his colleagues to forge a new approach which foregrounded the processes and techniques of research. What the case of Tout's Manchester School of History demonstrates, then, is the importance of institutional contexts in shaping how academic disciplines were defined and practised.

The third section, 'Society Journals', highlights the importance of societies and their journals for the development of the disciplines, in particular zoology and anthropology. Societies and journals were perhaps more significant earlier in the century, when the universities were not yet at the centre of the organization of knowledge. David Lowther addresses the role of the journal focussing on two notable episodes in the relatively short life of the *Magazine of Natural History*, founded in 1828 by John Claudius Loudon. In 1844, Hugh Strickland published 'The Strickland Rules', an innocuous-looking document that laid the foundations of modern zoological classification and established the authority of a new class of 'professional' naturalist. Lowther treats it as the culmination of a highly visible battle for dominance, played out in the natural history periodicals that flourished from 1820 onwards. Enjoying a wide circulation that extended far beyond the rarefied world of London's scientific institutions, 'middle-brow' publications such as the *Magazine of Natural History* were important scientific forums in which scientific reputations were made and broken. Encouraged by commercially minded editors, Strickland and his principal opponents, Nicholas Vigors and William Swainson, engaged in a heated war of words in which abstruse zoological theory was interwoven with venomous personal invective. This chapter analyses how the ruthless entrepreneurial practices of journal editors, including Loudon and Edward Charlesworth, often drove the pace of scientific debate in these important transitional years. Taking as his focus the writings of Strickland, Vigors, and their supporters in the *Magazine of Natural History* and *Magazine of Zoology and Botany*,

Lowther demonstrates that science publishers acted not as passive agents but as knowledge brokers, whose concern to cater for their audiences had a profound impact on the development of zoology at the dawn of the Victorian age.

Moving from the debates within zoology during the 1830s, Efram Sera-Shriar examines the anthropological schism of the 1860s as a critical event in the disciplinary history of British anthropology. During this period, researchers on either side of the debate fervently argued over the theoretical and methodological scope of the emerging science. Sera-Shriar spotlights the role of the periodical press in shaping the dispute. His chapter examines the significance of the *Anthropological Review* (AR) against the backdrop of the schism. In 1867 the executive members at the Anthropological Society of London (ASL) invited the philologist and engineer Hyde Clarke to join their council. Clarke was reluctant to accept the position unless he was allowed to look over the society's financial records. He discovered that the ASL was deeply in debt and that they owed their printers over £1,700. According to Clarke there were two reasons for this deficit. First, the society failed to collect regular subscription payments from its members, and second the executive council was paying the publishing costs of the *AR*. Clarke did not understand why the ASL was paying for the debts accrued by the *AR* because it was not an official ASL publication but, as the periodical routinely argued, an independent journal free from the politics of the society and designed for the open exchange of anthropological ideas in Britain. Sera-Shriar discusses how Clarke approached several leading members of the executive council about this monetary discrepancy, who avoided answering any of Clarke's queries. Frustrated by his multiple failed attempts to uncover the reasons behind this apparent misuse of societal funds Clarke began publishing a series of letters in the *Athenaeum* demanding answers regarding the relationship between the ASL and the *AR*. This chapter shows how the scandal involving the management of the *AR* publicly exposed the corruption occurring at the ASL, led to the eventual downfall of James Hunt as a disciplinary figurehead, and resulted in the end of the schism and the beginning of a new era in British anthropology. Both Lowther and Sera-Shriar demonstrate that journals were key factors in the definition of British anthropology and zoology, and were an essential part of the identity of these disciplines during the critical years of their formation.

The fourth section, on 'Literary Genres', explores Victorian archaeology and child psychology. Whereas the Daunton collection explicitly excludes consideration of the popularization of knowledge, Davies sees the representation of archaeology for a broad reading audience in the periodical press to be of particular importance.[39] Davies examines the relationship between literary genres in Victorian popular culture and the development of disciplines, specifically how evidence from the Victorian popular press fits with existing accounts of the development and separation of archaeology as a discipline. Of the numerous ruined cities uncovered and imaginatively revivified in Victorian Britain, Homer's Troy was the most hotly disputed. Drawing on newspaper reports and periodicals, aimed at children as well as adults, Davies examines the range of British reactions to Homer's Troy as a test case for public perceptions of archaeology and antiquarianism. She traces the extent to which archaeology emerged as a discrete, commonly accepted, discipline in the press: while adverts listed archaeology as a subject for public women's lectures, boys' journals presented archaeologists as heroic role-models and *Girls Own Paper* ran a lengthy series explaining 'Archaeology for Girls'; yet 'the antiquarian and archaeologist' often appeared inseparable or interchangeable. Classical archaeology offers a particularly complex, and visible, example of print media's active formation of the publicly recognized identities of new disciplines and their popular understandings in nineteenth-century Britain.

Roisín Lang's analysis of the two-way traffic between autobiography and child psychology continues the examination of literary genres and disciplines. The investigation of evolutionary theory following the publication of Darwin's *Origin of Species* in 1859 instigated the revolutionary process of reimagining the Christian soul as the psychological 'self'. The clearest expression of this self was found in the Victorian idea of childhood. The emergence of a specific psychology of the child was therefore inevitable. The same search for selfhood in childhood accounts for the proliferation of autobiographical accounts of the child's interiority from mid-century onwards. The invention of Child Study seems to have been propagated by debates about language acquisition. Laing's chapter demonstrates that the process of language acquisition offered a specifically progressive model of selfhood, because it demarcated a clear line dividing the developing child from the self that is its end.

Laing discusses how in Frances Hodgson Burnett's autobiography, *The One I Knew the Best of All* (1893), and in the work of James Sully and fellow pioneers of Child Study, the remembered child is portrayed as the self before language. By acquiring language, and using it to articulate the child's experience, the adult resolves the disjunction between self and language which this Other self, the childhood self, represents. In other words, Child Study and Victorian autobiography presented selfhood as the adult expression of a childhood impression of the self. Each thus informed the other to offer a model of selfhood in which the child is the origin to the adult self as an end.

The fifth section takes us from literary genres to 'Disciplinary Boundaries'. Both Simon Goldhill and Joan Richards deal with the theme of how disciplines were demarcated. In the case of Goldhill, classics and theology fought over the same territory: antiquity. For Richards, boundary work took place within mathematics itself when different generations of practitioners held to opposed conceptions of what core questions to be answered by the discipline. Goldhill explores the interconnections between the two dominant disciplines of the nineteenth-century university, namely, classics and theology. Although Christian theology had an unending and constantly anxious gaze at the classical world in which it took shape – in opposition and in appropriation – in the nineteenth-century university there was a particular and particularly intense interaction between these fields as the institutionalization, professionalization, and intensification of border disputes between disciplines come to dominate the landscape of scholarship. Goldhill's chapter traces the nineteenth-century configuration of the long battle between classics and theology as approaches to antiquity, as systems of values, and as understandings of the world – and argues that the two fields acted in a hybrid, intermingled way which stands against the standard story of increasing disciplinary separation and fortification. It begins with a general introduction that explores the basic facts of how the university's curriculum was dominated by these two fields, and how these two fields together played an especially vibrant role in the cultural imagination of Britain. Understanding the past of antiquity was fundamental to the historical self-understanding of the nineteenth century, and this made the study of antiquity the battleground on which were contested major political issues (democracy, for example, or Empire), cultural issues (what opera or the theatre should be), and religious belief (what was the early church). Next the chapter looks at the lived experience of the academic leaders of Victorian scholarship; at methodology, and the shared approaches to the study of antiquity and especially its texts that worked to set philology as the queen of sciences in the eyes of the university; and, finally, at how the interpretation of Greek tragedy was constantly informed by theological presuppositions and agendas. In sum, the chapter shows how continually embroiled classics and theology remain as disciplines – even until today, even when studiously disavowed by both sides. Disciplinary boundaries are difficult to maintain.

In her study of Victorian mathematics, Richards tracks the epistemological changes that redefined the discipline. Mathematics was one of the oldest disciplines. It was an essential part of the curriculum of the medieval universities, and unlike music, for example, maintained that position through the seventeenth century and beyond. Richards insists that it would be a mistake to take its longevity as a mark of constancy, however; she shows that mathematics was a properly plural word and a many-splendoured thing. A myriad of complex negotiations were hidden behind its apparent stability. The creation of mathematics as a discipline in the Victorian nineteenth century is an excellent example of this kind of negotiation. At the beginning of the century the mark of a legitimate mathematical statement was that it was ***true***, in some way that could be directly grasped; by the end of the period that same legitimacy meant that it could be ***proved*** within a well-defined mathematical framework.

This shift was essential to the creation of modern mathematics. Whereas the mathematics of truth was a subject without limits, the mathematics of proof was a subject with clearly defined boundaries. These boundaries were the prerequisite for the creation of mathematics as a discipline. Richards's chapter considers the career of Augustus De Morgan as a locus for this development in nineteenth-century England.

The final section moves from the construction of disciplinary boundaries to a discussion of 'Interdisciplinarity' in literature and musicology. Both the previous section and this one raise questions about the notion that a simple story about specialization can accurately describe the development of disciplines in the nineteenth century. Of course specialization is not some inevitable law of intellectual development, especially when disciplines were so mutable in this period. Instead, Miller and Zon depict the period as one in which a dynamic interdisciplinary ideal was still in play. Miller's chapter begins with the debate between Thomas Henry Huxley and George Henry Lewes on the value of specialization. In January 1854, Huxley used his first column in the *Westminster Review* to criticize Lewes for lacking a practitioner's experience required to write knowledgeably about contemporary science. George Eliot and Lewes rejoined by characterizing Huxley as a narrow specialist. Against this backdrop, Miller argues that *Middlemarch* (1871–2) provides a view into Eliot's interdisciplinarity. Setting her novel in the years 1829 through 1831, Miller asserts, allows Eliot to consider science before it had crystallized as a discipline. However, Miller shows that interdisciplinarity is only fathomable in a world of disciplines, and that interdisciplinarity in *Middlemarch* is informed by disciplinary developments that the British Association for the Advancement of Science, which was founded in 1831 to represent an emerging class of professional scientists, reflected and shaped in the forty years between the novel's setting and its writing. In this context, the character Tertius Lydgate represents a union of art and science as well as medicine and biological research that would prove unsustainable, while the Reverend Farebrother represents a union of science and religion that would be rent asunder over theories of evolution. This chapter examines how a particular novel engaged with the emergence of disciplines in the nineteenth century. It explores the ways in which literary genres and narrative forms were shaped by the rise of disciplines, and how literary genres and narrative forms contributed to how such disciplinary lines were both drawn and crossed.

Bennett Zon also deals with the issue of interdisciplinarity, but this time in the discipline of musicology. He meditates on one of the most rhetorically arcane proclamations of its time: Walter Pater's declaration that 'All art constantly aspires towards the condition of music'. Pater, Zon argues, relies upon two complementary concepts to justify his claim, ekphrasis and anders-streben. Ekphrasis 'produces images for the mind's eye by means of words'; anders-streben, literally other-seeking, is 'a partial alienation from its own limitations, through which the arts are able, not indeed to supply the place of each other, but reciprocally to lend each other new forces'. Together they form one of the earliest theorizations of Victorian interdisciplinarity. If all arts aspire to the condition of music, do all disciplines aspire to the condition of musicology? This chapter hazards an answer by utilizing contemporary musicology to exemplify the epistemic contradiction at the heart of Victorian disciplinarity, interdisciplinarity. An introduction investigates Pater as interdisciplinary exemplar; a main section applies his theories to (a) the development of professional organizations like the Musical Association; (b) developments in university education at Oxford, Cambridge, and London; and (c) popularization through academic and non-academic musical presses; and a conclusion locates Pater as the theoretical ancestor of the term 'interdiscipline'.

Notes

1 Thomas Henry Huxley, *Science and Culture, and Other Essays* (New York: D. Appleton & Company, 1882), 13.
2 Huxley, *Science and Culture*, 13–14.
3 Robert Anderson, *British Universities Past and Present* (London: Hambledon Continuum, 2006), 106.
4 Bernard Lightman, 'Science and Culture', in *The Cambridge Companion to Victorian Culture*, ed. Francis O'Gorman (Cambridge: Cambridge University Press, 2010), 12–13.
5 John R. Gibbins, '"Old Studies and New': The Organisation of Knowledge in University Curriculum', in *The Organisation of Knowledge in Victorian Britain*, ed. Martin Daunton (Oxford: Oxford University Press, 2005), 258.
6 Cassidy R. Sugimoto and Scott Weingart, 'The Kaleidoscope of Disciplinarity', *Journal of Documentation* 71/4 (2015), 775.
7 James Chandler, 'Critical Disciplinarity', *Critical Inquiry* 30/2 (Winter 2004), 360.
8 Ronald Schleifer, 'Disciplinarity and Collaboration in the Sciences and Humanities', *College English* 59/4 (April 1997), 444.
9 Christina Nadler, 'Deterritorializing Disciplinarity: Towards an Immanent Pedagogy', *Cultural Studies ↔ Critical Methodologies* 15/2 (2015), 145.
10 Sarah Burton, 'Becoming Sociological: Disciplinarity and a Sense of Home', *Sociology* 50/5 (2016), 988.
11 Ken Hyland, *Disciplinary Identities: Individuality and Community in Academic Discourse* (Cambridge: Cambridge University Press, 2012), 22–23.
12 Jerry A. Jacobs, *In Defense of Disciplines: Interdisciplinarity and Specialization in the Research University* (Chicago and London: University of Chicago Press, 2013), 13.
13 Donald T. Campbell, 'Ethnocentrism of Disciplines and the Fish-Scale Model of Omniscience', in *Interdisciplinary Relationships in the Social Sciences*, eds. Muzafer Sherif and Carolyn W. Sherif (Chicago: Aldine Press, 1969), 328–348.
14 Robin Valenza, *Literature, Language, and the Rise of the Intellectual Disciplines in Britain* (Cambridge: Cambridge University Press, 2009), 5.
15 Jean Lave and Etienne Wenger, *Situated Learning: Legitimate Peripheral Participation* (Cambridge: Cambridge University Press, 1991), 89–118.

16 Stephen Bulick, *Structure and Subject Interaction: Toward a Sociology of Knowledge in the Social Sciences* (New York: Marcel Dekker, 1982), 20.
17 Tony Becher and Paul R. Trowler, *Academic Tribes and Territories: Intellectual Enquiry and the Culture of Disciplines*, 2nd edn. (Buckingham: Open University Press, 2001).
18 Erica L. Frisicaro, 'Constructing Composition: History, Disciplinarity, and Ideology' (PhD diss., University of Wisconsin-Milwaukee, 2003), 13. See also David R. Shumway and Ellen Messer-Davidow, 'Disciplinarity: An Introduction', *Poetics Today* 12/2 (Summer 1991), 201–225.
19 Robert Post, 'Debating Disciplinarity', *Critical Inquiry* 35/4 (Summer 2009), 751.
20 Sugimoto and Weingart, 'Kaleidoscope of Disciplinarity', 775–794.
21 Allen F. Repko and Rick Szostak, *Interdisciplinary Research: Process and Theory*, 3rd edn. (Los Angeles: Sage, 2017), 6–7.
22 Repko and Szostak, *Interdisciplinary Research*, 6.
23 Peter Osborne, 'Problematizing Disciplinarity, Transdisciplinary Problematics', *Theory, Culture & Society* 32/5–6 (2015), 4–9.
24 Marta B. Calas and Linda Smircich, 'The Journey to Neo-Disciplinarity', *Organization* 3/2 (1996), 168.
25 Martin Daunton, 'Introduction', in *The Organisation of Knowledge in Victorian Britain*, ed. M. Daunton (Oxford: Oxford University Press for the British Academy, 2005), 9–10.
26 Ibid., 12–13.
27 John Pickstone, 'Science in Nineteenth-Century England: Plural Configurations and Singular Politics', in *Organisation of Knowledge in Victorian Britain*, ed. M. Daunton (Oxford: Oxford University Press, 2005), 29–60.
28 John R. Gibbins, '"Old Studies and New": The Organisation of Knowledge in University Curriculum', in *Organisation of Knowledge in Victorian Britain*, ed. M. Daunton (Oxford: Oxford University Press, 2005), 242.
29 Carol Atherton, 'The Organisation of Literary Knowledge: The Study of English in the Late Nineteenth Century', in *Organisation of Knowledge in Victorian Britain*, ed. M. Daunton (Oxford: Oxford University Press, 2005), 221. Atherton's account is shaped by T. W. Heyck's influential book, *The Transformation of Intellectual Life in Victorian England* (New York: St. Martin's Press, 1982).
30 See Mark Schoenfield, 'Introduction: Romanticism and the Boundaries of Disciplinarity', *The Wordsworth* Circle 32/1, Romanticism and Interdisciplinarity: Centres and Peripheries: Selected Papers from the 15th Annual Conference of the Interdisciplinary Nineteenth-Century Society (Winter 2001), 2–4.
31 Thomas F. Gieryn, *Cultural Boundaries of Science: Credibility on the Line* (Chicago and London: University of Chicago Press, 1999), xi, 40, 62–63.
32 Schoenfield, 'Introduction: Romanticism and the Boundaries of Disciplinarity', 2.
33 Robert Young, 'The Historiographic and Ideological Contexts of the Nineteenth-Century Debate on Man's Place in Nature', in *Changing Perspectives in the History of Science*, eds. Mikulas Teich and Robert Young (London: Heinemann, 1973), 344–438.
34 William Whewell, '*On the Connexion of the Physical Sciences.* By Mrs. Somerville', *Quarterly Review* 51 (1834), 58–60.
35 Rens Bod, *A New History of the Humanities: The Search for Principles and Patterns from Antiquity to the Present* (Oxford: Oxford University Press, 2013), 6.

36 Bod, *New History of the Humanities*, 7.

37 https://news.virginia.edu/content/nines-project-enhances-tools-digital-research-humanities; and http://www.springer.com/series/15607; for more information on NINES centrality see Jerome McGann, 'Information Technology and the Troubled Humanities', in *Defining Digital Humanities: A Reader*, eds. Melissa Terras, Julianne Nyhan and Edward Vanhoutte (London and New York: Routledge, 2013/2016), 49–66.

38 Daunton, 'Introduction', in *Organisation of Knowledge in Victorian Britain*, ed. M. Daunton, 24.

39 Daunton's justification for excluding the popularizing of knowledge is that it can only be undertaken 'when the bounds of legitimate knowledge have been determined; alternative and competing knowledge systems can only be marginalised and subordinated when official knowledge has been properly validated and methods established to police the boundaries'. This not only gives priority to the scholarly study of what he refers to as official and legitimate knowledge, it also depicts popularizations as separate from all other forms of knowledge. This position is no longer tenable given recent scholarship on the popularization of science, which has shown how these different types of knowledge have grown together in the same period, mutually shaping each other. See Daunton, 'Introduction', in *The Organisation of Knowledge in Victorian Britain*, ed. Daunton, 10; Bernard Lightman, *Victorian Popularizers of Science: Designing Nature for New Audiences* (Chicago: University of Chicago Press, 2007), 495.

Section I

Professional Validation

1 The Evolution of the Scientific Disciplines

Bernard Lightman

In the final chapter of the *Origin of Species*, where Charles Darwin recapitulated the 'chief facts and inferences' of his book, he concluded by offering his readers a stunning vision of unity. 'When the views entertained by me in this volume . . . are generally admitted', Darwin declared, 'we can dimly foresee that there will be a considerable revolution in natural history'. It is a revolution, Darwin believed, that would unite naturalists by resolving long-standing divisive issues. Squabbling between systematists, for example, over what constituted a real species, would simply disappear. But Darwin's revolution would not only strengthen the bond between naturalists, it would also provide coherence to the sciences. Since individuals of the same species were descended from one parent, Darwin was convinced that even 'the differences between the inhabitants of the sea on the opposite sides of a continent' could be understood by naturalists in light of their family relationship. Geology would become the imperfect record of how individuals of the same species had descended from their parent. Psychology would be 'securely based on the foundation already well laid by Mr. Herbert Spencer, that of the necessary acquirement of each mental power and capacity by gradation'. Darwin offered his readers an exhilarating glimpse of how the scientific disciplines could be united by evolutionary theory. In the final paragraph of the book, where he developed the concept of the 'tangled bank', Darwin claimed that the unity in science was but a reflection of the true state of nature. Although the natural world was filled with 'elaborately constructed forms, so different from each other, and dependent upon each other in so complex a manner', they had all been produced by the law of evolution.[1] The seemingly impenetrable tangled bank concealed a oneness at the heart of nature that could only be discerned by the evolutionist, and not by those who relied on the flawed theological concept of the unity of design.

Darwin's dream of a revolution touching all areas of science provides some sense of the massive disciplinary changes that took place in the nineteenth century. As Laing shows in Chapter 8 of this volume, evolution played a significant role in the origins of child psychology. But even Darwin may have been unaware of the full extent of disciplinary change when he wrote the *Origin*, despite his reflections on the future impact of evolutionary theory. For in the *Origin*, Darwin frequently referred to his area of study as 'natural history', not 'biology'. The term 'biology' never appears in the book. At the same time that evolutionary theory led to a debate about what unified knowledge, there was also a significant reconfiguration of the scientific disciplines. At the beginning of the nineteenth century what we call natural science was divided into two bodies of knowledge, natural philosophy and natural history. But by the end of the century, increasing specialization had led to the creation of a series of new scientific disciplines and the decline of both natural philosophy and natural history as commonly used designations. The shift in emphasis is captured in visual form by Google Ngrams, which are produced by an online search engine that charts the frequency a term used in the printed sources in Google's corpus of digitalized texts. If we search for the terms 'natural history' and 'biology' between 1800 and 2000, we see a general pattern of decreased use of 'natural history' and an increased use of 'biology' (Figure 1.1). The terms 'natural philosophy' and 'physics' follow a similar pattern (Figure 1.2). Biology doesn't begin to be used significantly until the end of the century and steadily climbs upwards from then on, while physics, in use already in 1800, also moves upwards throughout the course of the century.

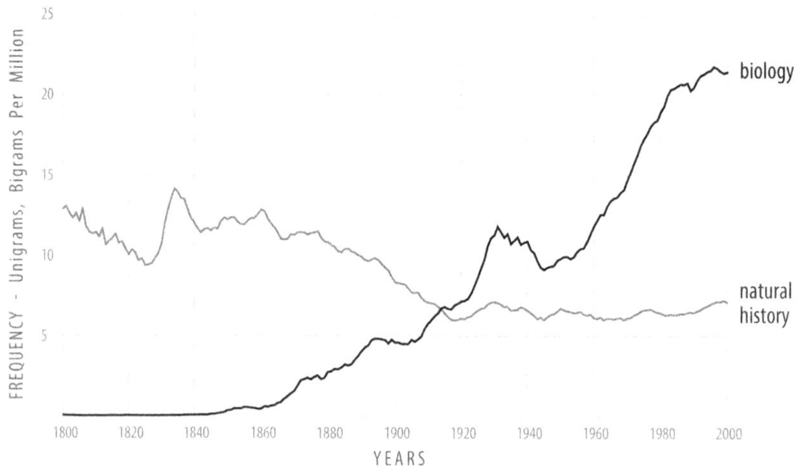

Figure 1.1 Charting the frequency of use of 'Natural History' and 'Biology' in printed sources 1800–2000. As of approximately 1915, the use of the term 'Biology' is clearly on the rise, while the term 'Natural History' is in decline. Based on a Google Books Ngram Viewer chart for 'Natural History' and 'Biology' that summarize the total n-grams each year, not a percentage of books. Here and in Figure 1.2 reporting has been changed to be case-insensitive, and the units have been standardized between the charts to 'n-grams per million' so that the y-axis units are consistent for comparison between charts. Graphics made by Rhumb Line Maps, using Google N-grams, 2019.

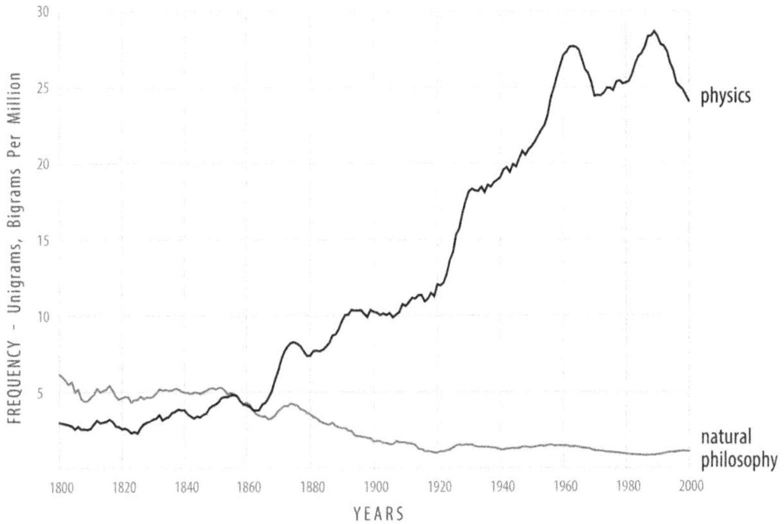

Figure 1.2 Charting the frequency of the use of 'Natural Philosophy' and 'Physics' in printed sources 1800–2000. As of approximately 1870, the use of the term 'Physics' is on the rise, while the term 'Natural Philosophy' is in decline. Based on a Google Books Ngram Viewer chart for 'Natural Philosophy' and 'Physics'. Graphics made by Rhumb Line Maps, using Google N-grams, 2019.

As the historian of science Jan Golinski has observed, the period from 1780 to 1850, sometimes referred to as the 'second scientific revolution', was a time in which 'new scientific disciplines such as geology, biology, and physiology were founded and existing ones (especially physics and chemistry) dramatically reconfigured. Remarkable changes in conceptual content and practice occurred in institutional settings that were themselves being transformed'.[2] Behind the move away from natural history and natural philosophy lies a complex story of institutional, as well as social, generational, and cultural transformation. Examining the reconfiguration of the scientific disciplines during the nineteenth century allows us a rare glimpse into the making – and redefining – of knowledge. I want to explore one crucial aspect of this process: the interplay between the creation of new disciplines and the enduring desire to unify science. In the first half of the century religious concepts provided the glue that integrated natural philosophy and natural history into a coherent whole. This vision of unity was propagated by institutions that were tied to the wealthiest and most powerful segments of society. During the second half of the century some Victorian scientists continued to cultivate a similar vision of unity, though against the backdrop of the decline of natural history and natural philosophy. But at the same time another group of Victorian scientists, largely Darwin's supporters, pushed for a more thorough-going redefinition of science that grounded unity in more secular principles. Their goal was to transform the disciplinary landscape, which required that they challenge the institutions that supported the old vision of unity.

The Great Empire of Science: The Disciplines before Mid-Century

In an anonymous review of Mary Somerville's *On the Connexion of the Physical Sciences* (1834), the Cambridge polymath William Whewell warned of the dangerous 'tendency of the sciences' towards 'separation and dismemberment'. Science was like 'a great empire falling to pieces' as it was 'endlessly subdivided, and subdivisions insulated'. The mathematician had turned away from the chemist, and the chemist from the naturalist. Left to himself, Whewell insisted, the mathematician 'divides himself into a pure mathematician and a mixed mathematician, who soon part company'. The same process of subdivision was at work in chemistry and the other physical sciences. As a result, science 'loses all traces of unity'. Whewell praised Somerville, a popularizer of science, for attempting to 'remove the evil' by 'showing how detached branches have, in the history of science, united by the discovery of general principles'.[3] Illustrating the connexion of the physical sciences was 'a noble object'.[4]

Whewell did not discuss in this review what lay behind the general principles unifying science. But Somerville was more forthcoming. She observed that the progress of modern science had tended to 'simplify the laws of nature, and to unite detached branches by general principles'. Magnetism, electricity, light, and heat were 'so connected' that they would 'ultimately be referred to some one power of a higher order, in conformity with the general economy of the system of the world, where the most varied and complicated effects are produced by a small number of universal laws'. Since it was possible to imagine a universe in which matter might have been moved according to an infinite variety of laws, Somerville concluded that natural laws like gravitation could only have been 'selected by Divine Wisdom out of an infinity of others, as being the most simple, and that which gives the greatest stability to the celestial motion'. Grasping natural law through mathematics was the most direct way to ascertain the divine unity in nature. The mathematical formulae which summarized the laws of nature were 'emblematic of Omniscience' as they condensed 'into a few symbols the immutable laws of the universe'. These fundamental axioms 'eternally existed in Him who implanted them in the breast of man when He created him after His own image'.[5] An omniscient, omnipotent, and benevolent Creator lay behind the unity in nature that modern science was beginning to uncover. As James Secord has remarked, Somerville's goal was to demonstrate that the higher mathematical analysis of the French did not lead to atheism but instead to a more profound understanding of divine creation.[6]

Somerville's notion of divine unity was widely accepted by both natural historians and natural philosophers even though they were commonly seen as adopting two very different approaches to studying nature. Natural history was understood to be about collecting, cataloguing, and describing the natural world. By contrast, natural philosophy, associated with experiment, was supposed to concern itself with causal explanation. However, in the eighteenth century, Peter Dear observes that 'the descriptive work of the naturalist had begun to bleed over into the explanatory work of the natural philosopher'.[7] In England, the closer relationship between natural history and natural philosophy was promoted by natural theology, which encouraged the use of apparent designfulness in the natural world as evidence of the hand of a benevolent Creator. Though English theologians may have been interested in natural theology, many natural historians and natural philosophers did not see their goal as demonstrating God's existence to their readers. They adopted a theology of nature, which conceived of science as being a mode of knowing firmly embedded within a religious framework. A theology of nature could draw upon the 'discourse of design' in order to illustrate a world full of divine purpose, and the unity that was the result of the actions of a single creator. Theologies of nature can be seen in representative texts from natural history and natural philosophy.[8]

Take, for example, John Herschel's *A Preliminary Discourse on the Study of Natural Philosophy*, which was published in 1830 as volume one of Dionysius Lardner's *Cabinet Cyclopedia*. An eminent astronomer, Herschel was read enthusiastically by Michael Faraday, Charles Darwin, and John Stuart Mill.[9] In the past, the *Preliminary Discourse* was treated by scholars as part of a tradition of philosophical reflections on the scientific method of induction and metaphysics.[10] More recently, Secord has suggested that the book was seen by contemporaries more as a conduct manual about how to develop the habit of strict investigation.[11] Whether it was a book on scientific method or a conduct manual, or both, Herschel explores many of the same themes to be found later in Somerville's *Connexion*. He opens the book with the assertion that nature is 'a system disposed with order and design' that led to the 'conception of a Power and an Intelligence superior to his own'. The study of natural philosophy through the use of natural reason placed 'the existence and principal attributes of a Deity on such grounds as to render doubt absurd and atheism ridiculous'. Like Somerville, one of his central themes in the book is the 'mutual relation and dependency' of the sciences. When scientific progress is made

> we are at length enabled to trace parallels and analogies between great branches of science themselves, which at length terminate in a perception of their dependence on some common phenomenon of a

more general and elementary nature than that which form the subject of either separately.

Herschel begins to focus more on this theme in part three of the book, which is titled 'Of the Subdivision of Physics into Distinct Branches, and Their Mutual Relations'. Here, while he runs through each sub-discipline of natural philosophy, including geology, chemistry, magnetism, and electricity, his main interest is in how different fields could overlap to produce more general laws. The convergence of magnetism and electricity, for example, is 'perhaps, the most satisfactory result which the experimental sciences have ever yet attained'. Herschel insisted that no natural phenomenon could be studied by itself but, 'to be understood, must be considered *as it stands connected with all nature*'. He concluded the book with a powerful image of unity, looking forward to future 'advances to the discovery of general laws, and to the inclusion of what is already known in generalizations of still higher orders'. This would provide insight into the 'sublime simplicity' of nature's divine plan.[12]

While Herschel's book is a good example of how natural philosophy was conceptualized in the first half of the nineteenth century, William Swainson's *A Preliminary Discourse on the Study of Natural History* (1834) provides us with a representative natural history text. This book was also published in Lardner's Cabinet Cyclopaedia as a companion to Herschel's discourse on natural philosophy.[13] Swainson believed that restricting scientific research to distinct portions of nature was required since the limited power of the human mind rendered the study of 'universal nature' impossible. 'Hence', Swainson declared, 'has originated the necessity of instituting those numerous divisions in natural philosophy, respectively assigned to the astronomer, the chemist, and the physiologist'. Those pursuits were no longer considered as forming a part of natural history, which embraced 'all that concerns the three great divisions or kingdoms of nature,–the animal, the vegetable, and the mineral'.[14]

However, Swainson argued, the necessity of creating scientific disciplines should not blind the reader to the fundamental unity of nature. 'One of the first impressions which arises on studying natural history', Swainson asserted, 'but more particularly animals, is the conviction of *design* in their creation'. The conviction of *design* in nature led inevitably to a Designer, 'or, in other words, the atheistical doctrines of chance and of self-development, vanish like a mist'. Since design could '*never be partial*', it ran throughout all nature. Each branch of the animal kingdom was 'dependent the one upon the other, and this dependence produces the most inconceivable harmony'. The chief purpose of the vegetable kingdom was to supply food to the animal kingdom. This pointed to the 'the great outlines of *design* through every branch of the animal kingdom'. This is why Swainson held that although he mainly discussed zoology in the book, his insights could be considered as being 'equally applicable both to the vegetable and the mineral'.[15]

Herschel and Swainson's division of knowledge into natural philosophy and natural history, unified by design, was pervasive throughout English culture in the first half of the century. It was embedded in educational institutions, especially the Anglican universities, Oxford and Cambridge, where William Paley's natural theology was influential, and professorships in natural philosophy, natural history, or a sub-discipline within one of them were typical. Whewell, Master of Trinity College, Cambridge, and Herschel, a graduate of Cambridge, were key figures in the formation in 1831 of the British Association for the Advancement of Science (BAAS), which became a powerful scientific society for the rest of the century. A theology of nature was widely favoured among members of the BAAS.[16] It not only provided a basis for investigating nature, it could also be used to shore up the political and social status quo when the French Revolution continued to cast a long shadow. The design in the natural world was paralleled by a design in the social world. They were following the lead of William Paley, an influential natural theologian, who had urged the British workers to be content with their lot in life. It was impious to complain about 'the necessity to which human affairs are subjected' since it was God who had 'contrived, that, whilst fortunes are only for a few, the rest of mankind may be happy without them'.[17]

The creation of new specialist societies in London in the early nineteenth century is often referred to as evidence of increasing specialization. The Geological Society (founded 1807), the Astronomical Society (founded 1820), the Zoological Society (founded 1826), and the Geographical Society (founded 1830) were among the most important. The BAAS quickly moved to a sectional format based on a disciplinary structure. By 1836 there were seven sections, mathematical and physical science, chemistry and mineralogy, geology and geography, zoology and botany, medical science, statistics, and mathematical science. Although the sections varied slightly in subsequent years, the number remained at seven.[18] But, as Pickstone has pointed out, this organization of the new analytic disciplines into distinctive bodies of knowledge was by no means a rejection of scientific unity. Each of the specialties was seen as a component of a 'single hierarchy with common methods'.[19] By the second quarter of the nineteenth century encyclopaedias had also seemingly departed from the ideal of the unity of knowledge.[20] But Herschel and Swainson recognized that natural history and natural philosophy could be subdivided into smaller bodies of knowledge. To them, as well as to Whewell and Somerville, there remained a larger unity beneath the disciplines that was guaranteed by divine design. We should therefore be careful when we refer to specialization in this period. It did not mean the creation of new bodies of knowledge that could be studied in isolation from the rest of nature. The emphasis was far more on the unity of design that allowed natural philosophers and natural historians to conceive of subdivisions within their fields of study.

Unity in the Second Half of the Century: Continuities

In 1874 the experimental physicist James Clerk Maxwell turned to the history of science for an example of key books that articulated, though not in definitive form, a way forward for scientists. These 'suggestive books' put into a 'definite, intelligible, and communicable form, the guiding ideas that are already working in the minds of men of science, so as to lead them to discoveries, but which they cannot yet shape into a definite statement'. Strikingly, Maxwell referred to Somerville's *On the Connexion of the Physical Sciences* as one of those 'suggestive books'. The sales of the book revealed 'that there already existed a widespread desire to be able to form some notion of physical science as a whole'. For the purpose of *Connexion* was to demonstrate 'the mutual dependence of the different sciences on each other, a knowledge of the elements of one being essential to the successful prosecution of another'. According to Maxwell, Somerville also showed in her book that mathematical analysis provided a 'common method' for the sciences.[21] Given Maxwell's central role in the development of physics in the second half of the century, and his devout evangelicalism, his interest in Somerville, and in the relationship between the branches of science, is important. It points to a continuing interest in unity grounded in religious concepts even after the publication of Darwin's *Origin of Species* in 1859, and not just in the physical sciences.

Unlike natural philosophy, the natural history tradition persisted well into the nineteenth century and beyond. Indeed, the period from 1880 to 1900 has been seen by the historian of science Paul Farber as the golden age of natural history. The strength of the tradition is evident in the construction and expansion of natural history museums in the late 1800s, including the opening of the Natural History Museum in London in 1881. The success of natural history museums, the rise of celebrated zoological and botanical gardens, and the proliferation of cheap books dealing with natural history themes reflected wide public support for this field of study. Although some scientists considered natural history out-of-date, the discipline still had its champions.[22] Take, for example, the Oxford educated Reverend Francis Orpen Morris (1810–1893), parson naturalist, prolific writer on over twenty natural history books, and vigorous opponent of evolutionary theory.

Morris's books are filled with expressions of admiration for the 'beautiful sights in which the Benign Creator displays such infinite wisdom of Almighty skill'.[23] His *Book of Natural History* (1852) would have met with Swainson's approval. Morris discusses the religious significance of the 160 animals described in the pages of his book. They are all designed in some way, whether we know it or not. 'How wonderful indeed are the various endowments with which God has gifted His creatures', Morris asserted, 'many of them obvious to us as to their utility, but other often entirely hidden from us as to any such, yet doubtless, all useful to their possessors in some way or degree or other'.[24] Darwin's *Origin* presented a threat to the unity of design that Morris saw in the animal kingdom. He began to voice his opposition to evolutionary theory in the late sixties when he perceived a concerted effort by Darwin's supporters to take over the British Association, an institution that had previously been a key power base for supporters of a theology of nature like Whewell and Herschel. Referring to himself as a 'Life Member of the British Association' since its second meeting, he believed he could speak on behalf of

> a large number of the members, that Section D should no longer be left in the hands of a small busy-body clique who have banded themselves together to cry down every attempt to disabuse the public mind of the pernicious principles to which the doctrines in question necessarily tend.

Morris worried that the Darwinians aimed to control the entire association, and not just Section D. He claimed that many of his BAAS colleagues reacted to the appointment of T. H. Huxley to the presidency for the year 1870 with a sense of 'foreboding'. In his *Difficulties of Darwinism Read Before the British Association at Norwich and Exeter in 1868 and 1869* (1869) Morris insisted that species had remained basically the same over time and that Darwin's supporters could not answer key questions about the theory of natural selection.[25]

The interest in unity of design was also influential in natural philosophy in the second half of the nineteenth century. Although those working on the physical sciences in that period didn't routinely identify themselves as natural philosophers, a significant number of them shared much in common with Herschel. William Thomson (1824–1907), later Lord Kelvin, was appointed professor of Natural Philosophy at the University of Glasgow in 1846 at the age of twenty-two. In his 'Introductory Lecture to the Course on Natural Philosophy' he laid out the traditional division of natural science into natural history and natural philosophy. Whereas natural history involved the 'description and classification of facts observed with reference to the various kinds of matter of which the properties are to be investigated', natural philosophy aimed to establish 'general laws' by 'induction from the facts collected in natural history'. Natural Philosophy included the study of mechanics, kinetics, statics, heat, electricity, and magnetism, as well as the science of optics. Optics, Kelvin declared, offered the best opportunity to trace 'the proofs of design in the adaptation of our organs of vision in accordance with the physical laws of light to receive the impressions by which we see external objects'. However, progress in all of the sciences throughout history was testimony to the divine gift given to humanity to investigate 'the laws established by the Creator for maintaining the harmony and permanence of His works'.[26] Thomson's commitment to a religious framework for science continued throughout his long and successful career. He was still referring to the discipline of natural philosophy in the 1860s. His *Treatise on Natural Philosophy*, published in 1867, was co-authored with Peter Guthrie Tait, and was intended to be, as Crosbie Smith puts it, the first volume in 'a complete state-of-the-art account of physical science in four volumes'.[27] Chapter 2, on 'Dynamical Laws and Principles', aimed to make the conservation of energy the unifying law upon which the entire foundation of dynamics rested.[28]

Maxwell shared Thomson's attraction to the emphasis on unity of design from the old natural philosophy tradition. In his book *The Science of Energy*, the historian of science Crosbie Smith has convincingly argued that the group of Scottish figures who constructed the science of energy from the 1850s to the 1870s promoted a natural philosophy in harmony with Christian belief. This 'North British' group was composed of natural philosophers Thomson, Maxwell, Peter Guthrie Tait, and the engineers Fleeming Jenkin and Macquorn Rankine. Bearing the impress of Scottish Presbyterianism, representing Whig and progressive values, and linked to the industrialists of northern Britain, these men were prepared to enter into an alliance with Cambridge Anglicans to undermine the authority of naturalistic evolutionists like Huxley.[29] Maxwell almost embodies the alliance between Oxbridge and the North British physicists. Maxwell had studied mathematics at Trinity College, Cambridge, took up the Chair of Natural Philosophy at Marischal College, Aberdeen in 1856, moved to Kings College, London, in 1860, returned to Scotland in 1865, and then moved back to Cambridge in 1871 to become the first Cavendish Professor of Physics. Maxwell was responsible for developing the Cavendish Laboratory, intended to be a state of the art experimental physics laboratory.

In his inaugural lecture as the Cavendish Professor of Physics in 1871, Maxwell highlighted the importance of experimental research, the object of which was 'to measure something which we have already seen'. Maxwell assured his Cambridge audience that despite his emphasis on measurement and experimental research, rather than the reliance on book learning that had produced distinguished Wranglers in the past, that the work in his laboratory would nevertheless lead to God. Experimental research, Maxwell argued, provided evidence for the existence of innumerable particles that, when examined and measured, turned out to be identical in their properties. Since neither the cause of their existence nor the identity of their properties could be ascribed 'to the operation of any of those causes which we call natural', experimental research led the physicist directly to a supernatural cause.[30] In his letter to C. J. Ellicott, Bishop of Gloucester and Bristol, dated November 22, 1876, Maxwell was even more explicit. Atoms were manufactured articles whose uniformity was 'accomplished by the same wisdom, and power of which uniformity, accuracy, symmetry, consistency, and continuity of plan are as important attributes as the contrivance of the special utility of each individual thing'.[31] Strikingly, Herschel had made a similar argument in his *Preliminary Discourse*. There he proclaimed that atoms of the same kind were identical, as if each of them was a '*manufactured article*', and therefore precision measure supplied evidence of divine creation.[32] For both Herschel and Maxwell we see design through the uniformity revealed by science. Unity was an indication of God's hand.[33]

But Maxwell's debts to Herschel and other earlier natural philosophers go further than just his 'new natural theology of precision measurement', which is historian of science Simon Schaffer's playful reference to this aspect of his work.[34] Maxwell's major achievements in electromagnetic theory illustrated the deep connections between branches of natural philosophy, thereby confirming the unity to which Herschel, Somerville, and Whewell had all tried to call attention. In the early 1860s Maxwell began to develop a mechanical model that unified electricity, magnetism, and light.[35] Maxwell had an abiding faith that behind the unity discovered by science lay an interconnected natural world. In an essay written in 1856 he considered whether nature was analogous to a book or to a magazine. If nature was like a magazine, then it would be 'foolish to suppose that one part can throw light on another'.[36] In a magazine, the separate articles written by different authors might have no connection to each other. There would be no reason to believe that understanding magnetism would help us understand electricity or any other branch of science.[37] However, if nature was like a book, 'the introductory parts will explain those that follow, and the methods taught in the first chapters will be taken for granted and used as illustrations in the more advanced parts of the course'.[38] Looking at nature as if it was like a book guaranteed that there was a common thread running throughout the physical world that could be used to interpret and understand the whole. Maxwell was certain that nature *was* like a book and, as the historian of science Matthew Stanley asserts, 'that its individual elements should be seen as manifestations of deeper unified principles'.[39]

Moving Forward Without the Unity of Design

Maxwell and Morris aimed to perpetuate a concept of unity within science, despite increasing disciplinary specialization, that drew upon the older traditions in natural history and natural philosophy. But during the middle of the nineteenth century important scientific figures began to search for a new notion of unity that did not rely on religious principles. Darwin's vision of how evolutionary theory could integrate the disciplines provided one option for those seeking a new principle of unity. In his ambitious system of knowledge, the philosopher of evolution Herbert Spencer attempted to flesh out the vision for the future laid out in the

Origin of Species, though in ways that would not have been acceptable to Darwin. Whereas for Darwin, evolution could be applied across the disciplines to show the grand explanatory power of his theory, for Spencer's evolution was the key to a totalizing system of knowledge and even a new world view. Spencer believed that evolution was at work in every stage of the development of the natural world, from the formation of the solar system by the condensation of white-hot nebular matter into planets (the nebular hypothesis), to the geological forces that determined the nature of the earth's crust, and to the development of life, from monad to man. Even the intellectual and cultural achievements of humanity, including science, were a part of the cosmic evolutionary process.

Spencer laid out this vision of cosmic evolution in his multi-volume *System of Synthetic Philosophy* (1862–1896), which was intended as a synthesis of all knowledge connected through the concept of evolution. In the first book of the system, *First Principles* (1862), he searched for truths that would allow him to synthesize scientific knowledge into one system. For Spencer, it is biology, and not physics, that provides the key theoretical underpinning of his entire system. He rejected the idea that the Newtonian universe, composed of matter, force, and motion, could provide the unifying truth that he sought. Instead, he concluded that 'the universal law of distribution of matter and motion' is 'evolution', which meant that evolutionary law was more fundamental than Newton's law of gravity.[40] This philosophical deduction was then empirically verified by empirical proof drawn from astronomy, geology, biology, psychology, and sociology. Spencer concluded that all phenomena were subject to the evolutionary process. 'Alike during the evolution of the Solar System', he declared, 'of a planet, of an organism or a nation, there is progressive aggregation of the entire mass'.[41] Evolution in its broadest sense, therefore, became the organizing principle for all of the sciences, including the social sciences, connecting them into a unified whole. However, even Spencer's closest allies, who like him accepted some version of evolutionary theory and defended Darwin, were not prepared to swallow the synthetic philosophy whole. For example, in Huxley's opinion, attempts to construct a philosophy of evolution in the second half of the nineteenth century were 'premature'.[42] John Tyndall and Thomas Henry Huxley conceived of themselves as evolutionists, and rejected the unity of design, but they did not use evolution, as Spencer did, as the glue holding the disciplines together. Instead, they pointed to the unifying force of natural law and the naturalistic scientific method.

Tyndall was appointed Professor of Natural Philosophy at the Royal Institution in 1853, and he remained in that post until 1887. In some ways, he resembled natural philosophers from earlier in the century. At times, Tyndall equated natural philosophy with physics. In a lecture on 'Elementary Magnetism' he referred to the 'large department of the system of Nature which forms the chief subject of my own studies. . . that of physics, or natural philosophy'.[43] Like earlier natural philosophers,

Tyndall's varied research projects led him to move across disciplines. During his career Tyndall conducted research on diamagnetism, glaciers, radiant heat, atmospheric gases, sound, electricity, and spontaneous generation. His experiments drew on an extensive knowledge of chemistry, physics, and biology. But unlike natural philosophers, or experimental physicists like Maxwell, Tyndall had no use for religious concepts in science. In fact, Tyndall held to a rigid distinction between science and religion. Science, part of the realm of intellect, dealt with facts, while religion, along with poetry and art, belonged to the province of feeling. Rightly conceived they could not come into conflict. Problems arose only when theologians tried to embody feelings in concrete facts.[44] So for Tyndall, no religious principle, including the unity of design, could possibly function as a key to unifying science.

In his essay 'On the Study of Physics' (1854), Tyndall spelled out the territory covered by physics and the other physical sciences. 'The term Physics', Tyndall stated,

> as made use of in the present Lecture, refers to that portion of natural science which lies midway between astronomy and chemistry. The former, indeed, is Physics applied to 'masses of enormous weight,' while the latter is Physics applied to atoms and molecules.

Physics, then, is identified by Tyndall as a bridging discipline between astronomy and chemistry, as its method spans all three. Physics therefore unifies the physical sciences. Tyndall then goes on to specify the subjects of 'Physics proper' as those that 'lie nearest to human perception:–light and heat colour, sound, motion, the loadstone, electrical attractions and repulsions, thunder and lightning, rain, snow, dew, and so forth'. Physics deals with those phenomena that we are most familiar with, and since these phenomena 'lie nearest to human perception', Tyndall emphasizes the importance of observation. Tyndall also asserts that physics exercises and sharpens the powers of observation, trains its students to use exhaustive logic, and demands precision. Unlike the study of classical languages and literature undertaken at Oxbridge, which ends 'in a mere game of intellectual gymnastics', physics tends 'to the mastery of Nature'.[45] For Tyndall, the study of physics disciplines the mind. Physics is united by a common naturalistic method, which emphasizes observation and other mental skills.

Fourteen years later Tyndall was again discussing the scientific disciplines, this time in his presidential address to the Mathematical and Physical Section of the British Association, which was meeting at Norwich that year. Here he tackled the unity of all sciences and not just the unity within physics. Tyndall observed that before him sat men who all pursued natural knowledge, but each had chosen 'one subject for the exercise of his own original faculty—one line, along which he may carry the light of his private intelligence a little way into the darkness by which all knowledge is surrounded'. The geologist dealt with rocks; the biologist with the conditions and phenomena of life; the astronomer with stellar masses and motions; the mathematician with the relations of space and number; the chemist pursued his atoms; 'while the physical investigator has his own large field in optical, thermal, electrical, acoustical, and other phenomena'. Each scientific discipline, Tyndall was asserting, was defined by its different objects of study. But what followed was a metaphor for the unity of science. 'The British Association then', Tyndall proclaimed, 'as a whole, faces physical nature on all sides, and pushes knowledge centrifugally outwards, the sum of its labours constituting what Fichte might call the *sphere* of natural knowledge'. Although the Association had found it necessary to 'resolve this sphere into its component parts' through the creation of its seven sections, nevertheless, they all were contained in a single geometrical figure and were grouped around a common center. But what connected them? Tyndall answered this question by pointing to the nature of the laws that could be found in nature. All natural phenomena, whether observed in the region of sense or imagination, were 'in the long run reducible to mechanical laws'.[46]

If Tyndall was critical of the older conception of natural philosophy, Huxley made a similar case for the problems with natural history. In 1854 Huxley was comfortable titling one of his essays 'On the Educational Value of the Natural History Sciences'. But in his 'On the Study of Biology' (1876) he characterized natural history as an outmoded term and recommended it be superseded by the term 'biology'. This was not just a change in terminology. Huxley maintained that natural history had become a victim of its own success. The 'marvelous progress' of the subjects that were an integral part of natural history, such as physical geography, geology, mineralogy, the history of plants, and the history of animals, at the 'latter end of the last and the beginning of the present century', led 'thinking men' to realize that 'very heterogeneous constituents' had been included 'under this title of "Natural History"'. It was possible to 'obtain an extensive knowledge of the structure and functions of plants and animals, without having need to enter upon the study of geology or mineralogy and *vice versa*'. Moreover, 'as knowledge advanced', it was realized that botany and zoology were very closely allied since they both dealt with living beings. They could therefore be united 'into one whole' and dealt with 'as one discipline'. Huxley credited Gottfried Reinhold Treviranus, the German naturalist and botanist, with being the first to work out completely the conception of biology as a separate discipline in 1802, when he published the first volume of his *Biologie*. 'That is the origin of the term "Biology"', Huxley declared. And it had led to the adoption by 'all clear thinkers and lovers of consistent nomenclature' of the term 'biology' to denote the 'whole of the sciences which deal with living things, whether they be animals or whether they be plants'. Only the muddled thinkers and lovers of inconsistent nomenclature retained 'the old confusing name of "Natural History"', which had 'conveyed so many meanings'.[47] Huxley's account of the origins of biology banished natural history to the dustbin of history. It conceived of a scientific discipline as being united by objects with similar characteristics. They could be understood without reference to knowledge of objects studied in other disciplines.

In presenting biology as an autonomous discipline, Huxley seemed to lose the possibility of finding a larger unity. But when Huxley was tasked with being one of the editors of a series of elementary scientific textbooks organized around the disciplines, he had to articulate what united all of the sciences. The *Science Primers* included volumes on chemistry, physics, physical geography, geology, physiology, astronomy, botany, logic, and political economy. Huxley's volume, simply titled *Science Primers: Introductory* (1880), was divided into three main sections. Huxley wrote to one of his series co-editors in 1879 that the idea in the book 'is to develop Science out of common observation, and to lead up to Physics, Chemistry, Biology, and Psychology'.[48] The first section explained basic terms such as 'cause', 'effect', 'natural order', and the 'laws of nature'. Huxley made it clear that the goal of science was to obtain knowledge of the laws of nature by using observation, experiment, and reasoning. Science was therefore unified by a common, naturalistic methodology, used to detect natural laws. Section Two dealt with what Huxley referred to as the 'two great provinces of nature', inorganic and organic material objects. These he further subdivided into the disciplines dealt with in the primers.[49] Section Three focussed on immaterial objects, or psychology, which involved the examination of mental phenomena that could be treated in the same way that material objects were studied, as subject to the relations of cause and effect. The final sentence of the book is a powerful affirmation of naturalistic method. 'All the phenomena of nature are either material or immaterial, physical or mental', he argued, 'and there is no science, except such as consists in the knowledge of one or other of these groups of natural objects, and of the relationships which obtain between them'.[50] Biological objects could be studied together apart from inorganic and immaterial objects. But they were all a part of nature ruled by discernible laws. Huxley's point was that it was not necessary to rely on unity of design to envision what connected the different branches of science. Nor did Huxley see the need to follow Spencer by basing unity on evolutionary theory – he aimed for something broader. For Huxley, evolutionary law was only one law among many.

Huxley was keenly aware that uprooting the natural history tradition in Britain would require institutional reform. One obstacle was the power of natural history in museums. Men like Richard Owen, who spent his career in natural history museums, were a constant thorn in Huxley's side. Another problem was the state of the British universities. Huxley argued that the German university system, with its emphasis on research training as a form of discipline, offered a model that should be imitated. When Huxley was given the opportunity in 1871 to set up a teaching laboratory in South Kensington, he adopted the German model and began to drill his student on how to observe with microscopes in the proper manner.[51] Whereas the German universities had set the standard, the British universities, particularly Cambridge and Oxford, were, in Huxley's mind, among the major impediments to progress. Even Cambridge, which had introduced the Natural Science Tripos in 1848, had the reputation long into the nineteenth century of lagging far behind the best European universities when it came to science education.[52] At one point, Huxley had high hopes that Cambridge would make steady progress towards becoming a leading centre for biological research when Francis Balfour was appointed Chair of Animal Morphology at Cambridge in 1882. Huxley saw Balfour as his possible successor – 'the only man who can carry out my work'. But Balfour died shortly afterwards in a tragic climbing accident in the Alps. Huxley spent the three days after Balfour's death 'utterly prostrated', unable to eat or sleep.[53] Without Balfour, Huxley feared that Cambridge would again decline. Huxley questioned why the British scientific disciplines had to be defined in the universities, and he also, like Tyndall, doubted that Oxbridge provided the proper form of discipline due to its emphasis on classical languages and literature.

When Huxley served as a member of the Royal Commission on Scientific Instruction and the Advancement of Science from 1870 to 1874 he was particularly harsh in his questioning of the faculty from Oxford.[54] He hoped that his work on the commission would lead to significant educational reform that undermined the power of natural history and the theology of nature that grounded it. His many controversies with Christian opponents over the autonomy of science were part of his attempt to redefine knowledge. His defense of Darwin was more about pushing for a naturalistic approach to science than an acceptance of the theory of natural selection. In the 1880s Huxley recollected that his circle's interest in the *Origin of Species* was due to Darwin's attempt to bring the organic world under the authority of natural law.[55] 'That which we were looking for', he declared, 'and could not find, was a hypothesis respecting the origin of known organic forms which assumed the operation of no causes, but such as could be proved to be actually at work'.[56]

Concluding Reflections: Principles for Unity

As the unity of design became less and less attractive during the second half of the nineteenth century, many alternative principles for unity were explored. Huxley and Tyndall looked to naturalism and natural law as a suitable replacement. Spencer and Darwin believed that a single natural law, evolution, provided the best alternative. In his presidential address to the British Association of 1866, the physical scientist William R. Grove offered a new candidate for the ultimate natural law: the law of correlation. Extending Cuvier's doctrine concerning the 'relations of the different parts of an animal to each other' to all nature, Grove saw this as an indication that 'all the phenomena of inorganic and organised matter might be expected to be so inter-related that the study of an isolated phenomenon would lead to a knowledge of numerous other phenomena with which it is connected'.[57] Interest in the issue of unity was not limited to Britain. Ernst Haeckel's advocacy of monism, that mind and matter were two modes of a single substance, was another attempt to unify knowledge.[58] Finally, the concept of the ether, a superfine, invisible fluid in which light was propagated, was viewed as a principle of unity. For physicists at Cambridge, the ether became the basis of a scientific spiritualism. Later, in the early twentieth century, the physicist Oliver Lodge became unsatisfied with just one principle of unity. In his *The Making of Man: A Study in Evolution* (1924) he aimed to integrate evolution into a synthesis he had been developing that had previously relied on the ether. The issue of unity continued to be a hot topic well into the twentieth century. The historian of science Peter Galison has argued that a unity of science movement arose in the inter-war period, led by polymath philosophers of science Rudolf Carnap, Otto Neurath, and Charles Morris, was a response to the rise of fascism. But he traces modern talk of unification in the sciences back to the German-speaking countries of the mid-nineteenth century, and figures like the physician and biologist Rudolf Virchow, who lived in the midst of a political struggle to unify Germany.[59]

However, the British nineteenth-century story is also important. Three striking features of that story stand out that illuminate our understanding of the disciplines in that period. First, perhaps surprisingly, the scientific disciplines were extremely fluid and malleable. Both Lowther (Chapter 5) and Richards (Chapter 10) confirm this point in relation to, respectively, natural history and mathematics. It might have been expected that of all the disciplines they would have been the most stable and that they would have provided stability to the non-scientific disciplines. However, the disaggregation of natural philosophy and natural history represented a significant transformation of the disciplinary landscape. Once the scientific disciplines had hardened by the end of the nineteenth century, they retained the appearance of permanence thereafter. Second, and seemingly in contradiction to my first point, that disaggregation may not have occurred without an abiding faith in an underlying principle of unity. Those who aimed to redefine the disciplines offered a new principle that offset the loss of the unity of design. It could be the unifying force of evolutionary theory, the law of correlation, the ether, monism, naturalistic method, or even the order underwritten by all natural laws. The search for some principle of unification continued into the twentieth century and beyond, as the physical and life sciences each attempted to provide a solid basis for a new vision of oneness. That was the point of finding a theory of everything or of establishing a modern evolutionary synthesis. Third, and finally, the redefinition of the scientific disciplines and the move away from the unity of design were part of critical institutional and cultural changes over the course of the nineteenth century.[60] Resolving disagreements over what constituted a scientific discipline was a high stakes cultural and political game. It had profound implications for the fate of Christian institutions, the universities, the museums, and learned societies, not just the questioning of particular scientific theories or practices. The disciplinary reorganization of science in the nineteenth century, it could be argued, played a central role in the creation of modern culture and society.

Notes

1 Charles Darwin, *The Origin of Species* (London: Penguin, 1985), 452, 455, 457–459.
2 Jan Golinski, *Making Natural Knowledge: Constructivism and the History of Science* (Cambridge: Cambridge University Press, 1998), 67.
3 [William Whewell], '*On the Connexion of the Physical Sciences.* By Mrs. Somerville', *Quarterly Review* 51 (1834), 58–60.
4 Ibid., 58.
5 Mary Somerville, *On the Connexion of the Physical Sciences*, 7th edn. (London: John Murray, 1846; reprinted New York: Arno Press, 1975), vii, 377, 432, 435.
6 James A. Secord, *Visions of Science: Books and Readers at the Dawn of the Victorian Age* (Chicago: University of Chicago Press, 2014), 129.
7 Peter Dear, 'The Natural Philosopher', in *A Companion to the History of Science*, ed. Bernard Lightman (The Atrium, Southern Gate, Chichester, West Sussex, UK: Wiley Blackwell, 2016), 80.
8 Bernard Lightman, *Victorian Popularizers of Science: Designing Nature for New Audiences* (Chicago and London: University of Chicago Press, 2007), 24.
9 Richard Yeo, 'Reviewing Herschel's *Discourse*', *Studies in History and Philosophy of Science*, 20 (1989), 541.
10 See, for example, Yeo, 'Reviewing Herschel's *Discourse*', 541–552.
11 Secord, *Visions of Science*, 81, 92.
12 John F. W. Herschel, *A Preliminary Discourse on the Study of Natural Philosophy* (Chicago and London: University of Chicago Press, 1987), 4, 7, 94, 221, 259, 324, 360–361. See also Yeo, 'Reviewing Herschel's *Discourse*', 546–548.
13 Swainson refers positively to Herschel's discourse several times. See William Swainson, *A Preliminary Discourse on the Study of Natural History* (London: Longman, Rees, Orme, Brown, Green & Longman, 1834), 150, 152.
14 Ibid., 95.
15 Ibid., 95, 109–110.
16 Jack Morell and Arnold Thackray, *Gentlemen of Science: Early Years of the British Association for the Advancement of Science* (Oxford: Clarendon Press, 1981), 227.
17 William Paley, *The Complete Works of William Paley, D.D.* (London: J. F. Dove, 1825), vol. I, 429.
18 Jack Morell and Arnold Thackray, *Gentlemen of Science* (Oxford: Clarendon Press, 1981), 453–454.

19 John Pickstone, 'Science in Nineteenth-Century England: Plural Configurations and Singular Politics', in *The Organization of Knowledge in Victorian Britain*, ed. Martin Daunton (Oxford: Oxford University Press, 2005), 29–60, on p. 46. Pickstone's otherwise excellent account of the changing disciplinary structure of nineteenth-century British science is flawed by its lack of attention to the crucial role of religious concepts.
20 Richard Yeo, 'Reading Encyclopedias: Science and the Organization of Knowledge in British Dictionaries of Arts and Sciences, 1730–1850', *Isis* 82/1 (March 1991), 48.
21 J. C. Clerk-Maxwell, 'Grove's 'Correlation of Physical Forces', *Nature* 10 (August 20, 1874), 303.
22 Paul Lawrence Farber, *Finding Order in Nature: The Naturalist Tradition from Linnaeus to E. O. Wilson* (Baltimore and London: Johns Hopkins University Press, 2000), 87–88, 94, 97–98.
23 Rev. F. O. Morris, *A History of British Butterflies* (London: Groombridge & Sons, 1853), 84.
24 Rev. F. O. Morris, *Book of Natural History; Containing a Description of Animals and Birds* (London: Groombridge & Sons, 1853), 34.
25 Rev. F. O. Morris, *Difficulties of Darwinism Read Before the British Association at Norwich and Exeter in 1868 and 1869* (London: Longmans, Green, & Co., 1869), v, vi, 4, 14.
26 William Thomson, 'Introductory Lecture to the Course on Natural Philosophy', in *The Life of William Thomson*, ed. Silvanus P. Thompson (London: Macmillan and Co., 1910), vol. 1, 240, 244–245.
27 Crosbie Smith, *The Science of Energy: A Cultural History of Energy Physics in Victorian Britain* (Chicago: University of Chicago Press, 1998), 193.
28 Smith, *The Science of Energy*, 199.
29 Smith, *The Science of Energy*.
30 James Clerk Maxwell, 'Introductory Lecture on Experimental Physics', in *The Scientific Papers of James Clerk Maxwell*, ed. W. D. Niven (New York: Dover Publications, Inc., 1965), vol. 2, 244, 247, 254.
31 Lewis Campbell and William Garnett, *The Life of James Clerk Maxwell* (London: Macmillan and Co., 1882), 393.
32 Schaffer, 'Metrology, Metrication, and Victorian Values', 446; Herschel, *Preliminary Discourse*, 38.
33 Matthew Stanley, *Huxley's Church and Maxwell's Demon: From Theistic Science to Naturalistic Science* (Chicago and London: University of Chicago Press, 2015), 43.
34 Schaffer, 'Metrology, Metrication, and Victorian Values', 465.
35 Margaret Morrison, 'A Study in Theory Unification: The Case of Maxwell', *Studies in History and Philosophy of Science* 23 (1992), 110, 117–118.
36 Campbell and Garnett, *Life of James Clerk Maxwell*, 243.
37 Stanley, *Huxley's Church and Maxwell's Demon*, 41–42.
38 Campbell and Garnett, *Life of James Clerk Maxwell*, 243.
39 Stanley, *Huxley's Church and Maxwell's Demon*, 41–42.
40 Herbert Spencer, *First Principles of a New System of Philosophy*, 4th edn. (New York: D. Appleton, 1882), 285.
41 Ibid., 307–311, 327, 556–558.
42 T. H. Huxley, *Science and Christian Tradition* (New York: D. Appleton & Company, 1894), 41.
43 John Tyndall, *Fragments of Science: A Series of Detached Essays, Addresses, and Reviews* (London: Longmans, Green, & Co., 1892), vol. 1, 344.
44 Bernard Lightman, *The Origins of Agnosticism: Victorian Unbelief and the Limits of Knowledge* (Baltimore and London: Johns Hopkins University Press, 1987) 131.

45 Tyndall, *Fragments of Science*, vol. 1, 282, 293.
46 Ibid., vol. 2, 76.
47 Thomas Henry Huxley, *Science and Education* (New York: D. Appleton, 1894), 263, 266–268.
48 Leonard Huxley, *Life and Letters of Thomas Henry Huxley*, 2 vols (New York: D. Appleton & Company, 1900), vol. 2, 2.
49 Professor Huxley, *Science Primers. Introductory* (New York, Cincinnati, Chicago: American Book Company, n.d.), 92–93.
50 Ibid., 94.
51 Golinski, *Making Natural Knowledge*, 72, 76.
52 Roy Macleod and Russell Moseley, 'The 'Naturals' and Victorian Cambridge: Reflections on the Anatomy of an Elite, 1851–1914', *Oxford Review of Education* 6 (1982), 177–195.
53 L. Huxley, *Life and Letters of Thomas Henry Huxley*, vol. 2, 40–41.
54 Bernard Lightman, 'Huxley and the Devonshire Commission', in *Victorian Scientific Naturalism: Community, Identity, Continuity*, eds. Gowan Dawson and Bernard Lightman (Chicago and London: University of Chicago Press, 2014), 114–116.
55 Stanley, *Huxley's Church and Maxwell's Demon*, 58.
56 T. H. Huxley, 'On the Reception of the *Origin of Species*', in *The Life and Letters of Charles Darwin*, ed. Francis Darwin (New York: D. Appleton, 1911), vol. 1, 182.
57 W. R. Grove, *Address to the British Association for the Advancement of Science 1866*, 2nd edn. (London: Longmans, Green, & Co., 1867), 73.
58 Todd H. Weir, 'The Riddles of Monism: An Introductory Essay', in *Monism: Science, Philosophy, Religion, and the History of a Worldview*, ed. Todd H. Weir (New York: Palgrave Macmillan, 2012), 2.
59 Peter Galison, 'Introduction: The Context of Disunity', in *The Disunity of Science: Boundaries, Contexts, and Power*, eds. Peter Galison and David J. Stump (Stanford, CA: Stanford University Press, 1996), 1, 3.
60 Pickstone's emphasis on the importance of the relation of science to the state and professional institutions leads him to perceive a third phase in the development of the disciplines that takes place after 1870. As in my account, he locates the first phase in the early nineteenth century, when, led by natural philosophers, the gentlemen of London and Cambridge sought to control the centrifugal tendencies of the new analytical disciplines through institutions such as the British Association for the Advancement of Science. The second phase begins when Huxley and his allies arrive on the scene in the middle of the century. They operated largely through state-institutions and pushed for a secular concept of science that was not based in the ancient universities. Pickstone adds a third phase, when disciplinary research schools, based on German models, arose in a few of the universities in the wake of the Devonshire Commission of the early seventies. His examples are both from Cambridge: Foster's physiology laboratory and the physics laboratory first run by Maxwell and then later by Lord Rayleigh. But, as Pickstone acknowledges, Foster was part of a group of young biologists who had helped to run Huxley's South Kensington summer schools for schoolteachers. Foster, then, was putting Huxley's vision of a research school into practise at Cambridge. I see Pickstone's second and third phases as part of the same development. See Pickstone, 'Science in Nineteenth-Century England', 50–60.

2 Disciplining Terpsichore

Moves Towards the Study of Dance in Victorian Britain

Theresa Jill Buckland

Dancing in Victorian Britain was a widespread activity throughout much of the social scale. Evidence of its practice abounds across various media, both public and private, yet during the nineteenth century dancing never became a recognized subject for academic attention. Terpsichore, the ancient Greek muse of dancing, to whom Victorian writers on dance were frequently fond of referring, remained an outsider in Victorian academia in spite of her oft-stated classical credentials by her votaries. Unlike her sister arts of music and painting, with whom dancing was often compared, attempts to create a discipline of standing with its associated hallmarks of national schools and professional associations, syllabi and examinations, dedicated societies, critical literature, and sustained university presence were only to be fully realized later in the following century. This chapter seeks to identify and explore the factors that prohibited the emergence of dance as a discipline in the Victorian era, raising comparative issues for consideration in understanding how disciplines are formed.

Searching for Relevant Scholarship

Examination of Victorian culture for traces of discipline building is limited in British dance historiography. Janet Adshead's *The Study of Dance* (1981), for example, notes relevant Victorian writings but does not address the period in any detail. Peter Brinson's *Dance as Education: Towards a National Dance Culture* (1991) refers to the late nineteenth-century positioning of dance within physical education in the British school curriculum, but his principal purpose is to provide historical background to the contemporary situation and potential for future discipline development. By contrast, American publications on the nineteenth century background are more numerous, largely as a result of the establishment of dance within their higher education sector as early as 1926.[1]

Dance studies as an academic discipline in Britain, however, dates from only the last third of the twentieth century, its relative youth and small scale mitigating against the range and depth of specialisms to be found in other more established university-located arts and humanities disciplines. Furthermore, dance's principal research *topoi* in Britain have been increasingly driven to underpin courses that favour contemporary rather than historical practice.[2] Responding to undergraduates' desire to continue their dancing while at university and to the need to champion practice-as-research as an art in academia, many degree courses in the early twenty-first century address the nurturing of independent practitioners; this has tended towards privileging practical studio sessions over sedentary lectures and seminars where dance history, philosophy, and analysis were formerly taught.[3] In such a climate, dance genres and their practice and evaluation in nineteenth-century Britain have seemingly little applicability and as consequence, any traces of building a discipline in that period have received scant scholarly attention.

Significant too in understanding the tardy recognition of dance's disciplinary status are underlying cultural matters concerning the place and value of dance in British society, which have positioned the subject far down the hierarchical ladder of artistic status, often rendering its worth questionable.[4] These are not new attitudes but can be found circulating in Victorian cultural discourse and practice, and indeed earlier. They highlight the social fact that dance, realized through the moving human body, whether in conjunction with, or viewed by others, has the capacity to magnify cultural beliefs and attitudes, especially those regarding inter-related issues of gender, race, class, age, occupation, and religion. This nexus in which the Victorian dancing body was exercised entrapped Terpsichore. While sharing in the long history of European ambivalence towards the performing arts, dance has received particular censure over the centuries. As a non-linguistic mode of cultural practice typically produced without the means of instrument or text external to the body, the nature of dance as understood in European discourse draws full attention to the body, in a manner that is unlike its embodied counterparts of mainstream European music and drama.[5]

For most of the nineteenth century throughout Europe, the cultural field of dance was largely unable to boast a complement of traditional disciplinary hallmarks, such as a corpus of socially esteemed experts, dedicated societies and journals, consensus on the discipline's core, and a university presence. Nor were there nationally agreed standards of production and transmission, a canon of works for study, nor an extensive amount of critical writings in existence. Nonetheless, Terpsichore, as will be explored below, was making moves in Britain during the nineteenth century towards such markers. In the process, Terpsichore confronted the disciplining of her numerous manifestations by those antagonistic to her presence in contemporary Victorian life, at the same time as disciplining her votaries from within. Only through knowledge of the more general dance scene and Victorian attitudes to the dancing body can the abortive efforts to establish dance as meritorious in artistic and academic terms be broached. In the process of investigation, hopefully greater light can be shed on the Victorian legacies that lie beneath contemporary manifestations of the discipline.

British Victorian dance culture embraced ballet, the various novelty and so-called 'fancy' dances of the popular stage, the social repertoire of the ballroom and drawing room, and selected dances found in rural contexts that were later to be canonized as folk dance. Most academic publications on nineteenth-century dance in Britain address the genre of ballet, thereby reflecting mid-Victorian fascination with the ballerinas of the Romantic period and their repertoire. Ivor Guest, pioneer of historical study on the Romantic ballet, devoted several publications to ballet in London.[6] His perspective consolidates early twentieth-century opinion that from the 1850s onwards, ballet in Britain went into serious decline until the arrival of Diaghilev's *Ballets Russes* in 1911. This degeneration in ballet's fortunes was reversed, according to Guest and earlier writers,[7] only by the example of the Russians, which then led to the foundation of native ballet companies such as *Ballet Rambert* and the *Sadlers Wells Ballet* (later to be reinstituted as the *Royal Ballet*). This interpretation of a late Victorian and Edwardian cultural wasteland in theatre dance has been subject to considerable revision in the work of Alexandra Carter and Jane Pritchard.[8] The former has employed feminist perspectives on the socio-cultural and economic life of the late Victorian English ballet dancer and argues for a thriving ballet scene in the gentrified Victorian music hall of the Alhambra and Empire Theatres, London. Pritchard's publications arise from deep and extensive knowledge of primary source materials for much of nineteenth-century theatre dance in Britain, establishing not only the artistic and social conditions in which ballet flourished in venues and contexts no longer associated with so-called 'high' art but also explaining the legal framework in which it operated. Neither author is directly concerned with questions related to the difficulties of establishing dance as an academic discipline in the Victorian period; nonetheless, they provide essential material and commentary that may be drawn into a wider discussion on this topic.

Works by nineteenth century theatre historians may include reference to different genres of dance in the Victorian popular theatre and music hall, albeit mostly fleetingly, although there are notable exceptions.[9] Again, the authors' intention is not to address the state of dance as a discipline. Useful comparisons, however, might be made with drama and theatre historiography, using findings from research on the rising social status of the actor and growing respectability of the theatre during the same period.[10] Social dance studies are also sparse, ranking even lower as a subject of interest amongst most dance historians. The less technically complex dances than those of earlier centuries have exercised little appeal to scholars. My own monograph on dancing in English high society covers the late Victorian and Edwardian period with a strong

London emphasis and attention to the changing socio-cultural contexts. Of pertinence here is discussion of the differing expectations for young men and women which sheds light on societal values in relation to dance, gender, age, and race, and on the implications for any potential discipline formation of dance during this period.[11]

Over the border in Scotland, the vigorous social dancing scene in the nineteenth century features in general histories of Scottish dancing, but concentration on dance as a prospective discipline in Victorian culture is largely absent.[12] Doctoral theses by Catriona Scott and Patricia Ballantyne, however, have advanced the topic by providing valuable information on the late nineteenth-century formation of organizations of dancing teachers, the latter author proposing a useful model for the development of professionalization and regulation of dance.[13] This issue will be taken up later in this chapter, building on my earlier study of late nineteenth-century efforts by English dancing masters to professionalize dancing.[14]

A number of studies on Irish traditional dance have included critical analysis of the homogenization of dance practice, especially as aided by competitive structures, in the development of Irish nationalism and the role of cultural expression.[15] Again, dance as a university discipline in Ireland features late in the twentieth century.

The emergence of English folk dance as both an object of study and practice in the early years of the twentieth century (under the auspices of the English Folk Dance Society 1911) has been treated in a number of publications, the later of which have radically revised the often-hagiographical earlier literature on the Society's principal founder, Cecil Sharp. The more comprehensive and penetrating studies on the Edwardian folk dance revival have extended contextual understanding of the drive towards embracing a construct of essential Englishness in so-called folk culture further back into the Victorian era.[16] Many early twentieth-century advocates, calling for the professionalization of dance in other genres, also drew upon this strong nationalist sentiment that was progressively identifiable from the late Victorian period.

Sources on dance are comparatively plentiful in terms of reference to the various balls, dances, and tuition on offer that formed part of the social fabric of Victorian Britain. They are also often tantalizingly brief as is typical for a quotidian popular activity and scattered, for example, across newspapers, general periodicals, fiction, poetry, diaries, and autobiographies, while iconographic sources on dance are notoriously difficult to interpret. Such material does not provide rich pickings in terms of evidencing moves towards a discipline. Critical responses to theatrical dance performances published in the press tend to be of a generalist nature or else focus on the attributes of specific dancers. Only towards the end of the century does dance performance occasionally receive more regular and thoughtful commentary, as for example, in the writings of Arthur Symons and the Reverend Stewart Headlam.[17] Aside from occasional essays, numerous publications produced mostly by dance pedagogues exist as dance manuals, written for a general public, as well as a much smaller percentage addressed to those working within the profession in theatrical contexts. From the closing decade of the century there is a comparatively sudden increase in monographs and the arrival of dedicated periodicals which establish a basis for more in-depth study leading to the later emergence and privileging for study of specific dance genres, most notably those under the broad heading of Western theatre art dance.

In late twentieth-century dance history there is a tendency to isolate dance genres, often reflecting presentist classifications and values, rather than attempting a wider perspective in order to understand commonalities and differences across Victorian dance discourse. Since at least the eighteenth century, dance professionals, employed as dancers, choreographers, and teachers, often worked across dance genres and contexts of enactment as well as traversing European, and sometimes North American, boundaries. Further exploration of this international exchange lies beyond the scope of this chapter, which focusses upon the example of Britain, in anticipation of later comparative studies of pre-twentieth century disciplinary building. High profile dance professionals, often from dynastic families, travelled, spoke, and read other European languages, most notably French, learning not only of fresh dance repertoire but also of new theoretical approaches and models of professional association and practice.[18] Given that the dance profession had been international in character for some time, Victorian technological innovations served to strengthen such interchange and articulation of distinctive practices. One European country, however, cannot be ignored in considering the state of Victorian dance in Britain. The epitome of dance and its most sophisticated understanding was believed to flourish in France and it was to that country that social and theatrical participants in dance alike looked for the latest fashion and technical standards in dance performance.

The French Example: L'Académie Royale de Danse

France commanded an extensive and long lasting influence on dance as both an art and social accomplishment across Europe. Since the establishment of the Académie Royale de Danse in Paris in 1661, one of the country's first national learned bodies to foster and monitor cultural production, France had furnished most of the European courts, theatres, and opera houses with the best trained dancers and teachers. Regarded today as the first dance institution in Europe and North America,[19] the Académie, led by thirteen selected experts and under royal protection, had been formed to address the poor standards of dance tuition offered by unqualified teachers operating after a succession of wars. The early establishment of dance under the auspices of an academy in France, explicitly modelled on that dedicated to painting and sculpture, highlights the value of dance accorded by royal patronage, as well as the granting to its members of a national remit to regulate the practice of dance across the country.[20]

Although falling into abeyance subsequent to the French Revolution in 1789, the Académie provided a much-cited model for the organization and control of dance discourse and practice across Europe over the next two centuries. Prior to the Académie, dance tuition in France had been controlled by the minstrels' (by the seventeenth century this had become the violinists') guild with its origins in the fourteenth century. This arrangement underlines two factors in the struggle to establish dance as a discrete discipline: the very close association of dance pedagogy with that of musicians and the notion of dance as an artistic profession, not a trade. Direct royal patronage has undoubted advantages but Rose Pruiksma has plausibly argued that the initiative for the French academy as a separate organization out of the control of other artists owed more to the dancing masters' ambitions than to the personal intervention of Louis XIV.[21] Such a desire to control standards (and any potential rewards) for dance to be governed by its own professionals, thereby elevating their social status, was an argument to be echoed in Victorian Britain.

France's early institutional arrangements and cultural lead had ramifications for the development of dance in Britain. The Académie's initial directive to guarantee highly trained dancers for Louis XIV's *ballets de cour* had led to the separate institution of a dedicated and professionalized school for the training of dancers at the Paris Opéra in 1713. England could not compete, turning to France, especially during the eighteenth and early nineteenth centuries, to provide its leading theatrical dancers and the latest social dances from Paris.[22]

The *cachet* of being taught by a French dancing teacher, particularly ones who had enjoyed an international reputation as ballet dancers, resonated throughout the Victorian period. London's eighteenth- and nineteenth-century theatres typically lacked similarly long established and prestigious training schools of dance with a national remit and consequently drew many of their stars from the Paris Opéra. Dance, in its most artistic form, was decidedly perceived as French and in its theatrical form as ballet was judged, until much later in the nineteenth century, to be an elite activity in England, on the basis of the social composition of much of its audience, and in view of the long years of preparatory training for its dancers. In the wake of the 1789 revolution, several French dancing teachers had settled in England, but until the early twentieth century Paris continued to set the fashion for dance, particularly in the social realm.[23]

It is important to note that social and stage dancing in Europe shared a common technical basis in the principles of the opera ballet until the early twentieth century. Dancing teachers in Britain, as elsewhere in the

Eurocentric world, taught a comparatively wide range of dancing that shared a similar aesthetic: thus dancers from the opera ballet were expected to teach deportment, ballroom etiquette, and the latest social dances, whilst generalist teachers, working more consistently at various levels of society, gave instruction in basic ballet technique. By the early nineteenth century, however, there was a marked contrast between the skills of the professional opera ballet dancer and that of the most practised social dancer, a divergence that was to split yet further as the century progressed.

After the French Revolution, apart from a brief period in which dancers in high society sought to embody the virtuosic steps of the professional dancer in the drawing and ballroom repertoire, dancing in the social realm became progressively and literally more pedestrian. Dancing as a theatrical art became ever more distinguished by professionalism and a technique that tended towards the spectacular and was demanding of time and physical effort.[24] For the majority of dance teachers, however, their livelihood lay outside the theatre, offering less visibility, financial reward, and status. To understand the prejudices against establishing dance as a respected academic discipline in the Victorian era, it is necessary to consider the cultural baggage of the dancing master in the social realm.

Ambivalence and Ridicule: The Status of the Dancing Master

An essential ingredient in the emergence of a discipline is a critical mass of experts, widely respected for their specialist knowledge. The privileged social position that this esteemed command of knowledge might bring, however, mostly eluded the dancing teacher. In fact, the dancing master (typically a male occupation before the later nineteenth century although by no means exclusively so) characteristically occupied an ambivalent status among his social peers and superiors.[25] The majority were not leisured gentleman scholars but instead were paid to provide a service leading to social betterment, through instruction in visual signifiers of corporeal distinction – that is, deportment, etiquette, and fashionable dancing. Dancing teachers taught the outward signs of 'breeding' and gentility to those who, as royals, aristocrats, and gentry, were supposed to have inherited such traits and to those, lower down the scale, who wished to purchase such attributes. The dancing master's knowledge therefore was socially suspect, although it had been essential for several centuries for the correct practice of courtly ritual: his ability to ape genteel manners, his potential circulation among elite circles, and his physical proximity when instructing their womenfolk fostered fears of duplicity, pretension, and immoral behaviour. During the nineteenth century, the political significance of elite balls organized by dancing instructors (who sometimes doubled as bandleaders and composers) declined. The expert knowledge of Victorian dancing masters was also variable, mostly depending on the social class they served; instructors ranged from the sought-after theatrical dancers and writers of manuals to the 'jobbing' provincial teacher who might use dance tuition to supplement a job as stonemason or blacksmith.

The extent of knowledge expected from nineteenth-century dance teachers was also changing. By the early Victorian period, the desire to approximate the artifice of eighteenth-century French deportment and manners was being replaced by preference for a more 'natural' demeanour considered to be more indicative of the 'honest Briton'.[26] Hence, Charles Dickens's portrait of Old Mr Turveydrop in *Bleak House* (1853) ridicules the dancing master's anachronistic clothing, posture, and affectation, while his earlier depiction of Signor Billsmethi in *Sketches by Boz* (1836), who taught in the rough East End of London, signals the charlatan tendencies of individuals masquerading (for the gullible) as conduits to polite society, within a profession that operated without regulation.

Dancing in the eyes of many Victorians was a profession that was designed to engender fun rather than any claim to thought-provoking study; it was principally a pastime, an almost quotidian cultural activity that in the social realm was increasingly accessible to all.[27] When the real-life celebrated dancing master Baron (born Barnett) Nathan, Master of Ceremonies and Managing Director of the popular Rosherville Gardens in Gravesend, Kent, made known his plan to open a college of dancing, the satirical magazine *Punch* immediately seized the chance for a lampoon. This was illustrated with a cartoon of 'the Baron' dancing in gown and mortarboard[28] (see Figure 2.1). Not only are Nathan's pretensions to social status a subject of ridicule but also derided is the idea that dance could be a serious subject for study. A later satirical sketch in the magazine entitled 'A Dancing University' also relies upon its readers' recognition of the absurdity of the notion. References to classical literature in both pieces are not without significance in underlining the mockery.[29]

The adoption of the title of 'Professor of Dancing' by those, such as Nathan, who were considered, or were self-elected, to be at the top of their occupation might be thought another indication of personal aggrandizement, although the title was widely in use during the mid-nineteenth century by those professing music, phrenology, calisthenics, and even by the proprietors of Punch and Judy shows.[30]

In another *Punch* skit, a letter purportedly written by a dancing master suggests remedies to address the contemporary decline of education in dancing and manners.

> Nor is there a dancing professorship at any of our Universities. Can we wonder, then, at the general awkwardness of scholars? Is it astonishing that three-fourths of our clergy are unable to walk, and therefore unfit to *enter* the Church? Latin and Greek may be all very well, but

Figure 2.1 'The College of Dancing', *Punch,* October 16, 1847, p. 142. By courtesy of Punch Cartoon Library/Topfoto.

> they will not enable us to go into a room. Mathematics may be useful enough, but they will not teach us how to offer an arm to a lady.[31]

Such a parody underlines the utility and esteem of certain university-approved subjects, while at the same time mocking social graces once deemed essential in polite society. The letter's spoof author, who offers his 'genius', claims the distinctive qualification of MD, glossed here as 'Master of Dancing' and not the long respected title of Doctor of Medicine, conferred as a university degree.

Without a governing body within the dance profession that might judge and award titular honours, a master or professorship of dance was by no means comparable to such titles awarded to experts in the 'serious' subjects such as archaeology, engineering, international law, and even fine art, now increasingly to be found in the university sector. Terpsichore was not counted among their numbers; her temples for worship, as contemporary writers indicated, were in the schools, academies, and associated subscription balls. Neither were they in the form of learned societies open to enthusiastic amateurs anxious to learn more about the subject; Terpsichore's Victorian votaries met essentially to dance and not to read or discuss the activity. When London's Adelaide Gallery (ostensibly opened to instruct and amuse its audience in practical science) presented a lecture on dance, the satirical press poured scorn on the event's relevance and usefulness.[32] Further indication of the dismissal of dance as desirably utilitarian is evident in a cartoon of 1849 (See Figure 2.2) in which instruction in dance for the rural classes acts as a synecdoche to ridicule Lord Henry Brougham's Society for the Diffusion of Useful Knowledge.[33]

For those wishing to raise the stakes for a cultural activity which had been variously discussed from the eighteenth century in Britain as an art, as a social accomplishment, and as healthy exercise, it was essential to define dance as a distinct field with specific theoretical literature, methodology, objects, and practice of study as well as institutional apparatus and means of reproduction. To begin with, an organization such as the Académie Royale was needed.

THE DANCING LESSON.

Professor Brougham and his Agricultural Pupils.

"His Lordship is possessed by an honourable ambition to beat everybody and everything * * * If his Lordship can put a little more life into these gentlemen, he will do them good service."—See *Times*.

Figure 2.2 'The Dancing Lesson. Professor Brougham and His Agricultural Pupils', *Punch*, September 29, 1849, p. 126. By courtesy of Punch Cartoon Library/Topfoto.

Organizing and Protecting the Professionals

The organization of societies dedicated to specific subjects, as for example, zoology and anthropology, played a crucial role in disciplinary development (see, respectively, Chapters 5 and 6 by David Lowther and Efram Sera-Shriar). In the case of dance, however, initial attempts in Britain to found an organization for the discipline were propelled by concerns to protect livelihoods and standards of the services which dancing teachers offered. In contrast to most Victorian learned societies whose ranks were drawn primarily from a social and intellectual elite, dance society members in the nineteenth century were, almost without exception, non-university educated workers whose names were more often to be found in trade directories and newspaper adverts than in scholarly journals or periodicals.

The establishment of a society focused on working for the common good of dancing teachers and their profession was slow to emerge. A principal factor was the strong element of individual competition as teachers struggled to recruit and maintain a clientele in a livelihood that privileged fashion and reflected the social hierarchy which they served.[34] Indeed, the first known organization in the nineteenth century was more concerned with welfare issues than promotion of dance as a subject of potential serious study. The Provident Society of Dancers and Teachers of Dancing instituted in 1844 at a meeting held at the Literary Institution, Leicester Square, London was first and foremost one of many friendly societies in Britain established to support the financial concerns of its members should they fall upon hard times.[35] The dancing profession was especially prone to lapses in income as a result of injury and age, as well as the impact of itinerant careers, moving between short contracts in various theatres. Professional dancers supplemented income from their stage career by teaching deportment, movement etiquette, and the latest fashionable dances. Those at the peak or profiting from cultural memory of their earlier fame could command an exclusive clientele of sometimes royalty, the aristocracy and gentry. The renowned ballerina Marie Taglioni, for example, towards the end of her life in the 1870s taught members of Queen Victoria's family and circle in London.[36] During the annual dancing season which ran from October to May, regular advertisements for dance and deportment tuition appeared in the *Times* and *Morning Post* and other national and provincial papers, offering classes to both children and adults. Typically the more prestigious teachers 'begged to announce' their availability and proffered their credentials, referring to the theatres in which they had lately been employed and/or to the fact that they were recently returned from Paris with the latest dances (see Figure 2.3). The pedagogic profession followed a strict hierarchy that mapped onto the social class which they might instruct, according to a scale of *cachet* and potential income charges. Most dancing teachers received their training through

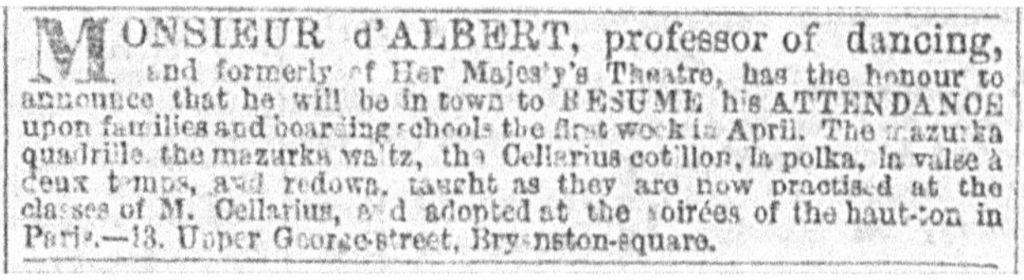
MONSIEUR d'ALBERT, professor of dancing, and formerly of Her Majesty's Theatre, has the honour to announce that he will be in town to RESUME his ATTENDANCE upon families and boarding schools the first week in April. The mazurka quadrille, the mazurka waltz, the Cellarius cotillon, la polka, la valse à deux temps, and redowa, taught as they are now practised at the classes of M. Cellarius, and adopted at the soirées of the haut-ton in Paris.—13, Upper George-street, Bryanston-square.

Figure 2.3 Advertisement from *The Times*, March 22, 1845, p. 8, column 2. By courtesy of The British Library Board.

being articled to a master, authority and competence being granted through interpersonal years of study rather than through membership of a guild, society, or organization which might award qualifications. By the 1840s, however, in the wave of 'polka mania', the latest dance craze that had flooded the dance pedagogic market with untrained foreign instructors, it was clear that British based dance teachers needed to protect their livelihoods.[37] Consequently, the 1844 Provident Society was not only designed as a relief fund subscribed to by its members; it also appended two 'branches', the first setting out regulations for 'one uniform method of teaching all fashionable dances' and the second setting up a 'Register Office' as an agency for out of work dancers. It also aimed to establish by donation a free 'Musical and Scientific Library' to 'consist of instructive, fashionable, and curious works, appertaining to the art of Dancing'. Further record of this proposed library is lacking in the subsequent press records of the meetings of the Society and proposals by Edgar Webster to establish a school of dancing and to award a prize for the best essay on dancing seem to not have been taken up.[38] The Society had more pressing concerns in terms of collecting subscriptions on time and raising funds for its activities, as well as finding sufficient employment for newly trained dancers.[39] Indeed, the reach and effectiveness of the Society appear to have been limited in its twenty-eight years of existence.

Over a decade after the Society's official closure, the drive towards recognition of competence within the profession bore fruit in the establishment in 1884 in Glasgow of the Scottish Association of Teachers of Dancing.[40] The need for regulation was largely the result of protectionism in a competitive market; the end of the nineteenth century witnessed an increase of interest in social dancing from a more moneyed lower-middle class with a corresponding increase in the number of unqualified teachers to meet the demand. A similar situation pertained in England as the activities of Robert Crompton to establish a national association for dance teachers in the early 1890s demonstrate.[41] One successful attempt was the British Association of Teachers of Dancing established in 1892 but its remit was much less ambitious than that of Crompton.[42] Crompton's plans to found a national association as a result of a three day

'Amateur Terpsichorean Congress' was due to be held in London with the support of the Westminster Orchestral Society in 1893. It included not only a ball to raise funds and secure patronage from leading society and parliamentary members but also, with a view towards disciplining Terpsichore, a day of papers to be presented by dancing teachers for discussion. Crompton even speculated on the prospect of a national headquarters for the art of dance pedagogy. The Congress was extensively advertised in Crompton's newly founded periodical *Dancing*, the chief aim of which, stated in the editorial of the first issue, was 'to secure for dancing the restoration of its ancient prestige, and an acknowledgement of its title to a prominent place among the fine arts'.[43]

For a variety of reasons, the Congress was aborted. It was not until 1904 that Crompton emerged as the president of a newly constituted Imperial Society of Dance Teachers (ISDT), mooted at a meeting in 1902, and supported at its inauguration at the Hotel Cecil in London by over two hundred teachers. With its provision of an annual Technical School and a dedicated professional bi-monthly publication the *Dance Journal* (from 1907), the ISDT largely overcame the professional jealousies within the pedagogic profession to become by 1918 the largest such society in the world.[44] Standardization and peer approval of dance training and its teachers were the Society's principal aims rather than any pretence to educational study; the institutional aspirations, paralleled to varying degree in the explosion of similar professional associations launched in the early decades of the twentieth century, were to nurture Terpsichore within the framework of vocational rather than academic training.

This is not to say that the ISDT ignored the need to educate its members on the history and technical literature of dance. The *Dance Journal* followed the lead of *Dancing* and *The Dancing Times* (1894–1902), edited by dancing master Edward Humphrey, in publishing extracts from earlier treatises by historically significant dance masters, and its editor Charles d'Albert, vice-president of the ISDT, undertook the Society's 1910 resolution to compile the *Encyclopaedia of the Art of Dancing*, the first such British publication on dance.

Heading the ISDT's list of objectives, recalling Crompton's earlier goals, was that of the 'elevation and advancement of the Art of Dancing, and the preservation of its ancient prestige and dignity'.[45] Among the other ten objectives primarily fashioned to regulate the conduct of the profession were the publication and dissemination of the *Dance Journal* and also '[l]ectures and the reading and discussion of papers upon Dancing and kindred Arts'.[46] Such goals were addressed to dance pedagogues, rather than to any wider audience with a non-professional interest in the subject.

Partaking in the general wave of interest in dance in Britain at the turn of the nineteenth and twentieth centuries were the founders of the

Edwardian revival of English folk dance and song. They rapidly succeeded in establishing a number of the hallmarks of discipline building. Within less than two decades, the folk dance revivalists, who operated outside of the tradition of professional dance teaching, had secured folk dance instruction within the Board of Education syllabus (1909); a dedicated national organization the English Folk Dance Society (1911) with subsequent regional branches, open both to those earning their livelihood as folk dance teachers and to amateur enthusiasts; publication of books containing notations and interpretive history (from 1907); syllabuses of competitions and examinations; and a dedicated journal (from 1915).[47] This rapid success has to be understood within the wider climate of enthusiasm for dance and particularly as nationalist tinged and enjoyable alternatives to the moribund state of waltzing in most ballrooms and, from 1910, the craze for ragtime and African American-sourced social dances and music such as the Onestep and Tango. Its leading proponent, Cecil Sharp, a member of the existing English Folk Song Society, university educated and with excellent social connections, had gathered around him a similar social class of enthusiasts who shared his aims of the revival of folk dance as artistic performance.[48] Although English folk dance was readily taken up in university extra-curricular contexts and had been given national official approval in the education syllabus of schools, dance remained outside the walls of higher academia.

Establishing Written Discourse on Dance in Victorian Britain

In the formulation of a discipline, a dedicated literature with and to which specialists can contribute and critically engage is essential. Theoretical writings on the technical practice and composition of dance did exist prior to the nineteenth century. In Britain, the most influential texts were those by dancer, choreographer, and teacher John Weaver (1673–1760), whose publications were mined and reproduced, often wholesale without acknowledgement, over almost two centuries. Appearing in various treatises on dancing, most notably those by Giovanni Gallini (1762) and Francis Peacock (1805), Weaver's observations were often cited in nineteenth-century dance manuals.[49]

Mostly written by dancing masters as guides to the contemporary ballroom, manuals often included a short introductory section on the value and history of dancing in society. Arguably, this tradition of constant recycling of written material hindered further extension of dance knowledge and theory. In any case the purpose of these texts, which included advice on deportment and ballroom etiquette, was not to further theory or knowledge of the subject of dance itself. They were primarily short, often repetitive and addressed to a public with scant knowledge of dance. Dancing teachers might read and refer to the latest volumes to be able to pass on new dances as a lucrative commodity to their clientele but there was little scope for theoretical exposition to such a readership.

Within the burgeoning magazine and periodical industry, demand for lengthy copy on the history, meaning, and theory of dancing was also limited. Readers, especially those later in the century, of the dedicated women's columns, were more likely to enjoy information on the latest fashions in dress, dances, and the dancing activities of aristocrats and celebrities from Paris.[50] The lifestyle of dancing teachers also militated against regular, sustained discourse on dancing. Frequently itinerant, taking individual lessons during the day and classes by night, as well as organizing balls, dances, and musicians (a number were themselves composers and bandleaders), dancing teachers were left with little time or motivation to develop a critical literature on the subject. In the theatre, similar constraints on time prevailed. As a predominantly oral and kinetic tradition, dancing was not generally considered to require written text.

The absence of a commonly accepted written recording system for dance within the profession has frequently been cited as a major hindrance in precluding acceptance of dance as an area of academic study. The absence of written scores of dance works, unlike the case in Western European mainstream music, has, so the argument goes, prevented comparable sophisticated communication and detailed analysis: dance's supposed ephemerality has shut off the past and occluded the present.[51] There are undoubtedly elements of truth in this consideration, especially given the complexities of recording bodies in motion and the lack of film and synchronized sound until the early twentieth century. The point here, however, is to understand the views of Victorian dancing masters on this issue.

Certainly the better educated in their occupation, whether through reading existing literature or knowledge gained through oral tradition, were aware of earlier forms of notation, most notably Feuillet notation.[52] By the end of the eighteenth century this system was obsolete, as the technique of dancing had widely diverged from a notation designed to record that of earlier times. The first dance notation to emerge in nineteenth-century London and which was harnessed to the contemporary technique of ballet was by dancer and dancing master E. A. Théleur (1831). His professed aim for dance was 'to snatch the art from the imputation of being illiterate and mechanic' and to 'reduce it to systematic principles, so that it may take its place among scientific arts'.[53] Théleur's notation, which he called chirography, was based on abstract symbols (see Figure 2.4), an approach that was later taken up more comprehensively in the twentieth century.[54] Less extensive dance notations existed in social dance manuals but these principally comprised diagrams and verbal notations that, even though expressed in language familiar to author and reader, were often perplexing. Dancing master and theoretician Edward

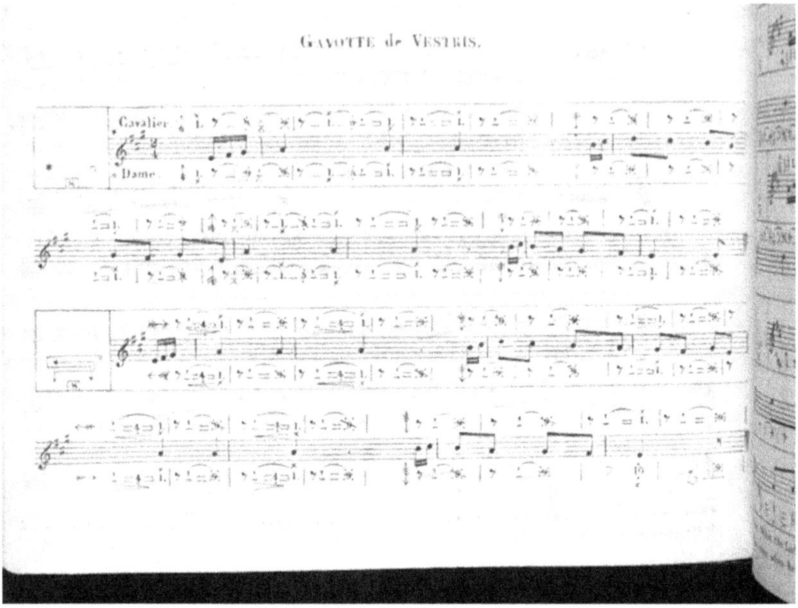

Figure 2.4 E. A. Théleur, 'Gavotte de Vestris', *Letters on Dancing* (London: Sherwood, 1831), p. 72. By courtesy of The British Library Board 558*.c.41.

Scott (1852–1937) criticized such efforts on the grounds of inadequacy and inaccuracy.[55] Lacking in correct analytic observation and linguistic precision, such descriptions were little more than aide-memoires for the amateur dancer.

Other attempts at devising workable notations were made outside Britain and in 1891 Crompton attempted to promote the system by Frederick Zorn of Odessa whose *Grammar of the Art of Dancing* (1887), published in German and Russian, had been translated into English in America. Crompton argued for the adoption of Zorn's system in order to facilitate rapid and accurate transmission of new dances between teachers,[56] signalling ease of vocational practice rather than pursuit of theoretical study commensurate with academic goals. The dancing profession continued to be resistant to learning notation – the creation and teaching of dance was an incorporated tradition, reliant upon interpersonal contacts, and not upon inscription. Busy schedules were not compatible with long hours studying symbols. In any case, dance composition primarily took place on bodies not on paper – thus, attempts to establish dance as a recordable art form comparable with music were of limited relevance.

Part of the legitimization process in demarcating an academic discipline in the arts and humanities lies in establishing a canon of works judged worthy of study. As philosopher of dance Anna Pakes has argued, however, the notion of dance's autonomy as an art form looks to be a twentieth-century formulation.[57] Citing musicologist and music historian Marian Smith's work on the Parisian ballet and opera in the 1830s and 1840s, Pakes notes the contemporary production of such now famous works as *Giselle* (1841) as less a dance work in which dancing forms the principal medium than a 'mimed musical drama with dancing'.[58] It is easy to forget today that such works were known at the time as ballet-pantomimes and that the technique in which dancers were trained was referred to as operatic dancing even in the early twentieth century. Victorian ballet as experienced in Britain was not the separate art form as understood today. This shift towards discrete recognition did not occur until almost a hundred years or so later when the figure of the choreographer gained prominence as the 'auteur' of a bounded, repeatable dance work. Drawing inspiration from Lydia Goehr's analysis of the production of European art music around 1800, Pakes thus questions the supposed cultural continuity of the concept of the dance work.

For the Victorians, dance as a recorded stable and single authored artwork did not exist for the exercise of analytic and reflective consideration. Dances were noted as being arranged not choreographed in nineteenth-century Britain, indicating that dance, if not always at the service of the other arts, was nonetheless not always the leading focus. The 'author' in this composite form contributed to the whole creative production not in the manner of the twentieth-century understanding of 'choreographer'.

Along with the notion of sole authorship is that of an original or authentic work.[59] Although the notion of authenticity was current in nineteenth-century British theatre, it was only towards the end of the century that interest turned towards replicating past dances. This, though, was principally in the context of theatre productions, especially in staging works by Sheridan and Shakespeare.[60] To modern eyes, this was a curious interpretation of the concept of authenticity: historical material was still adapted for contemporary audiences rather than presenting it in a more academic manner of as close as possible a rendition of the sources. The nineteenth-century dancing master John D'Auban, for example, consulted manuscripts in the British Museum in order to re-create dances of the seventeenth century in a revival of an early English masque. Descriptions and illustration of the result look more Victorian than Jacobean or indeed Elizabethan (the two reigns were collapsed). Nonetheless, the initiative indicates the beginnings of serious study of the past through locating and studying primary source materials and contributed to the establishment of the twentieth-century historical dance movement in Britain. The purpose in late Victorian Britain was principally to perform the 'ancient' dances. New careers even if on a somewhat restricted scale emerged from this interest, paralleling in limited degree that of the early music revival and its close companion the folk dance revival.[61]

Both the folk and historical dance movements were manifestations of a growing interest in the past history of dance. Producing written discourse on the history of dance helped to lay the groundwork for the formulation of a discipline of dance, legitimizing present practice and ameliorating its value as a serious subject. Three books were published in London in the last decade of the nineteenth century: Lilly Grove's *Dancing* (the first world history of dance, 1895), Edward's Scott's *Dancing in All Ages* (1899), and a translation from the French of Gaston Vuillier's *A History of Dancing* (1898). The latter two were written in the same European historical tradition, frequently seen more briefly, in dancing masters' manuals that traced earliest traces of dancing to the ancient Egyptians, Greeks, and Romans. Grove's vision of dance's history, as I have discussed more fully elsewhere re-cast dance's value in a different history – that of the evolution of mankind.[62] Dance was now apportioned a seriousness largely hitherto denied, as the headline 'The Dance Treated Scientifically' to a report on a lecture by Grove to the British Association (Anthropological Section) made clear.[63]

Undoubtedly this new perspective opened the subject up to further discourse by non-dance professionals but it arguably positioned dance yet further as the earliest and therefore lowest form of art in what would become a standard modernist interpretation of dance as non-verbal, emotionally expressive, non-rational, and essentially primitive. Terpsichore in such terms would appear only to be taking small steps in the progress of European civilization. Dance was now linked mainly by scholars without specialist knowledge to the non-powerful in European society – non-European primitives, women, and children – each regarded by white, often university-educated men as displaying excessive interest in and facility for dancing. Aside from the issues rehearsed above that pertain to the professional practice of dancing, inter-related and deep-rooted obstacles to the development of a discipline lay enmeshed in long-standing attitudes towards dance in Victorian society that focussed upon values of embodied gender.

Dance, Religion, and Education

Pervasive attitudes to dance in Victorian society stemmed from Christianity and from ancient Greek philosophy. The Church had a centuries-old history of opposition to dance and to the theatre, which was intensified in the Puritan tradition that, from the eighteenth century, took further form in the evangelical movement. Theatre professionals were perceived to possess dubious morals, especially the women, whose dancing on stage, positioning themselves as objects of the male gaze, was often viewed as tantamount to prostitution. There is no doubt that the so-called protection of male admirers in the nineteenth century, often encouraged by mothers keen to capitalize on the short careers of daughters enjoying the limelight, was a pathway to financial security in an age where marriage and a spinster's life looking after elderly relatives were often dominant outcomes for women to achieve respectability and a home.[64] The ranks of the English corps de ballet were less likely to attract a rich and socially well-connected lover, but even if the dancers led a blameless life their occupation was still tainted with the widespread perception of their occupation as a dancing or ballet girl, a euphemism for a prostitute. The dress of the ballet girl encouraged such attitudes. The shorter skirts of the late nineteenth-century ballet dancer facilitated performance and viewing of the increasingly virtuosic pirouettes and higher leg extensions but also encouraged further condemnation of indecency and ugliness in a dance style that by some was viewed as artificial, graceless, and acrobatic.[65] Not all churchmen were against the ballet. Most notably, the Reverend Stewart Headlam, Anglican priest and Christian Socialist, openly campaigned for better conditions for dancers and appreciation of the ballet as an art form.[66]

Social dancing also had its religious critics within the Anglican Church. The Reverend W. H. Finney considered that 'there was no place where jealousies and heartaches were so fostered as the dancing room' believing dancing to be contrary to spiritual growth.[67] Bodily contact between men and women in popular round dances such as the waltz and polka deeply troubled Reverend James Davies, the Anglican rector of Abbenhall, Gloucestershire, as late as 1870 when such dances had been staples of the ballroom for most of the century.[68] Some vicars refused to allow dancing on premises associated with the church even when the dances were intended to raise funds for charitable purposes.[69] In the nonconformist tradition in particular, dancing was deemed to be frivolous, a misuse of time and of one's body, both of which should be devoted to worship.

It is no surprise then that a familiar trope in religious tracts and fiction is that of the young girl who dies following her visit to the ballroom when she should have heeded her parents or stayed at home to say her prayers.[70] The giddiness induced by constant whirling in the waltz was thought by opponents to threaten not only the maintenance of what was deemed to be lady-like behaviour but was also injurious to the health of the weaker sex.[71] Social and moral order in the eyes of those expressing more extreme religious certainties was under threat when people met to dance.

Indeed, moves to discipline potential dancing had been enshrined in law since the mid-eighteenth century through the Disorderly Houses Act (Act Geo. II, c. 36) whereby those wishing to hold public dances were required to apply for a licence from the magistrates. Unlicensed dancing between the sexes in public spaces was thought conducive to drunkenness, sex, prostitution, theft, and civil disorder; numerous cases were brought to court throughout the century, increasing towards the end when legal powers for reinforcement passed to local authorities in the expanding towns and cities. Instructors holding dances in their academies frequently fell afoul of the law, mistakenly believing that their occupational activities were exempt largely as a result of often unsystematic prosecution. Newspaper reports of court cases against unlicensed dancing academies did nothing to elevate the social esteem of local dancing masters, nor was the general image of dancing helped by reports of trials against prostitutes and thieves who frequented public dancing halls.[72] For those nonconformist middle-class families especially, dancing by no means offered a career route towards improvement but embodied unproductive spent time and an undisciplined threat to social and spiritual standing.

Such attitudes, however, were not widespread in the power base of the aristocracy, whose endless round of balls during the London season from early May to the end of June enabled dynastic marriages to be brokered. Nevertheless, it was within this social milieu that reasons for the failure of dance to be legitimized as a serious subject were at their most effective. Among the male social elite, classical philosophy helped to shape cultural values, a tenet that was enshrined in the Victorian education system. Competence in Ancient Greek and Latin was essential to attend Oxford and Cambridge and, later in the century, to enter government services. Versed in a classical education since preparatory school, men inevitably assimilated attitudes of antiquity towards the male dancer, which were ambivalent to say the least. Apologists for dance might have 'cherry-picked' antique and biblical references in praise of dancing, as classical scholar Edith Hall has argued, but as she concludes, 'dance has been associated with decadent pleasure-seeking, unmanliness, and the arousal of sexual desire from its very first appearances in western cultural history'.[73] The oppositional juxtaposition between dancing and fighting in antiquity that she cites resonated into the Victorian period where one anti-dance writer called upon 'Nature' to underline the essential masculinity of war in contrast to femininity which, the author felt, was best expressed in dancing.[74] Furthermore, the seven liberal arts of Plato's Academy taken as a basis for Western education did not include dance.[75] The complex of military training, which in the Renaissance period had included dance and sword play, diminished with the increasing introduction of fire-arms, further situating dance instruction for the purposes of social and recreational activity while team games, drill, and gymnastics became valued as being more effective for modern warfare.[76] Increasingly feminized throughout the nineteenth century, dancing as a subject lay outside the interests and values of those in power. Women were largely excluded from university education in the nineteenth century and even when accepted were unlikely to be in a position or even wish to advance the cause of a subject that was held in low cultural esteem. Nor did most women, unlike men, wield economic power. If, as indicated, high ranking ladies were slow to help the dancing masters of the Provident Society of the 1840s financially through acting as patrons to their balls, it was highly unlikely that a rich male patron could be found to endow a university professorial chair, as had happened in the mid-century in the case of music.[77] Dancing masters might aspire to the status of gentleman, playing as an extremely accomplished violinist with upper-class amateur musicians, as in the case of Louis D'Egville, or relentlessly parading classical knowledge, as did Edward Scott in his publications,[78] but given such cultural legacies of exclusion, dance was never to be the focus of the male Victorian scholar. Any new discipline, at Oxford University for example, was expected to 'transform[ing] immature young men into responsible and capable leaders, at home and within the empire',[79] while utilitarian outcomes for those lower down the social scale, especially in schools chimed with notions of citizenship and nation-building.

Where dance might contribute to the latter aims was in the development of good health through physical exercise, a claim that had been touted by dancing masters for centuries. Recognition of, and alarm over, the nation's poor physical health at the end of the nineteenth century prompted the introduction of physical education, including dance, into schools in 1909, creating a national need for teachers able to deliver such a curriculum. Given that this was to be implemented in state elementary schools, girls' public schools, and teacher training colleges, thus institutions offering career route for young women, dancing once again fell into the sphere of the under-valued. Teacher training colleges did not offer scope for the development of disciplinary theory untied to educational aims and objectives as in a university discipline. In any case, unfavourable comparison was already being made between the science of gymnastics and that of the lack of systematic technique in the more eclectic syllabus of dancing which ranged across step patterns from historical and ballroom dances to national and folk dances.[80]

Terpsichore: Undisciplined in Victorian Academia

In classical antiquity, Terpsichore was not only the muse of dancing, but also of choral song. The classificatory system and performance of the arts in ancient Greece and Rome, even if it were possible to retrieve them from the historical record, did not automatically map onto modern practice and understanding.[81] By the nineteenth century, the muse's acknowledged stewardship of choral music, indeed of music at all, had dropped away in popular reference, leaving only dancing to be signified by evocation of Terpsichore. Yet dancing without music of any kind was unthinkable to the Victorians, either as an art or pastime, so integral was music to the manifestation of dancing; nonetheless, sustained theoretical considerations of choreo-musical relations or, indeed, of dance's exact connection to the other fine arts in British Victorian discourse were extremely limited. From the eighteenth century, dancing had theoretically been included within the system of fine arts, ostensibly shedding its medieval shackling to the mechanical arts, to become an equal art alongside poetry, music, and painting.[82] Yet noted Victorian art critic Walter Pater, for example, only fleetingly refers to dance in his writings. His essay on 'The School of Giorgione', which opens with the now famous dictum that '[a]ll art constantly aspires to the condition of music', does not interrogate dancing as part of his argument.[83] This is in spite of dancing's close association with music and rich potential in terms of illuminating the inter-related concepts of ekphrasis and ander-streben, employed by Pater to advance his argument that music alone of the arts collapses content and form. Bennett Zon (see Chapter 12 in this volume) identifies an alternative interpretation of Pater's treatment of these ideas, leading instead to the Victorian origins of musicology as an interdiscipline. In several respects, for Victorian apologists of dancing, its highest artistic manifestation, whether in classical antiquity as pantomime or on the Victorian stage as ballet, might suggest a focus for interdisciplinarity. Both ancient pantomime and the Victorian ballet-pantomime drew together the arts, requiring, as Victorian dance historian and writer Edward Scott argued following the tradition of Lucian, its performers, creators, and pedagogues to be knowledgeable in not only her 'sister arts' but also 'with anatomy, geometry, dynamics, and science generally'.[84] Such an extensive palette of interdisciplinary research potential and Victorian understanding of dance in relation to the arts and sciences, however, awaits fuller investigation. Suffice it to say here, that in relation to dance and moves towards professional validation in the nineteenth century, any aspiration of expert followers of Terpsichore towards the condition of music was targeted more towards the achievement of comparable social esteem and cultural standing, rather than towards any clear formulation of the study of dance as an interdiscipline, on either aesthetic or evolutionary grounds of interdisciplinarity.

Cultural value and legitimacy among social and intellectual elites are fundamental to the acceptance and development of a discipline; Terpsichore, although often revered by Victorians for her ancient Greek origins, was often reviled by the more extreme of Christian and classical disciples while progressively regarded as marginal to socio-political ritual in a democratizing age. Dance was increasingly feminized and infantilized, valued by scholars principally for a perceived primitivism in the narrative of human evolution and frequently considered a frivolity of no consequence; it is not at all surprising that Terpsichore failed to take her place in academia alongside music and fine art in Victorian Britain. Indeed, traces of such attitudes can be encountered today, stemming from a long inter-relation of once mainstream European thinking towards the moving body, sex, and gender.

If dance's progress towards the status of a discipline was impeded during the nineteenth century, largely through insistence on expectations of gendered behaviour and a privileging of logocentric activities in academia, nonetheless, there were moves made to shake off such prejudices and thinking. Such steps include the organization towards professionalization, the increase in specialist journals, the growth of scholarly literature, the championing of dance by notable writers and clergy, the eventual inclusion of dance in state schools, dance's national distinction as an expressive and historical practice, and the growing insistence upon dance as a serious art and not just as a mere amusement. The present overview in this chapter highlights the need for further research to be undertaken in examining the frequent paradoxes in the cultural status and practice of dance in nineteenth-century Britain, especially in relation to cognate disciplines. As a consequence, it is hoped that comparative studies may be undertaken and greater insight gained into the persistent inheritances and legacies of Victorian culture and the associated disciplinary origins of dance.

Notes

1 See, for example, the following written by dance educationalists: Thomas K. Hagood, *A History of Dance in American Higher Education: Dance and the American University* (New York: Edwin Mellen Press, 2000), Chapter 2, and Janice Ross, *Moving Lessons: Margaret H'Doubler and the Beginning of Dance in American Education* (Madison, Wisconsin: University of Wisconsin Press, 2000), Chapters 2 and 3. See also dance historians Nancy Lee Chalfa Ruyter's *Reformers and Visionaries: The Americanization of the Art of Dance* (New York: Dance Horizons, 1979), Chapters 5 and 6, and Linda J. Tomko's *Dancing Class: Gender, Ethnicity, and Social Divides in American Dance, 1890–1920* (Bloomington and Indianapolis: Indiana University Press, 1999), Chapter 1.

2 See Stephanie Jordan's polemic on the narrowing of dance research in UK universities in *The Dancing Times* (July 2017) 15.

3 This phenomenon (which may also be tied to potential dance careers in a neoliberal economy) has not yet received extensive scholarly analysis but see Suzanne Burns, *Mapping Dance: Entrepreneurship and Professional Practice in Dance Higher Education* (Lancaster: Palatine, Higher Education Academy, Subject Dance, Drama and Music, 2007) and Fiona Bannon, 'Starting from Here: Dance in Higher Education from the Inside Out', *Dance Dialogues: Conference Proceedings, Conversations across Cultures, Artforms and Practices* 2008, published 2011 as http://ausdance.org.au/articles/details/starting-from-here-dance-in-higher-education-from-the-inside-out accessed 21/7/2017.

4 As example, regrettably in academia, see the letter headed 'Amazing Dancing Profs', *Times Higher Educational Supplement* (November 24, 1995), 15. The cultural history behind such an attitude is explored in this chapter.

5 I am aware that what constitutes 'dance' is an ontological and cultural issue but discussion of this complexity lies beyond the scope of this chapter; similarly, outside the chapter's parameters lie examination of the historical and cultural issues, often shared with dance, surrounding the tardy acceptance of both music and drama as valuable assets in British society and their eventual formulation as university disciplines. On Victorian music and drama see, respectively, Rosemary Golding, *Music and Academia in Victorian Britain* (Farnham, Surrey: Ashgate, 2013) and Jonas Barish, *The Antitheatrical Prejudice* (Berkeley and London: University of California Press, 1981), Chapter 10.

6 See especially Ivor Guest, *Ballet in Leicester Square: The Alhambra and the Empire 1860–1915* (London: Dance Books, 1992).

7 Guest was following an interpretation already established by Cyril W. Beaumont and Arnold Haskell. I am grateful to Jane Pritchard for reminding me of this fact.

8 Alexandra Carter, *Dance and Dancers in the Victorian and Edwardian Music Hall Ballet* (Aldershot, Hampshire: Ashgate, 2005); Jane Pritchard, 'The Empire in Manchester', *Dance Research* 8/2 (1995), 11–27, 'Collaborative Creations for the Alhambra and the Empire', *Dance Chronicle* 24/1 (2001), 55–82, and '"The Great Hansen": An Introduction to the Work of Joseph Hansen, a Forgotten European Choreographer of the Late Nineteenth Century, with a Chronology of His Ballets', *Dance Research* 22/2 (2008), 73–139.

9 See, for example, J. S. Bratton, 'Dancing a Hornpipe in Fetters', *Folk Music Journal* 6/1 (1990), 65–82; Caroline Kershaw, '"They've done me, they've robbed me, but, thank God, I'm the champion still!" Clog Dancing in the Victorian Music Hall', *Border Tensions: Dance and Discourse, Proceedings of the Fifth Study of Dance Conference*, University of Surrey, compilers Janet Adshead-Lansdale and Chris Jones (Guildford, Surrey, UK : Dept. of Dance Studies, University of Surrey, 1995), 199–207; Catherine Hindson, *Female Performance Practice on the Fin-de-Siècle Popular Stages of London and Paris* (Manchester: Manchester University Press, 2007).

10 See Michael Baker, *The Rise of the Victorian Actor* [1978], (Abingdon, Oxon and New York: Routledge, 2016).

11 Theresa Jill Buckland, *Society Dancing: Fashionable Bodies in England, 1870–1920* (Basingstoke, Hampshire: Palgrave Macmillan, 2011).

12 See, for example, George S. Emmerson, *A Social History of Scottish Dance: Ane Celestial Recreatioun* (Montreal and London: McGill-Queen's University Press, 1972).

13 Catriona Mairi Scott, 'The Scottish Highland Dancing Tradition' (PhD diss., University of Edinburgh, 2005); Patricia Ballantyne, 'Regulation and Reaction: The Development of Scottish Traditional Dance with Particular Reference to Aberdeenshire, from 1805 to the Present Day' (PhD diss., University of Aberdeen, 2016).

14 See Theresa Jill Buckland, 'Crompton's Campaign: The Professionalisation of Dance Pedagogy in Late Victorian England', *Dance Research* 25/1 (2007), 1–34.

15 See, in particular, Catherine E. Foley, *Step Dancing in Ireland. Culture and History* (Farnham, Surrey: Ashgate, 2013), Chapter 5.

16 For example, Roy Judge, 'Merrie England and the Morris, 1881–1910', *Folklore* 104 (1993), 124–143 and '"The Old English Morris Dance": Theatrical Morris 1801–1880', *Folk Music Journal* 7/3 (1997), 311–350; Vic Gammon, '"Many Useful Lessons": Cecil Sharp, Education and the Folk Dance Revival, 1899–1924', *Cultural and Social History* 5/1 (2008), 75–97; Anne Blomfield, 'The Quickening of the National Spirit: Cecil Sharp and the

Pioneers of the Folk-Dance Revival in English State Schools (1900–1926)', *History of Education* 30/1 (2001), 59–75; Theresa Jill Buckland, 'Pioneering England's Dances among Late Victorian Youth: On the Early Work of Mary Neal and Grace Kimmins', in *(RE)searching the Field: Festschrift in Honour of Egil Bakka*, eds. Anne Margrete Fiskvik and Marit Stranden (Berg, Norway: Fagbokforlaget, 2014), 319–330.

17 Jane Pritchard, '"More Natural than Nature, More Artificial than Art": The Dance Criticism of Arthur Symons', *Dance Research* 21/2 (2003), 38–89; Richard Ralph, 'Stewart Headlam – the Dancing Priest', *About the House* 7 (Christmas 1984), 56–61.

18 For a general introduction to the figure of the dancing master see entry in *International Encyclopedia of Dance* [hereafter *Int. Encyc.*] (Oxford: Oxford University Press, 1998) and Foley, *Step Dancing*, Chapter 2.

19 See entry by Régine Astier on the Académie in *Int. Encyc.*

20 Maureen Needham, 'Louis XIV and the Académie Royale de Danse, 1661 – A Commentary and Translation', *Dance Chronicle* 20/2 (1997), 173–190.

21 Rose A. Pruiksma, 'Generational Conflict and the Foundation of the *Académie Royale de Danse*: A Reexamination, *Dance Chronicle* 26/2 (2003), 169–187.

22 There were, of course, eminent English dancers but the palm was always awarded to the French who were able to command high salaries. For an overview of the early eighteenth century see Jennifer Thorp, 'Dance in the London Theaters, c.1700–1750', in *Dance, Spectacle, and the Body Politick 1250–1750*, ed. Jennifer Nevile (Bloomington and Minneapolis, MN: Indiana University Press, 2008), and for the nineteenth century, Ivor Guest, *The Romantic Ballet in England* (London: Pitman, 1972).

23 See the example of the famous Noverre family, Trevor Fawcett, 'Provincial Dancing Masters', *Norfolk Archaeology* 35 (1973), 138–141.

24 See Sandra Noll Hammond, 'Clues to Ballet's Technical History from the Early Nineteenth-Century Ballet Lesson', *Dance Research* 3/1 (1984), 53–66, and her 'Dances Related to Theatrical Tradition', in *The Extraordinary Dance Book T B. 1826. An Anonymous Manuscript in Facsimile* (Stuyvesant, NY: Pendragon Press, 2000). On the lack of social distinction afforded by the nineteenth-century ballroom repertoire see Lawrence M. Zbikowski, 'Music, Dance and Meaning in the Early Nineteenth Century', *Journal of Musicological Research* 31 (2012), 147–165, especially 162–165.

25 On the well-established image of the dancing master in England see Richard Leppert, *Music and Image: Domesticity, Ideology and Socio-Cultural Formation in Eighteenth-Century England* (Cambridge: Cambridge University Press, 1988), Chapter 5, and more specifically Jennifer Thorp, 'Borrowed Grandeur and Affected Grace': Perceptions of the Dancing-Master in Early Eighteenth-Century England', *Music in Art*, Dance and Image, 36/1/2 (2011), 9–27. See also Cheryl A. Wilson, *Literature and Dance in Nineteenth-Century Britain* (Cambridge: Cambridge University Press, 2009), 22–24.

26 Buckland, *Society Dancing*, 119–122.

27 For the wider dance landscape of the Victorian era see Buckland, *Society Dancing*, and Philip J. S. Richardson, *The Social Dances of the Nineteenth-Century in England* (London: Herbert Jenkins, 1960).

28 'The College of Dancing', *Punch*, October 16, 1847, 142.

29 'A Dancing University', *Punch*, January 27, 1849, 38.

30 The use of the title was not restricted to men; see, for example, newspaper adverts for Miss Leonora Geary, Professor of Dancing and Deportment, *The Lady's Newspaper*, January 9, 1847, 34 and Mr. William Webster and Miss

Webster, Professors of Dancing in *Manchester Guardian*, January 20,1877, 5. Accusations of self-aggrandizement were common: see, for example, 'The Dancing Master', *The Penny Satirist*, April 29, 1843, 3.

31 'Dancing for the Million', *Punch* 3 (July–December 1842), 114.

32 'The Flight of Science – Dancing Illustrated', *The Satirist, the Censor of the Times*, October 20, 1844, 334.

33 'The Dancing Lesson. Professor Brougham and His Agricultural Pupils', *Punch*, September 29, 1849, 126. See too *Punch*'s (January 19, 1856, 49) mockery of Francis Mason's arguments (*A Treatise on the Use and Peculiar Advantages of Dancing and Exercises, Considered as a Means of Refinement and Physical Development* (London: Sharp and Hale, 1854).

34 This even extended to competing family members – see Buckland, *Society Dancing*, p. 88. For more general background on the nineteenth-century dancing teachers see Chapters 7 and 8.

35 *Laws and Regulations of the Provident Society of Dancers and Teachers of Dancing of the United Kingdom and Ireland. Instituted Midsummer 1844* (London: Provident Society of Dancers and Teachers of Dancing, 1849). Copy in British Library, London.

36 See Buckland, *Society Dancing*, 80, and Sarah C. Woodcock, 'Margaret Rolfe's Memoirs of Marie Taglioni: Part 1', *Dance Research* 7/1 (1989), 3–19, and 'Part 2', *Dance Research* 7/2 (1989), 55–69.

37 Reference was made to this situation in the annual meeting. *The Era*, July 29, 1849, p. 15. On polka mania see Libby Smigel, 'Minds Mad for Dancing: Polkamania on the London Stage', *Popular Culture* 30/3 (1996), 197–207.

38 *The Observer*, January 11, 1847, 5.

39 *The Observer*, July 29, 1849, 6. The Provident Society was dissolved in 1871, *Marylebone Mercury*, April 15, 1871, 2.

40 See Ballantyne, 'Regulation and Reaction', 231. Details on the formation of this association are elusive but teachers were advertising their certification by 1888, see *Kirkintilloch Herald*, January 4, 1888, 2.

41 See Buckland, 'Crompton's Campaign'.

42 Bryan Isaac, *The British Association of Teachers of Dancing. A Brief Review of One Hundred Years* (Glasgow: British Association of Teachers of Dancing, 1992).

43 *Dancing*, June 8, 1891.

44 Charles d'Albert, 'The Imperial Society of Dance Teachers. Its History, Objects and Its Future', *The Dancing Times* (May 1918) 245, 247. For a list of similar contemporary organizations see Buckland, 'Crompton's Campaign', 20–21.

45 d'Albert, 'The Imperial', 247.

46 Ibid.

47 On the Edwardian revival of folk dance and song see, Georgina Boyes, *The Imagined Village: Culture, Ideology and the English Folk Revival* (Manchester: Manchester University Press, 1993); Gammon, '"Many Useful Lessons"'; Roy Judge, 'Mary Neal and the Espérance Morris', *Folk Music Journal* 5/5 (1989), 545–591 and 'Cecil Sharp and Morris 1906–1909', *Folk Music Journal* 8/2 (2002), 195–228.

48 Derek Schofield, '"Revival of the Folk Dance: An Artistic Movement": The Background to the Founding of the English Folk Dance Society in 1911', *Folk Music Journal* 5/2 (1986), 215–219.

49 See introduction in Richard Ralph, *The Life and Works of John Weaver. An Account of His Life, Writings and Theatrical Productions* (London: Dance Books, 1985).

50 On the literature and readership of the later nineteenth century, see Buckland, *Society Dancing*, 16–19.
51 See Ann Hutchinson Guest, *Choreo-Graphics. A Comparison of Dance Notation Systems from the Fifteenth Century to the Present* (New York: Gordon and Breach, 1989), and for lucid argument on the value of notation, see Judy Van Zile, 'What is the Dance? Implications for Dance Notation', *Dance Research Journal* 17/2 and 18/1 (1985/1986), 41–47, and Brenda M. Farnell, 'Ethno-Graphics and the Moving Body', *Man* 29/4 (1994), 929–974.
52 Sometimes known as the Beauchamps/Feuillet system, this form of dance notation was published by Raoul Anger Feuillet as *Le Chorégraphie, ou L'art de décrire la danse par caractères et signes démonstratifs* in 1700 and was translated into several European languages.
53 E. A. Théleur, *Letters on Dancing* (London: Sherwood, 1831), p.[i].
54 Most notably Labanotation. Théleur's system is viewed as transitional – between that of Feuillet and Saint-Léon and Zorn, see Guest, *Choreo-Graphics*.
55 *Dancing as an Art and Pastime* (London: George Bell and Sons, 1892).
56 *Dancing*, November 1891, 63–64.
57 'Dance Works, Concepts and Historiography', in *Re-Thinking Dance History: A Reader*, eds. Geraldine Morris and Larraine Nicholas, 2nd edn. (London: Routledge, 2017).
58 Smith cited in Pakes, 'Dance Works', 65.
59 See Pritchard, "The Great Hansen". This practice was also common in the production of dramatical works.
60 For discussion see my 'Dance and Cultural Memory: Interpreting *Fin de Siècle* Performances of 'Olde England'', *Dance Research* 31/1 (2013), 29–66 (especially pp. 41ff.).
61 See, for example, the pioneers of the early dance movement in Britain, Mabel Dolmetsch and Melusine Wood.
62 'Dance and Evolutionary Discourse in Late Victorian Discourse', in *Evolution and Victorian Culture*, eds. Bernard V. Lightman and Bennett Zon (Cambridge: Cambridge University Press, 2014).
63 *The Woman's Herald*, September 28, 1893, 512.
64 See Lynn Garafola, 'The Travesty Dancer in Nineteenth-Century Ballet', *Dance Research Journal* 17/2 and 18/1 (1985/1986), 35–40.
65 See Carter, *Dance and Dancers*, 57–61.
66 Ibid., 111–112.
67 Quoted in *Dancing*, January 1893, 233.
68 Rev. James Davies, *On the Modern Mode of Dancing* (Gloucester: E. Nest, 1870). For a general study of Christian attitudes towards dancing, though with an American bias, see Ann Wagner, *Adversaries of the Dance: From the Puritans to the Present* (Urbana: University of Illinois Press, 1997).
69 Rev. Dalton, Vicar of Stepney, London reported in *The Dancing Times*, January 1897, 9.
70 See, for example, *The History of Will Worthy and Nancy Wilmot* (Chelsea: Religious Tract Society, [1820]) copy in Angus Library, Regent's Park College, University of Oxford.
71 For an overview see Mark Knowles, *The Wicked Waltz and Other Scandalous Dances* (Jefferson, NC and London: McFarland, 2009), 51–53.
72 For more detail see Buckland, 'Crompton's Campaign', 13–15.
73 '"Heroes of the Dance Floor"': The Missing Exemplary Male Dancer', in *The Ancient Dancer in the Modern World. Responses to Greek and Roman Dance*, ed. Fiona Macintosh (Oxford: Oxford University Press, 2010), 168.
74 W. P., *Dancing*, March 1893, 262.

75 Graham Pont, 'Plato's Philosophy of Dance', in *Dance, Spectacle, and the Body*, ed. Nevile; see also Francis Sparshott, 'On the Question: "Why Do Philosophers Neglect the Aesthetics of the Dance?" *Dance Research Journal* 15/1 (1982), 5–30.

76 The interrelation of dance and the military in Europe is a complex and under-investigated topic, but see Margaret M. McGowan, *Dance in the Renaissance. European Fashion, French Obsession* (New Haven and London: Yale University Press, 2008), 122–126, and Mathew McCormack, 'Dance and Drill. Polite Accomplishments and Military Masculinities in Georgian Britain', *Cultural and Social History* 8/3 (2011), 315–330. Dancing masters continued to teach fencing well into the nineteenth century.

77 *The Observer*, January 20, 1850, 5. On women and dance in society generally see Buckland, *Society Dancing*, Chapters 9 and 10.

78 Buckland, *Society Dancing*, pp. 81–82 and Theresa Buckland, 'Edward Scott: The Last of the English Dancing Masters', *Dance Research* 21/2 (2003), 3–35.

79 Reba N. Soffer, 'The Development of Disciplines in the Modern English University', *The Historical Journal* 31/4 (1988), 933.

80 For a more detailed analysis of dance in schools in the early twentieth century which drew on ideas from Spencer and the educational philosophy of Friedrich Fröbel see Anne Bloomfield, 'Health or Art? The Case for Dance in the Curriculum of British State Schools 1909–1919', *History of Education* 36/6 (2007), 681–696.

81 As example of the difficulties of studying written records of antiquity in relation to dance see 'Introduction',Karin Schlapbach, *The Anatomy of Dance Discourse. Literary and Philosophical Approaches to Dance in the Later Graeco-Roman World*, (Oxford and New York: Oxford University Press, 2018).

82 See Charles Batteux, *The Fine Arts Reduced to a Single Principle* [1746] trans. James O. Young (Oxford and New York: Oxford University Press, 2015). Such ideas were already circulating in the century but percolated to later authors through, in particular, the work of ballet-masters and theoreticians Jean-Georges Noverre, *Lettres sur la Danse* (1760) and Carlo Blasis, *The Code of Terpsichore* (1830).

83 In Adam Phillips, ed. *The Renaissance: Studies in Art and Poetry* (Oxford and New York: Oxford University Press, 1986), 86.

84 Edward Scott, *Dancing as an Art and Pastime* (London: George Bell and Sons, 1892), 213.

Section II

University Education

3 Positivism and Early Chairs of Art History in Europe

1860–1880

Barbara Larson

Art history emerged as an academic discipline in the second half of the nineteenth century. At that time, the few existing art historians teaching within universities or art institutions rarely claimed to be teaching in a specialization (even if they gravitated towards a particular area of study), but rather were regarded as generalists. Institutional professorships were followed by chairships in Germany, Austria, France, and Great Britain as art history consolidated as a field of study and gained recognition as a discipline with a future. Early art history chairs formulated, lectured on, and wrote about chronologies and approaches to art that demonstrated their recent attachment to the field of history. They either based texts on documents and 'facts', theories of cultural history that cited regional or geographical psychologies, or the social purpose of cultural products, methodologies in mid-nineteenth century history.[1] However, they attempted to create a separate identity for art history and give it greater credibility – since it also carried with it the burden of former associations with aesthetics and philosophy, now perceived as subjective and flawed – through an alignment with scientific ideas. While a 'positivist' turn within the humanities in the nineteenth century in the direction of objectivity and analysis (history and art history included) has been discussed in the literature of discipline formation, art history's complex early relationship with scientific ideas deriving from natural history has not been fully explored.[2] This chapter argues that in its initial phase as an institutionalized discipline certain early art history chairs capitalized on positivist modes of thought, which allowed the field to benefit from the growing authority of the natural sciences. In German-speaking states an admiration for a 'Cuvier-based' model of connoisseurship was promoted by early chairs, while in France the first permanent chair of art history recast past notions of geographical psychology (Montesquieu) according to new scientific ideas, and in Britain the first chair attempted to apply Herbert Spencer's popular evolutionary approach to society to the history of art.[3]

Older ideas based in the natural sciences can be found in the earliest art history texts beginning with Giorgio Vasari's *The Lives of the Most*

Excellent Painters, Sculptors, and Architects (1550). Though basically an account of artist-geniuses, especially those of the Italian Renaissance, its premise was based on the idea that art developed through time and followed cycles from youth to maturity to old age. Johann Winckelmann (1717–1768), the first modern art historian, also saw art as a journey of progress representing the evolution of the thought of a given period and following a cycle similar to that of organisms. This early application of biological metaphors to art was given new life in the middle of the nineteenth century through ideas on the development of societies in sociology, anthropology, and economic theory as well as geology and organic evolutionism. As Asa Briggs has noted of the rise of critical history and historical consciousness, the interconnectedness of structures and sequences, along with developmental processes, was now taken for granted.[4]

The positivism of some of art history's earliest chairs, rooted in new scientific methods and ideas in biology, had the uniform goal of objectivity.[5] However, the approach varied. Philosophical positivism beginning with Auguste Comte holds that science provides the model of real knowledge – what we can know of reality (including past products of human history) is what we observe and what we can conclude from those observations.[6] Assertions must be empirically verified. In art history these assertions might concern accurate attributions of paintings or sculptures, or explaining logically and factually (i.e. without subjective interpretation) the development of art forms, media, and style. In German-speaking countries in the middle of the nineteenth century, for example, key early art history chairs were especially interested in primary sources and in scientific attributions that helped them piece together the puzzle of art history. They emphasized connoisseurship and demonstrated a growing interest in Cuvier's ideas on discrete morphological parts that can be compared within a taxonomy to deduce 'types', wherein an organism can be theoretically rebuilt from a single element (the art historical translation would be that the style of a painted earlobe or a fingernail, for example, would provide irrefutable clues about the identity of the artist).[7] France's earliest long-term art history chair, alternatively, used studies from the natural sciences to develop a deterministic theory: art is a direct result of the specific time period and region in which it is found – successful art is like a plant that thrives in a given environment.[8] Britain's earliest art history chair focussed on developing a theory that historical art was a concrete result of social forces that consolidated in communal celebrations. Though the deep history of art was rooted in animal instincts, Gerard Baldwin Brown asserted that the play instinct, the aesthetic instinct, and mimicry rose to a new level that allowed for human artistic expression under the intense social stimulation of the festival.[9]

Positivist Roots of *Kunstwissenschaft* (Scientific Study of Art)

From 1860 to 1874 eight chairs of art history were established in what would become Germany and Austria.[10] The creation of these chairs within the university system corresponds to the rise of a secular middle class with a growing interest in art and its history along with government reform policies in education that promoted a modern agenda.[11] Early chairships dedicated exclusively to art history in Germany were occupied by Anton Springer (University of Bonn in 1860, University of Strasbourg in 1872, and the University of Leipzig in 1873), who had written the much respected *Handbook of Art History* in 1855, one of the first attempts to describe a whole history of art.[12] The *Handbook* was still embedded in the aesthetic notion of 'the progress of beauty', and Springer had attempted to reconcile this with 'the creative imagination of various nations'. His perspective on national temperaments came from the popularity of geography and cultural history within the discipline of history, but he soon attempted to distinguish art history from history itself through a foregrounding of connoisseurship, the trained critical eye.[13] In the decades to follow, Springer turned increasingly towards primary source documents and individual works of art along with connoisseurship rather than speculative and nationalistic cultural history in his attempt to be scientific. His growing admiration for the Italian art connoisseur Giovanni Morelli would influence the direction of his work, though this alone would not be a sufficient source in understanding a work of art in its totality. Morelli had studied physiology and comparative anatomy and was a friend and companion of the Swiss-American biologist and geologist Louis Agassiz. He first began to publish on connoisseurship in the 1870s, and was influenced by Cuvier on how peripheral details can be used to reconstruct an entire organism. For Morelli, the study of seemingly insignificant details such as the shape of earlobes or fingers or feet in a given painting could be used to discern the hand of a specific artist and identify the attribution of a work of art. And he likened the positioning of artists and art schools to taxonomies of species and genera. In 1881 Springer wrote an article praising Morelli, recognizing how his kind of methodology was similar to that found in medicine and the natural sciences and was thus scientific.[14]

Dedicated to the detachment of art history from its parent discipline history, Springer continued to move away from contextual studies, finding a more secure history in form itself and the relationship of works of art to one another, and the relationship of studies to the final image. He based his art history on the reality of object-based studies and this along with his admiration for methods within the natural sciences provided an important direction laid out for such early art historians in Germany as eminent turn-of-the-century scholars like Alois Riegl and Heinrich Wölfflin, who ultimately chose formalism as a direction over cultural history.[15] As early as the late 1880s the 'scientific study of art' (*kunstwissenschaft*) expanded beyond connoisseurship to include *stilkritik* (the scrutiny of objects and their physical properties) and iconology (the study of types or themes in a cultural context).[16]

Moriz Thausing, early chair of art history in Austria (University of Vienna 1873), was another admirer of the methods of Morelli (whom he befriended) and defined art history as a 'positive' science.[17] Thausing applied the historical-critical method originally derived from history emphasizing archival documents, but expanded the concept to art itself as visual documentation of cultural history. He employed dispassionate comparative analysis and called on the methods of the natural sciences by way of example: observation must 'lead to continuous comparisons, similar to those which the most real of our sciences, the natural sciences, use in practice'.[18] Morelli provided him with the platform he used to argue against aesthetics in stylistic observations on behalf of factual evidence; he dedicated his book *Wiener Kunstbriefe* (1884) to Morelli.[19] While Morelli's principles were used as a method of attribution as had been the case with Springer, Thausing added to this his evolutionary ideas on the history of sight and practice. Trained as a cultural historian, he diverged from positioning art as merely embedded within a culture and cited art works as factual documents or artefacts in the history of evolving visual perception (both biological and cultural). The idea that art provides documents in the history of seeing would also influence the direction of Riegl and Wölfflin.[20] Thausing regarded the very emergence of the discipline of art history as evidence that the eye had now evolved to an advanced state of sensitivity. Moreover, the art of painting was relatively modern and related to ocularity whereas sculpture, representing an older era, was tied to the tactile. Thausing was central to the emergence of the Vienna School of Art History, which attempted to put art history on a 'wissenschaftlich' basis.

The empirical researchers Wilhelm Wundt (Germany) and Ernst Mach (Austria), both major contributors to physiological psychology, studied the sensations involved in viewer response in a laboratory setting in the second half of the nineteenth century – they too were important contributors to positivism and the scientific pursuit of art history as it developed around the turn of the century. Perceptual psychologists Gustav Fechner and Hermann von Helmholtz, both from Germany, are other scientists who sought to demonstrate the embodied experience of visual culture. While each of the figures discussed earlier contributed to the development of *kunstwissenschaft* as it came to be understood after 1860, that approach is more complicated than a positivist orientation alone and its fruition belongs more properly to the subsequent era of formalism.[21]

France

A positivist disciplinary approach to art history is also clear in the work of the first chair of art history in France. This chairship was established in 1863, though not in the university, but rather at the venerable art academy the École des Beaux-Arts of Paris. Beginning in 1864, the original long-term occupant was the unlikely Hippolyte Taine, who was celebrated as a philosopher and a chronicler of English and French cultural history, but hardly thought of in terms of art or art history. Yet he remained in this position until his retirement twenty years later. In fact, Taine had had a contentious relationship with universities in general and any appointment there would have been unlikely since his brand of positive philosophy was not compatible with French academic studies in the 1850s and 1860s, decades in which eclectic philosophy was mainstream. Taine believed art had 'precise conditions and fixed laws', and could be understood from the deterministic position that an artist and his audience had the same formative influences and are located in the same environment and thus are perfectly suited. He was driven to create 'an analogy between human history and natural history'. Like Morelli and his followers, Taine was influenced by Cuvier, but for him Cuvier's idea that a creature could be reconstructed from a single bone was applied not to assigning attributions to single works of art based on peripheral details, but to working backward to society through art to understand the circumstances of its creation. Therefore, one could use individual works of art to analyze an entire culture. Taine was also interested in the senses and responses to works of art, both in the present and in past populations. He was a member of the French Society of Psychophysiology and cited Helmholtz on optics. Given his interest in natural histories, he came to believe aesthetics were ingrained within the nervous system of a given people; thus, one could scientifically talk about 'national sentiments'. In his book *De l'Intelligence* (1870), written in the 1860s, he detailed physiological responses to colour and line.

Taine's appointment, and along with it the institutionalization of art history as a discipline in France, was part of the state's agenda concerning promotion of science and its preeminence in the production of visual culture including design in industrial production. The establishment of an art history chair was the outcome of reform efforts by the Ministry of Public Instruction.[22] Taine was nominated by his friend Victor Duruy who headed this government agency. Taine made his positivist stance clear to students at the outset:

> The modern method which I will follow. . . consists in considering human works, and in particular works of art, as facts and products of which it is necessary to indicate the character and search for the

> causes, nothing further. Thus understood, science neither proscribes nor pardons, it observes and explains.[23]

Art, as a product of the conditions in which it was created, adheres to the scientific law of cause and effect.

The École's direction had been a conservative one up to 1863; the classical, the Renaissance, and the neo-classical provided the standards for artists to follow. By contrast, Taine argued that all artists who rose to prominence were very much of their own time. Taine's theories and histories were based in his reading of the evolutionary philosopher Herbert Spencer in the 1850s (on the social environment and social psychology); of philosopher and social theorist John Stuart Mill (on the importance of observation); and of the natural sciences (Geoffroy Saint-Hilaire and Cuvier on the interrelationship of parts to the whole, Lamarck on the environment and evolutionism, and Darwin on natural selection), appealing sources at a moment in which positivism was gaining in popularity and seemed to offer objective study of its various subjects.

Taine discussed art in biological, environmental, and medical terms. In applying his general method 'race-milieu-moment' he likened the relationship of a people to its environment and the period of time in which it is found to that between a plant and its species and surroundings. As an early French Darwinist Taine applied natural selection to art. In his opening lectures at the École he stated:

> Physical temperature acts by elimination and suppression—in other words by *natural selection*. Such is the great law by which we now explain the origin and structure of diverse existing organisms—a law as applicable to moral and physical conditions, to history as well as to botany and zoology, to genius and character as well as to plant and animal. In short, there is a moral temperature, consisting of the general state of mind and manners. . . a moral temperature makes a selection among different species of talent, allowing only this species or that to develop, to the exclusion of others. It is through some such mechanism that you see in artistic schools at certain times the sentiment of the ideal.[24]

By 'the ideal' Taine meant that an artist selects out a given object from the environment and renders it artistically according to intuited logic of internal proportions, having grasped an aspect of the phenomenal world, its laws, and causes. The object is then rendered according to the temperament of the artist and the appropriateness to the period of time: 'The end of a work of art is to manifest some essential or salient character', he wrote, 'consequently some important idea, clearer or more completely than is attainable from the real object'.[25] In this way the idea becomes the ideal. The best art of a given period expresses an ideal everyone can relate to and enduring masterpieces touch the very bedrock of humanity itself. The current artist should reflect his circumstances. Taine ended his first series of lectures with a quote from Goethe: 'Fill your mind and heart however large with the ideas and sentiments of your age and the work will follow'.[26]

Taine's interdisciplinary rhetoric included issues affecting national health. The Greeks were a healthful people who were devoted to protecting individual cities – thus, there was an emphasis on the strong, perfect physiques found especially in sculpture wherein even the gods were thought of as built along these lines. Architectural monuments were relatively small since spaces were humanizing. The middle ages, on the other hand, were dark ages – a time of despair in which the dim and towering cathedral with an emphasis on unhealthy mystical thinking dominated. Christianity represented pain in life—its psychology was depressive. Then there were the Italians of the Renaissance who desired peace, and focussed on heroic nudities and 'terrible muscularities' (Michelangelo) or healthy madonnas (Raphael).

While generations changed, the psychological underpinning of a given people remained intact so that one could even make a connection between Italians of the Renaissance and those of the classical period: the Renaissance imagination was classic, Latin, and existed in the kingdom of form. Taine wrote of the Italians of the Renaissance,

> energetic character and passionate habits suited to giving knowledge of and taste for beautiful, physical forms, constitute the temporary circumstances which, added to the innate aptitudes of the race, produced in Italy the great and perfect painting of the human form.[27]

In his first series of lectures after the introductory 'Philosophy of Art', Taine addressed the Italian Renaissance in detail. In terms of his ideas on 'race' and the Italians – like the nearby Greeks, they responded to the warm local climate and were joyful. Of Taine's concept 'moment', while medieval Italians had been mystical, and created ecstatic figures and flattened forms (Fra Angelico), improved economic circumstances and the age of humanism brought Italians back to their pagan past. Love of naturalism and clarity of form took priority during the Renaissance, a transition that could be observed from Cimabue to Giotto. Then, in the prosperous period to follow one found a cultivated lifestyle and a love of beauty. Never-the-less, external dangers threatened, making of the Italians a passionate people capable of producing the art of the High Renaissance. Still, Italians could be distinguished from one another. The Venetians differed in that their climate was wetter and milder, which pacified the nervous system. Therefore, these Italians were more sensual and prone to pursuing pleasure. The vaporousness of the location encouraged painterliness. Though they shared in common with their neighbours in Florence a certain joyfulness and love of the empirical, the Venetians were drawn to tactility, sensuality of the flesh, and an engagement with the present.

Taine divided the superior European south from the inferior north. Yet he turned to Netherlandish Renaissance art seeking the best of the Germanic (northern) race. On the whole, those of the north tended to be sluggish and fleshy; in mental habits they were slower and more methodical. Much of this had to do with the cold climate and struggles with a difficult terrain. As Protestants, their religion did not provide a background privileging corporeal form. However, the Netherlands itself was the best of the Germanic lot. The climate was more humid and this had a positive effect on the nerves; the senses were heightened. In addition, they were prosperous and tended towards secularity. Looking outwards, they were drawn towards naturalism and produced paintings of day to day life in minute detail or landscapes. Dressed up as they were in a chillier climate, the beautiful nude body was quite beyond them. The Netherlandish artist excelled at the optical essence of the physical world.

In his first lecture cycle, Taine ended with the Greeks; but in the future he would begin here. Despite his rebellious history against convention Taine revealed his love of Greek art, a trend among many early art history scholars who admired the work of that first modern art historian Winckelmann who found classical art to be superior to all others. Taine followed Winckelmann on a narrative of birth, growth, and decline. He also followed the classical scholar on eras of ancient art: the archaic, the early classic leading to high classical art, then Hellenistic and Roman imperial art.

Winckelmann had been interested in climate theory as it could be applied to temperament and, as we have seen, Taine was convinced of this as well, though through updated scientific ideas on adaptation.[28] Taine described the Greek race and its artistic products as the result of geography and climate. As Taine put it, 'We are led to regard the environment of the Greek plant in order to ascertain whether the soil and atmosphere which have nourished it do not explain the peculiarities of its form'.[29] And, of course, Taine found that it did. Greek thought and art forms could be explained as follows: the Greek eye was inherently predisposed to grasping relationships clearly given the lack of obstructions it encountered (low mountains, clear skies, a manageable sea). Nature itself prepared the Greek mind towards fixed and precise conceptions, and since the atmosphere was transparent and the climate mild, the Greek individual was joyous, vital, and had conscious energy. Taine wrote, 'The aptitudes and tendencies which she [nature] firmly implants in him are precisely the aptitudes and tendencies she daily satisfies'.[30] Thus formed, the Greek had delicacy of perception, the ability to seize relationships with a sense of gradation, and he loved life, celebrating the body. Following scientific principles, the remaining effects (art and architecture) of the original cause (the formation of the ancient Greeks) were symmetrical temples, sculptures of muscular athletes, and harmonious low relief processions that demonstrated the racial ability to grasp precise relationships and the tendency of the collective to celebrate a healthful, balanced life lived in sunshine. Taine offered a way of understanding the history of art through a combination of social psychology and positivism, an approach in keeping with the scientific agenda of the late Second Empire and early Third Republic.[31]

Great Britain

As Buckland (in Chapter 2) demonstrates the importance of French models for the development of dance in Britain, and Jones (Chapter 4) shows how German conceptions of historical scholarship were influential in the creation of the Manchester School of History, continental factors played a significant role in the founding of art history chairs across the channel. In Britain, the first art history chair was as interested in scientific explanations for art-making as had been the case with Taine. Gerard Baldwin Brown, who from 1880 occupied the Watson Gordon chair of art history at the University of Edinburgh (established by the family of the late painter Sir John Watson Gordon, former president of the Royal Scottish Academy of Art), held a degree in the highly respectable field of classical studies.[32] His inaugural lecture 'Fine Art as a Branch of University Study' (1880) only hints at what would be the unorthodox approach he would take in the next fifty years, 'I shall not merely give a history of Greek art, but try to show, using the Greeks as an example, what it is that the artist is dealing with, and how art grows up and is related to the life of a people.'[33]

In this seemingly benign introduction were the seeds of his positivist approach to art history: as exemplified in his 1891 book *The Fine Arts* social forces lie behind the creation of art forms. While social histories were also central to Taine's work, for Baldwin Brown artistic products were the result of communal celebrations which brought about a rush of creativity with roots in animal instincts.

Not unlike the case of Germany, Austria, and France, the gradual professionalization of British art history can be tied to the nineteenth-century history of modernism and modernity, itself rooted in the industrial revolution and manifested in economic and social histories. The British government established the Science and Art Department (1853–1899) and the South Kensington System of art education and museum displays, with the goal of elevating the working class and promoting better industrial design. The rise of the middle class with the subsequent commercialization of art and a growing interest in arts' classification and display were instrumental as well.[34] And the establishment of artists' societies and the rise of dealers' galleries promoted the growth of painting. The expanding art market, which catered to various genres and styles, was another result of economic change.[35] These transformations in the perception and display of art along with broadening possibilities of the purchase of art helped make the history of art a legitimate academic discipline in Great Britain and no doubt did much to secure the continuity of the Watson Gordon chair.[36]

Like Taine Baldwin Brown was interested in social histories and social psychology, but instead of Taine's 'plant that flourishes in a given environment and time period' approach, he thought of the communal in terms of collective celebrations and agreed upon socially meaningful art forms. In *The Fine Arts* (1891) Baldwin Brown maintained that civilization and the intellect came out of the religious, tribal, and domestic celebrations of the early ages. His was another early example in the field of art history of an attempt to establish the new discipline within recent theories of society based in scientific ideas – in this case the tandem evolution of mind, brain, and culture that Herbert Spencer had argued was the case. Though *The Fine Arts* is not a survey text per se it participated in the attempt to position art on a vast developmental scale. A section of Baldwin Brown's book is also devoted to physiological response to form and colour. He cited both Spencer (*Principles of Psychology*) and James Sully (*Sensation and Intuition*) on nerve stimulation, and he described mass as giving a general corporeal impression, including sublime structures such as cathedrals, pyramids, and the Eiffel Tower. The 'beautiful' applies to one's response to formal order, but the 'significant', which has to do with corporeal impressions that generate associative meaning, matters too.

In *The Fine Arts* Baldwin Brown speculated on the transition from rudimentary early forms of art (for example, crude doll-idols) to later developed forms (Greek sculptures of gods); embroidered decoration attached to monuments to later sculptural decoration; and altars to temples. He tended to connect certain modes of creation with given eras: sculpture with the Greeks, mural paintings with the medieval Florentines, architecture with northern populations of the Gothic period, for example, all of it 'straight from the hearts of the people'. However, he had little to say about transitions from one historical period to another. His central concern was with communal celebration and art forms that best captured those moments and helped to make them permanent. As a positivist he referred to his ideas on art as 'laws of artistic production'.[37] The importance of society to the development of art through the ages was central to Baldwin Brown; his focus in *The Fine Arts* is on the role of the festival and the need of members of society to adapt to a social state.

In his text Baldwin Brown brought up Friedrich Schiller on art as a form of play from *The Aesthetic Education of Man*, but this was in support of the writings of Herbert Spencer. Spencer's reputation in 1890 was significant in Great Britain, and he had enormous influence in many areas of the world as well.[38] However, the associate who might have brought Spencer's synthetic philosophy on the evolution of society to Baldwin Brown's attention in regard to the arts may have been Patrick Geddes.[39] Geddes, socialist, biologist, evolutionist, utopian town planner, and leader of an art movement, established the Edinburgh Socialist Union, with which Baldwin Brown became involved, and he was a follower of Spencer.

In *The Fine Arts* modes of expression (decoration, architecture, sculpture, and painting) followed the needs of a given society and, as with Spencer, psyche and society moved forward in tandem. Baldwin Brown also drew from the last section of the second edition of Spencer's *Principles of Psychology* of 1872. Spencer had directly addressed art and aesthetics in a section of this chapter entitled 'Corollaries', the first part of which was called 'Aesthetic Sentiments'. From the outset of his 1891 volume Baldwin Brown stated that art was indulged in for its own sake, an idea advanced by Spencer – he maintained like Spencer that art was a spontaneous product of human nature and neurological urges that had once been directed entirely at issues of survival before humans emerged from the ape. Echoing Spencer, Baldwin Brown wrote, 'Art affords gratification to instincts and feelings which only find their sphere of exercise when material needs are satisfied'.[40] Spencer, however, had little interest in describing the art of different periods; this is what Baldwin Brown addressed.

To find the beginning of art's history, according to Baldwin Brown, one must find the beginning of free activity or play, when a surplus of vigour no longer necessary for the maintenance of life urged release. In addition to superfluous energy, however, one also needs harmony or order to produce art, and such arrangements necessitate human mental power. Referencing Darwin, another scientist Baldwin Brown admired, the art historian pointed out that birds are non-human creatures with an aesthetic instinct, but even in the case of the bower bird who builds elaborate structures out of sometimes shiny items, these creatures do not space out objects in patterns as humans do and, therefore, do not create art.[41] In addition to the ability to create harmonious patterns that transform the aesthetic instinct into artistic abilities, humans build upon the instinctive roots of play and mimicry to create art forms. How does art come about in the first place? According to Spencer and Baldwin Brown, it comes from human social stimulation. Baldwin Brown cited Darwin on dance and music as the earliest and most universal forms of art.[42] He recounted a story from one of his sources regarding a South African tribe, 'Often in the midst of conversation, if a man happens to become excited, he will sing instead of speaking what he has to say. . . while the company around murmurs a chorus in unison. . . clapping, undulating their bodies, and perhaps dancing'.[43] He quoted Spencer's *Descriptive Sociology*, 'So sensitive are the negroes of the African coast that any regular recurring sound like the hammering of a carpenter will set them dancing in unison'.[44] Like many of his generation Baldwin Brown equated 'savages' of the present with prehistoric cave dwellers; thus, the examples he gives he considered appropriate for the prehistoric period as well.[45] While Taine did not feel it necessary to go back to the beginnings of art, for Baldwin Brown beginnings dictated all that was to follow (play, order, communal life with permanent symbolism).

Decoration was another early form of art, which at first was used to attract the opposite sex.[46] Eventually decorative objects were used on important buildings or on objects handed down in the family that came to be considered sacred. Decorative objects in civic life inspired patriotic and communal feelings. According to Baldwin Brown, eventually decorative objects as connected with religion came to be understood as the 'pledge of a deity'. Decoration wove a spell around material objects in a household or a city.[47] He favoured Gottfried Semper's theory that painted decoration originated from embroidery designs used in festivals.

Reminding the reader that it is social feeling that sets in motion a wave of sentiment which stirs the mind to artistic expression now that the important issue of survival had been replaced by effusive energy, Baldwin Brown focussed on the role of the festival. The communal feeling involved in festivals stimulated the origin of buildings and monuments, paintings, and sculptures. Even dolmens expressed the drive towards permanent expression of communal celebration. Sculptures and paintings were originally created to commemorate an occasion and bring to mind the festival. The communal spirit of the festival explains not only the Egyptian temple but also the painted relief upon it, before painting and sculpture diverged. Imposing dolmens, temples, and cathedrals were all the results of religious festivals and all make use of free, spontaneous expression – surplus energy stimulated by social activity – with order, thus are art. Baldwin Brown wrote,

> Art is a condition of excitement in which the individual is carried out of the circle of his ordinary existence—the contagious nature of this excitement intensified in the festival and artists made monuments, recorded deeds in pictures and glorified through statues.[48]

Art evolved as a response to communal emotional life. Baldwin Brown could not hide his enthusiasm about the classical: 'The most important monument in the whole history of art is the Greek Temple'.[49] The Greek Temple was a clear demonstration of the principle of order.

Baldwin Brown used the biological concept of mimicry to discuss the development of naturalistic art, including prehistoric carvings. Mimicry also explains the attempt to personify gods in dance and drama. Baldwin Brown mentioned Winckelmann on ancient art, but found his focus on ideal beauty as a generalizing characteristic in ancient sculptures to be somewhat off track. He claimed that the ancient artist created *individual* types, based on personalities of the gods. The artist attempted to mimic this personality. Pose and gesture, originating in the dance, were significant when it came to sculptural types. In the specific personality type and its handling in sculpture one finds a marriage of inner and outer characteristics. Baldwin Brown lingered over the classical expressing his admiration for it. That perspective had not been shared by Spencer, who believed the art of antiquity appealed to base emotions easily taken in by the heroic.[50] However, for Baldwin Brown even the figurative art of the Renaissance paled by comparison with ancient art: 'We find even the efforts of the greatest men to be tentative and vague, when we compare them with the majestic achievement of the Greeks'.[51]

Baldwin Brown turned next to medieval Florence where the classical lived on in festivals. Pageantry and an emphasis on the spiritual brought out a communal emphasis on painted murals with multi-figure compositions. However, from the sixteenth century forward art no longer expressed popular feeling and communal ideals so aptly presented in the festival. Instead, art became a private luxury. Current Impressionism, for example, was a 'creature of the hour'. Both Taine and Baldwin Brown preoccupied themselves largely with the eras their Western audiences found most fitting – antiquity, the medieval period, and the Renaissance. Baldwin Brown exhibited similar prejudices as did Taine, with ancient art as the best art by far and medieval art as exhibiting some anxiety. Though he did not spend a great deal of time on national character Baldwin Brown did touch upon it. The Greeks had great intellectual depth and a predilection for definite form. The Florentines of the medieval period were restless. They had a keen intellect, but not a profound one.[52] Despite their preoccupation with spiritual life Florentines never-the-less were healthful and satisfied with the kind of life they led. Defining national temperament was not Baldwin Brown's primary goal, however, as it had been with Taine.

Baldwin Brown added a lengthy introduction to new editions beginning in 1902 with the second edition of *The Fine Arts* citing literature that he felt had updated his field in the first decade since the book was first published, and that had led him to believe that Spencer's 'art for art's sake' principle and its evolutionary implications of increasing complexity were 'unsatisfactory'.[53] He cited Henry Balfour's *The Evolution of Decorative Art* (1893), which had convinced him that schematic decorative patterns had often come from complex imagery originally rather than vice versa. He added that it was best, therefore, to keep the terms evolution and development out of the picture of art. Yet, despite this cautionary language, he maintained the same categories of art-making, including modes of production and eras and nearly identical arguments throughout the remainder of the text. He also adhered to his original central principle: art represents an effort of the human spirit, under the stimulus of excitement, to externalize itself in some outward form or act, the resulting activity or product being always controlled by the principle of Order that ultimately brings a beautiful result.

Baldwin Brown also tempered his ideas on play by referencing a new literature that connected the behaviour in humans with that of animals in a more serious way and demonstrated to him that play was an ongoing aspect of society. For example, Karl Groos's books *The Play of Animals* (1896) and *The Play of Man* (1898) argued that play as deeply instinctive prepared one for the realities of life. Ernst Grosse's *Beginnings of Art* (1894) also addressed the practical aspect of play. Still, within constraints of practical purpose art, whether ancient or modern, could still demonstrate freedom. Work, play, and art began to converge for Baldwin Brown. He noted Karl Büchner's book *Work and Rhythm* (1897) on the 'savage' who alleviates dull labour through art such as by chanting. He revealed himself to be less enamoured of Spencer's theories of art as 'effervescence'. Rather than introduce his new editions with many references to art and the play impulse as so much extra energy as he had in 1891, he wrote about the kinds of activities that bring art about. Baldwin Brown maintained a social and biological explanation for art-making through the centuries that remain within the parameters of positivist thinking even by the turn of the century, a time in which the field of art history began to turn towards formalism.

Conclusion

The establishment of chairs of art history in institutions of higher learning from Austria to Great Britain within the span of two decades marked the institutionalization of this nascent discipline. Scientific validation of the emerging discipline was key here, just as it was in the cases of the establishment of Tout's new approach to history, discussed by Jones (in Chapter 4), and the origins of a child psychology grounded in evolutionary theory, examined by Laing (in Chapter 8). Positivistic models of art history provided by the natural sciences ensured rigorous methodologies subject to laws and objective observations and eschewed the subjective implications of aesthetics and philosophy. The fledgling field would no longer be thought of as attached to dilettantism, moralizing, taste, or recondite antiquarianism, a common perception in the early years of the nineteenth century. Early chairs of art history may not yet have represented actual departments, but they elevated art history to an academic field of study with a respectable means of interpreting the past. The two main methodologies that were pursued by the early chairs were roughly based on models from the field of history – cultural and social histories (Taine, Baldwin Brown) or documents and 'facts' (Springer, Thausing); yet art historians went further in the direction of science, foregrounding its recent philosophies. While for the most part positivism faded from the humanities (art history included) by the late 1890s, the legacy of the scientific enterprise of the history of art can be found in the methodologies of some of the most eminent of art history scholars in the early twentieth century and indeed in the formalist turn of the field in general in which rigorous stylistic analysis became the main direction of the discipline.

After 1900 the focus among art historians was mainly on the history of form and laws of stylistic development. The rhetoric of selection, adaptation, and descent with modification is integral to emerging formalist art history among scholars after 1900; in German-speaking countries it can be found in the writings of Riegl, Wölfflin, and Conrad Fiedler.[54] Darwinian thinking had worked its way into art historical thought. French formalist Henri Focillon believed that styles evolved from the simple to the complex, a Lamarckian or Spencerian approach to change through time. He often used biological metaphors regarding metamorphosis in art. His thoughts are summarized in *The Life of Forms* (1934). Focillon directly influenced some of France's leading art historians including Philippe Verdier and André Chastel. Early twentieth-century formalist Bernard Berenson was steeped in the methods of Morelli. Each of these art historians distanced themselves from the cultural histories of Taine or Baldwin Brown, but instead foregrounded the analysis of colour, line, and form. Roger Fry, leading British formalist of the early twentieth century and champion of modernism, also saw his project as a scientific one. Psychophysiology and Helmholtz on optics were referred to to demonstrate that effective art did not communicate through mimesis of nature, but by forms that created equivalencies for life.[55] He stated of his approach at his inaugural lecture as Slade Professor at the University of Cambridge, 'scientific methods will be followed wherever possible, where at all events the scientific attitude may be fostered and the sentimental attitude discouraged'.[56]

While a discussion of formalism is beyond the scope of this essay, further research remains to be done on how the positivist platform of the nineteenth century fed formalist currents in the early twentieth century, including theories of stylistic analysis and the evolution of form. Ways in which early positivist art historians may have influenced one another internationally have not been fully explored. Not only were their writings available to one another, with key texts published in various editions, but the first international congress of art history took place as early as 1873 (Vienna). While the institutionalization of art history in art academies and universities is but one strand in the professionalization of the field, museological work and art criticism representing other avenues, it does signal the moment when art history crystalized as an acknowledged discipline recognized by the public (named chairs) and the state (educational initiatives, including the establishment of chairs). Positivist thinking by early art history chairs at a critical moment in discipline formation helped to build the field's credibility through alignment of its methodologies with those of medicine and the natural sciences.

Notes

1 On the establishment of history as a discipline see Asa Briggs, 'History and the Social Sciences', in *A History of the University in Europe*, ed. Walter Rüegg (Cambridge: Cambridge University Press, 2004), vol. III, 459–492.

2 On positivism, the humanities, and art history see Robert Frodeman (ed.), *The Oxford Handbook of Interdisciplinarity* (Oxford: Oxford University Press, 2010), 134–135, and S. Kraft, 'Interdisciplinarity and the Canon of Art History', *Issues in Integrative Studies* 3/7 (1989), 57–71. The pairing of evolutionism with traditional notions of the 'progress' of art has attracted the greatest attention among scholars interested in biological models and their pertinence to the history of art. Among these publications are T. Munro, *Evolution in the Arts and Other Theories of Culture* (Cleveland: Cleveland Museum of Arts, 1950); P. Steadman, *The Evolution of Designs. Biological Analogy in Architecture and the Applied Arts* (Cambridge: Cambridge University Press, 1979); Eric Fernie, 'Art History and Evolution from Henri Focillon to Stephen Jay Gould', in *Raising the Eyebrow: John Onians and World Art Series*, ed. Lauren Golden (Oxford: Archaeopress, 2001), 65–83; Lauren Golden, 'Science, Darwin, and Art History', in Ibid., 79–90; and Robert Bork, 'Art, Science, and Evolution', in *Making Art History: A Changing Discipline and its Institutions*, ed. Elizabeth Mansfield (New York and London: Routledge, 2007), 187–202.

3 In her recent book on British landscape art Anne Helmreich examines the pervasive influence of science not on art history but rather on art itself during the Victorian period. In earlier years around mid-century the attention to close observation that characterized scientific naturalism (the scientific movement that eschewed religious interpretations of nature in favour of an inductive method) influenced artists, though this gives way to an awareness of the fallible eye and the importance of psychology and the imagination. She does credit the naturalists, which include in her discussion, Herbert Spencer, with the deployment of science in culture. The present chapter addresses how a positivist philosophy of science – a belief in mechanical laws and the scientific method – was used to shape the discipline of art history. See Anne Helmreich, *Nature's Truth: Photography, Painting, and Science in Victorian Britain* (University Park: Penn State University Press, 2016), on artists response to scientists during the Victorian period.

4 Briggs, 'History and the Social Sciences', 459.

5 On the sudden rise of objectivity in the nineteenth century see Lorraine Daston and Peter Galison, *Objectivity* (New York: Zone Books, 2007).

6 On positivism see Walter Simon, *European Positivism in the Nineteenth Century: An Essay in Intellectual History* (Cornell: Cornell University Press, 1963); Peter Dale, *In Pursuit of a Scientific Culture: Science, Art, and Society in the Victorian Age* (Madison: University of Wisconsin Press, 1989); D. G. Charlton, *Positivist Thought in France during the Second Empire: 1852–1870* (Oxford: Clarendon Press, 1959); and J. Blühdorn and J. Ritter, eds., *Positivismus im 19. Jahrhundert: Beiträgezu seiner geschichtlichen und systematischen Bedeutung* (Frankfurt am Main: Suhrkamp, 1971).

7 Michael Hatt and Charlotte Klonk, *Art History: A Critical Introduction to Its Methods* (Manchester: Manchester University Press, 2006), 51, and Elizabeth Mansfield (ed.), *Art History and Its Institutions: Foundations of a Discipline* (New York and London: Routledge, 2002), 22–23.

8 Philip Walsh, 'Viollet-le-Duc and Taine at the École des Beaux-Arts: On the First Professorship of Art History in France', in *Art History and Its Institutions*, ed. E. Mansfield (New York and London: Routledge, 2002), 96.

9 Gerard Baldwin Brown, *The Fine Arts* (New York: Scribner's, 1891), 22.
10 Heinrich Dilly, *Kunstgeschichte als Institution: Studien zur Geschichte einer Disziplin* (Frankfurt am Main: Suhrkamp, 1979), 237.
11 See Matthew Rampley, *The Vienna School of Art History: Empire and the Politics of Scholarship* (University Park: Penn State University Press, 2013), passim, and Elizabeth Mansfield, 'Introduction', *Art History and Its Institutions*, 2.
12 Gustav Waagen (University of Berlin) is sometimes credited with occupying the first chair of art history, beginning in 1844. However, this chairship was unique rather than permanent. Waagen was a pioneer of the 'historical critical' method (the use of primary source materials).
13 On German historical thinking see Georg G. Iggers, *The German Conception of History: The National Tradition of Historical Thought from Herder to the Present*, rev edn. (Middletown, CT: Wesleyan University Press, 2012).
14 Anton Springer, 'Kunstkenner und Kunsthistoriker', *Im Neuen Reich* 11/2, (1881), repr. In Anton Springer, *Bilder aus der neueren Kunstgeschichte*, 2 vols., 2nd edn. (Adolph Marcus, 1886), I: 1–40.
15 On continuing tensions between cultural history and formalism in Germany in the early professional years of art history, along with a discussion of Springer's followers, see Kathryn Brush, *The Shaping of Art History: Wilhelm Vöge, Adolph Goldschmidt, and the Study of Medieval Art* (Cambridge: Cambridge University Press, 1996), 19.
16 Kathryn Brush, 'German Kunstwissenschaft and the Practice of Art History in America after World War I: Interrelationships, Exchanges, Contexts', *Marburger Jahrbuch für Kunstwissenschaft* 26 (1999), 13–16.
17 Thausing replaced the very first chair of art history at the University of Vienna (and first chair in art history in Austria), Rudolf von Eitelberger, who began to teach in this position in 1852. Eitelberger paved the way for positivism in Austria in art history through an emphasis on object description over subjective aesthetics, and a foregrounding of archival research and analysis. He initiated the publication of 'Source Texts' in thirteen volumes (1871–1882). Beginning in 1854 Eitelberger began to teach in the Institute for Historical Research at the University of Vienna. For more on Eitelberger see Matthew Rampley, 'The Idea of a Scientific Discipline: Rudolf von Eitelberger and the Emergences of Art History in Vienna, 1847–1873', *Art History* 34/1 (2011), 54–79.
18 Moritz Thausing, *Wiener Kunstbriefe* (Leipzig: Seeman, 1884), 11.
19 His inaugural lecture of 1873 'Die Stellung der Kunstgeschichte als Wissenschaft', in which he calls for art history as a separate discipline is also published here. See Thausing, *Wiener Kunstbriefe*, 1–20.
20 On Thausing see especially Rampley, *Vienna School of Art History*, 33–34.
21 On the complex components of *kunstwissenschaft* and the era of formalism see Mitchell Frank and Daniel Adler, eds., *German Art History and Scientific Thought: Beyond Formalism* (Farnham, VT: Ashgate, 2012); Richard Woodfield, 'Kunstwissenschaft versus Ästhetik: The Historians' Revolt against Aesthetics', in *Re-Discovering Aesthetics*, eds. Francis Halsall, Julia Jensen and Tony O'Connor (Stanford: Stanford University Press, 2008), 19–33; and Emil Utitz, *Grundlegung der allgemeinen Kunstwissenschaft*, 1914, ed. W. Henckmann, 2nd edn. (Munich: Wilhelm Fink Verlag, 1972). On positivism, Riegl, and Wölfflin see Hans Berthold Busse, *Kunst und Wissenschaft: Untersuchungen zur Ästhetik und Methodik der Kunstgeschichtswissenschaft bei Riegl, Wölfflin, und Dvorák* (Mittenwald: Mäander Kunstverlag, 1981).

22 Among the scholars that have written about the emergence of art history in France and a state political agenda are Albert Boime, 'The Teaching Reforms of 1863 and the Origins of Modernism in France', *Art Quarterly* 1/6 (1977), 1–29; J. Laurent, *A Propos de l'École des Beaux-Arts* (Paris: École nationale supérieure des Beaux-Arts, 1987); M. Segré, *L'Ecole des Beaux-Arts XIXe et XXe siècles* (Paris: L'Harmattan, 1998); and Philip Walsh, 'Viollet le Duc and Taine at the Ecole des Beaux-Arts: On the First Professorship of Art History in France', in *Art History and Its Institutions: Foundations of a Discipline*, ed. E. Mansfield (New York and London: Routledge, 2002), 85–100.

23 Hippolyte Taine, *Philosophie de l'art*, 10th edn. (Paris: Hachette, 1903), 12.

24 Hippolyte Taine, *The Philosophy of Art*, 2nd edn., translated by John Durand from *Philosophie de l'art* (New York: Henry Holt & Co., 1884), 93–94.

25 Ibid., 76

26 Ibid., 165.

27 Ibid., 131.

28 Climate theory dates back at least to the time of Aristotle, the Hippocratic theory of physiology, and more recently Montesquieu (1689–1755). See Clarence Glacken, *Traces on the Rhodian Shore: Nature and Culture in Western Thought from Ancient Times to the End of the Eighteenth Century* (Oakland: University of California Press, 2011), and Thomas Kaufmann, *Toward a Geography of Art* (Chicago: Chicago University Press, 2004).

29 Hippolyte Taine, *Art in Greece*, trans. John Durand (New York: Henry Holt & Co., 1873), 12.

30 Ibid., 33.

31 On Taine's influence see Donald Preziosi, *Rethinking Art History: Meditations on a Coy Science* (New Haven: Yale University Press, 1989), 88–90.

32 Lectureships in the fine arts (the still prestigious Slade Professorships) were introduced at the Universities of Oxford, London, and Cambridge beginning in 1869, but these were three year positions featuring a limited number of lectures, not permanent chairs. The Slade Professorships were held mainly by artists and critics. Baldwin Brown's interests beyond providing a scientific theoretical model for the development of art included historic preservation and early art and architecture in England. After the turn of the century, he authored the six-volume series *The Arts in Early England* (1903–1930).

33 Quoted in George Macdonald, 'Gerard Baldwin Brown', *Proceedings of the British Academy* 21 (1935), 377.

34 Elizabeth Mansfield, 'Art History and Modernism', in *Art History and Its Institutions*, ed. E. Mansfield (New York and London: Routledge, 2002) 17–27.

35 Ibid.

36 The history and longevity of this chair (which continues to the present day) have been virtually forgotten, and Baldwin Brown is rarely mentioned by art historiographers. Indeed, the art historian Nikolaus Pevsner, writing in the 1950s about the history of British art history, bypassed Baldwin Brown entirely, placing the birth of art history as an academic discipline in the United Kingdom at 1931 – with the establishment of the Courtauld Institute of Art. See Nikolaus Pevsner, 'An Un-English Activity? Reflections on Not Teaching Art History', *The Listener* 47/1233 (October 30, 1952), 716.

37 Brown, *The Fine Arts*, 1.

38 See Bernard Lightman, ed., *Global Spencerism: The Communication and Appropriation of a British Evolutionist* (Leiden and Boston: Brill, 2015).

39 See C. Renwick, 'The Practice of Spencerian Science: Patrick Geddes Biosocial Program, 1876–1889', *Isis* 100/1 (March 2009), 36–57.
40 Brown, *The Fine Arts*, 2.
41 Ibid., 10.
42 Ibid., 19.
43 Ibid., 20. From Winwood Reade, *The Martyrdom of Man* (Melbourne: E. W. Cole, 1884), 441.
44 Brown, *The Fine Arts*, 20, n. 2; Herbert Spencer, *Descriptive Sociology* (London: Williams and Norgate, 1874), vol. II, 24.
45 Brown, *The Fine Arts*, 4.
46 Ibid., 21.
47 Ibid., 22.
48 Ibid., 39.
49 Ibid., 33.
50 Mark Francis, *Herbert Spencer and the Invention of Modern Life* (Cornell: Cornell University Press, 2007), 80.
51 Brown, *The Fine Arts*, 68.
52 Ibid., 130.
53 Gerard Baldwin Brown, *The Fine Arts*, 3rd edn. (New York: Scribner's, 1910), 6.
54 Barbara Larson, 'Introduction', in *Darwin and Theories of Aesthetics and Cultural History*, eds. Barbara Larson and Sabine Flach (Farnham, VT: Ashgate, 2013), 8. On Riegl see Marsha Morton, 'Art's "Contest with Nature": Darwin, Haeckel, and the Scientific Art History of Alois Riegl', in Ibid., 53–68.
55 Roger Fry in Roger Fry, Clive Bell, and Boris von Anrep, *Catalogue of the Second Post-Impressionist Exhibition* (London: Grafton Galleries, 1912), 26. On Fry and science see Adrianne Rubin, *Roger Fry's 'Difficult and Uncertain Science': Aesthetic Perceptions* (Pieterlen and Bern: Peter Lang Academic Publishers), 2013.
56 Roger Fry, address delivered October 13, 1933, *Art History as an Academic Study* (Cambridge: Cambridge University Press, 1933), 8. While formalism became the dominant direction in early twentieth-century art history, cultural and social histories of humankind and their works of art did have some adherents. For example, Elie Faure rejected positivism, but applied a neo-Lamarckian perspective to his anarchist belief in the progressive evolution of people and their artistic products, which he perceived as being part of nature, towards global unification (*Histoire de l'art*, Paris: Éditions Denoël. 1909–1927). See Serena Keshavjee, 'Natural History, Cultural History, and the Art History of Elie Faure', *Nineteenth Century Art Worldwide* 8/2 (2009), n.p.

4 The Manchester School of History

Victorian Origins of a 'Modernist' Discipline

H. S. Jones

There is a standard way of explaining how and why knowledge came to be organized in disciplines. The established narrative in the literature holds that the map of knowledge which we have inherited dates from the closing decades of the nineteenth century and the early twentieth century. It was then that specialist departments began to proliferate in universities, first of all in Germany and then in the United States; and it was then that the range of degree courses available to undergraduates massively expanded. The impetus came from several sources. As the frontiers of knowledge were pushed back rapidly, the old vision of a common liberal education appropriate for all undergraduates came to seem both outdated and obviously incapable of meeting the needs of an industrial economy for trained scientists and engineers. Equally, there was a clear connection with the contemporaneous development of the research university emphasizing the importance of graduate studies. If an undergraduate education could still, at a pinch, aim at integration, research could advance only through specialization and differentiation. The new universities of this period, such as Johns Hopkins in Baltimore (1876), explicitly saw the mastery of a specialism as the essential attribute of a professor. As disciplines subdivided and spawned new ones, so they reinforced their status through the creation of professional associations, learned societies, and scholarly journals.[1] This model of disciplinary specialization driven by research took root first in Germany and the United States, and especially in the sciences, and from there it spread more or less rapidly to other countries and to other disciplines.

In the British case, the process of professionalization and specialization was uneven and in some ways curiously slow. Reba Soffer has argued that the Oxford history school, dominated as it was by the college tutors rather than the university professors, was principally focussed even into the inter-war period not on a specialist training in history but on a historical education as a school of citizenship.[2] This became, she argues, the hegemonic view of the historical profession in Britain.[3] More recently, James Kirby has emphasized the centrality of the Church of England – its clergy and its committed laymen – to historical scholarship in Britain right up to the First World War. A significant proportion of learned research in history was conducted not in universities and colleges but in vicarages, rectories, and cathedral closes, not least by such luminaries as Bishop Stubbs, Bishop Creighton, and Archdeacon Cunningham.[4] Creighton left his Oxford tutorship to take a college living in Northumberland because he thought it would give him more time for writing.[5]

If there was a bastion of the cause of professionalism among the university historians of this period it was to be found in the School of History at Owens College, later (from 1904) the University of Manchester, and it offers the strongest rebuttal of Soffer's interpretation. Under the leadership of the medievalist Thomas Tout, Professor of History from 1890 to 1925, the Manchester History department pioneered an approach to the practice of history that looks self-consciously modern in advocating professionalized training, specialization, and a focus on original research as the central mission of the academic historian. As a scholar, Tout was best known for his work in the administrative history of medieval England, culminating in his *Chapters in the Administrative History of Medieval England* (6 vols, 1920–1931), and indeed his department is often identified, rather misleadingly, with a focus on administrative history.[6] But in fact, Tout and his department were much wider-ranging than that: the department was, for example, an important pioneer in economic history and in urban history. In any case Tout's distinction as a scholar was less important than his energy as an academic organizer, and as an organizer who was inspired by a clear and compelling idea of his discipline and of the university.

Michael Bentley has propounded a powerful and influential view of the significance of Tout's School of History. For Bentley, modernism in historiography stood for 'the destruction of what went before', and 'the substitution of an aggressive new methodology'.[7] Bentley depicts the age of Tout as the first age of modernism, an age when the Whiggish pieties of Stubbs and Freeman were displaced in the name of a professionalism that laid claim to scientific authority grounded in specialization. Bentley sees Tout as one of the key figures in the creation of this 'modernist' historiography. He was 'the most determined anti-whig'.[8]

Much of this seems incontestable. Although Tout was an Oxford graduate, the pupil at Balliol of one of Soffer's protagonists, A. L. Smith, and retained close Oxford connections, Tout was quick to recognize the opportunity to build a very different approach to historical teaching at Manchester.[9] He was a pioneer of what is now called research-based teaching at the undergraduate level, and was also an early advocate of graduate studies. After the First World War, with the new title of 'Director of Advanced Study', he devoted himself to the development of the new degree of PhD, with striking success. His language was often unashamedly modernistic, as when he advocated the establishment of 'historical laboratories' organized around libraries equipped to house and support seminar teaching. Like the art historians studied by Larson

(Chapter 3), he appealed, in positivistic fashion, to the natural sciences for validation. He insisted that the research ideal is 'no less applicable to history than to physics and chemistry'. 'One way of raising the level of the academic study of history in this country is to follow more closely the methods by which British exponents of the physical sciences have made their mark'.[10] By that he meant, above all, that the research-teaching nexus should be strengthened, through a greater emphasis in historical education upon 'the processes by which history is studied', as opposed to the results of those investigations.[11] He was instrumental in the establishment of Manchester University Press, serving as its first chairman, and promoting the Press as a flagship expression of the University's commitment to original research in the humanities.[12]

We find here the overt professionalism and perhaps also the positivism that are commonly associated with the 'modernist' renewal of the discipline of history. Tout was a leading contributor to the *Dictionary of National Biography*, the *English Historical Review*, and other collaborative enterprises; and indeed his *magnum opus*, the *Chapters in the Administrative History of Mediaeval England*, culminated in a grand collaboration, since volume five, published posthumously, was as he intended the work of 'a syndicate of old pupils', including his daughter and his sister-in-law.[13] He was a key advocate of both collaboration and specialization, and when he was elected Fellow of the British Academy in 1911 he pressed these causes on the Academy. Writing to its secretary, Israel Gollancz, in 1914, he supported the expansion of the Academy, a cause he thought would facilitate the promotion of collaborative projects; but he warned that a scheme effecting this without structural reform 'would not be suited to the claims of specialists'. The existing Section 1 (History and Archaeology) was 'already so large that the specialists on any branch of historical learning are sure to be outvoted by those whose studies are on different lines'. The use of sub-sections was his preferred remedy.[14] He was notably active in the Academy's sponsorship of collaborative scholarly projects, and chaired the Academy's committee to supervise the British contribution to a new Dictionary of Medieval Latin.[15]

And yet something important about Tout is missed by the depiction of him as an unalloyed modernist. In particular, it over-emphasizes the rift separating Tout from his predecessors. Bentley's narrative sets the 'modernist' historians in opposition to the 'Whigs', the pre-eminent ones when Tout was a young man being two successive Oxford Regius professors, Stubbs and Freeman. They were, it should be added, Whigs in the historiographical sense only: neither was a Whig in politics, for Stubbs was a High Church Tory, Freeman a Gladstonian Liberal.[16] But Tout, unlike some other modernists, such as his Balliol contemporary J. H. Round, was never inclined to rubbish his predecessors, and he had an especially close relationship with these two. When an undergraduate at Oxford, he was taught by Stubbs, who, as well as being

Regius Professor, was chaplain of Balliol – and much preferred tutorials with Balliol undergraduates to giving university lectures. Tout had an enduring regard for Stubbs, 'the greatest historian who taught history during the last generation', and this was fully reciprocated.[17] He also wrote a reverential obituary of Freeman for the *Manchester Guardian* in 1892. Freeman had been a vocal supporter of Owens College, notably in its struggle (only partly successful) for independent university status in 1875–1880.[18] After his death his library was bought for the College by the Whitworth Trustees, through the agency of Adolphus Ward, Principal and Vice-Chancellor and Tout's predecessor in the chair of History. The Freeman library, which consisted of some six thousand volumes, was central to Tout's conception of a 'historical laboratory', in which specialist seminar teaching would take place in the midst of a research library.[19] Thus, one of Tout's most ostensibly modernistic innovations paid tribute to an archetypal high Victorian Whig historian.

In fact, this fidelity to the legacy of Stubbs and Freeman is by no means as paradoxical as Bentley's account would lead us to suppose. As Ian Hesketh has demonstrated, both Stubbs and Freeman were actively engaged in the kind of 'boundary work' that was crucial in demarcating scientific history from 'literature', and Stubbs in particular saw it as his mission to create a cadre of trained historians.[20] One of Tout's favourite and apparently most modernistic locutions, the 'historical worker', was derived from Stubbs's inaugural lecture at Oxford in 1867, in which Stubbs introduced himself 'not as a philosopher nor as a politician, but as a worker at history', and referred enthusiastically to 'the great German hive of historical workers'.[21] The connection to German scholarship is reminiscent of how continental influences played a significant role in the cases of the development of dance (Chapter 2) and art history (Chapter 3).

In building on the legacy of Stubbs and Freeman, Tout's department did indeed offer something new and distinctive, but far from breaking radically with the past it was powerfully shaped by some characteristically Victorian struggles to define universities and their functions, and in particular to define the scholarly virtues required in a modern academic.[22]

Origins of an Academic Ideal

The conception of the academic life that we find in Tout's Manchester has obvious affinities with the oft-invoked 'German idea of the university' that is conventionally traced to Wilhelm von Humboldt's establishment of the University of Berlin in 1810. The German model loomed large in Victorian debates about university reform, and the German connection was probably at its strongest at Manchester, where there was a sizeable German community. Both Thomas Ashton (mill-owner, and the key lay figure in the extension of Owens College) and Henry Roscoe

(Professor of Chemistry, later Liberal MP) were educated at Heidelberg. So, later, was the German-born professor of physics, Arthur Schuster, who studied at Owens College first.

There is certainly no reason to play down the importance of the German influence, but an influence is not a causal relationship. If we are to explain why the German idea of the university really had traction in the context that Owens College found itself in, we need to attend also to what gave it special appeal to the academic community there. I contend that the successive struggles which led first to the creation of the Victoria University (1880) and then to its dissolution into independent universities (1903–1904) were decisively important in shaping the identity of academics in civic universities, Manchester in particular – and, crucially, not just in the sciences, but in the humanities too. Both these struggles were constructed in Manchester as struggles over the meaning of the idea of the university, and that was a key context for the formation of disciplinary identities.

Owens College had been founded in 1851, in execution of the will of John Owens, a wealthy textile merchant who had died five years before. In its first fifteen years or so, it struggled: as historians now recognize, it was founded at an unpropitious time, and it was only in the 1860s that demand for higher education started to pick up. It is sometimes suggested that what revived the College's fortunes was its decision, at the instigation of the chemist Henry Roscoe, to embrace technical education as its salvation, and to work more closely with local industry. But in reality what really made a difference was the fact that by the 1860s the educational environment was much more favourable, as the growth of secondary schooling fuelled demand for university education.[23] That was when Greenwood, Roscoe, and others launched an ambitious programme of expansion, relocating the College away from the city centre, where it was based in Richard Cobden's old house in Quay Street, to a more spacious location a mile to the south in Chorlton-on-Medlock.

As the College's student numbers expanded and new professors were appointed, it began to set its heights higher, and in 1875 it launched a campaign for independent university status, throwing off its relationship with the University of London, for whose degrees Owens prepared those of its students who wanted to graduate. But the initiative encountered resistance from Yorkshire, which was jealous of the prospect of Manchester having university status if Leeds did not. So the federal Victoria University was founded, based in Manchester but with constituent colleges (eventually three: Owens College, Manchester; Yorkshire College, Leeds; and University College, Liverpool). That was the institution that Tout joined in 1890, moving from St David's College, Lampeter, where he had served nine years as Professor of Modern History. The Owens College that he joined had been profoundly shaped by the drive for university status. But it is clear that he chafed from the outset at the status difference between a college in a federal university on the one hand and an independent university on the other hand. When Edinburgh and Glasgow both advertised new chairs in History in 1894, he was tempted by both, even though the Scottish universities had little tradition of historical teaching and research. He decided to defer to George Prothero in the former case but applied for Glasgow, where he lost out to his Balliol contemporary Richard Lodge.[24]

When the issue of the dissolution of the federal university into separate universities arose, Tout therefore threw himself enthusiastically into the cause. This campaign was formative in defining Tout's academic mission. He was right at the forefront in making the case for independence – along with his wife, Mary, who played a major role in canvassing the opinions of women graduates in particular.[25] The campaign gave Tout the opportunity to establish himself as one of the foremost figures in the academic politics of his time, one whose significance far transcended the boundaries of his own discipline. In its aftermath he was a figure of great power in the new university, serving notably as the first Dean of its Faculty of Arts.

The crisis was initiated by University College, Liverpool, which was the first to declare its desire to separate from the federal university and to set itself up as an independent University of Liverpool. The context was the establishment of an independent University of Birmingham in 1900, which offended Liverpool's civic pride. Significantly, the leaders of the Liverpool campaign were historians: chief among them, the Rathbone Professor of History, John Macdonald Mackay, who had played an important role in supporting Birmingham's case, and his junior colleague, Ramsay Muir, who had briefly taught for Tout's department a few years previously and who would later return as the first Professor of Modern History in 1914, before leaving to launch a career in Liberal politics.[26] It was Muir who made the fullest case for independence, in a sequence of articles for the *Liverpool Courier*, published soon afterwards in pamphlet form as *The Plea for a Liverpool University*.[27] Muir, who had been brought up in Merseyside and who was beginning to specialize as an historian of Liverpool, was well able to give voice to the dismay felt by the Liverpool's civic notables that Birmingham had acquired university status first: 'we do not altogether relish the idea of being worsted by a city inferior to our own in size, in wealth, and in dignity'.[28] His *Plea* set out some of the essential arguments which would be deployed by advocates of independence: that the essential functions of the university were teaching and research, whereas examining was incidental; that federal universities such as London and the Victoria were anomalous in the history of universities; and that federal universities got in the way of the civic mission of universities, because they lacked the essential bond between one university and one city that would enable universities to tap into civic patriotism.[29]

Liverpool was soon joined by Owens College, which felt that it had a prior claim to university status by virtue of the fact that it had first made the case a quarter of a century previously, as well as on grounds of its size. Owens therefore proposed the dissolution of the Victoria University, a proposal that was resisted both by Yorkshire College, Leeds – which felt that it was not ready for independence – and by a substantial body of graduates of the Victoria University, who believed that their degrees would be devalued by the abolition of the Victoria University. They were led by the young Manchester barrister and Tariff Reform campaigner, W. Barnard Faraday, and for a time they seemed to have the backing of the members of Convocation.[30] In the end, however, the proponents of separation were successful, both in Convocation and before the Privy Council.

When the opponents of the dissolution circulated a pamphlet to Convocation members trying to take apart the case for independence, it was Tout and Muir who sprang to action to make the case with renewed force. Muir was the author of the key pamphlet, but it was inspired by discussion with Tout and amended in line with Tout's revisions, as their correspondence indicates. It turned out to be a crucial pamphlet which played a decisive role in winning the vote in Convocation.[31] Significantly, Muir framed the dispute as one that hinged on the very idea of the university. The recalcitrant graduates asserted that a university was being destroyed, but for Muir this made no sense. No teaching or research would cease to take place: all that was being dissolved was an apparatus for examining and awarding degrees. 'The essential mark of a University is that it teaches and researches, and until the old University of London was created there has never been a University in the world which did not answer to this definition'. He ridiculed the narrowly insular conception of the university invoked by his opponents: the idea that the university was essentially an examining body defied the experience of 'twenty generations of the learned world'. The dissolution of the Victoria University would not entail the abolition of 'a teaching and researching corporation'; instead, the proposal would bring to completion three incomplete universities. And Muir was vociferous in denouncing the 'old retrograde examination-worship', the 'degrading fetish-worship of examinations', which he believed underpinned the resistance to the proposal.[32]

The case made by Muir was echoed, in remarkably similar terms, by Tout and his distinguished colleague Samuel Alexander, the Professor of Philosophy, who was a close collaborator in the independence campaign.[33] In particular, they denounced what Tout called 'the mischievous fetish of examination worship', and Alexander 'the dreary Chinese ideal which identifies the university with an apparatus for examination'.[34] Just as London University stood for the 'Chinese ideal' in the 1870s, so did the Victoria University a quarter of a century later. The Victoria University had accomplished a great deal: after all, there was a big difference between Owens professors preparing their students for an examination devised by a committee in London and preparing their students according to a curriculum they had helped devise for an examination set by a committee in Manchester on which they served with Leeds and Liverpool counterparts. But it still embodied the old and deleterious separation between the examining function and the teaching function, and thus in Tout's words 'falls short of the academic ideal'. For 'a real University is something much less mechanical than a federation of teachers for the sake of giving degrees of a uniform quality and seeing that their colleagues are much more than this'.[35] Examinations were a necessary part of university life, but 'we should not set before the University teacher the ideals of the crammer preparing his pupils to pass, or the director of a racing stable training his steeds for the race'.[36]

Research was central to the 'academic ideal' espoused by Tout and Alexander: what ultimately defined the worth of universities were 'the contributions made by their members to the sum of human knowledge and the enlargement of the range of human thought'.[37] The educational dimension was crucial too, but what characterized the educational work of a university was not mechanical teaching to the demands of an examination but 'the contact of mind and mind, of teacher and student, without as well as within the lecture-room, and living as far as may be the common social, as well as the common intellectual, life'.[38]

Tout, Alexander, and Muir shared, to a striking degree, a common sense of what was at stake in the contest over the creation of separate universities. They insisted, first of all, that this was a contest that turned on rival conceptions of the university. They asked, 'what is a university?', whereas their opponents maintained that the question was a purely practical one about the organization of higher education.[39] For the advocates of independence, the struggle was fundamentally about the coming to maturity of the three colleges as teaching and researching corporations. That entailed their emancipation from their subordination to an outside organization, the federal university. Critically, it was also about the recognition of the maturity of the professorial staff of the three universities. It was degrading to them, as researchers with established reputations for original work, to be deemed unfit to frame a syllabus for themselves in accordance with their own conception of their subject. 'When you have got a good man', wrote Muir, 'you must leave him, in teaching advanced students, to use his own methods. To impose upon him the methods of other men, even of men as good as or better than, himself, will only hamper him'. Independence would therefore enhance 'the freshness and effectiveness of the teaching in our local University'.[40] What was at stake, in short, was what German academics defined as one of their essential freedoms: *Lehrfreiheit*, or the freedom to teach what they regarded as true and important.

It is highly significant that Tout's most influential programmatic statements on the practice of the discipline of history date from the years during and immediately following the battle for independence: his paper on 'History at Owens College' in February 1902; his *Manchester Guardian* piece on 'The Historical Teaching of History', a review of Charles Firth's inaugural lecture at Oxford, which appeared in December 1904; and, finally, his piece on 'An Historical "Laboratory"', in January 1910.[41] To an extent there is a humdrum reason for this: now that he was professor at a unitary and independent university, he had – with his colleague James Tait – the power to shape the curriculum for himself, so this was a propitious time for reflection on what kind of history should be taught at university, and how it should be taught.[42] But, more importantly, there was a direct connection between the arguments deployed in favour of independence and the way in which Tout set about reshaping the curriculum. Advocates of independence pointed out that the existence of an external examining body led to a reliance on the traditional unseen examination, since the ethos was to separate the function of examining from the function of teaching. There was no room for (in modern terminology) the assessment of coursework or the production of pieces of independent research for examination. The Manchester physicist Arthur Schuster, in his evidence to the Privy Council, argued that the need to balance the interests of students from the different colleges in the federal university prevented 'a proper recognition of research work' in the examination of degrees, and the recognition of laboratory work undertaken by the student.[43] This was a key point. Defenders of the status quo maintained that there was no reason why the Victoria University examination should not accommodate the different teaching practices of the constituent colleges, but the system they defended was one that separated the examining from the teaching function and implicitly required the teacher to teach to the examination. Tout, who was close to Schuster, saw his opportunity, and once independence was achieved, he adopted the thesis as a compulsory and distinctive feature of the Manchester curriculum. Significantly, it was something he discussed with Muir, who told him that his Liverpool colleagues would welcome this initiative: it would be 'would be hailed with delight as fully satisfying everything that has been asked for from this side'.[44]

In other words, there was a powerful structural connection between the separation of the examining function from the teaching function in English universities and the survival of a model of historical education that concentrated on teaching the results of historical investigation as opposed to the techniques and methods of historical research. The dissolution of the federal university was therefore the prerequisite for an experiment with a new kind of historical education in which students would be taught research methods and would undertake a small-scale piece of historical research for themselves.

In addition, advocates of independence were clear that the dissolution of the federal university was necessary if universities were to be brought into a more lively contact with their civic environment: making curricular innovations to serve the distinctive needs of the local economy, attracting new endowments from local notables, shaping the intellectual life of the city, and in general serving as a focus for civic patriotism. In all these respects the civic colleges were hampered by the sense that they were something less than universities, and dependent upon a federal university that lacked a clear geographical identity. Tout, Alexander, and Muir all shared a powerful sense of the social responsibility of the university, and that social responsibility was focussed above all on the city. That could have implications for the academic content of research and teaching: Muir, for instance, became a specialist in the history of Liverpool, and urban history in a broader sense was an important focus in Tout's department.[45] But even more important was the idea of the scholar as citizen. Tout, like Alexander, had been taught by the influential idealist philosopher T. H. Green at Oxford, and as his widow put it, he learnt from Green 'that the academic man owes civic service in the widest sense'.[46] This is a significant point. Tout and his allies were proponents of professionalism, specialization, and the duty of the academic to be a researcher. But they were also clear that the new university they wanted to create must reach outwards and build new bonds with the local community. In this sense the example of Tout's Manchester challenges the antithesis that Reba Soffer has set up between history as a specialist research discipline and history as a school of citizenship.

It is striking that the three intellectual leaders of the campaign were all from arts faculties. That is not to say that scientists were peripheral: Tout's friend, the physicist Arthur Schuster, was very much of the same mind, and gave testimony to the Privy Council in support of separation, as did other leading Manchester scientists such as the chemist Harold Baily Dixon.[47] But Tout, Alexander, and Muir were in no sense subordinate to the scientists, and in the role they played in the campaign we see their growing self-consciousness and confidence about their professional identity as humanities academics.

This point deserves emphasis, because the history of the English civic universities has been written in such a way as unduly to marginalize the place of the humanities. Thus Peter Burke, in his admirable *Social History of Knowledge*, states that Owens College was 'originally founded by a local textile merchant to teach practical subjects'.[48] This is a curious misapprehension apparently grounded in an ingrained assumption that this is what the 'redbrick' universities must have been about. John Owens was indeed a local textile merchant, and while much about his motivation in endowing the college remains obscure, he was quite explicit about its subject coverage: it should instruct 'young persons of the male sex. . . in such branches of learning and science as are now and may be hereafter usually taught in the English Universities'.[49] Owens College was punctilious in following this injunction, establishing chairs in classics, history, and philosophy from the outset. It is well-known that the chemist Henry Roscoe – later Liberal MP for South Manchester – did more than anyone to shape the intellectual reputation of the College, and also played a decisive role, along with scientifically educated industrialists such as Thomas Ashton, in the movement for the extension of Owens College in 1870.[50] But alongside Roscoe's role should be set the fact that the four very able men who served as Principal were all humanists: the theologian and philosopher Alexander Scott, the Greek scholar Joseph Greenwood, the historian Adolphus Ward, and the lawyer Alfred Hopkinson.[51] The Senate in the wake of the college extension was equally balanced between the sciences and the humanities. Influential humanists in the early decades included Richard Copley Christie and James Bryce, both of whom were distinguished both as historians and as lawyers. Christie, who held chairs of Law, History, and Political Economy, and later served for many years as a member of Council, was notably important in shaping Owens College as a place of humane learning. He funded the construction of a library, named the Christie Library, and left his own collection that made the library a major resource for research in Renaissance studies.[52] As one of the Whitworth trustees he was also instrumental in the acquisition of Freeman's library, consisting of over 6,000 volumes, for Owens College.[53] Meanwhile Bryce, who held a part-time chair of law concurrently with the Regius Professorship of Civil Law at Oxford, was engaged to draft a constitution for Owens College at its extension in 1870. His constitution enshrined the balance of lay and academic influence in governance, and the tripartite separation of Court, Council, and Senate, that have subsequently become the model for English universities.[54]

The First Independence Moment

The English civic universities that were founded in the first few years of the twentieth century were driven, then, by a distinctive vision of the purposes of a university and of the academic's vocation. The interdependence of teaching and research was an essential part of that vision; so too was a sense of the organic relationship between the university and its civic environment. This vision was shaped by the struggle against the federal idea of the university, which ruptured the relationship between teaching and research, and the relationship between the university and the city. The immediate context was the struggle for independence from the Victoria University, which for University College, Liverpool and Owens College, Manchester embodied the federal idea. But a quarter of a century before, when Owens College made its first bid for independence, it was the University of London that stood for the federal idea. To achieve a full understanding of the origins of the Tout-Muir-Alexander vision of the university, we have to go back to the debates of the 1870s which led, as a compromise, to the formation of the Victoria University. They anticipated with a striking accuracy the arguments that finally achieved the formation of independent universities in 1903–1904. Tout, in particular, was acutely aware of the earlier history of the struggle for independence, and several times he lamented the fact that Owens College had too easily accepted the compromise solution of a federal university with its seat at Manchester.[55]

To understand how arguments about academic organization could turn on distinctive visions of the university, we have to consider the kind of case that was put against the creation of an independent university. It came from those who defended the University of London model – who held, in other words, that a university should be conceived as an examining body, and that it was desirable that the functions of teacher and examiner should be kept strictly apart. Until 1900 London University was purely a degree-awarding and not a teaching university. Its relationship to University College, King's College, and the other London colleges was the same as its relationship with Owens College and the other colleges that entered students for London degrees; and hence it was quite different from the relationship of the University of Oxford with Balliol, Magdalen, or St John's. Only in 1900 did the several London colleges become *part of* the University, and that organizational change transformed the University's relationship to the city.[56]

The case against a new university was propounded must trenchantly by the former Chancellor of the Exchequer, Robert Lowe, MP for London University since 1868.[57] Lowe certainly spoke for the interest of London University in resisting the establishment of a new university with degree-awarding powers of its own, but there was more to his position than that. As a young man he had established an academic reputation as the most successful private coach in Oxford, after he had to relinquish his college fellowship on marriage, and this experience made him look with favour on private provision in a competitive market as the institutional structure most conductive to educational efficiency. Ideologically he was a leading proponent of market-driven meritocracy – as Vice-President of the Privy Council's Education Committee under Palmerston he was responsible for the introduction of the notorious system of 'payment by results' for teachers, and he was a staunch opponent of endowments, which he held to be a restraint on the operation of the free market and hence of the stimulus of competition.[58]

In the Victorian period, written examinations started to flourish and became almost ubiquitous as markers of objective standards, for example in determining access to the professions.[59] In defending the London University model, Lowe drew on this cult of the examination. He argued in favour of the strict separation of the teaching function and the examining function – a separation that was embodied in the University he represented, which had no registered students of its own, and indeed admitted to its examinations candidates who were not registered students at any college. For Lowe, teaching was a burdensome occupation, and it was natural for the teacher to try to minimize his teaching load. Students were equally naturally inclined to excuse indolence and laxity on the part of their teachers. The only effective stimulus to efficient teaching, therefore, is the knowledge that without it one's students will perform badly in their examinations. But if those who do the teaching are also responsible for setting and marking the examinations, their interest is to lower standards so as to maintain the flow of students and hence of income. This is what happened, he thought, at Oxford and Cambridge: the university, as the examining power, ought to act as the check on the teaching of the colleges, but in practice it was 'in the power of the colleges', whose interest was to keep student numbers high by keeping examination standards low. 'Thus the teachers of the two great universities are virtually the judges of their own work, and treat it with an amount of tenderness and consideration which cannot but be extremely gratifying to their pupils, as well as agreeable to themselves'.[60] The power of 'self-government' which Owens College sought in emulation of Oxford and Cambridge was, according to Lowe, nothing more than 'the allowing teachers to put their own value on their own work'.[61]

Owens College mobilized its supporters against the ascendancy of the London University model, and in doing so generated a highly illuminating debate about the nature of the university. As in 1901–1902, this was not a purely technical question of the internal organization of universities. Rather, on this debate hinged the identity of the emergent academic profession. It engaged major national figures on the Owens side – Edward Freeman, Mark Pattison, Lyon Playfair, as well as a sequence of editorials in the recently founded science journal, *Nature*. It was, in fact, much more of a national campaign than that which would follow a quarter of a century later. Two central arguments were put forward by the Owens side.

The first focussed on the personal influence of teacher on student as an integral element in a university education. This point was made against London University's claim to be an authentic – indeed *the* authentic – university. For its critics, the problem was not simply that London University was not a teaching university, but crucially that it decided in 1857 to admit to its examinations candidates who were not registered students of any college. What this meant, so it was argued, was that London degrees were certificates of knowledge demonstrated, but not of an education received. The Owens sub-committee entrusted with the task of drawing up the proposal was highly critical of London's decision to do this, for it had abandoned an 'indispensable' element of a university education, namely 'the direct influence of teachers upon students', as well as of students on their fellow students'.[62]

The second point was that the ability to shape the curriculum was an integral part of the professional autonomy of the university professor, and constituted a fundamental distinction between the academic and the schoolmaster. After all, it might be said in response to the first argument that whether or not London University might admit non-collegiate candidates to its examinations, those students who were registered at institutions such as Owens College were indeed subject to the personal influence of academically distinguished teachers. What was lacking, however, was one of the means by which that influence could be exerted, namely the framing of a curriculum in accordance with current research. It was professionally demeaning for a distinguished professor at Owens College to be enslaved to a curriculum devised by 'a random collection of examiners, whatever their individual eminence, gathered temporarily in an office in London'.[63] In other words, defenders of the University of Manchester proposal held that what was important about university status was not simply the power to award degrees per se, but what that power implied, namely the ability of the Senate to frame a curriculum for itself according to its conception of the subjects it teaches. John Nichol, Regius Professor of English Literature at Glasgow, while recognizing that external examiners were an important check, maintained that 'a Professor in a University abdicates all that should distinguish him from a common schoolmaster when he consents to work up to a standard over which he has no control'.[64] The Manchester sub-committee, responding to press criticism of their proposal, insisted that degree-awarding powers would strengthen the college's ability to act as 'an independent source of intellectual culture and activity' in Manchester and its region. This was because that influence 'can hardly become strong and permanent, or, still less, develop into schools of thought, research, and study, where the teacher is fettered by the necessity of conforming, even in details, to a rigid system imposed upon him from without'.[65] So the argument here was that autonomy and self-government – qualities that Lowe sneered at – were indispensable if universities were to achieve their higher purposes, in teaching and research but also in civic engagement.

This argument was put forcibly in a series of articles in *Nature* in July 1876, presumably written by the editor, the astronomer Norman Lockyer. The London University system, which separated teaching from examining and gave London University power over the curriculum of each provincial college, was inconsistent with 'the true theory of a University', being incompatible with freedom of teaching and with the originality expected of an academic. 'Indeed it would be a mistake for such institutions to have at the head of their departments teachers of originality and power of research. Teaching of the kind to suit this system is incompatible with research'. This was because the curriculum would by definition encompass only 'the best known and most widely diffused results of knowledge – not that which is growing and plastic, but that which has already grown and hardened into shape – the knowledge in fact of a past generation which has become sufficiently well established to be worthy of this species of canonisation'.[66]

The central argument was that, for a college that possessed a mature professoriate – 'men of great originality', for Lockyer – the members of which had achieved nationwide or international recognition for their scientific or scholarly work, it was demeaning to be subordinated to the demands of an externally constructed curriculum.[67] This was precisely the time when the 'endowment of research' movement was taking shape, and the claims of research to be a fundamental part of the university's mission were being formulated for the first time in England. When Lockyer declared that teaching adapted to an externally determined syllabus was 'incompatible with research', he was explicitly pointing to the conflict between the London University model and this new understanding of the university – with 'the true theory of a University'. As Mark Pattison – Rector of Lincoln College, Oxford, patron of the endowment of research movement, and ardent supporter of the Manchester cause – put it, the London connection seriously impaired 'the freedom and originality of our instruction'.[68] So here we find 'Lehrfreiheit' – the freedom to shape the curriculum in accordance with one's own conception of the discipline – being positioned as a core value of the emergent academic profession. Pattison was one of the earliest and most caustic critics of the Victorian cult of the examination, and his conception of the university – in particular, his conception of the academic's vocation – surely helped inspire the proponents of the case for an independent university.[69]

These debates took place more than a decade before Tout's appointment at Manchester. But they already helped define the kind of values into which Tout would become socialized upon his arrival at Manchester. It was by no means just the scientists who espoused them. One of the key figures in the campaign for a University of Manchester was his predecessor as Professor of History, Adolphus Ward, who was one of the four professors who in 1875 initiated the campaign. He later served as Principal of Owens College (1890–1897) and Vice-Chancellor of the Victoria University. On Tout's account Ward was 'more than any other man, the true founder' of the independent University of Manchester established in 1904 – even though he had by that time retired from Owens and been elected to the Mastership of Peterhouse, Cambridge.[70] Tout attributed to Ward a formative role, too, in shaping the School of History – above all in 'planting. . . the spirit of historical investigation in the minds of so many able men'.[71] Tout was equally conscious of the role of Ward's predecessor, Christie – a pupil of Pattison's at Oxford – who had 'held up the ideal of history as a preparation for life, and of historical research as the life work of a scholar'.[72] And while Christie resigned his professorial appointments by 1869, he remained a formidable lay influence in the governance of both Owens and the Victoria University.

Conclusion

Disciplines took shape in a number of different contexts, including learned societies and the journals they established. By no means all those who played important roles in discipline-formation were academics. But universities were certainly among the key contexts, as Buckland (Chapter 2), Larson (Chapter 3), Goldhill (Chapter 9), and Zon (Chapter 12) have shown in the cases, respectively, of dance, art history, classics and theology, and musicology. This essay has set out to trace the ways in which particular disciplinary practices were formed in the context of large-stake contests about what defines a university, and about what characteristically distinguished the role of the academic. Tout was very much part of a Manchester project, and we can only understand the genesis of his distinctive conception of the practice of history by locating it in the context of Manchester's struggles for independence. Tout saw his opportunity to shape an approach to history which exploited the distinctive advantages of the newly independent civic universities. Freed from the sway of an examining body remote from the teachers, these universities had the chance to integrate research and teaching in a way that was hard to achieve either at the ancient universities or at those colleges subject to London University examiners. This vision was self-consciously professional and focussed on the importance of research to the historian's vocation. But it was also outward-looking and inspired by a sense of the importance of engagement with the civic environment. What the case of Tout's Manchester School of History demonstrates, then, is the importance of institutional contexts in shaping how academic disciplines were defined and practised.

Notes

1 This paragraph is principally based on Peter Burke, *A Social History of Knowledge, Volume II, From the Encyclopédie to Wikipedia* (Cambridge: Polity, 2012), 169–170, and James Turner, *Philology: The Forgotten Origins of the Modern Humanities* (Princeton: Princeton University Press, 2014), 231–235.
2 Reba Soffer, 'The Development of Disciplines in the Modern English University', *Historical Journal* 31 (1988), 933–946. The point is stated explicitly at 936–937.
3 Reba Soffer, *Discipline and Power: The University, History, and the Making of an English Elite, 1870–1939* (Stanford: Stanford University Press, 1994), 206–208.
4 James Kirby, *Historians and the Church of England* (Oxford: Oxford University Press, 2016), especially Chapter 3.
5 Louise Creighton, *Life and Letters of Mandell Creighton by His Wife* (London: Longmans, Green, & Co., 1904), vol. I, 143.
6 For example, Soffer, *Discipline and Power*, 29, 219 n. 34.
7 Michael Bentley, *Modernizing England's Past: English Historiography in the Age of Modernism, 1870–1970* (Cambridge: Cambridge University Press, 2005), 1.

8 Bentley, *Modernizing England's Past*, 101.
9 Soffer in my view overstates the extent of Tout's agreement with the Oxford school: Soffer, *Discipline and Power*, 57.
10 Article in *The Standard*, January 3, 1910, reprinted in Thomas Frederick Tout, *The Collected Papers of Thomas Frederick Tout with A Memoir ad Bibliography*, 2 vols. (Manchester: Manchester University Press, 1932), vol. I, 79–84 (henceforth *Collected Papers*).
11 T. F. Tout, 'An historical "laboratory"', *Collected Papers* I: 80.
12 H. B. Charlton, *Portrait of a University, 1851–1951: To Commemorate the Centenary of Manchester University* (Manchester: Manchester University Press, 1951), 94–95.
13 T. F. Tout, *Chapters in the Administrative History of Mediaeval England*, 6 vols. (Manchester: Manchester University Press, 1920–1933), vol. v, vi. See also the stimulating article by D. Vance Smith, 'Marx and T. F. Tout, Household, City, and History at Manchester', *Journal of Medieval and Early Modern Studies* 24 (2004), 523–547, especially 535.
14 Tout to Israel Gollancz, March 3, 1914, British Academy Archives BA 357.
15 F. M. Powicke, 'Memoir', *Collected Papers* I: 18 n. 1.
16 See J. E. Kirby, 'An Ecclesiastical Descent: Religion and History in the Work of William Stubbs', *Journal of Ecclesiastical History* 65 (2014), 84–110; James Kirby, *Historians and the Church of England: Religion and Historical Scholarship, 1870–1920* (Oxford: Oxford University Press, 2016); G. A. Bremner and Jonathan Conlin (eds.), *Making History: Edward Augustus Freeman and Victorian Cultural Politics* (Oxford: Oxford University Press for the British Academy, 2015).
17 T. F. Tout, 'Schools of History', *University Review* March 1906, reprinted in *Collected Papers* i: 108; F. M. Powicke, 'Memoir', *Collected Papers* i: 2.
18 Edward A. Freeman, 'Owens College and Mr Lowe', *Macmillan's Magazine* 35 (1877), 407–416.
19 On this, see Maurice Powicke, 'Manchester University 1851–1951', *History Today* 1 (May 1951), 55. Powicke was an undergraduate and research fellow at Manchester, and then succeeded Tout as Professor of Medieval History.
20 Ian Hesketh, *The Science of History in Victorian Britain* (London: Pickering & Chatto, 2011), especially Chapter 4 for 'boundary work'.
21 William Stubbs, *Seventeen Lectures on the Study of Medieval and Modern History and Kindred Subjects* (Oxford: Clarendon, 1887), 15, 13.
22 Here I am indebted to Léjon Saarloos, 'Virtue and Vice in Academic Memory: Lord Acton and Charles Oman', *History of Humanities* 1 (2016), 339–354, especially 342.
23 William Whyte, *Redbrick: A Social and Architectural History of Britain's Civic Universities* (Oxford: Oxford University Press, 2015), 99; Matthew Paul Andrews, 'Durham University: The Last of the Ancient Universities and the First of the New (1831–1871)' (D.Phil thesis, University of Oxford, 2016), Chapters 6 and 9.
24 For Tout's candidature at Glasgow, see his letter of application and testimonials at John Rylands Library Tout papers TFT/1/418; also TFT/1/36/38-46, 49–50, letters from Charles Firth to Tout between April 13 and July 6, 1894.
25 The numerous letters written to Thomas and Mary Tout, and to some of their fellow campaigners, are collected in several unlisted folders in the Tout papers at the John Rylands Library: in particular those labelled TFT/MT Independent University of Manchester, and MT Independent University of Manchester.
26 On Mackay, see Thomas Kelly, *For Advancement of Learning: The University of Liverpool 1881–1981* (Liverpool: Liverpool University Press, 1981),

118–119; *A Miscellany Presented to John MacDonald Mackay, LLD, July 1914* (Liverpool: Liverpool University Press, 1914), and Muir, *Autobiography*, Chapters 4–8. On Birmingham's debt to Mackay, see E. A. Sonnenschein, 'Birmingham University and Mackay', in *Miscellany*, 77–79.

27 Ramsay Muir, *The Plea for a Liverpool University* (Liverpool: C. Tinling, 1901), University of Liverpool Archives D 119/1/9. Muir's six articles appeared anonymously in the *Liverpool Courier* between March 21 and May 13, 1901. They are collected in a scrapbook of newspaper cuttings in University of Liverpool Archives D 51/5/15.

28 Muir, *Plea*, 8.

29 Ibid., 40–43, 66–67, 83–86.

30 On Faraday, see 'Mr W. B. Faraday', *Manchester Guardian* June 19, 1953, p. 5. Ironically, the obituary recorded that he was a graduate of 'Manchester University'.

31 The pamphlet was Ramsay Muir, *The Case for the Establishment of Independent Universities of Manchester, Liverpool, and Yorkshire* (Manchester: University of Manchester Archives OCA/25/2, 1902). For its gestation, see Ramsay Muir, *An Autobiography and Some Essays* (London: Lund Humphries, 1943), 47–48; and Muir to Tout, n.d. [1902], TFT/1/842/1-2.

32 Ramsay Muir, *The Case for the Establishment of Independent Universities*, 8, 15, 17.

33 Alexander, an Australian graduate of Balliol, had also studied in Germany: At Freiburg-im-Breisgau, during the tenure of his fellowship of Lincoln College, Oxford.

34 T. F. Tout, 'The future of the Victoria University', *The Pilot*, 1902, reprinted in *Collected Papers* I: 49.

35 Tout, 'The future of the Victoria University', 48.

36 T. F. Tout, 'Schools of History', 96; Tout, 'The future of the Victoria University', 49.

37 Tout, 'The future of the Victoria University', 48.

38 Ibid.

39 This question was posed by Tout, 'The federal university', 47–48, and in his interview with the *Daily Despatch*, January 9, 1902, in Tout papers, 'Dissolution Victoria University Cuttings'.

40 Muir, *Plea*, 55–56.

41 These are all reprinted in *Collected Papers* volume 1.

42 Peter R. H. Slee, *Learning and a Liberal Education: The Study of Modern History in the Universities of Oxford, Cambridge and Manchester 1800–1914* (Manchester: Manchester University Press, 1986), 155.

43 'Proof of Professor Schuster, F.R.S. on Behalf of the Owens College, Manchester', University of Manchester Archives FVU/4/21.

44 Muir to Tout, June 11, 1907, TFT/1/842; Slee, *Learning and a Liberal Education*, 156–159. Oxford, at the initiative of the Regius Professor, Charles Firth, also introduced an undergraduate thesis in 1907, but this was optional and only a very small proportion of candidates offered one.

45 Ramsay Muir, *A History of Liverpool* (London: Williams & Norgate, 1907).

46 Mary Tout, 'T. F. Tout as a citizen', *Collected Papers* I: 27.

47 See the documents collected in University of Manchester Archives FVU/4/21.

48 Burke, *Social History of Knowledge*, ii: 134.

49 Quoted by Whyte, *Redbrick*, 93.

50 W. H. Chaloner, *The Movement for the Extension of Owens College Manchester 1863–1873* (Manchester: Manchester University Press, 1973); also

Henry Enfield Roscoe, *The Life and Experiences of Sir Henry Enfield Roscoe* (London: Macmillan, 1906), 110–111.

51 On the first two in particular, see J. W. Rogerson, 'The Manchester Faculty of Theology 1904: Beginnings and Background', *Bulletin of the John Rylands University Library of Manchester* 86/3 (2004), 9–22.

52 'The Christie Library and Whitworth Hall, Owens College', *Manchester Guardian* June 21, 1898, p. 12, and Moses Tyson, *The Manchester University Library* (Manchester: Manchester University Press, 1937), p. 16.

53 'Mr Richard Copley Christie', *Manchester Guardian* January 10, 1901, p. 10.

54 The relevant papers are in University of Manchester Archives OCA/7. See also David R. Jones, *The Origins of Civic Universities: Manchester, Leeds & Liverpool* (London: Routledge, 1988), 146.

55 T. F. Tout, 'Sir Adolphus William Ward 1837–1924', in *Collected Papers* i: 152.

56 On which see Negley Harte, *The University of London 1836–1986* (London: Athlone Press, 1986).

57 Robert Lowe, 'Shall We Create a New University?', *Fortnightly Review* 21 (February 1877), 160–171. For other 'London' perspectives, see e.g. W. B. Carpenter (Registrar of the University of London') to J. G. Greenwood, June 6, 1876, OCA/23/3, pp. 12–16, and Sir John Lubbock (Vice-Chancellor the University of London, and member of parliament for the University, to Henry Roscoe, April 29, 1876, OCA/23/3, 32.

58 For the general argument, Robert Lowe, *Middle Class Education. Endowment or Free Trade* (London: Bush, 1868). For the specific case of universities, see e.g. *The Times*, June 3, 1872, p. 11.

59 On this subject, see notably Gillian Sutherland, 'Examinations and the Construction of Professional Identity: A Case Study of England 1800–1950', *Assessment in Education: Principles, Policy and Practice* 8 (2001), 51–64; and Christopher Stray, 'The Shift from Oral to Written Examination: Cambridge and Oxford 1700–1900', *Assessment in Education: Principles, Policy and Practice* 8 (2001), 33–50.

60 Lowe, 'Shall We Create a New University?', 163.

61 Ibid., 165.

62 University of Manchester Archives OCA/23/2, pp. 3–4.

63 William Jack to A. W. Ward, May 8, 1876, reprinted in University of Manchester Archives OCA/23/3, p. 29. Jack was formerly Professor of Natural Philosophy at Owens College.

64 John Nichol to A. W. Ward, April 23, 1876, reprinted in University of Manchester Archives OCA/23/3, p. 36.

65 University of Manchester Archives OCA/23/4, p. 14.

66 'The University of Manchester II', *Nature*, July 20, 1876, 245–246, and July 27, 1876, 265.

67 'The University of Manchester III', *Nature*, July 27, 1876, 265.

68 'Owens College, Manchester', *The Times* July 23, 1877, 10.

69 On Pattison's conception of the academic's vocation, see H. S. Jones, *Intellect and Character in Victorian England* (Cambridge: Cambridge University Press, 2007), Chapters 4 and 5.

70 Tout, 'Sir Adolphus William Ward', 156. Ward was a member of the Court of the Victoria University.

71 Tout, 'The School of History, 73.

72 *Collected Papers* i, 65–66.

Section III

Society Journals

5 Un-Gentlemanly Science

Rhetoric and Rivalry in the Codification of British Zoology, 1830–1840

David Lowther

Introduction

That natural history was transformed in the early decades of the nineteenth century is by no means an original observation. Lightman (Chapter 1 in this volume) observes that the scientific disciplines were surprisingly fluid throughout the entire century, while Richards (Chapter 10) comes to a similar conclusion about the development of nineteenth-century mathematics. However, the process of transformation itself in the case of natural history, and the heated rhetoric which surrounded it, still has the capacity to surprise and, moreover, to change the way we think about disciplines, both as historical constructs and as present-day academic realities. From our vantage point in the twenty-first century, in the codification of disciplines very human passions often seemed to triumph over cold and measured reason. Personal ambition and rivalries played a powerful role in pushing the boundaries of scientific debate. So too did wider considerations of national prestige. Although it would be facile to now suggest that 'modern' zoology developed within a strictly national framework, the product of one nation's combined genius, just such a narrative was harnessed and peddled to great effect by a cadre of British zoologists in the early years of the nineteenth century, and lay behind the establishment of some of Britain's most enduring scientific establishments, notably the Zoological Society of London (est. 1826).

As drivers of scientific change, personal and national ambition, and their political contexts, have received considerable attention by historians of science in recent decades. So too has the role of print culture, particularly in the years around and immediately preceding the 'Darwinian Revolution'. Print culture had an active role in the shaping of nineteenth-century science and did not merely serve as a passive organ by which scientific discoveries were disseminated. Indeed, driven by popular curiosity, scientific themes permeated almost every publishing genre. Newspapers carried extraordinarily detailed reports of the business of the annual meetings of the British Association for the Advancement of Science (BAAS): indicative of a real public appetite for news of scientific developments, and perhaps signs of a more serious age.

What have received rather less attention from historians are the specialist and non-specialist natural history journals, which acted as expansive forums for both reasoned debate and the pursuance of bitter personal rivalries.[1] Journals flourished in the early decades of the nineteenth century, partly as a result of a technological revolution in printing and the introduction of steam-driven presses, which drastically reduced costs and generally acted as forums in which primary research was first published. However, as David Allen has shown, scientific journal publishing was a brutal business, and the new technologies did not usher in the era of cheap learned journals that some had hoped for. Even with the introduction of steam-printing, costs were high and circulation often low, and many journals were of ephemeral life-spans.[2] Looking to their bottom line, editors and proprietors could resort to tactics which, even today, seem dubious, artificially stoking controversies in the hope of drawing in subscribers.

This paper addresses this largely under-studied issue by focussing on two notable episodes in the relatively short life of the *Magazine of Natural History* (*MNH*), founded in 1828 by John Claudius Loudon (1783–1843). The first, under his tenure as both editor and proprietor in 1830, erupted in a series of public letters exchanged between Nicholas Aylward Vigors (1785–1840), a prominent ornithologist and the powerful Secretary of the Zoological Society of London, and the author and zoologist William Swainson (1789–1855). Both men were passionate advocates of the then-fashionable and influential Quinarian theory of classifying animals, devised a decade previously by the entomologist William Sharp Macleay (1792–1865).[3] Despite significant differences in their interpretations of the theory, both men saw themselves as Quinarianism's principal torchbearer. The second exchange, under Edward Charlesworth's (1813–1893) editorship in 1840, drew Swainson into a bitter rear-guard action against the 'new men' of British zoology, led by the geologist and naturalist Hugh Strickland (1811–1853). Strickland's contempt for what he saw as Quinarianism's facile metaphysics, particularly the complicated variant peddled by the increasingly eccentric Swainson, boiled over in a number of articles which did much to destroy whatever credibility the theory (and Swainson) had left. By analyzing the different approaches adopted by Loudon and Charlesworth to these two key episodes in the history of 1830s zoology, it will be demonstrated that, almost inadvertently, their actions served to shape how the interested public perceived the outlines of scientific debate, as well as hardening divisions between opposing groups of naturalists and their competing visions of a newly emergent discipline.

Quinarianism and the Birth of 'British Zoology'

Before turning to the controversies which were so prominent a feature of zoology between 1830 and 1840, it is worth taking a wider view of the preceding decade and the state in which zoology entered the 1830s. Zoology began to emerge as a discipline at a peculiarly febrile moment in British history and, as it dealt broadly with questions of life, was politically and religiously charged. In Britain, after 1815 and the final defeat of Napoleonic France and French revolutionary radicalism, reaction and conservatism were in the ascendant in ruling circles. There was ample cause for concern. Between 1818 and 1821, years characterized by Robert Patten as 'the Georgian Hinge', Britain came closer to revolution than at any other moment in the long nineteenth century, and the summer of 1819 marked the high point of radical unity.[4] Recurring crises of government were precipitated by a deep, post-war economic recession; 'Peterloo', a political reform meeting in Manchester on 16 August 1819, broken up by the volunteer Yeomanry and resulting in seventeen deaths, the bloodiest political event of the nineteenth century on English soil; the extremely negative popular reaction to the repressive Six Acts (1819); the accession of a new and widely reviled monarch, George IV, and the Queen Caroline Affair; and finally the Cato Street Conspiracy to murder prominent members of the Cabinet. Embattled on all fronts, Lord Liverpool's Tory administration faced a scene of unparalleled social and political dislocation.[5]

As Dov Ospovat and other historians of scientific culture in these seething decades have emphasized, the spirit of philosophical and political reaction permeated deeply into Britain's scientific institutions.[6] This was partly a consequence of the men who controlled their affairs, the majority of whom were men of property and rank with a vested interest in maintaining social and political order. Clergymen also featured prominently in scientific circles, particularly in natural history. In the 1820s, for example, the Reverend William Kirby (1759–1850) and the Reverend Robert Hodgson (1766–1844), Dean of Carlisle, were both fixtures of the Linnean and Zoological Societies, with Kirby widely recognized as a world authority on entomology.[7]

However, it would be simplistic to infer from this that *all* of the most prominent naturalists were instinctive Tories or bastions of the established Church. Whilst it is true that Kirby cleaved to a 'Church and King' view of British society, the figures who emerged in the 1820s and 1830s at the head of British natural science represented a rag-bag of political and religious opinion. The early membership of the Zoological Society of London demonstrates this well. Its second and third Presidents, the Marquess of Lansdowne and the 13th Earl of Derby, were both moderate Whigs with tepid Reformist sympathies. Nicholas Vigors, who features largely in this paper and who served as the Society's founding Secretary, entered Parliament in 1832 as a radical Whig, and later aligned himself (to his cost) to the Irish leader Daniel O'Connell.[8] Into the 1830s, as Adrian Desmond has shown, the sympathies of the Council shifted to the conservative end of the spectrum, under the influence of figures including Richard Owen and Edward Bennett, and leading in 1836 to a clash with the Society's increasingly reformist ordinary membership.[9] Few, if any, of these men wanted to see the rise of the sort of scientific, Lamarckian materialism that had flourished so dangerously in France in the 1790s.[10]

First conceived by William Sharp Macleay as a means of circumventing exactly this danger whilst studying his father's collection of beetles, Quinarianism has been almost completely forgotten by historians of biology, and enjoyed a brief popularity between 1820 and 1840.[11] In this short period the theory, which was ostensibly directed to providing a 'natural' classification of insects (i.e. one which attempted to reflect their place in the 'natural' order of Creation), attained a level of influence which was far in excess of the numbers who took it seriously. It also generated quite extraordinary hostility in those who disagreed with its basic principles, giving rise to protracted conflicts, in print and in Britain's zoological institutions, which shaped the way in which zoology developed into the 1850s and 1860s.

Those basic principles can be simply expressed. Macleay saw an underlying regularity to the bewildering array of forms in his father's beetle collection. Some of the variations in appearance were minute, others startlingly apparent. Through what he was later at pains to present as a rigorously empirical study, Macleay began setting them into groups based on points of similarity and divergence. Eventually, he composed the species in the collection into families, each composed of five genera of five species each, with twenty-five species in each family. Despite not being well-versed in other branches of zoology, and similarly inexperienced in botany, he extended this privileging of the number five right across the animal and plant kingdoms, drawing points of analogy between the lowest forms of animal and the highest forms of plant. At each level of classification, from kingdom downwards, the five groupings are arranged in touching ('osculant') circles, the forms within each circle arranged according to gradations of similarity, or their affinities, to the next form (see Figures 5.1 and 5.2). Like Linnaeus before him, and Darwin after, Macleay saw only graduated shifts in nature, not saltations, or sudden leaps. Each circle was formed by a series of affinities which 'returned' upon themselves, hence the circular diagrammatic arrangement. By these means, Macleay argued, it was possible for naturalists to discern in nature 'the plan by which the Deity regulated the creation', and that they would thereby obtain 'a view of the universe as it was originally designed'.[12]

That Macleay's system did not sink into almost immediate obscurity was due largely to one man, Nicholas Vigors, a fellow of the Linnean Society and, in 1821, more interested in entomology than any other branch of natural history. Exactly at what point Vigors became convinced of Quinarianism's merits is difficult to pinpoint with any certainty, but by 1825 he had become its leading advocate, with Macleay

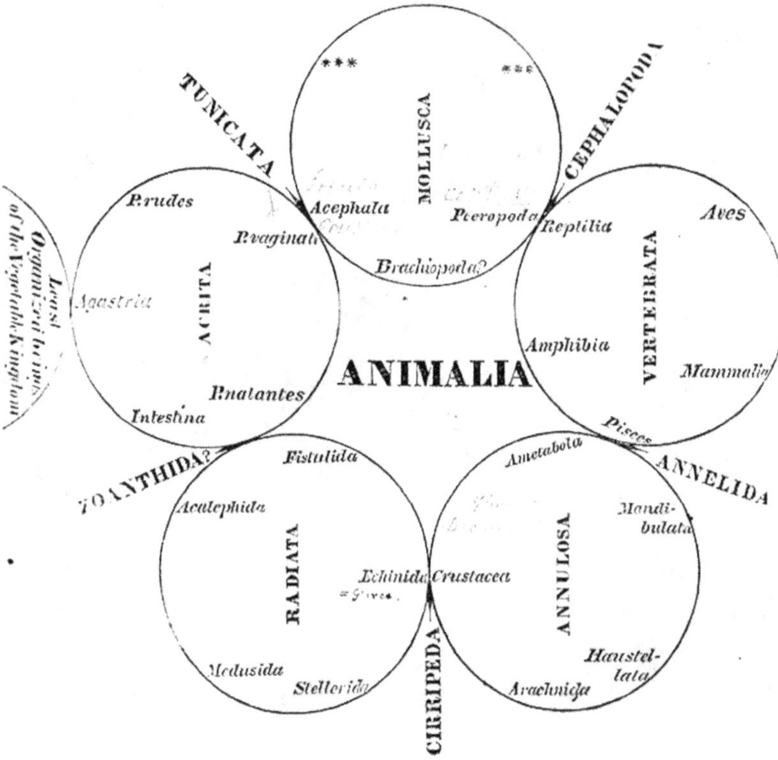

Figure 5.1 Macleay's Quinarian arrangement of the animal kingdom. W. S. Macleay, *Horae Entomologicae* (London: S. Bagster, 1819–1821), I., 2, p. 318. [Biodiversity Heritage Library.]

increasingly content to take a more detached role. By that year he had extended what was initially an entomological theory to ornithology, going some way to realize Macleay's ambition to apply it universally across the animal kingdom.[13] He had also become the leading figure in a splinter group of naturalists dissatisfied with the progress of zoology in the Linnean Society, then dominated by botanists, and had driven the formation of the Zoological Club in 1822, the first such assembly in Britain and as such a considerable influence in the early codification of the discipline. The Zoological Club's own in-house periodical, the *Zoological Journal*, edited by Vigors from 1827, allowed articles which discussed Quinarianism to be published quickly, and elevated the theory to prominence with astonishing rapidity, carrying Vigors's reputation along with it.[14]

Vigors's rise was observed with growing bitterness by one who should have been a natural ally. William Swainson also adhered to Macleay's

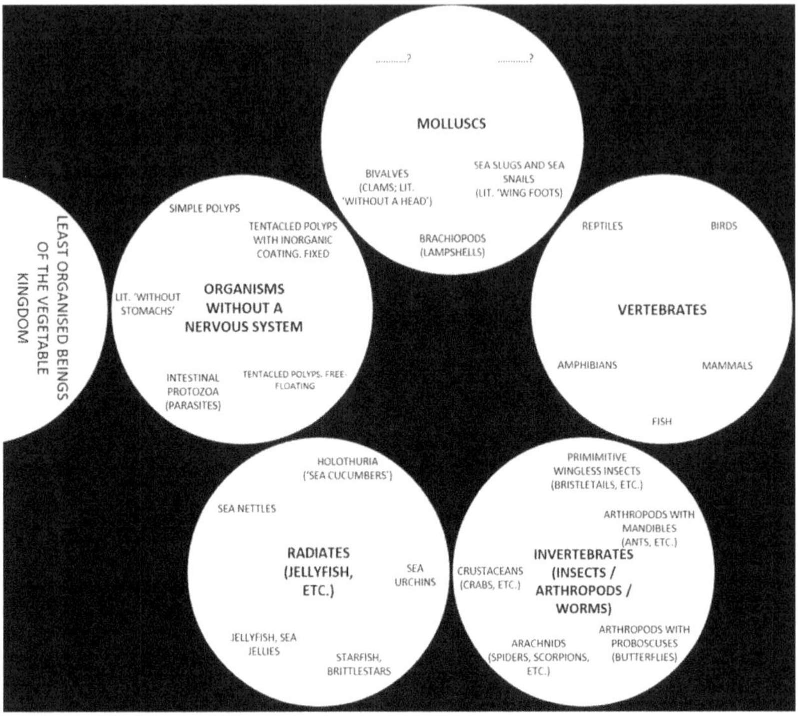

Figure 5.2 Macleay's arrangement of the animal kingdom (author's interpretation). It should be noted that many of the taxons used by Macleay in his original, latinate diagram have been superseded, incorporated into new taxons, or are now used to denote different animals. For example, Macleay's sub-kingdom 'Acrita', little known in the early nineteenth century, is here understood to include polyps and protozoa. Acrita is now understood to be a sub-kingdom encompassing unicellular eukaryotic organisms (protozoa). To avoid confusion, the author has adhered to Macleay's understanding of the terms as much as possible.

theory, but over time had developed his own variant which, to contemporaries, seemed to reach into the realms of the mystical (see Figure 5.3). The naturalist squire and popular author Sir Charles Waterton (1782–1865), who harried Swainson throughout the 1830s, decried the 'series of circles which would puzzle Sir Isaac Newton himself, and which will tend to scare nine-tenths of the votaries of ornithology clear out of the field. Your nomenclature', he added for good measure, 'caused me jaw-ache'.[15] So complex and laced with did Swainson's Quinarian interpretation become (see Figure 5.3) that one of the most recent scholars of early nineteenth-century taxonomy, Aaron Novick, has argued that Swainson was not a Quinarian at all.[16]

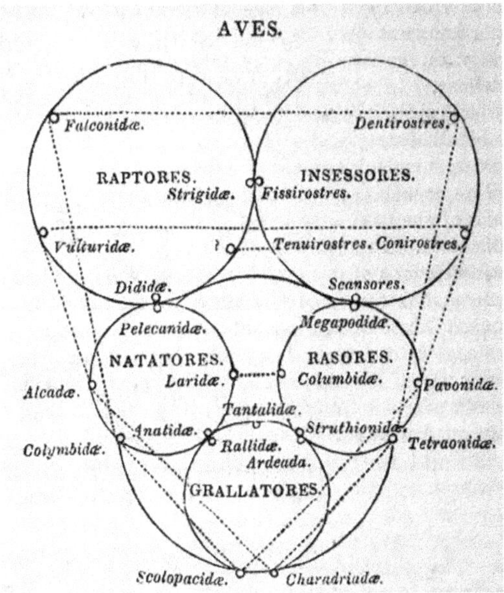

Figure 5.3 Swainson's Quinarian arrangement of birds, showing the complex web of analogies linking different 'tribes'. W. Swainson, *On the Natural History and Classification of Birds, Volume* 2 (London: Longman, Rees, Orme, Brown, Green, & Longman, 1837), p. 200. [Biodiversity Heritage Library.]

Allies Divided: Vigors, Swainson, and Competing Visions of a Discipline

The antagonism between Vigors and Swainson showed itself early on. A revealing exchange of letters in 1824, now in the Linnean Society archives, shows that Vigors attempted to recruit Swainson to the Zoological Club and received from him a promise that he would contribute an article on the ornithology of Mexico to the *Zoological Transactions,* which he adjudged 'an efficient instrument' for the dissemination of Quinarian systematics.[17] Swainson had recently published an article in *The Zoological Journal* in which he had praised Vigors's 'able disquisition' on the present state of ornithological nomenclature and made some scathing statements on the backwardness of zoology in Britain, particularly the insistence of zoologists on acting 'on the *spirit*, and not on the *letter*' of Linnaeus's work, that chimed with Vigors's own thoughts. For example,

> While Botany had been progressively advancing, Ornithology has remained nearly stationary. Our elementary books and our voluminous systems, as Mr. Vigors truly observes, speak the language of a

> remote period; and display a lamentable picture of our Zoological proficiency to the rest of Europe. Better indeed had there been no such terms as *Order* and *Genus*, for they have acted like a magical spell, upon minds that otherwise perhaps might have burst the trammels of nomenclature, and like Linnaeus, have "dared think for themselves".[18]

Swainson's contempt for the rigidity of the British Linneans and concern for the 'embarrassing' state of British ornithology seemed well-calculated to appeal to Vigors. Although Swainson's reply to Vigors's overture is missing, the tenor of the correspondence that followed suggests that he was happy to comply.[19] However, the subsequent deterioration of the relationship between the two ornithologists was rapid. Vigors's conception of his role as a champion of 'natural' systems made him unwilling to brook opposition or foot-dragging and his demands of Swainson, which had ballooned to include diagrams of his system and a paper on the *Laniidae* (shrikes and 'butcher birds'), were such that the latter was unable to keep up.

The break between Vigors and Swainson occurred two months later and can be attributed to more than a clash of personalities. In a previous letter, Vigors spoke revealingly about the importance of the British Museum to the success of 'our exertions in zoology', and hinted deliberately at the 'difficulties' that had existed between the museum and Swainson since 1822.[20] Having now also recruited Macleay and Thomas Horsfield (1773–1859), a botanist and close associate of both Vigors and Stamford Raffles, to contribute articles to the *ZTLS*, Vigors's loss of patience with Swainson is plain. '[W]e must all endeavour to pull together', he warned, ample indication that, already, the Quinarian camp was dividing.[21] He revisited the theme, with cold ferocity, a month later. Refusing to put forward Swainson's name for election to the Zoological Club, Vigors declared that '[w]e feel a disinclination to urge any man who is not an ardent volunteer in the same cause'. He continued:

> It is cordial and efficient cooperation that we require, & not cold and constrained compliance. Join us then, if you can, with perfect cordiality, with head & heart, with all the veins as the Irish now say. We shall rejoice to have you in our ranks, but hope we may not be considered as soliciting the union of any man with us merely to add a name to our list, or a paltry fee to our purse.[22]

This outburst marked the end of their tepid attempt at collaboration. Despite the Club's primary emphasis on ornithology, Swainson would play only a marginal role in the remaining five years of its existence, by which time it had been wholly superseded by the Zoological Society, which from the outset placed more emphasis on zoology as both a classificatory science and a means of demonstrating Britain's growing imperial commitment. By the end of the 1820s, with the Zoological Society and his own brand of Quinarianism seemingly well-established, Vigors could be forgiven for thinking that the future course of zoology in Britain was firmly set.

That this was not to be the case was demonstrated by a far louder, and far more public controversy between Vigors and Swainson which erupted in 1831. This had both personal and disciplinary foundations, and clearly flagged up the competing visions of British zoology that the two men had by now developed. The aggressor was Swainson, who took exception to the tone and content of an article written by Vigors in 1828 which attacked the reputations of the eminent French naturalists Rene Lesson (1794–1849) and Anselme Desmarest (1784–1838).[23] Vigors's motivations in publishing this cynical and slashing piece of invective, part of his campaign to establish a distinctively 'British' zoology with direct reference to the French 'other' whilst simultaneously boosting his own relative importance, were clear to Swainson. He had visited Paris in the early 1820s and had established friendly relations with Cuvier, Lamarck, and others at the Jardin des Plantes, and accordingly held less chauvinistic views about his French counterparts, although why he waited three years to launch into print remains a mystery.[24]

Whereas their previous clash took place via private correspondence, in 1831 Swainson chose to attack Vigors's in one of the most popular natural history journals of the day. The *MNH* was established in 1828 by John Claudius Loudon, one of the most remarkable men of the era. An extremely shrewd and energetic publisher, Loudon had a keen understanding of the opportunities and obstacles that faced specialist journals within the wider market. Having achieved considerable success with the *Gardener's Magazine*, Loudon hoped to repeat his good fortune with a natural history journal. Under his editorship and without an editorial board to consider, as would be the case with a journal of a learned society, for a brief time the *MNH* successfully navigated the fine line between 'popular' appeal to the interested amateur, and more specialist content that engaged Britain's growing class of dedicated gentlemen naturalists. Though it never enjoyed the same commercial appeal as the *Gardener's Magazine*, with which Loudon had earlier made his name, the *MNH* became a popular forum for the publication of detailed zoological research, methodological articles, and for the airing of private grievances, all of which offered competing visions of natural history as it began to coalesce into distinct disciplines.[25]

Loudon and his successor as editor, Edward Charlesworth, were careful to set aside a considerable portion of the *MNH* for letters, a tactic that was designed to stoke the sort of controversy between naturalists that would keep readers engaged. As Allen, Cantor, and Shuttleworth, amongst others, have noted, the life of the average early nineteenth-century journal was short and brutal. As in the illustrated folio market, competition between publishers was intense and editors were unscrupulous in their determination to keep circulation figures high.[26] This was particularly acute for 'general' publications including the *MNH*, a manifestation of a 'broad' scientific culture in which purely scientific concerns and demarcations between men of science, men of letters, and scientific popularizers were blurred.[27] However, as recent historiography seeks to demonstrate, and as the 1831 dispute between Vigors and Swainson highlights, the mission of these journals was more than mere popularization and dissemination. The medium shaped the message, and the journal was, in various ways, constitutive of knowledge. Zoological debate was made by zoologists in conjunction with editors and publishers, who had their own, often nakedly commercial agendas.[28]

Swainson's first article appeared in the *MNH* in March 1831. A brief letter he received from Loudon in October 1830, when the latter confirmed receipt and acceptance of Swainson's manuscript, reveals that Loudon was content to publish it. 'I am very happy', Loudon added, 'to find that you think favourably of the French [Lesson and Desmarest]', hinting that he shared more of Swainson's European outlook than Vigors's narrowly British conception of science.[29] From the outset, he attacked the whole culture of 'sententious oratory' and 'invective' that characterized zoology at this time and which, he believed, Vigors had so turned to his advantage.[30] Commenting upon the advances made in British zoology over the previous decade, Swainson acknowledged that it had indeed made strong gains but, he added, 'it is yet in its infancy'. Rather than Vigors's strident outbursts of invective, 'more calculated to foment bitter feeling among individuals, and to bring national reproach upon us all', Swainson advocated 'mildness and conciliation', which would 'insure [British zoology] respect, and its voice will then be listened to'.[31]

In contrast to 1824, Swainson was now convinced that Quinarianism represented a marked advance in man's understanding of the natural world. 'We have caught a glimpse of some mighty truths', he intoned. However, he again counselled caution.

> Yet, seeing but the shadow, we must not fancy we have caught the substance; or, to drop metaphor, because we have discovered a *part* of the natural system, we must not arrogantly imagine we have grasped the whole; that all further enquiry, discussion, or opposition is to cease.

He condemned Vigors's hostility to France, and his apparent belief that there existed a 'conspiracy' amongst French naturalists against their English counterparts, as rank foolishness.

> When personal and national invective is thus substituted for fair and temperate discussion, it is really time to be serious. We are certainly carrying matters too far; and our "infant school" may probably be compared to the boys in the story, who got possession of a little puddle, from which they bespattered every passenger who refused to take a *sup*.[32]

Swainson's scorn for Vigors's narrow parochialism contrasted with his deep respect for the two naturalists targeted by the latter's invective. Lesson, one of the great ornithologists of the age, was doubly admirable because he was 'not a man who merely theorises in his closet, and frames systems "called natural" within the walls of a museum'. This was a clear stab at Vigors, safe in his Bruton Street bailiwick, and Swainson twisted the knife by comparing Lesson's apparent readiness to quote and build upon the work of British naturalists, including Raffles and Horsfield, with Vigors's accusation that Lesson showed 'striking injustice to the merits of British naturalists'.[33] Desmarest was described in similarly glowing terms, and to Vigors's detriment. As for the charge of French national jealousy, one of the most important planks of Vigors's platform during the late 1820s, Swainson rejected it out of hand. He compared the Zoological Society of London's refusal to grant him access to its museum with the gracious largesse of Lesson at the Jardin des Plantes. 'Does such conduct, to a stranger and a foreigner savour of the accusations so repeatedly insinuated by Mr. Vigors?' Swainson demanded, 'or does it not rather evince how much the Institution, of which he is the secretary and the chief adviser is behind all the others, whether of France or of England, in the march of liberality?' If jealousy existed, he concluded, 'on which side of the channel is it most conspicuous?'[34]

This was strong stuff and, at this stage at least, seemed much to Loudon's taste, who ensured that the collected edition of the *MNH* for 1831 contained every instalment of the controversy which followed. What is important here is that the clear division which existed between Swainson and Vigors had its roots in more than mere personal animosity. At this stage, Swainson was the defender of scientific pluralism, and not only because of his cosmopolitan fondness for France. It was contingent upon naturalists, at a time when the boundaries of knowledge were being pushed further and further back, to consider the views of others and that 'the true lovers of science' France and England, the two most advanced nations in Europe, work together. Further, Vigors's attacks and 'unkindly feelings' had damaged Britain's reputation in the 'republic of science'. '[I]f the contagion be not timely checked', he warned, 'it will undermine all that is to give energy to individual exertion, and all that is to make us respected in the eyes of foreigners'. It was also, he added with what would soon become a habitual piety, an exercise of 'temperance, moderation, and self-denial' that was required of good Christians.[35]

Vigors's reply, in the next number of the *MNH*, was revealing. Vigors's professed abhorrence of any trace of 'personal animosity' in scientific debate must have raised eyebrows amongst even his closest supporters. In contrast to Swainson's vision of a British zoology made stronger by debate, Vigors advocated strength through unity, and deprecated open dissention of any sort.

> [H]ow disgraceful to the reputation of any country are all those internal dissensions, those "plus quam civilia bella," which degrade the fields of science into an arena of contention; - in order to prevent the continuance of such an evil, as far as I am myself concerned, I have made an appeal to the writer of the article in question [Swainson], through the medium of his friends, in the hope that, when the truth is laid before him, he may of his own accord make due reparation for expressions which I am fain to believe originated in some strange and untoward misconception.[36]

This was Vigors at his disingenuous worst, but allows us a valuable insight into his understanding of what constituted a 'national science'. Noting, with evident satisfaction, how many of his friends had rallied round both he and his 'cause', he invoked the 'cavaliers of older times', imagining the sense of 'exhilaration and triumph. . . to hear in the stress of war the generous cheers of their companions in arms advancing "to the rescue"'.[37]

Accusations that the Quinarians were a small and fractious clique were given added potency by what followed. Partisans of the two belligerents joined in the fray, although Swainson and Vigors continued to conduct the principal fighting themselves. In his next contribution to the exchange, Swainson decried the involvement, on Vigors's side, of Edward Turner Bennett (1797–1836), then the vice-Secretary of the ZSL and later Vigors's successor as Secretary.[38] He again asked whether 'such language' as Bennett had used of Lesson and Desmarest 'would not breed dissensions among us, or would not deeply injure the reputations of MM. Desmarest and Lesson, if left uncorrected'.[39]

Vigors responded to this 'unprovoked and wanton outrage' with a denunciation of Swainson and a spirited defence of his own record as a zoologist and a gentleman.[40] There was little 'scientific' about this, but again it reveals much about his approach, particularly as an editor.

> [Swainson] has the audacity to accuse another [. . .] of equally abusing the influence which he is alleged to possess as the ostensible agent of a scientific institution, by rendering that institution far behind all others, whether of France or England, in the march of liberality; of being the detractor of men of merit; of not acting in accordance with his own recorded professions; of rendering his professions of *truth*

> being his guide utterly worthless, by not putting them in practice... In the circle of society in which Mr. Swainson appears to revolve, such insinuations may perhaps be little regarded... but among gentlemen and men of honour the case is different.[41]

As a leading 'gentleman of science', Vigors also had little time for Swainson's 'cant' about the 'decline of science' in Britain. This was a recurrent theme in Swainson's writings and personal correspondence. In 1834, he wrote to Charles Babbage, the mathematician and fellow 'Declinist', lamenting the absence of a 'distinct Society composed *exclusively* of men of *known* and eminent talent where, in short, the Elite of the Science of the country should be *alone* admitted'.[42] Little could be more offensive to Vigors than this aspersion of the Zoological Society. '[W]hen did science, our science [zoology] at least, stand on a higher elevation than at present?' he asked.[43] That Swainson could regard himself as blackballed from the gentlemanly circles that Vigors moved in was made abundantly clear. '[H]e has heaped injury upon me in exchange for kindness; he has loaded me with insult in return for forbearance. On the head of the aggressor let the odium rest!'.[44]

Such episodes made for entertaining reading. By providing a forum for clashes between naturalists, and their proxies, publications such as the *MNH* provided a great service to zoology during these transitional years, bringing debates about the 'big' questions before a broad readership. Loudon's editorial policy also ensured that it avoided the financial abyss which claimed so many of its more determinedly specialist competitors. The *Zoological Journal*, for example, lasted only nine years despite having the weight of Britain's zoological elite behind it. It was the first British journal devoted exclusively to zoology, and informed its readers in 1824 that:

> Original Memoirs and Monographs will take the precedence in our pages. The subjects of Zoological Classification – Comparative Anatomy – particularly Class, Families, Genera, and Species – Animal Chemistry – Palaeontography and Nomenclature are amongst the most important.[45]

The editor of this high-minded journal was Nicholas Vigors.

Despite his initial encouragement of Vigors and Swainson to carry their dispute into the pages of the *MNH*, when the collected edited 1831 edition was published, Loudon sounded a tone of uncomfortable ambivalence. As early as June that year, he had taken steps to rein in the protagonists. Another brief note to Swainson, after the publication of the first round of articles and in response to the latter's request that space in the *MNH* be given to Desmarest and Lesson to weigh in, reveals his tactics. '[O]f course I shall admit replies from the gentlemen you mention',

Loudon reassured him. But he would not pay Swainson for any further contributions on the matter. 'I regret', he added rather ominously, 'that so much excitement has been produced by it'.[46] This was expressed publicly in the preface to the 1831 edition. Loudon told his readers that 'it is not without regret' that he had included a 'large proportion of controversial papers'. This regret, he went on, 'is less on account of the unsuitableness of these papers to this Magazine (because we are convinced that in the end they will do good), than because of the space they occupy'.[47] This is significant, for it is clear evidence that Loudon recognized the potential that such controversies had to push the boundaries of debate, even if they did, as in this case, go on for longer than he had anticipated.

Loudon's brief notice highlights the fundamental problem that controversies such as this repelled as many readers as it stimulated. His solution was simple. Such disputes would still be carried by the *MNH*, but no longer occupy the space usually reserved for 'hard' scientific articles. Instead, they would be shifted under a new heading, 'Retrospective Criticism', and be in 'small type' to take up less room and 'be passed over by those who do not take an interest in the subjects discussed'. 'We trust', Loudon concluded soothingly (and, as it turned out, mistakenly) that 'we shall henceforth have very little [controversy]'.[48] As for Lesson and Desmarest, the unwitting originators of all the trouble, they maintained a discreet silence. Lesson wrote to Loudon and flung a casual gibe in Vigors's direction, quoting a personal conversation with Desmarest. 'I shall take good care to not answer this', Desmarest reportedly said after reading Vigors's original article. 'If I write but one or two pages, they will come down upon me with a quarto volume at least'.[49]

Hugh Strickland and the Attack on Quinarianism

From his place at the centre of Britain's scientific firmament, Hugh Strickland observed the Quinarian squabbling with growing impatience. Although particularly interested in geology and ornithology, Strickland's pen ranged widely over the field of natural history, and from the middle of the 1830s he produced a stream of articles which addressed general questions of methodology and taxonomy. Solidly reasoned and written with a massive clarity, these would contribute to his being approached to be a member of the committee taxed by the BAAS in 1841 with drafting rules which would govern zoological nomenclature.[50] One of the first, written in 1835, established him firmly on the reforming wing of zoology. This addressed the then particularly acute problem of synonymy in taxonomy, or the widespread practice of ambitious (or careless) zoologists assigning scientific names to species already both discovered and described.[51] Strickland took a dim view of this habit, in which the Quinarian zoologists were particularly prone to indulge.

Strickland was also critical of the basis on which Quinarian and other natural classifications were established, which he viewed as bringing into disrepute the scientific credentials of British zoology. One of the most innovative aspects of Macleay's system was his dual theory of affinity and analogy. Empirical in his approach, Strickland sought to exclude analogy, and by extension symmetry, from the systematics altogether. For the Quinarians, affinity and analogy were equally important. Without either one, Swainson urged, no system of classification could be argued to be truly 'natural'.[52]

Strickland disagreed. In 1840 he published an article in the *MNH*, prompted by the appearance in an earlier issue of a paper by the entomologist John Obadiah Westwood (1805–1893).[53] Westwood was a late convert to Quinarianism. In 1841 he was to develop the principles of symmetry and analogy even further than had Swainson, resulting in a septenary system of ferocious complexity.[54] Strickland had as little time for Westwood's philosophical principles as he had for the other Quinarians, but he treated Westwood with a professional courtesy which he denied to Swainson. Westwood had attempted to clear up a perceived misconception in his contemporaries' understanding of analogy, particularly the apparent tendency to 'confound' the two, or even to give 'the higher rank' to analogies between species ahead of relations of affinity.[55]

Westwood saw several reasons for the difficulty, not the least of which was the 'dislike of uprooting long-established opinions' and the substitution of new ones which 'required from their supporters a far more extensive acquaintance with the objects of nature than was required in the old works of classification'.[56] With this Strickland doubtless agreed. What he did take umbrage with was Westwood's follow-up. 'Relations of affinity and analogy have their origin in more or less perfect resemblances of structure or habits', Strickland declared, 'and are of comparative or relative value; and hence that distinct relations, both of affinity and analogy, exist between the same groups'.[57] He went on to illustrate the principles with reference to several genera of animals, encompassing both vertebrates and invertebrates and including the swallow (*Hirundo*), dragonfly, and bat, 'all [of] which are distinguished by their large wings when extended in action, their rapid motions, large mouths, and insectivorous hawking flight'.[58] He argued that although there are clear dissimilarities in organized structure between these animals – what he terms relations 'of the first degree' – there are striking similarities when analyzed from the viewpoint of higher taxonomic levels. The former he viewed as an affinity, such as the relation between a swallow and a martin; the latter as an analogy, such as between a swallow and a dragonfly.

If there is something inescapably vague about Westwood's clarification, it is an impression not dispelled by his admission at the end of the paper that identification of affinity and analogy is largely down to the individual naturalist's perception of what constitutes a 'close' relation;

> It has long appeared to me to be most probably, that the fact of two animals or groups of animals thus exhibiting relations both of

affinity and analogy, was the chief cause which induced many persons to regard both these relations as of equivalent value, and as synonymous with resemblances.[59]

In his examination of Westwood's views, Strickland took careful aim at this idea that similarities, or 'representations', between animals in different classes or even sub-kingdoms were divinely ordained. However, the inescapable conclusion is that Strickland's real target was not Westwood, whose writings he characterized as 'distinguished for scientific accuracy', but rather Swainson. Though he does not directly mention the latter by name at any point in the main body of text, it is notable that all the contemporary zoological works cited in footnotes as particularly reprehensible were written by Swainson for Lardner's *Cyclopedia*, including his methodological and classificatory studies on birds.[60]

The evident relish with which Strickland dismantled the 'visionary and theoretical views' advanced by Swainson and his fellow Quinarians casts some light on the editorial practices of the *MNH* during this period of mergers and journal failures. Having dismissed Swainson as an a priori thinker who twisted facts to suit his system, in a scathing passage Strickland then dismantled the principle of analogy upon which Quinarianism was based.[61] 'This has always appeared to me one of the most unsound and unphilosophical of the doctrines maintained by the advocates of the circular system [i.e. Quinarianism]', Strickland argued.

> It seems derogatory to Creative Power to suppose that the principle of *representation* had any place in the scheme of creation, or that certain organs were given to species, not with a view to the discharge of certain destined functions, but for the apparently useless object of *imitating* or *representing* other species in a distant part of the system.

Having thus ridiculed Quinarianism's claim to represent the divine mind, Strickland then, and perhaps more importantly, attacked the empirical basis of the theory.

> Without wasting words upon the serious discussion of such puerilities, I will merely repeat my deliberate conviction that relations of analogy are not to be regarded as affording any evidence of *intention*, in the scheme of creation, but are mere coincidences of structure, incidental to the grand design of adapting a large number of organized beings to perform a comparatively limited number of functions.[62]

This wholesale rejection of 'metaphysical' reasoning marked a real shift in the development of zoology in Britain, which was until the late 1850s dominated by Strickland's more prosaic, if more critical approach to taxonomy.[63] To Strickland's mind, the highest taxonomic groupings – mammals, birds, reptiles – exhibited no real 'tendency to unite'; that no one vertebrate was any nearer to a mollusc, for example, than any other. Only at the very lowest taxonomic levels, such as genera and families, could naturalists see chains of resemblance. And these similarities, Strickland emphasized, must necessarily be so close to be affinities, rather than analogies.[64] Resemblances between one species of swallow and another were therefore to be taken more seriously than the entirely coincidental similarities, by virtue of their similar diets, between a swallow and a dragonfly.

All of this was grist to the mill of Edward Charlesworth, Loudon's successor as the *MNH*'s editor. Charlesworth, as Susan Sheets-Pyenson observes, 'made a point of searching out controversial material'.[65] As well as encouraging spats between authors, he was ever-ready to start controversies on his own initiative. Indeed, in the same 1840 edited volume of the *MNH* in which Strickland's and Westwood's articles appear, Charlesworth included a 72-page appendix in which a lengthy exchange of heated letters between himself and two of the luminaries of London geology and palaeontology, Richard Owen and Charles Lyell, is laid bare.[66] This particular controversy, characteristically framed by an aggrieved Charlesworth as 'Owen and Lyell *versus* Charlesworth', lay in disputed priority for the description of certain paleontological specimens. What is of relevance here is Charlesworth's lengthy prelude, in which he gives an invaluable account of the challenges he faced on becoming editor of the *MNH*, and which casts light on his willingness to encourage articles by rival naturalists.

In what takes the form of an *apologia* for his editorial policies, Charlesworth first made clear the distinction, as he saw it, between the periodical devoted to 'general literature' and a scientific journal. The majority of contributors to the former 'transfer their ideas to paper as an honourable means of subsistence'. In turn, the mass of its readers do so for 'self-instruction and amusement', and no further. By contrast, both readers of and contributors to scientific journals are driven by the higher ideal of laying new discoveries at 'the shrine of science'.[67] This was followed by a brief and selective survey of Charlesworth's early years at the *MNH*, which he bought from Loudon in 1838, becoming both proprietor and editor. Feeling that the direction of the *Magazine* under Loudon was uninspired and financially disappointing, Charlesworth determined that the second series (beginning in 1838) should 'embrace a larger share of the philosophy of the science, and a greater amount of those descriptive details which should enhance its absolute value to practical naturalists'.[68] Circulation, which had stood at 2,000 copies in 1828, had fallen to under 1,000 copies by 1836.[69]

To emphasize the change, the title of the journal was changed to the *Magazine of Natural History, Conducted by Edward Charlesworth* (see Figure 5.4). What this meant in practice was an increase in the total number of articles on 'general topics', a bracket which embraced disputes on methodological matters or spats about priority. This course

THE

MAGAZINE OF NATURAL HISTORY.

VOL. II.

NEW SERIES.

1838.

CONDUCTED

BY EDWARD CHARLESWORTH, F.G.S.

LONDON:

PRINTED FOR

LONGMAN, ORME, BROWN, GREEN, AND LONGMANS,

PATERNOSTER ROW.

1838.

Figure 5.4 Title page of the 1838 collected edition of the *Magazine of Natural History, conducted by Edward Charlesworth* (London: Longman, Orme, Brown, Green, & Longman, 1838). [Biodiversity Heritage Library.]

was further precipitated by actions of several of the most regular contributors to the first series of *MNH* who, on Charlesworth's elevation as editor in 1836, took their business to Sir William Jardine's rival publication, the *Magazine of Zoology and Botany* (*MZB*), founded earlier in that year. To add to Charlesworth's problems, a generalist journal, *The Naturalist*, was also launched in 1836 by Neville Wood, a man much in the same mould as Charlesworth himself. Noting the appearance of the two new journals, Charlesworth complained of Wood's attempts to undercut the *MNH* which, Charlesworth alleged, Wood viewed simply as a 'source of pecuniary emolument to Mr. Loudon' rather than a serious organ of science.[70]

Although Charlesworth pitched the *MNH* at an altogether more restricted audience than Knight's mass-market *Penny Magazine*, both productions were rooted in a common publishing context and their editorial practices share many features, not the least of which was the acute concern to balance quality of material with quantity of numbers sold. However, where Knight strove to avoid contentious material that might inflame his lower-class readership, Charlesworth was under no such restraint. In contrast to Loudon, who had felt compelled to apologize for giving space to the Swainson-Vigors controversy in 1832, Charlesworth actively encouraged his authors to publish controversial pieces, such as Strickland's strong attacks on the now-dwindling band of Quinarians. He also displayed considerable ruthlessness, attacking rival publications in print, including both *The Naturalist* and the *MZB*, making enemies along the way.[71] Yet under Charlesworth's ownership the *MNH* lasted only two years. In 1840 it was merged with the *Annals of Natural History* (formerly Jardine's *MZB*) to form the *Journal of Natural History*, still extant.[72]

Conclusion

In its short run, the new series of the *MNH* packed in a high proportion of articles that may be described as controversial, and if they ultimately proved to be unable to save the journal from amalgamation, they did serve to further clarify the rapidly shifting boundaries of debate during a crucial transitional period. By focussing attention on competing visions of a 'British' zoology in the pages of the *MNH*, both the Vigors-Swainson controversy, and Strickland's later, very public dismantling of Quinarianism, did much to define the disciplinary limits of zoology at successive stages of its early development. As work by Sheets-Pyenson has demonstrated, naturalists of the 1830s paid close attention to the content of natural history journals, as stimuli to their own work and a means of locating themselves within the wider scientific discourse.[73] By providing a platform to the Quinarians and their detractors, the *MNH* responded to a demand amongst Britain's growing and eclectic community of naturalists and zoologists for material relating to the newest and most novel theories of the day. In so doing, it shaped not only wider opinion of the debate on zoological classification, which began to shift decisively to the Quinarians' disadvantage from the mid-1830s onwards, but also helped to clarify and entrench points of division between the naturalists themselves. The *MNH* is just one example of a society journal that was central to the definition of a discipline through controversy, or otherwise. The *MNH* performed an analogous role for natural history in the 1830s as the *Anthropological Review* played for the development of anthropology in the 1860s (see Chapter 6) and the *Dance Journal* for the study of dance early in the early twentieth century (see Chapter 2).

As Quinarianism declined, so new theories rose to occupy its place. Strickland's own 'natural system', much influenced by Cuvier, held its ground for much of the 1840s and 1850s, providing a much-needed sense of unity until absorbed and superseded, in turn, by Darwin's theory of evolution in the 1860s.[74] Darwin himself, as his notebooks demonstrate, had been a keen reader of the *MNH* during Charlesworth's time, notwithstanding his own aversion to controversy. He paid particular attention to the articles written for Charlesworth by Edward Blyth (1810–1873), who presented intriguing information on hybridization and variation in birds.[75] Just as the magazine presented a forum for the discrediting of one theory, which within its own limits had propelled zoology forward, so too did it help shape the most profound transformation in nineteenth-century science.

Notes

1 The starting point for consideration of print culture and natural history remains D. E. Allen, *The Naturalist in Britain: A Social History* (Princeton: Princeton University Press, 1976). Important journal articles to consider include W. H. Brock, 'British Science Periodicals and Culture: 1820–1850', *Victorian Periodicals Review* 21/2 (Summer, 1988), 47–55; S. Sheets-Pyenson, 'Darwin's Data: His Reading of Natural History Journals, 1837–1842', *Journal of the History of Biology* 14/2 (Autumn, 1981), 231–248, which covers the *Magazine of Zoology and* Botany, *Annals of Natural* History, and the *Magazine of Natural History*; and S. Sheets-Pyenson, 'From the North to Red Lion Court: The Creation and Early Years of the *Annals of Natural History*', *Archives of Natural History* 10 (1981), 221–249. Useful recent studies on Victorian periodicals, which take a broader view of nineteenth-century publishing, including the scientific context, include: J. A. Secord, *Victorian Sensation: The Extraordinary Publication, Reception, and Secret Authorship of Vestiges of the Natural History of Creation* (Chicago, IL: University of Chicago Press, 2000); R. Cooter, S. Pumfrey, 'Separate Spheres and Public Places: Reflections on the History of Science Popularization and Science in Popular Culture', *History of Science* 32 (1994), 237–267; L. Brake and J. F. Codell (eds.), *Encounters in the Victorian Press: Editors, Authors, Readers* (London: Palgrave, 2005); G. Cantor, G. Dawson, G. Gooday, R. Noakes, S. Shuttleworth, and J. R. Topham (eds.), *Science in the Nineteenth-Century*

Periodical: Reading the Magazine of Nature (Cambridge: CUP, 2004); H. Fraser, S. Green, and J. Johnston, *Gender and the Victorian Periodical* (Cambridge: CUP, 2003); D. E. Allen, *Books and Naturalists* (London: Collins, 2010). More specialist studies focussing on particular aspects of 'popular' publishing and its economics include T. Weller, 'Preserving Knowledge through Popular Victorian Periodicals: An Examination of *The Penny Magazine* and the *Illustrated London News*, 1842–1843', *Library History* 24/3 (September 2008), 200–207; M. Demoor and K. MacDonald, 'Finding and Defining the Victorian Supplement', *Victorian Periodicals Review* 43/2 (Summer 2010), 97–110; D. Dixon, 'Children's Magazines and Science in the Nineteenth Century', *Victorian Periodicals Review* 34/2 (Fall, 2001), 228–238; S. Wadsworth, 'Charles Knight and Sir Francis Bond Head: Two Early Victorian Perspectives on Printing and the Allied Trades', *Victorian Periodicals Review* 31/4 (Winter, 1998), 369–386.

2 Allen, *Books and Naturalists*, 185–188.

3 W. S. Macleay, *Horae Entomologicae*, 2 vols (London: S. Bagster, 1819–1821). Studies of Quinarianism are thin on the ground. Hugh Strickland and Peter Rylands gave contemporary, if partial, accounts which are good introductions to both the theory and how naturalists interpreted it: H. E. Strickland, 'On the Progress and the Present State of Ornithology', *Report of the British Association for the Advancement of Science for 1844*, 14 (1845), 170–221; P. Rylands, 'On the Quinary, or Natural System, of McLeay, Swainson, Vigors, &c.', *Magazine of Natural History* 9 (1836), 130–138, 175–182. Several more recent historians engage with Quinarianism to a greater or lesser extent, the best being J. Coggon, 'Quinarianism after Darwin's "Origin": The Circular System of William Hincks', *Journal of the History of Biology* 35/1 (Spring, 2002), 5–42; M. P. Winsor, *Starfish, Jellyfish and the Order of Life* (New Haven, CT: Yale University Press, 1976), 83–84; P. F. Rehbock, *The Philosophical Naturalists: Themes in Early Nineteenth-Century British Biology* (Madison, WI: University of Wisconsin Press, 1983); and D. Ospovat, *The Development of Darwin's Theory: Natural History, Natural Theology, and Natural Selection, 1838–1859* (Cambridge: Cambridge University Press, 1981), 99–102.

4 R. L. Patten, 'George's Hive and the Georgian Hinge', *Browning Institute Studies* 14 (1986), 37–69.

5 There is a huge literature on the social and political dislocations of the late Georgian period. The best and one of the most recent surveys of the critical moment around 1820 is M. Chase, *1820: Disorder and Stability in the United Kingdom* (Manchester: Manchester University Press, 2013).

6 Ospovat, *Darwin's Theory*. Adrian Desmond's work on the dawn of a highly politicized zoological culture in the late-Georgian period made an invaluable contribution to this field of research. See A. Desmond, *Archetypes and Ancestors: Palaeontology in Victorian London, 1850–1875* (London: Blond & Briggs, 1982); A. Desmond, 'The Making of Institutional Zoology in London, 1822–1836', *History of Science* 23 (1985), 153–185, 223–250; and *The Politics of Evolution: Morphology, Medicine and Reform in Radical London* (Chicago, IL: University of Chicago Press, 1989). M. Blaisdell, 'Natural Theology and Nature's Disguises', *Journal of the History of Biology* 15/2 (Summer 1982), 163–189.

7 C. S. Varma, 'Threads that Guide or Ties that Bind: William Kirby and the Essentialism Story', *Journal of the History of Biology* 42/1 (2009), 119–149; J. F. M. Clark, 'History from the Ground Up: Bugs, Political Economy and God in Kirby and Spence's *Introduction to Entomology* (1815–1856)', *Isis* 97/1 (2006), 28–55.

8 O. Macdonagh, *O'Connell: The Life of Daniel O'Connell 1775–1847* (London: Weidenfeld & Nicolson, 1991), 421.
9 Desmond, 'Making of Institutional Zoology', 231–241; [Anon.], *Statement by the President and Certain Members of the Council of The Zoological Society, in Reply to Observations and Charges Made by Colonel Sykes and Others, at the General Meeting of the Society on the 29th of April Last, and at the Monthly Meeting on the 2nd of the Same Month* (London: Richard Taylor, 1835).
10 F. A. Steflau, 'Lamarck: The Birth of Biology', *Taxon* 20/4 (1971), 397–442; E. Mayr, 'Lamarck Revisited', *Journal of the History of Biology* 5/1 (1972), 55–94; P. Corsi, *The Age of Lamarck: Evolutionary Theories in France, 1790–1830* (Berkeley, CA: University of California Press, 1988).
11 See, for example, Macleay, *Horae, Part II*, 162–169, in which he discusses Lamarck's work. For background, Blaisdell, 'Natural Theology', 170.
12 W. S. Macleay, 'Remarks on the Identity of Certain General Laws Which Have Been Lately Observed to Regulate the Natural Distribution of Insects and Fungi', *Transactions of the Linnean Society of London* 14/1 (1825), 46–67. See also Macleay, *Horae, Part II*.
13 N. A. Vigors, 'Observations on the Natural Affinities that Connect the Orders and Tribes of Birds', *Transactions of the Linnean Society of London* 14/3 (May, 1825), 395–517. He elaborated further the following year: N. A. Vigors, 'Sketches in Ornithology; Or, Observations on the Leading Affinities of the More Extensive Groups of Birds', *The Zoological Journal* 2 (1826), 36–70, 182–198.
14 J. Bastin, 'The First Prospectus of the Zoological Society of London: New Light on the Society's Origins', *Journal of the Society for the Bibliography of Natural History* 5 (1970), 369–388; P. C. Mitchell, *Centenary History of the Zoological Society of London* (London: Zoological Society of London, 1929), 2–8.
15 C. Waterton, *An Ornithological Letter to William Swainson* (London: R. Nichols, 1837), 2.
16 A. Novick, 'On the Origins of the Quinarian System of Classification', *Journal of the History of Biology* (2015) [Epub ahead of print], 1–39.
17 Vigors to Swainson, October 16, 1824. LS, SC. 921.
18 W. Swainson, 'An Inquiry into the Natural Affinities of the Laniidae, or Shrikes; Preceded by Some Observations on the Present State of Ornithology in this Country', *The Zoological Journal* 1 (1824), 292.
19 Vigors to Swainson, August 20, 1824. LS, SC. 918.
20 Ibid., October 16, 1824. LS, SC. 921.
21 Ibid., October 16, 1824. LS, SC. 921.
22 Ibid., [undated] November 1824. LS, SC. 922.
23 N. A. Vigors, 'A Reply to some Observations in the "Dictionnaire des Sciences Naturelles", Upon the Newly Characterised Groups of the Psittacidae', *The Zoological Journal* 3 (1828), 91–124.
24 See W. Swainson, 'A Defence of "certain French Naturalists"', *Magazine of Natural History* 4 (March 1831), 105–106. Strangely, Swainson does not mention his Paris expedition in his brief 'memoir' in W. Swainson, *Taxidermy, with the Biography of Zoologists* (London: Longman, Rees, Orme, Brown, Green & Longman, 1840), 338–352.
25 Allen, *Books and Naturalists*, 186.
26 Ibid., 181–203. L. Henson, G. Cantor, G. Dawson, R. Noakes, S. Shuttleworth, and J. R. Topham (eds.), *Culture and Science in the Nineteenth-Century Media* (Burlington, VT: Ashgate, 2004); G. Cantor and S. Shuttleworth (eds.), *Science Serialized: Representation of the Sciences in Nineteenth Century Periodicals* (Cambridge, MA: MIT Press, 2004), 1–16.

27 Cantor et al., *Science in the Nineteenth-Century Periodical*, 28.
28 C. Hamlin, 'Review: Games Editors Played or Knowledge Readers Made?', *Isis* 96/4 (December 2005), 634–635.
29 J. C. Loudon to W. Swainson, October 10, 1830. LS, Swainson Correspondence. 578.
30 Swainson, 'A Defence of Certain French Naturalists', 97.
31 Ibid., 98.
32 Ibid.
33 Ibid., 99.
34 Ibid., 106.
35 Ibid., 107.
36 N. A. Vigors, 'A Letter to the Editor Respecting Art. I. of No. XVIII. of this Journal', *Magazine of Natural History and Journal of Zoology* 4 (1831a), 207.
37 Ibid.
38 W. Swainson, 'A Further Defence of "Certain French Naturalists", *Magazine of Natural History and Journal of Zoology* 4 (1831), 316–317; Bennett, E. T., 'Evidences in Proof of Certain Statements Contained in the "Gardens and Menagerie of the Zoological Society Delineated", In a Letter to the Editor', *Magazine of Natural History* 4 (1831), 199–206; J. C. Edwards, 'Bennett, Edward Turner (1797–1836)', *Oxford Dictionary of National Biography* (Oxford: Oxford University Press, 2004).
39 Swainson, 'A Further Defence', 319.
40 N. A. Vigors, 'A Reply to Art. I. No. XVIII of this Journal, in a Letter to the Editor', *Magazine of Natural History and Journal of Zoology* 4 (1831b), 319–337.
41 Ibid., 320–321.
42 W. Swainson to C. Babbage, April 8, 1834. Add. Ms. 37, 188, fol. 303. British Museum.
43 Vigors, 'A Reply to Art. I.', 336.
44 Ibid., 337.
45 N. A. Vigors, 'Introduction', *The Zoological Journal* 1 (1824), iv.
46 J. C. Loudon to W. Swainson, June 11, 1831. LS, Swainson Correspondence. 581.
47 J. C. Loudon, 'Preface', *Magazine of Natural History* 4 (1831), iii–iv.
48 Ibid., iv.
49 R. Lesson, 'Letter to the Editor, in Defence of certain French Naturalists', *Magazine of Natural History and Journal of Zoology* 4 (1831), 488.
50 See H. Strickland, 'Report of a Committee Appointed to Consider of the Rules by Which the Nomenclature of Zoology May be Established on a Uniform and Permanent Basis', *Report of the Twelfth Meeting of the British Association for the Advancement of Science* (1842), 110–111.
51 H. E. Strickland, 'On the Arbitrary Alteration of established Terms in Natural History', *Magazine of Natural History and Journal of Zoology, Botany, Minerology, Geology and Meteorology* 8 (1835), 36–40; H. E. Strickland, 'On the Inexpediency of Altering Established Terms in Natural History', *Annals and Magazine of Natural History* 1 (1837a), 127–131.
52 W. Swainson, *A Treatise on the Geography and Classification of Animals* (London: Longman, Rees, Orme, Brown, Green & Longman, 1835), 197. Italics in the original.
53 H. E. Strickland, 'Observations Upon the Affinities and Analogies of Organized Beings', *Magazine of Natural History* 2/4 (1840), 219–226; J. O. Westwood, 'Observations Upon the Relationships Existing Amongst Natural Objects, Resulting from More or Less Perfect Resemblance, Usually Termed Affinity and Analogy', *Magazine of Natural History* 4 (1840), 141–144.

54 See E. Newman, 'Further Observations on the Septenary System', *The Entomological Magazine* 4 (1833), 234–251 for a careful, contemporary evaluation of Westwood's system.
55 Westwood, 'Observations', 141.
56 Ibid.
57 Ibid., 142.
58 Ibid., 143.
59 Ibid., 144.
60 Swainson, *Classification of Animals*; Swainson, *Classification of Birds.*
61 Strickland, 'Observations', 219.
62 Ibid., 224.
63 See W. Jardine, *Memoirs of Hugh Edwin Strickland, M. A.* (London: John Van Voorst, 1858).
64 Strickland, 'Observations', 226.
65 Sheets-Pyenson, 'Darwin's Data', 237. See also R. Marsham, 'Notes on Edward Charlesworth, 1813–1893', *Ipswich Geological Group Bulletin* 18 (1976), 14–16.
66 E. Charlesworth, 'Appendix to the Thirty-Ninth Number of the New Series of the Magazine of Natural History: By the Editor', *Magazine of Natural History*, New Series, 4 (1840), 1–72.
67 Charlesworth, 'Appendix', 3–4.
68 Ibid., 5.
69 C. E. Jackson, P. Davis, *Sir William Jardine: A Life in Natural History* (London: Leicester University Press, 2001), 152.
70 Charlesworth, 'Appendix', 7.
71 Jackson and Davis, *Jardine*, 152–153.
72 N. L. Evenhuis, 'Publication and Dating of the Journals Forming the *Annals and Magazine of Natural History* and the *Journal of Natural History*', *Zootaxa* 385 (2003), 1–68.
73 Sheets-Pyenson, 'Darwin's Data', 231–248.
74 See M. P. Winsor, 'Considering Affinity: An Ethereal Conversation', *Endeavour* 39/1 (2014), 69–79; and M. A. Di Gregorio, 'In Search of the Natural System: Problems of Natural Classification in Victorian Britain', *History and Philosophy of the Life Sciences* 4/2 (1982), 225–254, especially 237–240.
75 See Sheets-Pyenson, 'Darwin's Data', 240–248; E. Blyth, 'A Few Remarks on Hybrids, in reference to Mr. Berry's Communication', *The Magazine of Natural History* 8 (1835), 198–202; E. Blyth, 'An Attempt to Classify the "Varieties" of Animals, with Observations on the Marked Seasonal and Other Changes Which Naturally Take Place in Various British Species, and Which Do Not Constitute Varieties', *The Magazine of Natural History and Journal of Zoology* 8 (1835), 40–54; and E. Blyth, 'Observations on the Various Seasonal and Other External Changes Which Regularly Take Place in Birds', *The Magazine of Natural History* 9 (1836), 399–406.

6 The Scandalous Affair of the *Anthropological Review*

Hyde Clarke, James Hunt, and British Anthropology in the 1860s

Efram Sera-Shriar

In the summer of 1868 a huge dispute unfolded in the pages of the London-based weekly journal, the *Athenaeum*. Two groups of anthropologists argued over the connection between the Anthropological Society of London (ASL) and the supposedly independent periodical, the *Anthropological Review* (*AR*), which was owned and edited by an unknown party. The origins of this debate began in 1867 when the president of the ASL, the speech therapist and physician James Hunt (1833–1869), invited the philologist and engineer Hyde Clarke (1815–1895), to join the ASL's council. Clarke had trepidations about accepting Hunt's offer until he had looked over the society's financial records. During the course of his investigation he discovered that the ASL was deeply in debt, and that a large proportion of the money it owed was accrued through its relationship with the *AR*. This financial strain was stunting the ability of the society to pursue its own publishing projects until these other liabilities were paid off. Given that the *AR* was not one of the ASL's official publications, Clarke did not understand why the society was burdening itself with this debt.

Clarke's initial inquiry into the connection between the ASL and the *AR* sparked a prolonged affair that implicated many figures and led to the publication of eight letters in the *Athenaeum* between August and October 1868, as well as numerous other reports in the pages of both the *AR* and the *Journal of the Anthropological Society of London* (*JASL*) between August 1868 and January 1869. The major revelation that emerged from these entries in the periodical press was that Hunt was abusing his power as president of the ASL for his own ends. As the story unfolded, it was discovered that Hunt had been hiding his identity as the proprietor and editor of the *AR*, so that he could broker a special deal that would require members of the ASL to buy copies of his own journal as part of their subscription fees. It was also revealed that he was misusing society funds in order to avoid amassing any personal debt by saddling the ASL with the majority of the *AR*'s production costs.[1]

Building on recent themes in the history of science that have emphasized the reciprocal relationship between print culture and the making and representation of science in nineteenth-century Britain, this chapter will examine the details of this story, and show its significance as a major event in the disciplinary formation of British anthropology during the nineteenth century. The chapter underscores the centrality of periodicals in both establishing and expanding Victorian anthropology.[2] Key to this examination are the analytical models outlined in the works of Jonathan Topham and James Secord who have conceived of science as a communicative act that is reliant on different forms of media for generating, revising, and expanding knowledge. Paying close attention to the role of different types of historical actors in this process is an essential part of these analytical models.[3] Very little scholarship has considered how the periodical press shaped the construction and representation of nineteenth-century British anthropology. The most extensive study is by Sadiah Qureshi, who looked at the intersection of print, advertisements, and foreign living people shows in nineteenth-century Britain.[4] In my book, *The Making of British Anthropology*, I have also looked at the reception of two significant ethnological texts from the 1850s, Robert Knox's *Races of Men* (1850) and Robert Gordon Latham's *Varieties of Man* (1850).[5] However, a study of the relationship between print culture and the formation of key learned bodies such as the ASL has never been undertaken. Because the ASL was one of the primary scientific institutions to disseminate anthropological literature in Britain during the middle of the nineteenth century, investigating the types of publications it was producing and the controversy surrounding its connection with the *AR* sheds important new light on the disciplinary history of anthropology in the nineteenth century.

James Hunt before the Schism

Before separating from the British ethnological community and becoming a disciplinary figurehead for British anthropology in the 1860s, Hunt had a successful medical practice in London.[6] He earned a substantial amount of money from speech therapy and even treated well-connected figures such as the historian and novelist Charles Kingsley (1819–1875).[7] This was significant because it helped him network with some of the more influential people in Victorian London. When Hunt eventually co-founded the ASL in 1863 with the explorer and geographer Richard Francis Burton (1821–1890), he invested much of his own wealth in the society. He recognized that as one of the anthropological community's largest patrons, he could direct the activities and methodologies of researchers.[8]

Hunt's foray into the scientific study of races occurred in 1856 when he joined the Ethnological Society of London (ESL). He was initially drawn to ethnology because of his interest in medicine and his concentration on speech and language. Both of these fields of inquiry were centrally important to ethnological research during this period.[9] The ESL was the first learned body in Britain to be strictly devoted to the scientific examination of human diversity. It was co-founded in 1843 by the Quaker abolitionist and physician Thomas Hodgkin (1798–1866), and the Arctic explorer and surgeon Richard King (1811–1876). Its formation was in response to the lack of opportunities at other learned bodies, such as the Royal Asiatic Society (f. 1824), and the Aborigines' Protection Society (f. 1837), to discuss in detail the scientific pronouncements of races.[10]

There was a strong Quaker presence at the ESL and this had a significant impact on the emerging science's theories and practices. As Michael Bravo stated,

> The driving force behind ethnology was a group of Quaker philanthropists (predominantly middle-class manufacturers and industrialists), whose commitment to religious tolerance (in contrast with the orthodox Anglicans of the day) inclined them to be relativistic and sympathetic to peoples holding religious beliefs other than their own.[11]

These sympathies were extended to different races and defined the theoretical foundation of the discipline. A key example was the theory of monogenism, which argued in favour of both the common origin of all humans, and the potential for each race to achieve the same level of civilization. This type of Quaker-influenced theoretical principle supplied researchers with a scientifically grounded argument against the exploitation of extra-Europeans and encouraged arguments in favour of racial equality through moral, physical, intellectual, and social improvement.[12]

Hunt's personal views on race, however, clashed with this ideological stance. He conceived of different races as being biologically distinct species that derived from separate origins. For Hunt, extra-Europeans were naturally inferior to Europeans and could never achieve the same heights of civilization. This theoretical perspective was a form of polygenism, which eventually put him at odds with some of the senior members of the ESL. However, in the early stages of his participation at the ESL, he got on amicably with his ethnological colleagues. As a young and ambitious practitioner, Hunt was very active at the society and consequently his status rose quickly. He was elected joint honorary secretary in 1859 and held this post until his resignation in 1862.[13]

For much of the first half of the nineteenth century, the physician James Cowles Prichard (1786–1848) was a guiding voice for British ethnology, and his famous book, *Researches into the Physical History of Man* (1813), was a seminal text for the emerging discipline. Prichard was also president of the ESL during the late 1840s.[14] However, in 1848 he passed away and the ESL struggled for several years to find a new figurehead to lead the science forward. Hunt recognized that there was an opportunity for him to position himself as a scientific reformer and leader, and he set out to establish and promote what he believed to be a new disciplinary foundation for ethnologists, built upon rigorous theoretical and methodological principles that prioritized anatomical and physiological examinations of races.

Hunt's commitment to reforming ethnology began to wane, however, and it was apparent by the start of the 1860s that he was frustrated with what he viewed as the central methodological focus of ethnology: an overemphasis on non-physical data such as linguistic evidence, and an overreliance on biblical explanations for the origin of humans.[15] Soon he and his supporters broke away from the ESL and formed the ASL, which was dedicated to promoting racial studies according to Hunt's disciplinary vision. Their polygenetic views and focus on comparative anatomy and transcendentalism were incompatible with those of the ethnological monogenists, who were increasingly interested in Darwinian evolutionary theory. This was a further hindrance for Hunt because among the new members who sought to redefine ethnology along Darwinian lines were some of the more influential scientific promoters of the day including the scientific naturalists Thomas Huxley (1825–1895), John Lubbock (1834–1913), and George Busk (1807–1886). Each would pose a threat to Hunt's authority within the ESL.[16] Moreover, against the backdrop of all of these issues was a debate about the content of the ESL's journal. This dispute ultimately led to Hunt's withdrawal from the British ethnological community and the founding of the *AR* and British anthropology.

Origin of the *Anthropological Review*

In his 1868 paper entitled, 'On the Origin of the Anthropological Review and its Connection with the Anthropological Society of London', published in the *AR*, Hunt gave a brief history of the formation of his journal. Long before the establishment of either the ASL or the *AR*, there were plans afoot to produce a major British quarterly for the open exchange of knowledge relating to human diversity. Hunt stated that

> It was the conviction that but little good could be achieved in arousing a spirit of inquiry into the most important scientific questions of the day without some organ specially devoted to the subject of the study of the races and science of man, that led to the organisation of our present periodical.[17]

He continued by discussing how during the 1850s the ESL had stopped producing its own periodical, the *Journal of the Ethnological Society of London* (*JESL*), because there were not enough members at the society to make the publication financially viable. However, this changed in 1858 when, according to Hunt, British ethnology began experiencing a renaissance. With a younger generation of practitioners interested in human variation studies, the ESL began to grow and by the following year members of the council started making arrangements to organize a new revitalized periodical. Hunt recalled, 'It was in the autumn of 1859 that a prospectus was first drawn up of a quarterly journal on these subjects, and was even put up in type – the proposed title being, "The Quarterly Journal of Ethnology"'.[18]

The journal, which was renamed the *Transactions of the Ethnological Society of London*, was delayed because of several logistical problems. Most notably, the original editor of the *JESL*, Luke Burke, was unable to commit to the publication because he was engrossed in other activities.[19] This postponed the release of the first volume of the new series, while the ESL council searched for a new editor. Eventually, the honorary secretary of the ESL, Thomas Wright (1810–1877), accepted the role of editor. Hunt was not involved in the scheme to revive the ESL's periodical until 1861 when he was asked to assist in the production of the subsequent volume. George Stocking has partly attributed Hunt's resignation from the ESL to his participation in helping to organize the second instalment of the society's new journal series. Likewise, I have shown that print culture was an important factor in causing the British anthropological schism of the 1860s.[20] Examining the details of Hunt's break from the ESL greatly enhances our understanding of mid-nineteenth-century ethnology and anthropology, and brings to the fore the centrality of scientific publishing within these disciplinary debates.

Just prior to the release of the second volume of the new series, a disagreement erupted in May 1863 between Hunt and several senior members of the ESL, including Hodgkin and the philanthropist and banker Henry Christy (1810–1865). The evidence is patchy, and the ESL recorded little detail of the disagreement. However, with the archival material available, it suggests that Hunt's view on the role of printed materials in the making of scientific knowledge played a central part in the debate. At the core of the dispute was a difference of opinion over the cost and the depiction of some lithographs from an article on the inhabitants of Sierra Leone, especially its positive portrayal of Africans.[21] The significance of this disagreement is more understandable when one considers the larger debates occurring at the ESL between Hunt, the racial determinist with polygenetic sympathies, and Hodgkin and Christy – both Quakers who were devout monogenists and supporters of abolitionism.

Hunt was increasingly interested in scientific discussions about human variation, and in several of his articles he propagated extreme racial views.[22] Hunt acknowledged that his racial theories were imbibed from his mentor, the anatomist Robert Knox (1791–1862), who had attributed all cultural and physical traits to racial determinism.[23] In addition, Hunt believed that there was insufficient observable data available to substantiate any theory that attempted to explain the origin of humans. Instead, researchers were to focus on the contemporary state of races. With this in mind, Hunt argued that Africans were probably a separate species because he viewed their current physical form as visibly different from

Europeans.[24] He also thought that Africans possessed inferior cognitive abilities than those of Europeans, and he argued that their capacity to become civilized was limited.[25]

In light of Hunt's contentious views on race and his ambition to reform the science according to his anthropological vision, we should reinterpret the debate regarding the use of the Sierra Leonean lithographs (see Figure 6.1) for the society's periodical as a conflict about scientific accuracy, and the role of printed materials in shaping ethnological

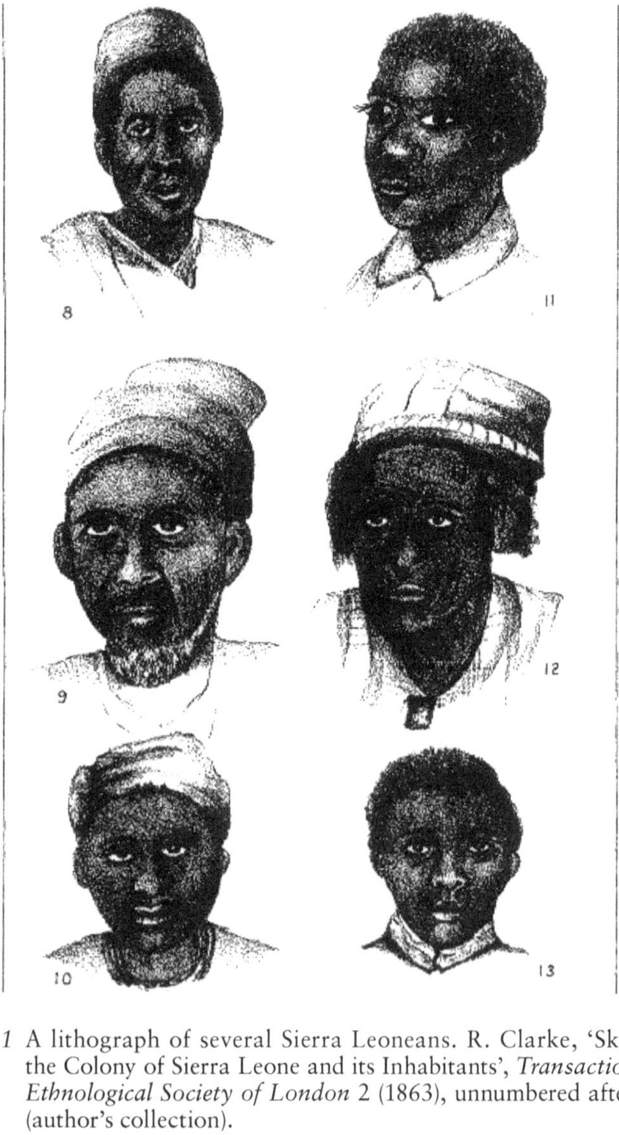

Figure 6.1 A lithograph of several Sierra Leoneans. R. Clarke, 'Sketches of the Colony of Sierra Leone and its Inhabitants', *Transactions of the Ethnological Society of London* 2 (1863), unnumbered after p. 352. (author's collection).

knowledge. The clash between Hunt and the senior members at the ESL – including Hodgkin and Christy – is further complicated by political motivations. Since 1787, Sierra Leone was a colony for the resettlement of free and emancipated Africans, and by the 1860s it was also a central location for abolitionists and humanitarians to demonstrate the unity of race.[26] Despite claims by extremists such as Knox and the American physician Josiah Nott (1804–1873) that Africans were unable to reach the same level of civilization as white Europeans, the African colony at Sierra Leone was stable.[27] For Hunt, the publication of the article on the people of Sierra Leone was problematic because it communicated to the readership a depiction of Africans, which he believed was wrong, and varied from his own perspective.

The ESL executive council met to consider Hunt's case for rejecting the images. Unsurprisingly, Hunt failed to convince the council, which included Hodgkin and Christy. The details of this debate are vague, and the ESL meetings record nothing of the dispute until 5 May 1863, when it was noted that there were some

> differences of opinions having arisen in relation to the woodcut design to illustrate the paper on the Natives of Sierra Leone by Mrs. Clarke, it was resolved that the arrangement of the question be referred to the Honorary Secretary Mr Wright.[28]

The ESL members elaborated no further on the issue and clearly considered it a closed matter. However, the conflict must have frustrated Hunt because after this meeting he resigned from the ESL. If Hunt wanted to reform the sciences relating to human diversity and disseminate his vision of the discipline, it would not be at the ESL, or through its journal. Therefore, Hunt formed the ASL in order to cultivate his version of the science with researchers who shared similar views, and, in turn, he founded his autonomous periodical the *AR* in order to circulate this research to a broader audience.

Because of the debates surrounding the lithographs of the Sierra Leoneans, Hunt was eager to produce an independent periodical that was separate from both the ASL and the ESL. This would afford him more control of the content of the journal because he did not have to receive any approval from either council. He could choose to publish any paper regardless of its socio-political orientation without worrying whether senior members of either society would block its publication. Equally, he could reject any paper that contained information that clashed with his racial prejudices. Because of the controversy surrounding both his exit from the ESL and the subsequent establishment of the ASL, Hunt chose to hide his identity as the proprietor and editor of the *AR*. His decision to conceal his identity provided him with the perfect cover for using the periodical for his own ends. Moreover, he believed that by producing the

AR anonymously he could attract more readers who might have been put off by his direct involvement in the periodical. This was all part of his strategy for taking a leading role in building British anthropology.

As Secord argued in *Victorian Sensation*, anonymity was a powerful tool that allowed actors to publish controversial ideas under the guise of an all-seeing objective voice.[29] Similarly, Gowan Dawson, Richard Noakes, and Jonathan Topham argued in the 'Introduction' to *Science in the Nineteenth-Century Periodical* that anonymous publishing masked the agenda of editors and authors, making it difficult for readers to ascertain the motives or biases lying behind a publication.[30] In Hunt's case, he had even arranged for his publisher and printer, Trübner and Co. and T. Richards, to hide his involvement in the production of the journal. If asked about the ownership of the *AR* they were to respond that it was a 'third party' and provide no further details.[31] Throughout his seven-year tenure as proprietor and editor of the *AR*, Hunt took advantage of this anonymity. He used the journal as an organ to promote his other publishing projects.[32] For instance, he regularly printed positive reviews of the translated books produced by the ASL. In the *AR*'s review of J. Frederick Collingwood's translation of Theodor Waitz's, *Introduction to Anthropology* (1863), Hunt – writing as an anonymous reviewer – praised the significance of the text for the emerging discipline, and he stated,

> The Anthropological Society, if they had done nothing else, and should cease their labours, would have effected very much Anthropological Science. Therefore, for the first time in the history of British scientific literature, we have a compendium for modern Anthropological science.[33]

For Hunt, who wanted control of the discipline, this manipulation of book reviews in his own periodical was an ideal publishing strategy for promoting the prestige of the ASL.

Hunt organized a two-part process for controlling both the production and reception of anthropological materials in Britain. First, as president of the ASL he could define the research scope of the field by helping to select which foreign books were translated and by whom. Second, he could print positive assessments of them in his own journal, which was the only quarterly review in Britain dedicated solely to anthropological research. By using the veil of anonymity throughout this whole process, all of these activities could be done furtively without receiving any direct criticisms from his opponents. Only a small group of friends knew his identity as proprietor and editor of the *AR*. The hope was that this devious system would increase the sales of these translations and raise the standing of the ASL and the discipline of anthropology.[34]

In an effort to strengthen further the illusion of his journal's impartiality, Hunt sent anonymous letters to both the ASL and the ESL offering them opportunities to publish their societies' periodicals alongside the *AR*. He recalled in his 1868 defence of the *AR* that

> When it was finally decided to publish the first number of this *Review*, a letter was addressed to the secretaries of the Ethnological and Anthropological Societies, offering to print their Journal or Proceedings at the end of the *Anthropological Review*. Identical terms were offered to both societies: one refused, and the other accepted.[35]

Hunt's anonymous letter presented this proposal as a cost saving measure because it was cheaper to print, bind, and distribute the journals together. Each issue of the *AR* was priced at 2s 3d, the same value that would be given to a joint publication. This arrangement would also ensure that members of each society received all of the journals as part of their subscription fees. Additionally, the letter stressed that the *AR* offered something different than either the *Transactions* or *JASL*. As a review journal its primary purpose was to publish short synopses of every new and important book on topics connected to ethnology and anthropology. Only a select number of original research papers would be part of the *AR*'s volumes. By contrast, the *Transactions* and *JASL* primarily published research essays, and the reports of the proceedings from their respective meetings. Very few book reviews were included in their pages.

There was little doubt over whether the ASL would accept the offer. Hunt was president of the ASL at the time of the proposal, and he was given a leading role in brokering a deal between the two parties. Thus, he was essentially negotiating a deal with himself.[36] The ESL by contrast declined the offer for joint publication. It is unclear what their reasons for passing on the deal were, but it is likely that the anonymity of the proprietor and editor concerned them. Hunt wasted little time in championing the value of the *AR* for the progress of British anthropology, and in his 'Introductory Address on the Study of Anthropology' from 1863 he stated,

> It is not a little remarkable, that amongst all the journals devoted to different branches of science, there has as yet been no independent journal for the interchange of communications from anthropologists in different parts of the world. The advent of our Society will enable such a journal to be founded. This journal will, however, not be under the influence of the Society, further than engaging to print our official reports. It will be for the use of, and a medium of communication between all anthropologists.[37]

For Hunt the development of British anthropology was reliant on printed works. Through the circulation of these materials, anthropologists would come into contact with new theories, methods, and data. The *AR* was central to this process, not only was it printing materials produced by the ASL and ESL, but according to its maxim, it published any information connected to ethnology and anthropology around the world.

After the publication of the first volumes of both the *JASL* and *AR* as a joint venture, the ASL's council decided to draw clearer distinctions between the two journals. They wanted to ensure that members of the society did not think that the *AR* was an official publication – only a linked one. A decision was made to change the pagination style of both periodicals to highlight their autonomy from each other. In the first annual report of the ASL it was stated that

> The Council, at the early part of the year, made arrangements with Messrs. Trübner and Co. to publish the Journal of the Society in connection with the *Anthropological Review*. This has hitherto been carried out, and the Council think that the connection between the *Review* and *Journal* will soon be better understood. At first the *Journal* was printed as part of the *Review*, but the Council have now made arrangements that the *Journal* shall be paged differently, and it will then be seen for which part of this publication the Society is alone responsible.[38]

In total there were eight volumes of the *AR*, produced between 1863 and 1870, and the vast majority of its articles were reviews of books. The *AR* also contained short news excerpts of anthropological activities throughout the world such as accounts of explorations, human fossil discoveries, and archaeological excavations, as well as descriptions of the proceedings of various anthropological societies across Europe.[39] The *AR* also published regular reports on ethnology and anthropology at the British Association for the Advancement of Science (BAAS).[40] Although it was technically an autonomous publication, its strong ties to the ASL were highly visible. An analysis of its content shows that its contributors were primarily members of the ASL, including Knox, Burton, the craniologist and physician Joseph Barnard Davis (1801–1881), the physician John Beddoe (1826–1911), and the comparative anatomist Charles Carter Blake (1840–1887).[41]

Although the *AR* had reasonable scholarly intentions, and achieved many of its aims – such as being the first quarterly review in Britain to focus strictly on anthropological and ethnological works, and publish material from all over the globe – its dubious ownership, suspicious management, and backhanded deals inevitably led to its downfall. Moreover, the cost of producing the journal was far too high for Hunt to fund with his own wealth. As a result, he relied on ASL subscription fees to finance its publication. This led to a growing debt at the society because Hunt and his friends on the council prioritized the *AR*'s and *JASL*'s liabilities over the money owed for translated works.[42] For instance, the ASL produced an English translation of Johann Friedrich Blumenbach's *Anthropological Treatises* in 1865, but the printing costs were not fully paid until 1867. Nevertheless, during this two-year period, the ASL's council continued to pay in full the publishing expenses of the *AR*.[43] It was because of these dealings that Hyde Clarke discovered the financial discrepancies at the ASL.

Financial Discrepancies

In 1867 the executive members of the ASL invited Clarke to join their council. Clarke was reluctant to accept the position until he had looked over the society's fiscal reports. The council agreed to his request and provided him with some access to the ASL's financial records. It was during his analysis of these documents that Clarke discovered that the ASL was deeply in debt, and according to his calculations owed their printers somewhere between £1,000 and £1,700.[44] Clarke identified two reasons for this deficit. First, the ASL was failing to regularly collect subscription fees from all of its members, and as a result many of its subscribers were in arrears. This was problematic because the ASL was still printing and circulating copies of both the *AR* and the *JASL* to non-paying members. It was only after Clarke identified the severity of this problem that the ASL restructured its collection policy and began seeking remuneration from its defaulters. In the annual report from 1868, the balance sheet showed that the ASL received £1,128 15s in back-payments. This was a significant boost to the society's flagging income. However, the second cause of the ASL's debt, which was far more concerning for Clarke, was that the council was paying the publishing costs of the *AR*.[45] Clarke did not understand why the ASL was settling the debts accrued by the *AR* because technically it was not an official publication of the society but – as Hunt routinely argued – an independent journal designed for the open exchange of anthropological knowledge in Britain.

Clarke approached several leading members of the council – including the newly re-elected president Hunt, the director Edward William Brabrook (1839–1930), the treasurer Dunbar Isidore Heath (1816–1888), and the secretary J. Frederick Collingwood – about these financial discrepancies and apparent misuses of the society's funds. However, he grew increasingly frustrated by the lack of cooperation he was receiving. Neither Hunt nor his friends on the council were willing to expound on the connection between the ASL and *AR*. After having failed to uncover any answers regarding the arrangement between the society and the periodical, Clarke decided in the summer of 1868 to expose this issue to the larger membership, who were for the most part unaware of the ASL's poor financial state. Clarke's ultimate aim was to push for a full-scale investigation into the matter, and finally reveal the mysterious relationship between the ASL and the *AR*. The entire story unfolded in the pages of three journals: the *AR*, *JASL*, and the *Athenaeum*.

In order to publicize the troubled financial condition of the ASL to its members, Clarke had to find a journal that was not under the influence of Hunt or his friends. He could not provide any information on the fiscal incongruities at the ASL in either the *AR* or the *JASL*, because Hunt and his inner circle would block its publication. The *Transactions* was an equally poor option because the British ethnological community stood in opposition to the British anthropological community. A notice about a suspicious financial arrangement between the ASL and the *AR* in the *Transactions* would have given the appearance that the ESL was purposefully spreading negative rumours about their rival. As a result, on 6 August 1868, Clarke sent a letter to the *Athenaeum* requesting that the ASL's council explain why they were paying for the *AR*'s publishing expenses, rather than settling its debts with the printers for the society's official publications, such as its translations of foreign books.

There were multiple reasons for why it was sensible for Clarke to publish his grievances in the *Athenaeum*. First, the *Athenaeum* regularly reported on the activities of London-based learned societies. Clarke's letter was not out of place in the periodical. Second, the *AR* and *JASL* specifically targeted a small specialist readership interested in anthropology. By contrast, the *Athenaeum* was a literary journal, publishing on a much broader spectrum of topics, and it had a wide general readership. By the 1860s it was selling over 7,000 copies per weekly issue.[46] Clarke hoped that by publishing his letter in the *Athenaeum* he would inform both members of the ASL and the larger scholarly community about this apparent financial scandal. Fundamentally, Clarke wanted to apply as much pressure as possible on Hunt and his friends in order to persuade them to address publicly the matter in the *Athenaeum* and reveal who was behind the *AR*'s production. Third, as a weekly journal his letter would be circulated fairly quickly and not have to wait a few months for the next issue to be released, as would be the case with a quarterly publication. This was ideal because it would limit the opportunity for the ASL's executive members to hide the apparent misuse of funds.

Clarke's letter, which was addressed to the executive members of the ASL, appeared in the *Athenaeum* nine days later on 15 August 1868. He wrote,

> it is known among some of ourselves that the *Anthropological Review* is not your property and not under your control, although we pay for it. It is not, however, known, although we pay for it through you, who are the proprietors of the *Anthropological Review*, - a matter of professed mystery to the Secretary, Director, and Council.[47]

Clarke wanted to unmask the identity of the *AR*'s editor and proprietor. He argued that

> The consequences of our having a *Review*, belonging to some unknown individual or individuals, edited by the same or other unknown individuals – a state of affairs unexampled in scientific societies – has been our subjection to such losses and liabilities as no other society has suffered.[48]

Because of these pecuniary woes, Clarke wanted the ASL to break its ties with the *AR*. In doing so, he believed that the ASL could steady its financial state and embark on new and more productive projects.

His letter was read at the next council meeting of the ASL on 18 August 1868, where the minutes state that

> The President [Hunt] drew attention of the Council to a letter by Mr Hyde Clarke which appeared in the "Athenaeum" . . . Resolutions were carried unanimously. . . [that the council] remained satisfied with the conclusions at which it has previously repeatedly arrived. . .[49]

What the council concluded was that there were no abuses of the society's funds for publishing purposes, nor were there any discrepancies with the society's financial records. The arrangement between the ASL and *AR* was deemed acceptable, and no further elaboration was necessary. It was not a closed matter, however, and more letters followed in the *Athenaeum*.

In the following issue of the *Athenaeum*, from 22 August 1868, Clarke received some responses to his letter. The first was from Hunt who stated that Clarke was alone in his views respecting the arrangement between the ASL and *AR*. According to Hunt, most of the society's members approved of the relationship between the ASL and *AR*. He wrote, 'Up to this period there has been a singular unanimity of opinion, both in the Council and amongst the Fellows of the Society generally, respecting the benefits derived from their connexion with the *Anthropological Review*'.[50] The core point in Hunt's reply to Clarke's allegations was an insistence that the council saw the *AR* as an essential resource for the emerging discipline. As such, its connection to the ASL was unproblematic and should be continued.

In the same issue of the *Athenaeum*, there was also a letter written by Brabrook that defended the arrangement between the ASL and *AR*. Brabrook rejected Clarke's claim that the *AR* was saddling the ASL with a large debt. Moreover, he dismissed the accusation that the details of the agreement between the two parties were not fully disclosed to all members of the ASL. According to Brabrook, Clarke's motivation for spreading these allegations was driven by his recent decision to join the ESL's council. To gain more authority in his new role, Brabrook contended that apparently it was in Clarke's interest to ruin the reputation of the ASL. As punishment for this calculated attack on the ASL, Brabrook proposed that Clarke be immediately expelled for his actions.[51]

It was not long before Clarke responded to both Hunt's and Brabrook's letters in the *Athenaeum*. In his second letter published on 29 August 1868, Clarke replied to Hunt's assertion that the council had unanimously supported the arrangement between the ASL and the *AR*. He wrote,

> there was no "unanimous" approval of the *Anthropological Review*, or of the proceedings of the Council, any more than there was a unanimous election of himself [Hunt]. I made very strong protest against the accounts, the financial management, the concealment of liabilities, [and] the *Anthropological Review*. . .[52]

Clarke's jibe at Hunt's electoral victory is significant because he was implying that coverage of the ASL's presidential election was misrepresented in the *JASL* – a periodical openly under the influence of Hunt. According to Clarke, the vote to re-elect him was split, but this information was absent from the *JASL*'s account. It was another example of Hunt's manipulation of both the *AR* and *JASL* for his own ends. Clarke was suggesting that if Hunt was twisting the report of his presidential re-election in the *JASL*, what else was he being dishonest about?[53]

In the same entry, Clarke also responded to Brabrook's letter by dismissing the claim that he was only discussing the affair publicly because he was a member of the ESL's council and wanted to ruin the ASL's reputation. Moreover, he reasserted that it was necessary for members of the ASL to know the identity of the *AR*'s editor and proprietor.[54] According to Clarke, there was enough evidence to indicate that there was serious corruption occurring within the ASL. Why else would Hunt and the other executive members of the council continue to avoid disclosing the identity of the *AR*'s owner and editor? If there were no transgressions, this information would be freely available and not concealed. The ASL's fiscal management was criticized in other ways. Clarke reiterated that the ASL was carrying a large debt created by its unclear link to the *AR*. Brabrook's insistence that this claim was untrue was simply an attempt to mask the fraudulent activities occurring at the ASL.[55] Clarke continued by expressing his concerns over the ASL's willingness to prioritize the *AR*'s outlays over its own liabilities, and he concluded his letter by advocating that members of the ASL should push for an independent investigation into whether Hunt and his friends on the council were engaging in any dishonest practices.[56]

On 5 September 1868, the *Athenaeum* published two more letters on the ASL scandal. The first was written by Henry Brookes, who was a member of the society, and one of its auditors for the 1867 annual financial report. As was the case with Clarke, he had also expressed concerns over the connection between the ASL and the *AR*. After having read Clarke's first letter in the *Athenaeum* on 15 August 1868, Brookes decided it was an opportune time to express his views on the management of the ASL and its suspicious link to the *AR*. He wrote,

> As one of the Fellows and a Member of the Council of this Society, I thank you for the publication of Mr. Hyde Clarke's letter in the *Athenaeum* on the 15th inst. Unless I am greatly mistaken, many others of the Fellows will feel equally obliged to him and to you for thus exposing to view one of the weakest points in our present position in order to have it thoroughly investigated and repaired.[57]

Brookes's letter echoed Clarke's earlier notice, and he wanted to know the identity of the *AR*'s proprietor and editor. He explained that when he questioned Brabrook and Collingwood about the matter, neither would provide him with a clear answer. In both cases each of them responded by stating that Hunt negotiated the agreement between the ASL and *AR*, but it was unknown whether he had a controlling influence in the journal. Finally, Brookes ended his letter by criticizing the governance of the ASL, and he remarked, 'The Anthropological Society of London belongs to the great body of anthropologists, and ought not to be governed – or misgoverned – by any clique or minority of partisans'.[58]

In the same issue of the *Athenaeum*, there was also a letter written by Brabrook who stated that the ASL was in the process of organizing a special committee to investigate Clarke's allegations. He wrote,

> [It was] resolved that a Committee of five Fellows, not members of the Council or friends of Mr. Clarke, be appointed to investigate his charges, the reply of the Council and the general financial state of the Society, and to report to a special meeting a month hence.[59]

What Brabrook did not mention in his letter was that Hunt personally selected the group of investigators. The entire investigation was therefore compromised from the onset. After concluding their investigation, the committee argued that Hunt and his friends on the council did not engage in any underhanded activities, nor was there any problem with the ASL's finances. According to the committee's report, the society's accounts were balanced.[60]

For several weeks, the *Athenaeum* continued to publish letters on the financial scandal at the ASL. Throughout the correspondence, Hunt,

Brabrook, Heath, and Collingwood avoided answering any of Clarke's or Brookes's questions regarding the editorship and ownership of the *AR*. There was a clear effort to hide Hunt's full connection to the journal. However, after weeks of publicly pressing the issue in the *Athenaeum*, Hunt finally revealed that he was both editor and proprietor of the *AR*. On 26 September 1868, Hunt wrote a letter to the *Athenaeum* affirming that he was the controlling party behind the journal. He stated that

> It will be saving me much in answering questions if you will allow me to inform those of your readers who do not know already, that I originated, and have since maintained, the *Anthropological Review*; that for six years I have been its sole responsible editor. . .[61]

Moreover, he asserted that his identity as proprietor and editor of the *AR* was a non-issue because the service it rendered to British anthropology far out-weighed any of the problems.[62]

Hunt sidestepped all of the charges laid against him for fraud and the embezzlement of society funds for his own ends. He did not offer to repay the ASL for any of the money he deceitfully took over the years to finance the publication of the *AR*. Instead he proposed that the council should buy the copyright of the *AR* and make it an official publication of the ASL. He discussed some of the benefits of having the ASL take control of the *AR*. He wrote,

> It is possible, however, that the Society could conduct the *Review* at a smaller expense than a private individual is able to. It is for this reason that I have urged, and still urge that the Anthropological Society to accept the copyright of the *Review* free from debts.[63]

Hunt continued by championing the value of the *AR*, not only for the progress of anthropology in Britain but also for anthropology around the world. He remarked, 'I am fully conscious of the important services which the *Anthropological Review* has it in its power to render to the progress [of] anthropological science, not only in this country, but throughout the civilised world'.[64] Hunt was attempting to manipulate the circumstances surrounding the *AR* by avoiding any mention of the corruption allegations against him. By professing the great merits of the journal, he hoped he could overcome the scandal without facing any serious consequences.

The disagreement between Clarke and Hunt persisted for a few more weeks. If this was to be the end of his disreputable reign as leader of the British anthropological community, he was going to take his opponent down with him. Hunt and his friends on the council worked tirelessly to oust Clarke from the ASL. Although Hunt's corruption was publicly exposed, he successfully managed to convince the council that because the internal investigative committee ruled in his favour, and stated that he had not engaged in any financial indiscretions, there were sufficient grounds to expel Clarke. On 3 November 1868, it was recorded in the ASL's minute book that it was

> Resolved unanimously that the Council is still of the opinion that there is good cause for the expulsion of Mr Hyde Clarke from the Society. . . [because he was] guilty of false and calumnious statements affecting the scientific reputation of the society. . . and the personal character of individual fellows.[65]

After much discussion, Clarke left the society for good. Nevertheless, despite being forced to admit publicly that he had been misusing both his presidency, and ownership and editorship of the *AR* for his own purposes, Hunt's power within the ASL remained strong until his sudden death in 1869 at the age of thirty-six. It was a quiet end to his vocal and libellous career as a prolific disseminator of British anthropology.

Conclusion

This chapter has examined the scandalous affair surrounding the ownership and editorship of the *AR* in the late 1860s, showing its significance as a major event in British anthropology's disciplinary formation.[66] What came to the fore in this analysis is that printed materials, such as the *AR* and the *JASL*, defined the intellectual and methodological scope of British anthropology, and were an essential part of the discipline's identity during the critical years of its formation. Through Hunt's total control of the ASL's periodicals, he could define the boundaries of the nascent discipline and forward his particular vision of anthropological science that prioritized direct observation, was grounded in a stalwart commitment to Baconian induction, argued for biological determinism, and promoted polygenesis.[67] He manipulated the press for his own ends, vilified anyone who dissented from his regime, and managed to avoid any punishment for his financial indiscretions. His adeptness as a propagandist was even apparent in periodicals that were not under his control. He presented himself in his letters to the *Athenaeum* as a martyr for the discipline, and he utilized his inner circle of friends to publicly support this characterization.

Nevertheless, although Hunt was an important founding figure for British anthropology, due to his central role in forming the ASL and producing some of the discipline's earliest specialist periodicals, his extreme socio-political views, aggressive attack on his opponents, and dishonest activities ensured that he would remain infamous in the secondary literature. Other factors also affected Hunt's anthropological legacy. Two years after his sudden death in 1869, the ESL and ASL amalgamated to form the Royal Anthropological Institute of Great Britain and Ireland.[68] One of the council's first acts was to cut all ties to the ESL's and ASL's periodicals in order to establish their new title, the *Journal of the Anthropological Institute.* With these major changes, Hunt's two biggest contributions to the disciplinary formation of British anthropology were gone. It marked the end of the anthropological schism, and a new era for British anthropology that was led by members of the X Club, grounded in evolutionary theories, and promoted monogenesis and the possibility of racial parity through cultural developmental processes.[69]

Notes

1 H. Clarke, 'Anthropological Society of London', *Athenaeum* 2129 (1868), 210; J. Hunt, J. F. Collingwood, and E. W. Brabrook, 'Anthropological Society of London', *Athenaeum* 2130 (1868), 239–240; H. Clarke, 'Anthropological Society of London', *Athenaeum* 2131 (1868), 271–272; H. Brookes and E. W. Brabrook, 'Anthropological Society of London', *Athenaeum* 2132 (1868), 32; C. Harding and D. I. Heath, 'Anthropological Society of London', *Athenaeum* 2133 (1868), 334; H. Clarke and H. Brookes, 'Anthropological Society of London', *Athenaeum* 2134 (1868), 368–369; J. Hunt, D. I. Heath, L. O. Pike, H. Clarke, and P. M. Duncan, 'Anthropological Society of London', *Athenaeum* 2135 (1868), 402–403; H. Brookes, 'Anthropological Society of London', *Athenaeum* 2136 (1868), 432–433; J. Hunt, 'On the Origin of the Anthropological Review and Its Connection with the Anthropological Society of London', *Anthropological Review* 6 (1868), 431–442; and Anonymous 'Report of the Committee of Investigation into the General and Financial Condition of the Anthropological Society of London', *Journal of the Anthropological Society of London* 7 (1869), i–xxi.

2 The focus on the intersection of print culture and disciplinary formation is similar to how Lowther (Chapter 5) demonstrates the key role of journals in the evolution of natural history earlier in the century, and Buckland (Chapter 2) points to the founding of the *Dance Journal* later in the early twentieth century as a milestone in the professionalization of dance training

3 J. Topham, 'Scientific Publishing and the Reading of Science in Nineteenth-Century Britain: A Historiographical Survey and Guide to the Sources', *Studies in the History and Philosophy of Science* 31 (2000) 559–612; J. Secord, 'Knowledge in Transit', *Isis* 95 (2004), 654–672.

4 S. Qureshi, *Peoples on Parade: Exhibitions, Empire, and Anthropology in Nineteenth-Century Britain* (Chicago, IL: University of Chicago Press, 2011).

5 E. Sera-Shriar, *The Making of British Anthropology, 1813–1871* (London: Picking & Chatto, 2013), 102–106. See also R. Knox, *The Races of Men: A Fragment* (London: Henry Renshaw, 1850); and R. G. Latham, *Natural History of the Varieties of Man* (London: John Van Voorst, 1850).

6 A tremendous amount has been written on James Hunt and the anthropological schism of the 1860s. See J. W. Burrow, 'Evolution and Anthropology in the 1860s: The Anthropological Society of London, 1863–1871', *Victorian Studies* 7 (1963), 137–149; G. W. Stocking, 'What's in a Name? The Origins of the Royal Anthropological Institute (1837–1871)', *Man* 6 (1971), 369–390; G. W. Stocking, *Victorian Anthropology* (New York, NY: The Free Press, 1987), 238–245; D. Lorimer, 'Science and the Secularization of Victorian Images of Race', in *Victorian Science in Context*, ed. Bernard

Lightman (Chicago, IL: University of Chicago Press, 1997), 214–218; R. Kenny, 'From the Curse of Ham to the Curse of Nature: The Influence of Natural Selection on the Debate on Human Unity before the Publication of the Descent of Man', *British Journal for the History of Science* 40 (2007), 367–388; H. Kuklick, 'The British Tradition', in *A New History of Anthropology*, ed. H. Kuklick (Oxford: Blackwell Publishing, 2008), 52–56; and E. Sera-Shriar, 'Observing Human Difference: James Hunt, Thomas Huxley and Competing Disciplinary Strategies in the 1860s', *Annals of Science* 70 (2013), 461–491. For an account of Hunt and his views on slavery and race consult D. Lorimer, *Colour, Class and the Victorians: English Attitudes to the Negro in the Mid-Nineteenth-Century* (Leicester: Leicester University Press, 1978); and Sera-Shriar, *The Making of British Anthropology*, 119–126. For an account of Hunt's views on women see E. Richards, 'Huxley and Woman's Place in Science: The Woman Question and the Control of Victorian Anthropology', in *History, Humanity and Evolution*, ed. J. Moore (Cambridge: Cambridge University Press, 1989), 253–284.

7 For more on Hunt's medical practice see J. Hunt, *Stammering and Stuttering, their Nature and Treatment* (London: Longman, Green, Longman, and Roberts, 1861), 157–160.

8 J. Hunt, 'Introductory Address on the Study of Anthropology', *Anthropological Review* 1 (1863), 14.

9 For more on the significance of language for ethnology see: M. Bravo, 'Ethnological Encounters', in *Cultures of Natural History*, ed. N. Jardine, J. Secord, and E. Spary (Cambridge: Cambridge University Press, 1996), p. 339; and Sera-Shriar, *The Making of British Anthropology*, 44–45.

10 R. King, 'Address to the Ethnological Society of London Delivered at the Anniversary, 25th May 1844', *Journal of the Ethnological Society of London* 2 (1850), 15. For more on the Ethnological Society of London see Stocking, 'What's in a Name?', 369–390; Stocking, *Victorian Anthropology*, 244–257; Lorimer, 'Science and the Secularization', 214–217; G. Cantor, *Quakers, Jews and Science: Religious Responses to Modernity and the Sciences in Britain 1650–1900* (Oxford: Oxford University Press, 2005), 133–138; Kenny, 'From the Curse of Ham to the Curse of Nature', 363–388; Qureshi, *Peoples of Parade*, 186–187; and Sera-Shriar, *The Making of British Anthropology*, 53–79.

11 Bravo, 'Ethnological Encounters', 339–340.

12 For more on the civilizing mission in nineteenth-century Britain see C. Hall, *Civilising Subjects: Metropole and Colony in the English Imagination, 1830–1867* (Chicago, IL: University of Chicago Press, 2002).

13 Hunt, 'On the Origin of the Anthropological Review', 432–434.

14 J. C. Prichard, *Researches Into the Physical History of Man* (London: John and Arthur Arch, 1813). For more on Prichard and ethnology see G. W. Stocking, 'From Chronology to Ethnology: James Cowles Prichard and British Anthropology 1800–1850', in J. C. Prichard, *Researches into the Physical History of Man*, ed. G. W. Stocking (Chicago, IL: University of Chicago Press, 1973), ix–cx; J. Efron, *Defenders of Race: Jewish Doctors and Race Science in Fin-de-Siècle Europe* (New Haven: Yale University Press, 1994), 44–45; H. F. Augstein, *James Cowles Prichard's Anthropology: Remaking the Science of Man in Early Nineteenth-Century Britain* (Amsterdam: Rodopi B. V., 1999); and Sera-Shriar, *The Making of British Anthropology*, 21–52.

15 D. Lorimer, 'Hunt, James 1833–1869', in *Dictionary of Nineteenth-Century British Scientists*, ed. B. Lightman (London: Thoemmes Continuum, 2004), 1034. For several examples of Hunt's criticisms of ethnology see Hunt,

'Introductory Address', 1–20; and Hunt, 'On the Origin of the Anthropological Review', 431–442.

16 Stocking, *Victorian Anthropology*, 254. For more on Hunt's professional rivalry with Huxley see Sera-Shriar, 'Observing Human Difference', 461–491.

17 Hunt, 'On the Origin of the Anthropological Review', 433.

18 Ibid.

19 Ibid.

20 Stocking, *Victorian Anthropology*, 238–245; Sera-Shriar, 'Observing Human Difference', 461–491.

21 Stocking, *Victorian Anthropology*, 247; Sera-Shriar, *The Making of British Anthropology*, 119–126; 4 March 1862, Minutes of the Proceedings of the Ethnological Society of London Meetings 1843–1871. Ethnological Society of London Archives, Royal Anthropological Institute, London, UK; May 5, 1863, Minutes of the Proceedings of the Ethnological Society of London Meetings 1843–1871. Ethnological Society of London Archives, Royal Anthropological Institute, London, UK.

22 The best example of Hunt's views on race was published in his first major scholarly contribution to anthropology: J. Hunt, *On the Negro's Place in Nature*, (London: Trübner and Co., 1863).

23 J. Hunt, 'On the Application of the Principle of Natural Selection to Anthropology, in Reply to the Views Advocated by Some of Mr Darwin's Disciples', *Anthropological Review* 4 (1866), 336. For more on Knox's racial determinism see Knox, *Races of Man*, 1–7.

24 For more on Hunt's criticism of Darwinian evolutionary theory see J. Hunt, 'On the Doctrine of Continuity Applied to Anthropology', *Anthropological Review* 5 (1867), 110–120; and Hunt, 'On the Application of the Principle of Natural Selection', 320–340.

25 Hunt, *On the Negro's Place in Nature*, 4, 27.

26 Stocking, *Victorian Anthropology*, 247–248; and Sera-Shriar, *The Making of British Anthropology*, 120.

27 Knox, *Races of Man*, 12.

28 5 May 1863, ESL Minutes; Stocking, 'What's in a Name', 376; and Sera-Shriar, *The Making of British Anthropology* 125.

29 J. Secord, *Victorian Sensation: The Extraordinary Publication, Reception and Secret Authorship of Vestiges of the Natural History of Creation* (Chicago, IL: University of Chicago Press, 2000), 367.

30 G. Dawson, R. Noakes and J. Topham, 'Introduction', in *Science in the Nineteenth-Century Periodical*, eds. G. Cantor et al. (Cambridge: Cambridge University Press, 2004), 28.

31 The arrangement between the ASL, *Anthropological Review* and the publisher and printer is discussed in Dunbar Isidore Heath's letter to the *Athenaeum* on September 12, 1868: Harding and Heath, 'Anthropological Society of London', 369.

32 For translations produced by the ASL see T. Waitz, *Introduction to Anthropology*, trans. J. Frederick Collingwood (London: Longman, Green, Longman, and Roberts, 1863); P. Broca, *On the Phenomena of Hybridity in the Genus Homo*, trans. C. C. Blake (London: Longman, Green Longman and Roberts, 1864); G. Pouchet, *On the Plurality of the Human Race*, trans. H. J. C Beaven (London: Longman, Green, Longman, and Roberts, 1864); C. Vogt, *Lectures on Man: His Place in Creation, and in the History of the Earth*, trans. J. Hunt (London: Longman, Green, Longman, and Roberts, 1864); J. F. Blumenbach, *The Anthropological Treatises of Johann Friedrich Blumenbach, Late Professor at Göttingen and Court Physician to the*

King of Great Britain, trans. Thomas Bendyshe (London: Longman, Green, Longman, Roberts, 1865). For reviews of the ASL's translations in the *AR* see J. Hunt, 'Waitz's Introduction to Anthropology', *Anthropological Review* 1 (1863), 465–472; Anonymous, 'On the Phenomena of Hybridity', *Anthropological Review* 2 (1864), 164–173; Anonymous, 'The Plurality of the Human Race by George Pouchet; Hugh J. C. Beavan', *Anthropological Review* 3 (1864), 120–132; and J. M. Allan, 'Carl Vogt's Lectures on Man', *Anthropological Review* 7 (1869), 177–184.

33 Hunt, 'Waitz's Introduction to Anthropology', 465.

34 After discovering that Hunt was secretly the proprietor and editor of the *Anthropological Review* Henry Brookes wrote a scathing letter to the *Athenaeum* scolding Hunt for his unscrupulous publishing tactics. See Brookes, 'Anthropological Society of London', 432–433.

35 Hunt, 'On the Origin of the Anthropological Review', 435.

36 Ibid., 436.

37 Hunt, 'Introductory Address', 14.

38 Anonymous, 'First Annual Report of the Anthropological Society of London', *Journal of the Anthropological Society of London* 2 (1864), lxxvi.

39 For examples of these different types of publications see W. W. Reade, 'Burton's Mission to Dahome', *Anthropological Review* 2 (1864), 335–343; E. B. Tylor, 'On the Discovery of Supposed Human Remains in the Tool-Bearing Drift of Moulin Quignon', *Anthropological Review* 1 (1863), 166–168; Anonymous, 'Human Remains in Lough Gur, County Limerick', *Anthropological Review* 2 (1864), 59–60; J. B. Davis, 'The Skulls of the Inhabitants of the Caroline Islands', *Anthropological Review* 4 (1866), 47–61; Anonymous, 'The Proceedings of the Anthropological Society of Paris', *Anthropological Review* 2 (1864), 141–145; M. N. Serrano, 'Spanish Anthropological Society: Translation of the President's Address', *Anthropological Review* 4 (1866), 186–197.

40 For examples of the AR's coverage of the BAAS meetings see Anonymous, 'Anthropology at the British Association', *Anthropological Review* 1 (1863), 379–464; Anonymous, 'Anthropology at the British Association, A.D. 1864', *Anthropological Review* 2 (1864), 294–335; Anonymous, 'On the Prospects of Anthropological Science at the British Association of 1865', *Anthropological Review* 3 (1865), 224–229.

41 All eight volumes of the AR are filled with entries by leading members of the ASL. For some examples of contributions by ASL members see R. Knox, 'Ethnological Inquiries and Observations', *Anthropological Review* 1 (1863), 246–263; R. Knox, 'On the Application of the Anatomical Method to the Discrimination of Species', *Anthropological Review* 1 (1863), 263–270; J. B. Davis, 'Italian Anthropology', *Anthropological Review* 2 (1864), 30–38; J. B. Davis, 'Dutch Anthropology', *Anthropological Review* 3 (1865), 202–218; J. Beddoe, 'On the Supposed Increasing Prevalence of Dark Hair in England', *Anthropological Review* 1 (1863), 310–312; C. C. Blake, 'Lunacy and Phrenology', *Anthropological Review* 1 (1863), 476–480; C. C. Blake, 'Organic Philosophy', *Anthropological Review* 2 (1864), 213–216; C. C. Blake, 'On a Human Jaw from the Cave of La Naulette, near Dinant, Belgium', *Anthropological Review* 5 (1867), 294–303; R. F. Burton, 'A Day Amongst the Fans', *Anthropological Review* 1 (1863), 43–54; R. F. Burton, 'Notes on Waitz's Anthropology', *Anthropological Review* 2 (1864), 233–250.

42 The official financial records of the ASL were published yearly in the *Journal of the Anthropological Society of London*. The reports for each year show

how much money was spent on publications, and includes information about the society's liabilities see Anonymous, 'First Annual Report', lxxiv–lxxx; Anonymous, 'Second Annual Report of the Anthropological Society of London', *Journal of the Anthropological Society of London* 3 (1865), lxxv–lxxxv; Anonymous, 'Report of the Council', *Journal of the Anthropological Society of London* 4 (1866), xlix–lix; Anonymous, 'Report of the Council', *Journal of the Anthropological Society of London* 5 (1867), xxxiii–xliii; Anonymous, 'Report of the Council of the Anthropological Society of London for the Year 1867', *Journal of the Anthropological Society of London* 6 (1868), lxv–lxxvi; Anonymous, 'Report of the Council of the Anthropological Society of London for the Year 1868', *Journal of the Anthropological Society of London* 7 (1869), lxxv–lxxxi; Anonymous, 'Report of the Council of the Anthropological Society of London for the Year 1869', *Journal of the Anthropological Society of London* 8 (1870–1871), lxxiv–lxxvii; Anonymous, 'Report of the Committee of Investigation', i–xxi.

43 See: Blumenbach, *Anthropological Treatises*; Anonymous, 'Report of the Council of the Anthropological Society of London for the Year 1867', lxv.

44 Clarke, 'Anthropological Society of London', 210.

45 Anonymous, 'Report of the Council of the Anthropological Society of London for the Year 1868', lxxv.

46 For more on the *Athenaeum* see J. Plunkett, 'The *Athenaeum*', in *Encyclopaedia of Nineteenth-Century Photography*, ed. J. Hannavy (London: Routledge, 2004), 92–93; and M. Demoor, 'The *Athenaeum*', in *Dictionary of Nineteenth-Century Journalism*, eds. L. Brake and M. Demoor (Gent: Academia Press, 2009), 26–28.

47 Clarke, 'Anthropological Society of London', 210.

48 Ibid.

49 August 18, 1868, Minutes of the Proceedings of the Anthropological Society of London Meetings 1863–1871. Anthropological Society of London Archive. Royal Anthropological Institute of London, UK.

50 Hunt, Collingwood, and Brabrook, 'Anthropological Society of London', 240.

51 Ibid.

52 Clarke, 'Anthropological Society of London', 271.

53 Hunt discusses his unanimous re-election in his presidential address from 1868: J. Hunt, 'The President's Address', *Journal of the Anthropological Society of London* 6 (1868), xcviii.

54 Clarke, 'Anthropological Society of London', 271.

55 Ibid.

56 Ibid., 272.

57 Brookes and Brabrook, 'Anthropological Society of London', 32.

58 Ibid.

59 Ibid.

60 The details of the ASL's financial investigation were published in *Journal of the Anthropological Society of London* in 1869. See Anonymous, 'Report of the Committee of Investigation', i–xxi.

61 Hunt, Heath, Pike, Clarke, and Duncan, 'Anthropological Society of London', 402.

62 Ibid.

63 Ibid.

64 Ibid.

65 November 3, 1868, Minutes of the Proceedings of the Anthropological Society of London Meetings 1863–1871. Anthropological Society of London Archive. Royal Anthropological Institute of London, UK.

66 Just as the heated controversy earlier in the century between Nicholas Vigors, William Swainson, and Hugh Strickland over the status of Quinarianism in the pages of the *Magazine of Natural History* defined the future of natural history (Chapter 5), the bitter debate between Hunt and Clarke on the financial situation in the *ASL* profoundly affected the development of anthropology from the 1860's onwards.

67 Sera-Shriar, 'Observing Human Difference', 481–482.

68 For more on the amalgamation of the Ethnological Society of London and Anthropological Society of London see Stocking, 'What's in a Name?', 369–390; Sera-Shriar, *The Making of British Anthropology*, 144–145.

69 Sera-Shriar, *The Making of British Anthropology*, 147–149.

Section IV

Literary Genres

7 'A subject which is peculiarly adapted to all cyclists'

Popular Understandings of Classical Archaeology in the Nineteenth-Century Press

Rachel Bryant Davies

'Archaeology is a subject', proclaimed a women's magazine in the mid-1890s, 'peculiarly adapted to all cyclists'.[1] This pronouncement signals archaeology's disciplinary identity as so well established that it could confidently be popularized as a hobby. The author, F. J. Erskine, aimed her article at New Women, for whom the current 'bicycle craze' symbolized female emancipation.[2] Defining archaeology broadly, as the study of 'relics of a past age', she argued that it was not 'a dry and uninteresting' academic pursuit.[3] Rather, this incipient authority on *Lady Cycling: what to wear & how to ride* passionately promoted 'archaeologising' as a 'wonderfully enticing' activity. 'Of course', she conceded, 'some branches of it are too deep for the average intellect, but the broad outline [. . .] is sufficiently clear to be grasped by anyone'. While learned archaeological societies were 'hardly the working man's milieu', the affordability of safety bicycles for 'lower-middle and working class cyclists' aided wider participation in archaeology, even as increasingly diverse readerships engaged in discourses surrounding the definition and practice of archaeology.[4]

In asking how archaeology was treated in newspapers and periodicals for different readerships, this essay examines the relationship between Victorian popular culture and the development of disciplines; in particular, how evidence from the Victorian popular press fits with existing accounts of the development and separation of archaeology as a discipline. Levine's pioneering account of amateurs and professionals in the antiquarian, historical, and archaeological discourses of national and regional learned societies, especially as preserved in their archives, uncovers the gradual individuation of all those terms through the century. Perceptions of these same participants and their discourses, in the cheap formats through which their activities reached larger and more varied audiences, reveal an alternative viewpoint of the 'formation and moulding' of recognizable disciplinary identities.[5] 'Periodicals are the best record', as Prince has noted about Shakespearean drama, 'of the ways in which the nineteenth century created a new public'.[6] Consistent formatting, interactive submissions, and often clearly expounded ideologies fostered readers' community spirit, while their rapidly sequential nature enabled the 'fine texture of debates'.[7]

Analysis of a representative sample of articles, with differing prices, agendas, and readerships, shows that popular and learned perceptions were defined; contended; and, often, mocked in the press.[8] Titles targeting specific audiences, such as *Hearth and Home: an illustrated weekly journal for gentlewomen* which printed Erskine's ideas for 'Cycling hobbies', proliferated in the mid- to late-nineteenth century. Both specialized titles and those which achieved huge circulation reached many more readers than books, and often included detailed book reviews. Articles were not necessarily factual or didactic: Noakes has highlighted how *Punch*'s satirical journalism 'shap[ed] and determin[ed] popular knowledge and opinions about science'.[9] Many journalists, as we shall see, played with, and subverted, readers' expectations of archaeology. Verbal and graphic jokes spoofed the satirical stereotype of obscurity; letters and stories told of site and museum visits; learned speeches were often printed verbatim; and readers' assumed knowledge was even tested in puzzles. These shifting portrayals of archaeological activities reveal a 'feedback loop' created by overlaps between practitioners and public, specialists and amateurs, readers and writers, which results in a multi-faceted, often convoluted, picture of both the development and wider adoption of disciplinary identities. Fluid understandings do not negate the role of public discourses in shaping academic disciplines. Rather, as the result of extensive, targeted journalism, their very openness affords crucial insights into the evolution of disciplines within the cultural imagination.

Expectations of what target readers should be taught, or already know, reveal how archaeology as a discipline was promulgated. As Shuttleworth and Cantor explain, 'each periodical fashions its response to science in the light of the intended readership'.[10] Children's titles and cheaper, more overtly didactic, publications, which consciously acted as 'conduits' of specialized knowledge, demonstrate how the discipline was shaped. Even as archaeology was demarcated from kindred disciplines, however, its precise definition varied: in particular, antiquarians and archaeologists often appeared interchangeable. A fruitful comparison is the disciplinarization of psychology, which 'remained almost as open' by the mid-1870s among educated and middle-class readers of 'thick' journals, despite focussed debate since the 1850s.[11] Widely reported antiquarian meetings, barrow digs, and Grand Tours 'heightened consciousness' of archaeological pursuits so that, like psychology, archaeology 'existed before academic institutionalisation as a scientific discourse of non-academic readers and writers'.[12] Smith locates psychology's appeal to 'public, non-specialist culture' in its facilitation of 'open-ended debate on the relation of knowledge to judgment'; similarly, it is clear that archaeology spoke strongly to contemporary anxieties over the relation of past to present, and of imagination to reality.

Public discourses shaping the demarcation of new disciplines were further fuelled by the visibility of, and hype surrounding, archaeological discoveries and their exhibition. Erskine perceived archaeology as an accessible hobby since cyclists required no special equipment to observe ancient remains in the landscape. Nonetheless it was, as Levine notes, 'the work of excavators that first fired the public imagination'.[13] Unearthing the past, whether through geology and palaeontology, or urban development and modern technologies, had caused cultural and religious upheaval. Classical excavations further complicated notions of historical time and disciplinary identity by suggesting the verification, through material evidence, of canonical, mythical literature. Even as finds arrived in London for display, categorization of the process by which they had been unearthed hovered between science, literature, history, and art.

It is no accident that archaeology's emergence as a discrete, commonly recognized, subject coincides with mid-nineteenth-century expansion of the press. Excitement over discoveries both fuelled and fed readers' interest in excavations. The sensational identification of Troy in 1874 would prove a particularly contentious watershed in popular understanding of, and controversial discourses surrounding, archaeology. Its identity had been hotly contested, through philological, topographical, and archaeological methods, long before Heinrich Schliemann funded excavations at Hissarlik (in modern Turkey), which had begun to be identified as the Homeric citadel.[14] Debate over efforts to locate this legendary city had filled monthlies and quarterlies since the early nineteenth century; this backstory, combined with the Homeric and Virgilian epics' educational centrality and their popularity as entertainment, conditioned journalists' and readers' responses.[15] Even as Schliemann's trench was seen as a trial for developing excavation methods, his constant advertisement of discoveries in newspapers, combined with enthusiastic support from British Prime Minister and Homeric scholar William Gladstone, increased public appetite for Schliemann's exhibition of 'Priam's Treasure' at South Kensington Museum in London (1877–1881).[16]

Modern histories of archaeology often condemn Schliemann as embodying the 'romanticism of the antiquarian era' or as an 'archaeological anachronism' using 'crude and destructive' methods, but others praise his pioneering of 'basic archaeological methods' to 'uncover a rich preclassical culture'.[17] Most pinpoint his excavations as an early example of the recently identified subdiscipline of 'historical archaeology' and 'significant. . .for public mythmaking about archaeology'.[18] Additional participants engaged with Schliemann's promotional campaigns, yet debates about different techniques used to locate Homer's Troy at Hissarlik, plus recent heated rhetoric about unearthing antiquity, had already focussed significant attention onto the purpose of excavation.[19] As readers of *Macmillan's Magazine* learned, Homeric 'devotees ask no longer "Where is Troy?" but "What do we learn of Troy from Hissarlik?"'.[20] Schliemann's self-publicity added fuel to the already-raging fire which shaped perceptions of the subject among wider publics – not least in designating what archaeology was not.

Closer examination of descriptions, explanations, and implied understandings – both of archaeology's disciplinary identity and examples of its practice – will begin to tell the story of how popular understandings evolved through the press. I focus here on classical archaeology, which dominated and shaped nineteenth-century archaeology: such culturally privileged sites were most visible, often underpinned wider definitions of archaeology, and generated controversy over the allocation of funding for overseas versus local excavations.[21] In addition, classical archaeology's disciplinary autonomy and allegiances are still contested: Victorian popular discourses highlight the murky overlaps perceived with antiquarianism (which fluctuated between obsolete forerunner, subdiscipline, and major archaeological activity of the majority of amateur archaeologists) that still colour 'caricatured' traducements of 'traditional classical archaeology'.[22] While levels of esteem for archaeological activities, as well as accuracy of perceptions to actual practice, fluctuated markedly between publications, the focus of discourse remained remarkably constant across the century. Popular definitions of archaeology were moulded, as we shall see, by judgements about the subject's accessibility and relevance to both author and implied reader; disciplinary discourses centred around participants and cultural relevance, especially as measured through funding.

'What Does the Ordinary British Taxpayer Care about the Site of Troy?': Contending the Relevance of, and Shaping an Audience for, Archaeological Excavations

The clearest British debate about the cultural relevance of archaeological excavation occurred almost entirely in newspapers and periodicals. Just months before reports of Schliemann's discovery of 'Priam's Treasure' reached the reading public in August 1873,[23] the Chancellor had refused the Society of Antiquaries funding to excavate burial mounds in the Troad. Provocative headlines such as 'Antiquarian Research at the Public Expense' prompted a nationwide discussion, far beyond the Society's elite membership.[24] This controversy highlights three central strands of archaeology's emergence in public discourse: the purpose of such researches; who should participate (and pay) for them; and the fluidity of its disciplinary identity.

In its concern for 'the ordinary British taxpayer', the *Daily News* pinpointed the utilitarian question. The Chancellor, Robert Lowe, had justified his rejection on account of the 'little or no chance of acquiring any possession for the public which would repay the search'. In previous expeditions, Lowe explained, 'the main object was the acquisition of specimens' and so he doubted whether 'excavations undertaken for the purpose of illustrating the *Iliad* [are] a proper object for the expenditure of public money'.[25] Such material concerns were damned by *The Graphic*. Despite general agreement that 'portable' treasures were unlikely to be found (since Calvert and Schliemann's excavations had hitherto proved unproductive), this weekly illustrated paper insisted that '[t]he pilfering of the curiosity hunter is but one degree better than the ravages of the barbarian invader'.[26] Many did, however, condemn the 'large number of wealthy English noblemen and gentleman' who subscribed to the Society of Antiquaries but had not financed excavations themselves.[27]

It is striking that this controversy largely avoids the terms 'archaeology' or 'archaeologist', especially since its ironic timing shaped analyses of Schliemann's archaeological methods. Despite the qualification 'thorough and scientific', the Society's proposed 'exploration of the tumular barrows' suggested a throwback to eighteenth-century excavations rather than testing the latest theories about Troy's location.[28] The fluidity of concepts of 'archaeology' and 'antiquarianism' is equally evident in responses. *The Graphic*, for example, recalled that 'Greek archaeology was quite an English speciality', but illustrated this assertion with 'explorers' and failed to distinguish research from the treasure-hunting it so roundly condemned.[29]

At this point, *Punch* entered the fray with a satirical meditation on *The Times*' complaint: 'Mr. Lowe's refusal to subsidise a pilgrimage for discovering the graves of Achilles and Hector, betrayed a deep and deplorable scepticism as to the historical accuracy of Homer'. In a pointed comment on public resources, John Tenniel adapted Hablot Knight Browne's illustration for Charles Dickens's novel *Martin Chuzzlewit*, showing two women taking tea. Tenniel added a brief dialogue, naming the two characters as Dickens's incompetent nurse Sairey Gamp and her friend Betsey Prig: here renamed 'Bobsey', after Lowe (who, as education minister, had challenged the dominance of classics in schools). Gamp's enthusiasm for reading Homer 'night and day' caricatures the Liberal Prime Minister William Gladstone, while the newspaper quotation conflates Homeric and biblical pilgrimages. Tenniel's contribution to this fiery debate emphasizes interaction between different parts of the press (where Dickens's novel originally appeared), as well as class tensions implied by interest in classical antiquity and also contemporary convictions that authenticating Homer's Troy validated religious faith in the Bible.[30] 'A Deplorable Sceptic' must have been shaped by, and viewed against, Tenniel's recent comment on Gladstone's Homeric scholarship (see Figure 7.1) which, in a later *Punch* compilation, was featured overleaf.[31]

CARTOON.—DECEMBER 14, 1872.
BAKERS
COAL MINERS
POLICE
"MY OLD FRIEND HOMER."
("*Every day must begin for me with my old friend* HOMER—*the friend of my youth, the friend of my middle age and of my old age—from whom I hope never to be parted so long as I have any faculties, or any breath in my body.*"—MR. GLADSTONE, Dec. 3, 1872.)
GHOST (*rises*). "But if a clamorous vile plebeian rose,
Him with reproof he checked, or tamed with blows,
'Be silent, wretch, and think not here allowed
That WORST OF TYRANTS, a USURPING CROWD.'
—*That is Mr. Pope's translation of a passage of mine, sir. What do* YOU *make of it?*"
Much of the dissatisfied feeling at this time prevalent amongst the working classes was attributed to the supineness of the Government.—1872.
No. 34.

Figure 7.1 'My Old Friend Homer', *Punch* (December 14, 1872), 247 (author's collection).

Only a few months earlier, Tenniel had depicted Gladstone dozing in his armchair.[32] Meanwhile, the ghost of the epic poet – identified by both title, 'My old friend Homer', and the book on Gladstone's desk – points to the mob of 'the working classes' in the background. Tenniel contrasts Gladstone's enthusiasm for classical scholarship with recent strikes by labourers, which the compiler claims was 'widely attributed to the supineness of the Government'. Homer's ghost quotes Alexander Pope's translation of 'my' *Iliad* in apparent support of Odysseus' beating of the 'vile plebeian' Thersites. In pointing the harsh disparity between dark, frantic background and serenely passive foreground, Tenniel questions the suitability of Gladstone's claim to read Homer '[e]very day', even as his later depiction of Gamp as Gladstone further highlighted the traditional inaccessibility of classical scholarship.[33]

It is likely that such problematic intermeshing of classical and political discourses prompted Lowe's refusal to use 'money wrung from the earnings of the poorest of the community'.[34] This explanation was supported by *The Times*, which echoed calls for privately funded excavations on the grounds that 'any aesthetic benefit. . .from the exhumation of old Troy. . .would be realized by classical scholars, and not the public at large'.[35] The conflation here between classical scholarship, antiquarian research, and excavations at Troy (soon to be labelled 'archaeological') underscores the problematic issue in this debate: the purpose and audience of unearthing antiquity.

Indeed, it seems class connotations influenced many distinctions between antiquarians and archaeologists, beyond the milieu of the learned society. In the wake of this controversy, *The Daily News* declared that

> [t]he order of topographical and archaeological research is quite uniform. First, we have the scholar who has been in possession of the Trojan plain for two thousand years and more; then the surveyor, who gives us the accurate features of the ground; and lastly, the man with the spade and pickaxe.[36]

This journalist expressed admiration for Schliemann's biography and, importantly, for his excavations at Hissarlik, even if he suggested those remains might not be of Homer's Troy. This makes the rather dismissive description of the excavator – presented as a rather newfangled non-expert against the surveyor's accuracy and the scholar's pedigree – all the more remarkable, but such embedding of class into terminology is consistent with Levine's and Heringman's accounts of attitudes towards 'professionalisation' and the elision of 'knowledge workers'.[37]

This was not the first time that the relevance of such investigations, and social status of participants and audiences, had been conflated, and contended, by journalists. Earlier descriptions of excavations shared concerns raised by the Antiquaries' controversy over the relevance of archaeological activity, social status of participants, and ultimate paymaster. In 1837, for example, a short item nestled between society notices complained of diplomats 'excavating the ruins of Carthage'. It continued, 'if the British Consul at Tunis is paid for poking about the ruins of Carthage, the sooner his "grog is stopped," and he is dismissed. . .the better'.[38] Repetition of Sir Thomas Reid's position emphasizes *The Age*'s indignation over this perceived misuse of public funds. Another 'cheap, radical, satirical journal'[39] was similarly incensed a decade later, asking whether 'archaeology. . .is the proper occupation for a well-paid dignitary of the Church?'. *The Satirist*'s rather lengthy complaint grumbled that '[a]rchaeology is doubtless mighty well in its way but to our minds. . .people have far greater missions in this world than going about grubbing up old bones and stones. . .with a genteel highwaymanship'. The real grievance, again, was funding. Of course it made better copy for journalists to assume priests and diplomats were neglecting their day jobs to indulge in amateur archaeology, which meant the taxpayer was effectively paying unauthorized bills: 'if people have other business of a high and important character, and for [which] *the public* right well pay them for, ought not the public to ask a query or two touching archaeology?' [emphasis original].[40]

Between these two complaints, *John Bull*'s description of 'archaiological research' [sic] reinforces popular perceptions (and reality, especially in the early nineteenth century) of an elite network of antiquarians engaged in the sort of treasure-hunting espoused by Lowe and the British Museum. 'At noon on Tuesday last' began the report, which was also sandwiched between society notes, 'a numerous company of noblemen, ladies, and learned antiquarians, with a retinue of five carriages, passed through Saffron Walden, from the princely mansion of Audley End. . .to visit the incomparable and celebrated Tumuli of the ancients'.[41] The labourers who presumably created the 'excavation three feet wide, seven high, and thirty-eight long' are not mentioned at all, despite the emphasis on the 'considerable expense' required to excavate all seven tumuli.[42]

Later in the century, *John Bull*'s 'Foreign Intelligence' column bemoaned the systematic lack of funding for British archaeology. The journalist, 'A Roman correspondent of the *Pall Mall Gazette*', contrasted French, German, and Italian budgets with 'the chance subscriptions' on which '[t]he English are entirely dependent'.[43] This emphasis on tourists – presumably the ladies 'new to Rome' who attended the lecture paraphrased here – is significant. In contrast to the armchair subscribers anticipated during the Antiquaries controversy, their presence indicates the changing dynamics of, and growing audience for, archaeology. Developing concepts of professionalization had led the British and American Archaeological Society to seek visiting lecturers from Oxford and Cambridge. At the same time, excitement sparked by Schliemann's display of 'Priam's Treasure', and the increased accessibility of travel, created larger audiences for archaeological research, which, in turn, was packaged for still wider readerships. This article acknowledged the financial crisis which made it an especially 'bad time' to seek 'assistance' with lecturers' travel expenses. The juxtaposition with details of this crisis renders even more striking the shift in implied approval ratings, which clearly indicates a change in the ways that excavations, archaeologists, and antiquarians were defined.

'The Foot and Hand of History' or 'The Science Which Treats of the Ancient World of Man': Shifting Descriptions of Archaeology[44]

Changing attitudes in the press towards the cultural status of excavations correlate to the proliferation of explanations which treated archaeology as a discrete discipline. Central to these definitions were accounts of the archaeologist's activities. Unsurprisingly, Schliemann's excavations at Hissarlik were crucial in shaping such discourses: only a few months after the Antiquaries' controversial funding request, *The Pall Mall Gazette* predicted that Trojan discoveries 'will certainly constitute an epoch in the study of archaeology'.[45] Seven months later, *The Daily News* described how '[t]he labours of Dr Schliemann have been conducted with that effective modern weapon of controversy, the spade'. Repetition of this Herculean phrasing emphasizes the heroic overtones of 'indomitable courage and perseverance' which successive biographies would uphold.[46]

Other accounts, however, saw Schliemann's 'enthusiasm and happy credulity' as symptomatic of a wider clash between amateurs and specialists.[47] These reveal the scientific, objective expectations increasingly implicit in understandings of archaeology. For example, *The Examiner* admitted 'that gentleman's ability as an explorer' but judged 'the enthusiasm which produces such splendid tribute from the past is just that very qualification which unfits the man from becoming an archaeologist of the first authority'.[48] The issue of 'archaeological judgment' also worried William Stillmann, writing for *Cornhill Magazine*, one of the most influential shilling monthlies.[49] Although excited by 'this mysterious site' of Hissarlik and keen to locate Homer's Troy, Stillmann was nonetheless convinced that '*this* is not the ruin of the sacred city' [emphasis original]. His lengthy, considered, analysis strikingly combines criticism of Schliemann's archaeological research with belief in the existence of Homer's Troy. Again, funding, or 'what most real archaeologists have not – money', emerges as 'an important point in archaeological research'. Yet even as responses to Schliemann generated clearer definitions of archaeology, criticisms that 'Homer was his guide-book' echo those levelled against much earlier topographers and antiquarians. Even as the scale of his excavations ushered in a new era, 'this inquisitive German' defined the opposite of Stillmann's archaeologist. 'It is unfortunate', he confided, 'that the enthusiastic Doctor has so little archaeological knowledge or judgment that we can accept none of his conclusions as of any authority'.[50]

Later definitions show that lines between antiquarianism and archaeology, associated with artistic enthusiasm and 'inductive process', respectively, continued to be fluid. In 1885, the 'inaugural address' of the British Archaeological Association's annual meeting – which was reported at length in *John Bull* – offered an official explanation of the discipline.[51] Sir James A. Picton, an architect and Fellow of the Society of Antiquaries, directly addressed the question 'What is archaeology?', which, he said, some members had recently been asked by tourists. *John Bull*'s generous paraphrase explained that:

> archaeology might be defined as that study which connected the past with the present by its visible monuments. It was distinguished from written history, which was the record of human actions and motives. Ancient architecture had been defined as history in brick and stone, but this was only one department of archaeology, which embraced in addition works of art of every description on which human minds and hands had been employed. . .The province of archaeology was to discover, arrange and classify these phenomena, and connect them with the written records of ages gone by. Beyond these records, where they failed entirely, the Cimmerian darkness was illuminated by the researches of the archaeologist, who took up the relics of the long-buried past, and, by the inductive process of arrangement, classification, and comparison, presented inferences as to the condition and progress of humanity in prehistoric times, not less certain, and in many respects more trustworthy, than the written records of history.[52]

It is noticeable that this confident definition – which implies excavation without using this term – relies on other disciplines while, despite emphasizing systematic categorization, its inclusion of 'works of art' would not exclude taking Homer's *Iliad* as a tour-guide. Furthermore, 'antiquarian wealth' and 'antiquarian research' feature later in this keynote speech, and the remainder of the article described stereotypically antiquarian 'pleasant excursion[s]', suggesting its implicit subsumption within this demarcation of archaeology.

The definition of archaeology against other subjects is a recurring feature of explanations, whether for adults or children, in expensive or cheap publications. *Kind Words*, a Sunday School Union publication, had offered a more capacious definition to its middle-class 'little readers' when explaining, two decades earlier, how the Grimm Brothers were 'the greatest philologists and archaeologists'. The general outline of 'these long titles', however, corresponds with that in Picton's lecture: 'as *archaeologists,* anything that was old or ancient attracted their attention' [original emphasis].[53]

As that lecture made clear, the line between archaeology and history had long been well defined: indeed, the account of excavations near Saffron Walden in 1840 suggested intense rivalry between 'our historians' belief in the tumuli's Saxon origin and the 'strictly Roman' contents unearthed by 'antiquarians'. The boundary between excavating antiquarian and archaeologist, on the other hand, continued to be blurred. Citing a dictionary entry from 1899, Levine notes this 'casual and common assumption that antiquarianism and archaeology were identical, particularly in antiquarian circles where so many belonged to what were dubbed archaeological societies, hindered the development and formation of a separate self-image'.[54]

In contrast, and despite the fact that many eighteenth-century antiquarians had been barrow-diggers, 'the most characteristic activity which classified archaeology throughout the century was excavation'.[55] Nonetheless, it was not only those who complained of Schliemann's enthusiasm or disagreed with his results who labelled his excavations as antiquarian. A piratical 'yarn' on 'hidden treasure' in *Every Boy's Annual* cautioned, in 1881, that 'it is not given to every seeker after wealth to come upon such a glorious "find" as that which has recently set agog the world of antiquarians; we refer, of course, to Mr Schliemann's well-earned success at Mycenae'.[56]

The much earlier casual conflation of 'the archaeologist and the antiquary' in *The Ladies' Cabinet* was understandable in relation to the Crystal Palace collections; however, several years after the Chair in Classical Archaeology had been established at Oxford, the editor of *Young Folks* perpetuated this fusion of 'antiquarian and archaeologist'.[57] This is more surprising since descriptions of antiquaries did not usually include excavation but focussed on collections. *Chatterbox*, a halfpenny magazine aimed at providing moral instruction to working-class children, did not paint a favourable picture. One story from 1870 classified 'The antiquary' as:

> an old gentleman who wanders about in a shabby coat, short trousers, dusty boots, a tall ill-shaped hat, an old-fashioned neck-cloth, and high collar. In his hand he carries a gingham umbrella, however fine the weather may be, lest the old books or engravings which he purchases should get wet.

This is a far cry from portrayals of Schliemann as exemplary hero – whether labelled archaeologist or antiquarian – in other children's periodicals. While the antiquary in this story made his living cheating poor families, another *Chatterbox* item two decades later added a comic spin to this dim outlook. In relating how a legacy of diaries left to the British Museum had been ignored, the writer asserted that all hundred volumes contained only 'ludicrous trifles'. Since the author specifically mentions a pet parrot, this misleading anecdote must have concerned William Cole's bequest, which specified his antiquarian manuscripts and diaries remain unopened for twenty years, until 1803.

These negative views of antiquarianism were challenged by more substantial definitions of archaeology's disciplinary origins and identity. *The Girls Own Paper*, which sustained a detailed series entitled 'Archaeology for Girls' in 1894–1895, began by reassuring readers that 'archaeology has rather an alarming appearance, and a learned sound, but in reality its literal meaning is simple enough'.[58] This article immediately signalled its – and the discipline's – scholarly pedigree by providing its etymology, in Greek script. It also differentiated archaeology and archaeologists from the

> kindred, we may almost say synonymous, words, "antiquarian" and "antiquary" [which] formerly were used in quite a different sense, and usually signified a collector or discoverer of antiquities. . .from a dealer in such wares, to a learned archibishop [sic].[59]

As the writer hastened to claim,

> [t]he word "archaeologist" has never been used in such a wide sense as this, though it is no longer restricted to its original signification, and although we call such men as Layard, Smith, Bonomi and Schliemann, archaeologists, yet we do not restrict the term to indicate those alone who discover and write about classical antiquities.[60]

Not long after, another British Archaeological Association keynote further elaborated on what marked out archaeology from previously defined areas of study. The speaker, the Venerable R. Thornton, Archdeacon of Middlesex, declared (according to *The Standard*'s paraphrase) that 'antiquarianism has become archaeology, and had changed from mere collecting of antiquities into a true science of investigation, and in this way, as chronology had been termed the eye, so archaeology had become the foot and hand of history'.[61] Fundamental to such definitions was the link between archaeology and science. Citing Schliemann's excavations at Mycenae, Thornton continued to explain '[t]he position of archaeology among the sciences'.[62] Similarly, the second instalment of 'Archaeology for Girls' (apparently forgetting the 'wide range' denoted by the eschewed term antiquarianism) explained that archaeology 'includes art, literature, history, manners and customs, and almost everything that relates to ancient peoples, their costumes and their monuments'.[63] Although the eighth instalment would caution that 'neither history nor archaeology are abstract sciences and what they tell or teach can at best be only approximately true', this chapter confidently asserted that '[t]his vast range of knowledge. . .certainly places it [archaeology] under the head of science rather than art'.[64]

Most tellingly, archaeology was casually included alongside other sciences when *St Nicholas* printed an invitation to join a scientific society which already boasted 5,000 members.[65] Its aim was that 'the boy who lives in the remotest village can send his bit of stone' to '[m]ore than fifty gentlemen representing all departments of science'.[66] While this letter juxtaposed archaeology with coleopterology (the study of beetles) and mineralogy, *The Monthly Packet*'s 'Letters on Geology' taught church members that '[a]rchaeology, or the science which treats of the ancient world of man may be said to. . .take up the world's history where geology leaves it'.

The most precise instance of disciplinary demarcation, however, appears in the first instalment of 'Archaeology for Girls'. The subject which was felt to encroach most upon archaeology's territory was architecture, especially of ancient buildings. A remarkable Venn diagram (see Figure 7.2) delineates each area's speciality and overlaps.[67] The variety of these definitions and perceived disciplinary interrelationships shows Shuttleworth and Cantor's 'conduit' model in action: especially in children's periodicals which assumed knowledge, or felt compelled to provide more or less detailed explanations. Archaeology's identity, in each case, was affected by that of participants and readers, as well as chronological developments.

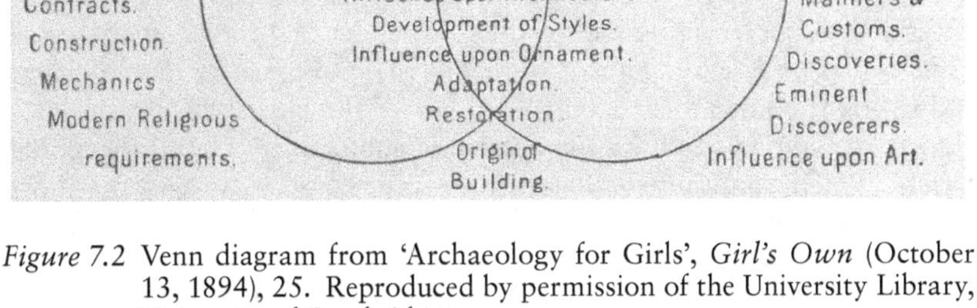

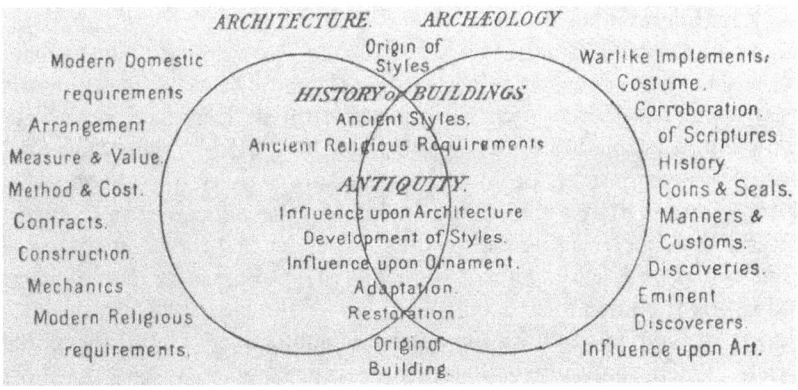

Figure 7.2 Venn diagram from 'Archaeology for Girls', *Girl's Own* (October 13, 1894), 25. Reproduced by permission of the University Library, University of Cambridge.

'Peculiarly Adapted to All Cyclists': Popular Acceptance of Archaeology as a Discipline

Widespread awareness of archaeology as a discrete academic discipline is signalled, just as effectively, by the number of casual references which relied on familiarity with a shared concept of the subject. From the 1880s, such detailed definitions were, often, no longer perceived as necessary. This is particularly striking in women's and children's publications. It is clear that this follows from the increasing accessibility and appeal of archaeology, not least through the opportunities and information perpetuated in these titles.

Reports of the burgeoning women's education movement routinely featured archaeology as an academic discipline. In 1878, the *Journal of the Women's Education Union* listed archaeology in its lecture-list; in 1880, *The Girl's Own Paper* included it as an optional subject for women studying at Cambridge University and in 1898 also explained it was one of the subjects taught in adult-education 'women's clubs' in America.[68] Moreover, the *Women's Penny Paper* in 1889 reported that 'Miss Annie E. F. Barlow. . .gave a very interesting description of her travels before the Lancashire and Cheshire Antiquarian Society'. Further on, when noting that 'Miss Brodrick gave her first lecture on Egyptology at the British Museum on Saturday', the compiler took the predominantly female audience as evidence that '[t]he taste for archaeology among women is rapidly increasing'.[69]

The accessibility of museums and sites, as well as formal education, was a major factor in heightened public interest in archaeology. Reports of first-hand encounters in the press, as well as fictional versions, reached still wider readerships. An American child's letter to *St Nicholas* revealed that viewing 'some of the things which Doctor Schliemann has dug up' was a highlight of her European trip.[70] A story in *Boy's Own Paper* featured a more melodramatic 'Trip to Mycenae'.[71] A very different 'archaeological excursion' was imagined by *The Ladies' Treasury*, in a romantic story which featured a protracted tour of a British 'Druidical' site.[72]

As the 'Cycling Hobbies' article illustrates, such 'archaeologising' was, thirty years later, promoted as a leisure activity for 'anyone'. Erskine enthused that archaeology (to which she allocated most space) 'gives a new zest to riding and reading'. The fact that this women's magazine contrasts '[r]eading about old ruins in a close, stuffy town library, and seeing the same after a sharp ride under the blue sky' substantiates reports of women studying the academic subject. Erskine's foresighted article, which maintained cycling had 'come to stay', is also the most striking example of when archaeology needed no explanation, even in a non-academic environment.

An emphatic instance of archaeology as a particularly suitable example of women's education features in a romance from *The Monthly Packet of Evening Readings for Members of the English Church*. Surprisingly, given this religious affiliation, Frances Awdry (aunt of *Thomas the Tank Engine*'s creator) presented her heroine's failure to attend church in a positive light. When her sister complained, her father 'hope[d] that the glow of delight Mr Carter's account of Schliemann's Trojan discoveries gave Lucy is worth the damage done'. Contemporary links between Homeric and biblical archaeology are not only taken for granted in the curate's courtship conversation, but made exemplary for the maxim (clearly intended to support women's education): 'it makes *all* women of far more use in the world to have cultivated minds'.[73]

Archaeology was often perceived as an archetypal serious subject. Acknowledging her fellow cyclists' likely idea of archaeology as 'dry and uninteresting' (drawing on the tradition of 'dryasdust' antiquarians, after Walter Scott's fictional dedicatee of *Ivanhoe* and source in *The Antiquary*), Erskine agreed: 'so it is – if one gets hold of a textbook crammed thickly with dates and periods, with a substantial dusting of technical terms and Latin to season it. . .then it is as dry as dry can be'.[74] She defended the subject rousingly, however, claiming that 'somehow, in archaeology one can take it pleasantly', especially after a bicycle ride.

Peter Parley's Annual for 1885 also exploited academic associations. Early in an eleven-page discussion of electricity, archaeology's reputation proved a point: 'you may call lead heavy, and you may call that lecture on archaeology you went to heavy, without mixing up the metal with the discourse'.[75] Five years earlier, *Peter Parley* had encouraged readers to try Schliemann's books, commenting that 'the Doctor's visit to Ithaca reads like a story'. Since this annual was a customary Christmas gift, many of its consumers probably received both volumes. As in the 'Cycling Hobbies' article, *Parley*'s readers were cautioned that Schliemann's accounts were 'full of dry archaeological details', but promised that his book 'also contains much more popular matters'. Using pictures of Schliemann's Trojan loot to jog readers' memories (or catch their attention), the article began by assuming that

> most of you no doubt heard of the name of Dr Henry Schliemann, the gentleman who claims to have found the real site of Homer's City of Troy, as well as the original treasure of the great King Agamemnon, which he recently exhibited at the South Kensington Museum.[76]

Avoiding any discussion of archaeology per se, this twenty-page discussion focussed on Schliemann as moral exemplar whose perseverance, determination, and hard work, along with divine intervention, turned bad luck into good fortune. Many similar didactic invocations of Schliemann also helped orient readers, usually more briefly as 'the discoverer of Troy' or 'the greatest excavator of modern days'.[77]

A biography published between these two examples, however, claimed that Schliemann's archaeological activities have 'been so fully open to the public that we need not say anything about it here'.[78] This was in *Boy's Own*, which catered to a diverse readership of 'boys, old and young'[79] and was celebrated by contemporary observers as 'the only first class magazine which has forced its way into the slums as well as the best homes'.[80] *Young England* also assumed readers' familiarity with archaeology as a discipline. As with *Peter Parley*'s explanation of electric light, archaeology provided the starting-point for detailed explanation: in this case, of the nature of coal. Before getting on to the details of its biological composition, the author used the layered ruins at Hissarlik to explain stratigraphy:

> The investigations of Dr Schliemann on the supposed site of the city of Troy furnish a good example of this method of research. He found lying, one on the top of another, traces of the existence of five successive communities of men, differing in customs and social development.[81]

This more detailed reference does draw out the relevance of the comparison for those who did not possess sufficient requisite knowledge. Nonetheless, it is striking that, once again, readers were expected to be familiar with Schliemann, and to understand the archaeological analogy as well as that of a 'messy cupboard in a tenanted house'.

The balance between knowingness and didacticism, especially in children's periodicals, was exploited in fiction too. This was often for comic effect: one story in *St Nicholas* commented that 'nowadays people are discovering everything' and cited the example of 'Dr Schliemann, who has discovered all the old kitchen-ware of the ancient Trojans', before introducing its fictional conceit: 'another explorer has just found out about some young Centaurs who went to old Chiron's school'.[82] Here, even as the Trojan finds are purportedly explained, the expectation is that some readers would appreciate the comic inaccuracy of the description of the current display of 'Priam's Treasure'.

A later archaeological adventure-story, aimed at older readers, played more extensively with their expected knowledge. The third chapter of an illustrated serial followed the exploits of a British family excavating overseas. Entitled 'in the trenches', it name-dropped excavations 'at Susa, at Mycenae, at Pompeii', before highlighting those at Hissarlik. The accompanying image, in the style of depictions of Schliemann's trench at Hissarlik, emphasized its scale (see Figure 7.3). As the 'little archaeologists' are forced to explain the value of excavation to a sceptical German professor, the hero scores a point: 'I need not remind you of the Trojan researches of your compatriot Schliemann'.[83] For readers familiar with criticisms of using Homer as a 'guide-book', the dialogue between young

A traveller was approaching.

Figure 7.3 'A traveller was approaching': Laurie, 'Mystery at Ecbatana', *Boy's Own* (March 21, 1891), 389. Reproduced by permission of the University Library, University of Cambridge.

hero and pompous German professor would have extended the comic reversal of the usual explanations and disparagements of Schliemann's research. The analogy between real and fictional excavation is strengthened by the fact that the supposed location, Ecbatana, was, like Troy, familiar from classical literature.[84] Additionally, it remained unexcavated until 1913, making Hissarlik the clear model for this story.[85]

These similarities are further pronounced by the debate between British excavator and German professor. Kerdic 'hold[s] that in a matter of archaeology tradition is one of the safest guides you can follow'. Echoing generations of Homeric pilgrims, he points to the 'plain. . .dotted with tumuli'. 'To an archaeologist', he explains, 'these tumuli speak in a loud voice; they say: "We cover ruins, old buildings, traces of palaces, of ramparts; scratch us, dig into us, turn us inside out, and you will find them!"'. The professor ridicules these 'accommodating tumuli [which] say what you wish them to say': it is significant for the overwhelming impression of sympathy with Schliemann's romantic perspective, however, that his criticism ironically echoes enthusiastic responses to Schliemann's excavations at Hissarlik, such as that published by Karl Blind, a German revolutionary refugee, who rejoiced that '[t]he very stones have spoken – *saxa loquuntur* – to say that Ilion once was'.[86]

This story, from 1891, was inspired by the learned discourses which surrounded Schliemann's excavations at Hissarlik and which shaped expectations and definitions of archaeological excavation. Literary journals *Cornhill*, *Fraser's*, and *Macmillan's*, as well as the weekly illustrated *Graphic* newspaper, had all printed detailed criticisms with comic overtones. The excavations on 'the mole-hill of Hisarlik' were openly dubbed an 'archaeological joke' while the 'so-called Scaean Gate, and Priam's Palace' was said to 'resemble rather a jumble of Irish hovels than a royal abode' and renamed 'the palace of Priam's pig'.[87]

It was not, of course, new for archaeologists and antiquarians to inspire jokes, but – as *Punch*'s cartoons about Gladstone's Homeric enthusiasm showed (see Figure 7.1) – shifts in the target of the satire offer a litmus-test for wider perceptions and knowledge of the subjects. In 1848, *The Satirist* had printed a poem in response to the recent unrolling of an Egyptian mummy at the British Archaeological Association's annual meeting.[88] The poem – which punned on the 'mummery' surrounding the dramatic revelation – lampooned the surgeon Thomas Pettigrew as one of the society's 'grave, solemn *savans*' pursuing, Frankenstein-like, 'the deep mysteries of science'. In mock-defence of this irreverent approach, the poet vowed in conclusion not to 'stoop to apology/For having thus dwelt on a subject so great/As that of sublime archaeology'.

A key complaint of this poem was that such Egyptological research 'puzzled the critics, though versed in reviewing'. The problem of perceived audiences for antiquarian and archaeological discoveries persisted, even as the expected level of awareness changed. By 1887, for example, a father who thought a Professor of Archaeology must study

Noah's Ark was the butt of a joke in *Boys of England*. This joke laboured his misunderstanding: since 'Bible says there ain't going to be no more floods. What do you want with arks?'. Importantly, while the joke highlights its biblical pun, it assumed that readers understood Dr Stoneage's subject. The penny paper *Funny Folks* not only expected its 60,000 readers to decipher anagrams of archaeologists' names and appreciate references to 'Dr. Stealman' and Schliemann's 'dis*con*veries' but even, in a parodic diary format mimicked by *Fun* the following month, mimicked the Homeric descriptions and specific identifications bestowed on objects unearthed by Schliemann at both Hissarlik and Mycenae.[89] The frequent lack of explanations in these cheap publications – *Fun* was even '[k]nown as the 'Poor Man's *Punch*' – suggests that their enormous readerships were expected to know, or infer, detailed knowledge about Schliemann's publicity.

Despite the increased circulation of such a wide variety of discourses surrounding archaeology, an 1881 cartoon sketch in *Fun* shows that the issue of who was perceived to know about archaeology was still a sore point with comic potential (see Figure 7.4). Entitled 'Caught Out', it depicts the meeting at a Roman Camp between an 'Archaeologist, who knows little of Cricket, and Intelligent Rustic, who knows nothing of Archaeology'.[90] The butt of this joke is not so much archaeology but, rather, the assumption or lack of knowingness which cuts both ways, across class boundaries. Punning on 'caught out' in cricket parlance, and on the shared name, Julius Caesar, of Roman emperor and recently deceased professional cricketer, this dialogue could have been ascribed to a historian, classicist, or antiquarian. The choice of archaeology further underscores its disciplinary identity within popular, as well as learned, discourses.

Archaeology, as well as antiquarianism had, as we have seen, been portrayed as archetypal serious subjects even before archaeology gained an independent identity. Back in 1848, *Punch* had mocked 'an energetic Archaeologian' for his interest in barrows and for the customary phrase of reading papers 'upon the wall'. The accompanying cartoon (see Figure 7.5) showed a portly gentleman and his audience perched precariously on a ruined, buttressed structure. *Punch* was not only spoofing the phrasing. Rather, the lecturer is described as a *savant*, as were those who witnessed the unravelling of Pettigrew's mummy earlier that year. *The Satirist*'s poetic tribute then had warned of the dangers of 'wander[ing] from truth in obliquity'.[91] Dwelling on the lecture's detail 'brick by brick. . .and hanging upon the coping with affectionate tenacity', *Punch* shares this concern with the dangers of obscurantism and specialist jargon.[92] After discovering his audience melted away, this unfortunate lecturer 'was wheeled home in what was supposed to be his favourite vehicle'.[93] The comic literalism, punning on barrow graves and wheelbarrows, underscores the real consequences of communication failures between specialists and wider publics.

F A F
CAUGHT OUT.
(SCENE—*A Roman Camp. Archæologist, who knows little of Cricket, and Intelligent Rustic, who knows nothing of Archæology, conversing.*)
Intelligent Rustic.—"AH! FINE CHAP 'E WERE, TOO, SIR, JULIUS CÆSAR!"
Archæologist.—"HE WAS, INDEED, MY FRIEND!"
I. R.—OI BESTED 'UN ONCE, THOUGH! FORTY YEARS AGO, MEBBE! PLAYIN' SUBSTITOOT. CAUGHT 'UN HOIGH UP IN AIR I' MY LEFT 'AND! SET OUT TO RUN, 'E 'AD!"

Figure 7.4 'Caught Out', *Fun* (May 25, 1881), 207. Reproduced by permission of the University Library, University of Cambridge.

Schliemann's self-promotion did clearly communicate his findings to newspaper readers. As this overview of archaeological jokes before and after the discovery of Troy suggests, his publicity made excavations at Hissarlik a clear watershed, not only for the formal emergence of the

Figure 7.5 'More Archaeology', *Punch* (August 12, 1848), 72. Reproduced by permission of the University Library, University of Cambridge.

discipline of archaeology itself but also for the public perceptions which continued to shape, and be shaped by, learned discourses. The combination of Schliemann's amateurism and enthusiasm alongside the high cultural stakes in proving the historicity of Homeric epic, even while regarded as joke by many, refocussed the debate about what archaeology could, or could not, hope to achieve.

Excavation as the 'Way to the Truth': The Cultural Importance of Popular Understandings of Archaeology

Troy's cultural importance had, in the early nineteenth century, been asserted primarily by elite writers. Towards the end of the century, their 'works. . .upon the subject' would be denounced by *The Morning Post* on the charge of 'form[ing] a literature to themselves'.[94] In contrast, *The Monthly Packet* assumed all its 'readers are well aware that there are two serious claimants for the honour of having been the very site' of Homer's city.[95] This assumption is rather odd, since its target market was young girls, whereas *The Pall Mall Gazette,* aimed at those more likely to have followed the controversy, confessed only two years later that '[t]o all but professed or amateur archaeologists, the purpose of Dr. Schliemann's repeated volumes on the Troad must seem rather hard to understand'.[96] Only expecting readers to remember 'some curious discoveries at Hisarlik', this journalist seems sensitive to the increasing disciplinarization and professionalization of archaeology as ever more scientific excavations seemed to close the brief window which had enabled so many to participate in complex debates over Troy's existence as well as to share in the wonder of discoveries.

'One of the most remarkable features of the present time', claimed an article entitled 'The Historian's Pickaxe', was how 'the pickaxe and the shovel are made to contribute to our knowledge of remote history, as exemplified in the recent marvellous discoveries of Dr. Schliemann on the supposed site of the City of Troy'.[97] Archaeology's new significance in the popular imagination was its ability to link two areas of cultural importance: the Bible and classical culture. John Murray's advert for *Troy and Its Remains* quoted *The Standard's* belief that '[i]t is questionable if any archaeological discovery of greater interest was ever made than that which Dr Schliemann has accomplished'.[98] Still more extravagant than this claim that 'interest in Nineveh and Babylon pales before that which we feel in Troy' was the *Methodist Quarterly*'s conviction that 'none have dug so satisfactorily to the classical scholar as Schliemann. . .[who] appealed to the logic not of the pen but of the pick ax and spade. . .[and] dug his way to the truth'.[99] The *Girl's Own* series on archaeology clearly also built towards affirming the 'corroboration which archaeology affords to the truth of Scripture narrative'.[100] In a telling overlap between adult and children's periodicals, it recirculated to a fresh audience *Quarterly Review*'s stark impression that Hissarlik 'stands henceforth as a lasting witness' not to modern progress, but rather, 'to the progressive decay of civilisation, industry and wealth among the successive races of the inhabitants'.[101] This is far more than a 'subtle fear of decay';[102] rather, Troy – as visible symbol of unearthed antiquity – became both 'a beacon and a warning'.[103]

Such anxiety over the implications of excavated evidence affected attitudes towards archaeology. Ancient discoveries intimated both longevity and failure of modern technologies: spoof articles '[b]y the Dr. Schliemann of the future' and serious proposals to create a 'Pompeii for the twenty-ninth century' by preserving artistic, literary, scientific, and technological endeavours in time-capsules beneath Salisbury plain both suggest sharpened anxieties over how the present fit between past achievements and future progress. 'Excavations into the mysteries of antiquity are the order of the day',[104] noted the *Methodist Quarterly* but, as a parodic report of the gold found at Mycenae warned, 'there are finds which are losses'.[105] Once again, *Hearth and Home*'s journalist would identify an important aspect of archaeology in the wider imagination. As she somewhat flippantly wrote:

> [i]t is the fashion to look on our forefathers as a set of semi-savages, but when archaeologising it begins to dawn on the mind, that if they had not had cycles, or trains, they were no fools for all that.[106]

Despite the variety of ways in which archaeological discourses were packaged in popular print media, these diverse items for heterogeneous readerships paint a similar picture of how contributors and readers responded to the emergence of archaeology as a recognizable discipline. Over the course of the nineteenth century, and particularly after debates over excavations in the Troad in the 1870s, different branches of the press played an important role in shaping, forming, and facilitating discourses about the identity and purpose of archaeology, as well as its perceived social relevance.

The nascent discipline of classical archaeology was delineated through the broadcasting, satirizing, adulating, and advocating of the activities of its practitioners to a variety of readerships. Because newspapers and periodicals marketed ephemeral content to lasting consumer-bases with established identities – even if readers disagreed with specific content – they offer potent insights into how wider publics engaged with the development of an academic discipline.[107] As wider understanding was fuelled by reports of excavations and descriptions of finds, public interest generated yet more archaeological content. This also created a sufficiently stable disciplinary identity among readers to enable satirical, comic content. While some explanations were influenced by, or deliberately exploited, still-fluid associations with 'antiquarian's spade' and 'historian's pickaxe', both archaeology and antiquarianism were, by the end of the century, confidently defined in didactic publications.[108] Such explanations, especially in children's periodicals which were 'one of the most widely consumed forms of entertainment in late Victorian Britain', provide vital evidence for assessing the circulation and popular perception of knowledge.[109] The complicated relationship between disciplines, in this case between antiquarianism and archaeology, echoes that between classics and theology (Chapter 9), science and literature (Chapter 11), and musicology and every other discipline (Chapter 12).

Erskine explained to her fellow female cyclists that 'it makes things so much plainer, and more real to see the relics of a past age'; she especially advocated the power of archaeology to 'compare the past with the present'. This was an era when travellers feared the fates of ruined classical sites might befall 'our own country'; Dore's depiction of Macaulay's iconic New Zealander in the ruins of London resonated powerfully. The articles surveyed here not only heighten our perception of the types of archaeological knowledge available and their social distribution but also show how such a contentious subject formed a vital part of the nineteenth-century cultural landscape. Classical archaeology offers a particularly complex, and visible, example of print media's active formation of the publicly recognized identities of new disciplines and their popular understandings in nineteenth-century Britain.

Notes

1 F. J. Erskine, 'Cycling hobbies', *Hearth and Home* (May 7, 1896), 997.
2 Lena Wånggren, 'The Freedom Machine: The New Woman and the Bicycle', in *Transport in British Fiction: Technologies of Movement, 1840–1940*, eds. Adrienne E. Gavin and Andrew F. Humphries (New York: Springer, 2015), 123.
3 F. J. Erskine, *Lady Cycling* (London: Walter Scott, 1897).
4 Philippa Levine, *The Amateur and the Professional: Antiquarians, Historians and Archaeologists in Victorian England 1838–1886* (Cambridge: Cambridge University Press, 1986), 57; Nicholas Oddy, 'The Flaneur on Wheels?', in *Cycling and Society*, eds. Dave Horton, Paul Rosen, and Peter Cox (Farnham: Ashgate, 2007), 97–112, on 103–105.
5 Roger Smith 'The Physiology of the Will: Mind, Body and Psychology in the Periodical Literature, 1855–1875', in *Science Serialised: Representation of the Sciences in Nineteenth-Century Periodicals*, eds. Geoffrey Cantor and Sally Shuttleworth *Periodicals* (Cambridge, MA: Massachusetts Institute of Technology, 2004), 81–110, on 83. As p. 84 points out, seeking an origin narrative could be 'misguided'.
6 Kathryn Prince, *Shakespeare in the Victorian Periodicals* (Abingdon: Routledge, 2008), 15.
7 Gowan Dawson, Richard Noakes and Jonathan R. Topham, 'Introduction', in *Science in the Nineteenth-Century Periodical*, Geoffrey Cantor, Gowan Dawson, Graeme Gooday, Richard Noakes, Sally Shuttleworth and Jonathan R. Topham (Cambridge: Cambridge University Press, 2004), 1–36, on 2.
8 Articles from GALE's *19thC UK Periodicals* and *British Library Newspapers* databases.
9 Richard Noakes, '*Punch* and Comic Journalism in mid-Victorian Britain', in *Science in the Nineteenth-Century Periodical*, Cantor, Dawson et al. (Cambridge: Cambridge University Press), 91–122, on 122.
10 Cantor and Shuttleworth, *Science Serialised*, 4.
11 Smith, 'Physiology of the Will', 82.
12 *Ibid.*, 83, 98.
13 Levine, *The Amateur and the Professional*, 88.
14 E.g. H. C.'s letter to *The Times* ('Greek Archaeology' (April 3, 1873), 12) emphasized Frank Calvert's prior excavations at Hisarlik. See further A. C. Lascarides, *The Search for Troy* (Bloomington, IN: Lilly Library, 1977); J. M. Cook, *The Troad* (Oxford: Oxford University Press, 1973), 14–44.
15 See Bryant Davies, *Troy, Carthage and the Victorians: The Drama of Classical Ruins in the Nineteenth-Century Imagination* (Cambridge: Cambridge University Press, 2018), 47–124.
16 See David Gange, *Dialogues with the Dead: Egyptology in British Culture and Religion, 1822–1922* (Oxford: Oxford University Press, 2013), 142–149.
17 Gillian Wallace, 'Archaeology and Society', in *Handbook of Archaeological Theories*, eds. R. Alexander Bentley, Herbert D. G. Maschner, and Christopher Chippindale (Lanham, MD: Rowman & Littlefield, 2009), 395; Brian M. Fagan and Nadia Durrani, *Brief History of Archaeology: Classical Times to the Twenty-First Century* (Abingdon: Routledge, 2015), 88–92, on 92; Steven R. Pendery, 'Urban Archaeology', in *The Oxford Companion to Archaeology*, eds. Brian M. Fagan (Oxford: Oxford University Press, 1997), 327; Linda Ellis, 'Classical Archaeology', in *Archaeological Method and Theory: An Encyclopaedia*, ed. Linda Ellis (Abingdon: Routledge, 2003), 102.

18 Charles E. Orser, Jr., 'Historical Archaeology', in *Oxford Companion*, ed. Brian M. Fagan (Oxford: Oxford University Press, 1997), 667–673, on 667; Wallace, 'Archaeology and Society', 395.
19 Susanne Duesterberg, *Popular Receptions of Archaeology: Fictional and Factual Texts in 19th and Early 20th Century Britain* (Bielefeld: transcript Verlag, 2015), 25, notes popularization as not solely a process of simplification, but creating additional discourses.
20 W. H. Mason, 'Homer and Dr. Schliemann', *Macmillan's Magazine* (September 1876), 454.
21 E.g. *The Times* ('Editorial' (March 27, 1873), 9) claimed to support public funding of Trojan excavations if they 'were on the coast of Great Britain'.
22 Anthony Snodgrass, 'What Is Classical Archaeology?', in *Classical Archaeology*, eds. Robin Osborne and Susan E. Alcock (Hoboken, NJ: John Wiley & Sons, 2012), 13–29, on 17.
23 E.g. 'The Treasures of King Priam', *Morning Post* (August 18, 1873), 7.
24 'Antiquarian Research at the Public Expense', *Huddersfield Daily Chronicle* (March 27, 1873), 3. *The Leeds Mercury* ('Royal Society of Antiquaries' (March 8, 1873), 11) printed a very full account of the paper and discussion on the same day as it appeared in *The Times* as 'The Siege of Troy' (March 8, 1873), 5.
25 'The Site of Troy', *Daily News* (March 26, 1873), 4.
26 J. Lewis Farley, 'Homeric Troy', *The Times* (March 27, 1873), 11; 'Topics of the Week', *Graphic* (April 4, 1873), 311.
27 'The Site of Troy', 4; Lewis Farley, 'Homeric Troy', 11.
28 See further: Bryant Davies, *Troy, Carthage and the Victorians*, 47–66.
29 'Topics of the Week', 311.
30 See David Gange and Rachel Bryant Davies, 'Troy', in *Cities of God: The Bible and Archaeology in Nineteenth-Century Britain*, eds. David Gange and Michael Ledger-Lomas (Cambridge: Cambridge University Press, 2013), 39–70.
31 Percival Leigh, ed., *The Rt. Hon. W.E. Gladstone, M.P.: Cartoons from the Collection of "Mr. Punch"* (London: *Punch*, 1878), No. 34. See image and further discussion in Bryant Davies, *Troy, Carthage and the Victorians*, 55–66.
32 'My Old Friend Homer', *Punch* (December 14, 1872), 247.
33 On Gladstone's Homeric scholarship, see Gange, *Dialogues with the Dead*, 12–18, 116.
34 'The Site of Troy', 4.
35 'Editorial', *The Times* (March 27, 1873), 9.
36 'London', *Daily News*, (April 24, 1874), 5.
37 Levine, *The Amateur and the Professional*; Noah Heringman, *Sciences of Antiquity: Romantic Antiquarianism, Natural History, and Knowledge Work* (Oxford: Oxford University Press, 2013).
38 'Table Talk', *The Age* (April 9, 1837), 115.
39 Noakes, '*Punch* and Comic Journalism', 96.
40 'Archaeology and Its Advantages(?)', *The Satirist* (August 4, 1849), 353.
41 'Ancient Tumuli', *John Bull* (April 27, 1840) 195. See Levine, *The Amateur and the Professional*, 96, for barrow-excavations as spectator-sport.
42 Ibid.
43 'Foreign Intelligence', *John Bull* (January 11, 1879), 19.
44 'The British Archaeological Association', *Standard* (September 22, 1896), 6; 'Letters on Geology: XI', *Monthly Packet* (November 1, 1866), 488.
45 'The Treasure of Priam', *Pall Mall Gazette* (October 2, 1873), 5.
46 'London', *Daily News* (April 24, 1874), 5.

47 William Stillmann, 'Homer's Troy, and Schliemann's', *Cornhill Magazine* 663–674 (June 1874), 670.
48 'Literature: Mycenae', *Examiner* (January 19, 1878) 77–79.
49 Ibid., p. 670.
50 Stillmann, 'Homer's Troy', p. 668; 674; 670; 666; 673. See Bryant Davies, *Troy, Carthage and the Victorians*, 5–7.
51 'British Archaeological Association', *John Bull* (August 29, 1885), 566.
52 Ibid.
53 'B.C.', 'Great Writers and Little Readers', *Kind Words* (June 7, 1866), 180.
54 Levine, *The Amateur and the Professional*, p. 31.
55 Ibid., p. 88.
56 Lieut. C. R. Low (late), 'The Hidden Treasure', *Every Boy's Annual* (1881), 585.
57 H. G. Adams, 'Courts of the Crystal Palace', *Ladies' Cabinet* (December 1, 1856), 309; Levine, *The Amateur and the Professional*, 171; 'The Editor's Chair', *Young Folks Paper* (September 22, 1888), 189.
58 'Archaeology for Girls [1]', *Girl's Own*, (October 13, 1894), 25.
59 Ibid.
60 Ibid.
61 'The British Archaeological Association', *Standard* (September 22, 1896), 6.
62 Ibid.
63 'Archaeology for Girls [2]', *Girl's Own* (November 17, 1894), 105; 'Archaeology for Girls [8]', *Girl's Own* (May 18, 1895), 521.
64 'Archaeology for Girls [2]', p. 105.
65 'The Letter-Box', *St Nicholas* (March 1, 1883), 396.
66 Harlan H. Ballard, 'History of the Agassiz Association', *Science* (January 28, 1887), 95.
67 'Archaeology for Girls [1]', p. 25.
68 'March and April Calendar of Classes open to Women in London', *Journal of the Women's Education Union* (March 15, 1878), 58; 'Our Own Colleges', *Girl's Own* (August 7, 1880), 502; Dora de Blaquière, 'After-School Education', *Girl's Own* (September 3, 1898), 772.
69 'Current News About Women', *Women's Penny Paper* (October 26, 1889), 2.
70 Mamie Charles, 'Letter-Box', *St Nicholas* (October 1, 1878), 828.
71 Revd E. E. Bradford, 'Our Trip to Mycenae', *Boy's Own* (September 19, 1896) 808.
72 'Too Rich for a Husband', *Ladies' Treasury* (June 1, 1866), 309.
73 Frances Awdry, 'Lucy's Romance', *Monthly Packet* 197–221 (December 1, 1881), 206.
74 Erskine, 'Cycling hobbies', 997.
75 'The Electic Light', *Peter Parley's Annual* 95–105 (1885), 95.
76 'Dr. Henry Schliemann', *Peter Parley's Annual* (1880), 82.
77 'Our Letter Box', *Young Folks* (October 25, 1879), 303; 'Reached His Goal', *Chums* (October 28, 1896), 156.
78 'Boys who have risen', *Boy's Own* (July 28, 1888), 699.
79 'Odd Fellow', 'Still more fun from the classics', *Boy's Own Paper* (March 17, 1883), 398–399.
80 Marjory Lang, 'Childhood's Champions: mid-Victorian Children's Periodicals and the Critics', *Victorian Periodicals Review* 13/1/2 (1980), 17–31, on 28.
81 J. Arthur Thompson, 'The Natural History of Coal', *Young England* (undated), 460.
82 Evelyn Müller, 'The Boys at Chiron's School', *St Nicholas* (November 1, 1879), 40.

83 A. Laurie, 'Maurice Kerdic; or the Mystery at Ecbatana', *Boy's Own Paper* (March 21, 1891), 388.
84 Herodotus, *Histories* 1.98–99.
85 Trevor Bryce, *Routledge Handbook of the Peoples and Places of Ancient Western Asia* (London: Taylor & Francis, 2009) 212.
86 Karl Blind, 'Troy Found Again', *Antiquary* (May 9, 1884), 202.
87 Mason, 'Homer and Dr. Schliemann', 456; Stillmann, 'Homer's Troy, and Schliemann's', 669; 'Simpson's Drawings in Asia Minor and Greece', *Graphic* (May 4, 1878); William Simpson, 'The Schliemannic Ilium', *Fraser's Magazine* (February 1878), 232.
88 'Archaeological Society. —Unfolding a Mummy', *Satirist* (September 9, 1848), 380.
89 'Hermetic Anagrams', *Funny Folks* (January 11, 1879), 10: 'Lady A. Harris' for 'Sir A H Layard'; 'Mrs. Ann Childe' for 'Dr. Schliemann'. 'With Dr. Schliemann', *Funny Folks* (January 6, 1877), 2; 'Multiple News Items', *Funny Folks* (March 24, 1877), 91; 'What We Hope Dr. Schliemann Will Discover', *Funny Folks* (February 3, 1877), 36; 'The Latest Relics', *Fun* (March 21, 1877), 116. See also 'The Hero of Mycenae', *Funny Folks* (May 12, 1877), 45 which vaguely explained Schliemann 'has won renown by finding a good many things'.
90 'Caught Out', *Fun* (May 25, 1881), 207.
91 'Unfolding a Mummy', p. 380.
92 Noakes, '*Punch* and Comic Journalism', 101; 108.
93 'More Archaeology', *Punch* (August 12, 1848), 72.
94 'Journals of Travel in Egypt and Turkey', *Morning Post* (July 26, 1869), 2.
95 George Washington, 'A Day in the Troad', *Monthly Packet* (July 1, 1881), 83.
96 'Troja', *Pall Mall Gazette* (December 28, 1883), 5.
97 'The historian's pickaxe', *Graphic* (July 3, 1875), 14.
98 'Troy and its Remains', *John Bull* (May 1, 1875), 296.
99 'Quarterly Book Table: *Troy and Its Remains*', *Methodist Quarterly* (July 1875) 521–522, on 521.
100 'Archaeology for Girls [2]'.
101 'Archaeology for Girls [5]', *Girl's Own* (February 16, 1895), 315.
102 Duesterberg, *Popular Receptions of Archaeology*, p. 328.
103 'The Trojan Horse; or Siege of Troy explained', *Blackwood's Edinburgh Magazine* (February 1836), 225.
104 'Quarterly Book Table', p. 521.
105 'The Hero of Mycenae', p. 45.
106 Erskine, 'Cycling Hobbies', p. 997.
107 James A. Secord, *Victorian Sensation: The Extraordinary Publication, Reception, and Secret Authorship of Vestiges of the Natural History of Creation* (Chicago: University of Chicago Press, 2000), 351.
108 'From our Constantinople Correspondent', *Times* (June 5, 1876), 12; 'The Historian's Pickaxe', 14.
109 K. Boyd, *Manliness and the Boys' Story Paper in Britain: A Cultural History, 1855–1940* (Basingstoke: Palgrave Macmillan, 2002), 49–50.

8 Victorian Autobiography, Child Study, and the Origins of Child Psychology

Roisín Laing

Introduction

In her study of Jean Piaget's clinical method, Susan Jean Meyer observes that Piaget's first book, *The Language and Thought of the Child* (1923/1926), opens, '[f]or whatever combination of reasons', with a detailed analysis of the speech of two six-year olds.[1] The combination of reasons for Piaget's interest in childhood language deserves more attention, in view of his influence on psychology. Mayer herself argues that Piaget's 'distinctive "clinical method" [that is, the clinical interview] generated the findings that created the field of developmental psychology and that continue to frame developmental research to this day'.[2] An examination of some of Piaget's antecedents in the late nineteenth century will illustrate that its focus on childhood language marks Piaget's clinical method as the product of an amorphous, interdisciplinary theoretical field which emerged as part of the non-Darwinian revolution.

It is no coincidence that there was unprecedented interest in childhood in the Victorian period. Peter Bowler has shown that Charles Darwin's *The Origin of Species* (1859) 'converted the scientific world to evolutionism'.[3] As Deborah J. Coon argues, this conversion instigated the revolutionary process of 'secularizing the soul . . . repackaging it . . . as the "self"', and thereby hastening the 'birth of psychology' in the late nineteenth century.[4] Carolyn Steedman has demonstrated that the clearest expression of the 'interiorized self' which was to replace the Christian soul is found in the idea of childhood in the nineteenth century.[5] The emergence of a specific psychology of the child, in the protean field of Child Study, was therefore inevitable in the final decades of the Victorian period.[6]

The same search for selfhood in childhood accounts for the proliferation of autobiographical accounts of the child's interiority which followed the pioneering opening chapters of Charlotte Brontë's *Jane Eyre* (1847).[7] As Jonathan Loesberg asserts, '[a]utobiography is self-making'.[8] That so many Victorians wrote fictional and non-fictional autobiographies suggests that self-making was a vital process in the period. That many such autobiographies open with detailed accounts of childhood experience suggests that, for many authors, the self was made in childhood. Child psychology and its counterpart in autobiography flourish in the late Victorian period because to study childhood was to study the self in an era in which that self was newly necessary.

Although, as this suggests, *The Origin of Species* had a revolutionary effect, it was not Darwin's non-progressive model of evolution by natural selection, but other, progressive models which revolutionized Victorian culture.[9] This chapter will lay out the argument that Child Study and autobiography of childhood experience are unmistakably inventions of the non-Darwinian revolution, because they both attempt to construct a specific type of selfhood. Within the specifically progressive evolutionary world view of the late nineteenth century, the Christian soul was replaced by a psychological self which was, likewise, fundamentally progressive.

In her analysis of the intersection between the emergent discipline of scientific Child Study and contemporaneous autobiographical accounts of childhood, Sally Shuttleworth observes, in passing, that '[t]he spur' for the invention of Child Study 'appears to have been evolutionary debates about language acquisition'.[10] This chapter will demonstrate that the emergence of disciplines devoted to the study of childhood during the period betrays a widespread effort, sustained across discourses, to formulate a specifically progressive model of selfhood, and that language acquisition is the 'spur' for this effort because it offers a clear line dividing the developing child from the self which is its end. In other words, the fascination with language acquisition in Child Study and in autobiography of childhood experience epitomizes the non-Darwinian revolution from which both discourses emerged.

Analyses of autobiographical work from the Victorian period have generally followed two major patterns which belie the significance of a progressive evolutionary model of childhood. First, most critics focus largely on autobiographical work by men like Charles Darwin, John Ruskin, Thomas Carlyle, John Stuart Mill, and John Henry Newman.[11] Jenny Bavidge has argued that 'authors of imaginative literature for children . . . [were] presumed to have a (childlike) insight into children's lives of feelings, [and] to be possessed of a unique ability to remember back into their own childhoods' in the period.[12] Many such authors were women.[13] To focus on the autobiographies of eminent Victorian men is therefore both to understate the centrality of childhood to the period's evolutionary discourse, and to disregard the prevalent view that children's authors had particular expertise in this area.

Second, those critics who do discuss autobiographies of childhood experience have largely focussed on the extent to which a Victorian ideology of childhood can be read in such work.[14] This chapter will show that the non-Darwinian revolution had a determining influence on the ideology of childhood, because it propagated that search for a progressive model of selfhood through which dedicated studies of childhood emerged in the late Victorian period.

To examine the role of progressive evolutionism on the invention of Child Study, and on autobiography of childhood experience, and to explore the characteristics of the ideology of childhood proliferated through these responses to the non-Darwinian revolution, this chapter will discuss the work of one of the most successful authors of the late Victorian period, Frances Hodgson Burnett, in comparison with the work of some of the most prominent practitioners of Child Study, and particularly the work of its leading pioneer in Britain, James Sully. Burnett was a prolific author, who wrote for a range of audiences, but she was, and remains, celebrated primarily for her novels for children.[15] As such, Burnett's autobiographical account of early childhood, *The One I Knew the Best of All* (1893), would have been considered at least as significant a contribution to debates about childhood as comparable accounts by more distinguished contemporaries. Through his major academic contribution to Child Study, *Studies of Childhood* (1895), and, more directly, through the many articles he contributed to such non-specialist journals as *Longman's Magazine*, Sully was perhaps the most effective advocate for the professionalization of Child Study in the Victorian period.[16]

Sully's work corroborates the suggestion that Burnett's views would have carried particular authority in Victorian debates about childhood. Although the claim that 'the grace of childhood may almost be said to have been discovered by the modern poet' is, inevitably, substantiated with reference to Wordsworth and Blake, it is clear that, from Sully's perspective, contemporary writers, including many women, have contributed work of more value for an evidence-based study of childhood.[17] George Sand receives particular attention in *Studies of Childhood* but Sully notes, regretfully, that'[s]ince this was written the authoress of *Little Lord Fauntleroy* has shown us how clear and far-reaching a memory she has of her childish experiences'.[18] Burnett's most successful work is a metonym for her expertise. While, as Sully notes, '[t]he appearance of Darwin's name among those who have deemed the child worthy of study' gives status to the science of Child Study, the autobiographical work of experts like Burnett is the evidence based on which Child Study can claim to be scientific at all.[19]

Through an analysis of Burnett's autobiography, Sully's discussions of contemporary autobiographical work by Pierre Loti and George Sand, and contemporary psychological studies of childhood and of selfhood, this chapter will demonstrate that the origins of child psychology in the revolutionary period following the publication of *The Origin of Species* are evident in the function which childhood performs, as an origin for a progressive model of selfhood, in autobiography and Child Study of the era. For Burnett, and for Sully and his peers in the field of Child Study, the remembered child is the self before language. By acquiring language, and using it to articulate the child's experience, the adult resolves the disjunction between self and language which this Other self, the childhood self, represents. In other words, Child Study and Victorian autobiography present selfhood as the adult expression of a childhood impression of the self. Each thus informs the other to offer a model of selfhood in which the child is the origin to the adult self as an end.

The implications of this model extended far beyond the individual child or self under scrutiny. First, one of the most prominent alternatives to Darwinian evolutionism in the late nineteenth century was the theory that ontogeny recapitulates phylogeny; that the development of the child recapitulates the development of the human species. Seen through this dominant theoretical filter, autobiographical and psychological studies of childhood as a progressive development towards adulthood are commensurate with studies of evolution as the progressive development of the human species. The recapitulation of progressive individual development in the evolution of the human species suggests that Child Study was invented, and autobiography revolutionized, in response to the late nineteenth-century need for a progressive model of evolution, in which the human species retained its place as the high-point and end.

Second, both the theoretical and the methodological characteristics of Victorian Child Study can be traced in twentieth-century developmental psychology. Marylène Bennour and Jacques Vonèche note that 'Piaget's only contact with Darwin came through the reading of [Henri] Bergson's (1907/1911) *Creative Evolution*, [in which evolution] . . . is meaningful and purposefully directed'.[20] In Bergson's work, there is 'a hierarchy of beings from the inferior to the superior culminating in spiritual life'.[21] Contemporary overviews of Piaget's theory of cognitive development indicate that it implies a comparable hierarchy of cognitive processes. A 'theory of the development of intellectual *competence*', the brilliance of which lies in the insight that children 'not only know *less*, they know differently'; Piaget's theory evidently at least allows cognitive development to be imagined as 'the *progressive* and increasingly complex *advancement*' of cognitive processes.[22] Ideas about progressive development constitute the theoretical basis of Piaget's clinical practice in 1923, and, through him, in developmental psychology throughout the twentieth century.

These ideas are evinced in the method which Piaget developed and which is now a cornerstone of clinical practice in developmental psychology. In his overview of the clinical interview, Herbert P. Ginsburg argues that 'the interviewer attempts to uncover the thoughts and concepts underlying the child's verbalizations. . . [The] goal is to understand the underlying thinking, to enter the child's mind'.[23] As will be argued, the clinical method in which the (adult) interviewer first elicits the (child) subject's 'verbalizations', and then interprets these to 'uncover' the child's thinking, is predicated on an idea of specifically progressive individual development, which thus recapitulates the non-Darwinian model of species development.

In 1855, Anna Jameson called for a view of the self in which childhood and adulthood were integrated. The seemingly paradoxical model of selfhood as a 'progressive whole', proposed by Jameson, is formulated in the symbiosis between Child Study and autobiography from which child psychology emerged.[24] The late nineteenth-century origins of child psychology offer a progressive model of selfhood, and thus illuminate the co-dependence of debates about human evolution and about child development in Victorian culture.

Autobiography and Child Study in the Victorian Period

As Richard Coe observes, '[e]very authentic account of childhood of necessity relies mainly upon memory'.[25] Of the problems this raises, 'the reliability (or arbitrary unreliability) of memory' was perhaps the most pressing for Victorian autobiographers, because of the intense scepticism with which memory was viewed in the psychology of the era.[26] William James, for example, insists that 'the object of memory is only an object imagined in the past . . . to which the emotion of belief adheres'.[27] George Stout and Wilhelm Wundt, James's peers in Britain and Germany, respectively, were comparably sceptical.[28] Shuttleworth has noted that Victorians in general were also 'obsessed with the horror of the lie'.[29] Victorian autobiographers were consequently required to present a convincing defence against the serious imputation that their work was misleading.[30]

Burnett's defence is simply to refute the premise on which the charge is based. Perhaps capitalizing on the credibility she enjoys as a prominent children's author, Burnett declares that 'after all the years that have passed I remember with equal distinctness the thoughts which were in the Small Person's mind'.[31] Whatever psychology might have uncovered about memory does not apply to Burnett, whose memory is entirely reliable.

It suits the purpose of Child Study to accept such claims. Burnett would undoubtedly have been among those authors who, Sully claims, have a 'gift of sympathetic insight' into the child-mind.[32] In 1891 Sully contributed an article about a recently published autobiography, Pierre Loti's *Le Roman d'un Enfant* (1890), to *Longman's Magazine*, in which he attributes to Loti the same powers of memory which Burnett will subsequently claim to authenticate her autobiography. Not only was the child Loti 'subject to powerful impressions which . . . remained indelibly graven on the memory'.[33] The narrative actually 'surpasses in retrospective reach all other records of childish experience' (p. 202).

As in *Studies of Childhood*, Sully invokes Darwin's name to lend scientific authority to such claims.[34] He points to the parallel between Loti's claim that 'the welling up of new childish emotion . . . causes the image of the moment to penetrate into the very texture of the mind, never to be dislodged', with the fact that 'Darwin tells us that he preserved to the end a picture of the exact aspect of the old tree or bank where, as a Cambridge undergraduate, he made a good capture of beetles' to validate the assertion that Loti has 'photographic registration of sense impressions' (p. 205). According to Sully's analysis, in *Le Roman d'un Enfant* Loti has offered the reader photographic, indelible, and exceptionally early memories of childhood experience. For Sully as for Burnett, the charge of falsity or fictionality simply does not apply to the autobiographical memories of that select group of adults who retain a rare degree of identification with their childhood selves. Victorian psychologists are only lately beginning to receive recognition for their influence on Sigmund Freud. Without wishing to perpetuate the view that Freud's work had no antecedents, the idea that anyone's mental processes are entirely reliable seems distinctly pre-Freudian, and unsustainable after Freud.

A second charge is less easily deflected, even before Freud, than the accusation of autobiographical deceitfulness. Coe claims that 'if there *is* any value in childhood experience, it lies in the fact that this experience is unique'.[35] If this had been the Victorian view, autobiographers of early childhood experience would have been unavoidably susceptible to the accusation of what Loesberg calls 'a morbid, debilitating over-involvement with self'.[36] However, Victorian autobiographies of childhood experience were valuable largely insofar as that experience was *not* unique. Shuttleworth notes that 'the representative quality of the individual portrait' lends scientific authority to autobiography, in a fundamentally symbiotic relationship where Child Study, reciprocally, can use autobiographical memories of an individual's childhood experience as evidence for claims about the child-mind in general.[37] This role in scientific study also enables the authors of autobiography of childhood experience to circumvent the accusation of self-obsession.

Thus, Burnett's autobiography is presented as 'an attempt to understand the working of the child-mind by studying one particular example in detail',[38] but this is not only, or even primarily, to invest her work with scientific authority. Indeed, when Burnett claims that 'I might fairly entitle [the autobiography] "The Story of *Any* Child with an Imagination"', she does so to insist that she is accordingly 'absolved from any charge of the bad taste of personality' (p. vii). Burnett's autobiography is not a testament to the uniqueness of her childhood experience, and consequently to her debilitating obsession with herself. It is, instead, a source of enabling insight into the child we all once were.

Burnett's claim that her self-portrait is representative deflects the charge of 'personality', but, once again, such claims also suit the purposes of Child Study. Sully asserts that the mind uncovered in Loti's autobiography might be that of any child: Loti has 'the true feeling' not just for his *own* 'child-nature' but 'for child-nature' itself, and 'its original way of envisaging things' (p. 200). Likewise, although Sully's review of George Sand's autobiographical *Histoire de ma Vie* (1855) opens with the admission that '[t]he reader need not be told that the child who was to become the representative among modern women of the daring irregularities of genius was an uncommon child', 'close inspection shows that the untamed and untameable "oddities" were, after all, only certain common childish impulses and tendencies exalted, or, if the reader prefers, exaggerated'.[39]

Sully's analyses of autobiographical accounts of Sand's childhood experiences can consequently be reproduced in his seminal contribution to the study of the child-mind itself. Although '[t]he early recollections of George Sand', which Sully summarizes in 'A Girl's Religion' (1890), 'furnish what is probably the most remarkable instance of childish daring in fashioning a new religion', this account forms the basis and main evidence for Sully's analysis of children's religious beliefs in general in *Studies of Childhood*.[40] In the latter text, Sand's experiences illustrate, 'no doubt, a true *childish* aspiration towards the great Unseen, and also an impulse to invent a form of worship which should harmonise with and express the little worshipper's individual thoughts'.[41]

In short, then, 'the gifted child seems not less but more of a child because of his gifts'.[42] Exceptionally intense childhood experience – which Loti, Sand, and Burnett all claim to have had – paradoxically epitomizes childhood experience itself and, conveniently, leaves an indelible trace on the adult's memory. The claims of Sully's Child Study are validated because they are based on the testimony of authors who are both extraordinarily able to recollect childhood, and representative in the experiences they had. Through this symbiosis with scientific discourse, the same authors circumvent many of the charges to which autobiographers in general were susceptible.

The Content of Children's Minds

The reciprocity between an emergent autobiography of childhood experience and the newly invented discipline of Child Study operated in the context of that revolution in humanity's understanding of itself propagated by Darwin's evolutionary theory. This context is palpable in the specifically progressive model of selfhood which is formulated at the interface between the two discourses. The defining features of the child as it is conceptualized in the study of language acquisition in both discourses enable a concept of growth as progress and adult as end. The child in both autobiography and Child Study individuates, reflects, and validates Victorian tenacity to the idea of progressive evolution.

Psychologists conducted their search for a progressive model of selfhood through what Sully, in a characteristically flippant essay entitled

'Baby Linguistics' (1884), calls 'venerable and learned disputes about the exact relation of speech to thought'.[43] Sully proposes that these disputes 'may some day be amicably settled by a reference to that most unimpeachable of testimonies, the babblings of infancy' (p. 111). He is fully aware that this is not an entirely 'fanciful . . . supposition' (p. 111). The earliest contributions to, and 'spur' for, Child Study – Darwin's 'Biographical Sketch of an Infant' (1877) and Hippolyte Taine's 'On the Acquisition of Language by Children' (1877) – were studies of the child's acquisition of language, and of what that process might say about the relationship between language and mind.[44] Nearly two decades later, in a major contribution to the now established discipline, William Preyer presents his analysis of the development of language in children as a response to exactly that question, '*Is there any thinking without words?*'[45]

The very title of Preyer's chapter, 'Development of the Child's Intellect Independently of Language', indicates that his answer to the question '*Is there any thinking without words?*' is a definite affirmative.[46] The introductory paragraph of the chapter actually dismisses the opposite view outright as a 'prejudice' which is 'at least unproved'.[47]

Sully's view is consistent with Preyer's. In *Studies of Childhood*, he argues that:

> [t]he growth of a child's speech means a concurrent progress in the mastery of words and in the acquisition of ideas. In this each of the two factors aids the other, the advance of ideas pushing the child to new uses of sounds, and the growing facility in word-formation reacting powerfully on the ideas, giving them definiteness of outline and fixity of structure.[48]

In 'Baby Linguistics', Sully claims that '[l]anguage is the "*instrument* of thought"' because a word can 'symbolise a whole class of objects' (p. 113). *Studies of Childhood* indicates that the instrument in this metaphor is both mechanical and musical. Language helps to produce thought, but it also expresses thought which has already taken place.

Two key points emerge from these studies. First, the child is, by definition, without words. Second, the child is nevertheless capable of abstract thought. Such a view is entirely consonant with what Burnett remembers about her own childhood self. That Small Person is also capable of thought, and incapable of articulation. Burnett states that 'I recognise that [the Small Person] was too young to have had in her vocabulary the *words* to put her thoughts and mental arguments into—and yet they were there, as thoughts and mental arguments are there today' (pp. 8–9). Similarly, recollecting 'the first social difficulty of the Small Person', in which she is confronted with 'the overwhelming problem of how to adjust perfect truth to perfect politeness', Burnett observes that '[l]anguage seems required to mentally confront this problem' (p. 10). Although 'the

Small Person cannot have had words', Burnett insists that it is '*certain* that she confronted and wrestled with it' (p. 10, emphasis added). As in foundational texts in the emergent discipline of Child Study, the child in Burnett's autobiography is a mute receptacle for insight.

This idea of the child's inarticulate insight reveals the interdependence of ideologies of childhood and debates about progressive evolution in the Victorian period. Herbert Spencer, a prominent contributor to both debates, encapsulates their co-dependency in the claim that 'the genesis of knowledge in the individual, must follow the same course as the genesis of knowledge in the race', 'hence the fundamental reason why education should be a repetition of civilization in little'.[49] According to Bowler, this theory of recapitulation 'was non-Darwinian in character because it encouraged the belief that evolution shares the progressive and teleological character of individual growth', but ontogeny can only recapitulate a teleological phylogeny if childhood is conceived as a primitive stage in the progress towards adulthood as a goal and end-point.[50] The developmental model of progressive species evolution depends on a concept of the child as a narratable origin to a stable end.

When Burnett, Sully, and so many others insist that the child has the capacity for thought but not for speech, they conceptualize the child in exactly these terms. They present the child as a primitive (because pre-linguistic) ancestor to the fully articulate adult. Piaget's clinical interview operates on the basis of comparable ideas. His method is based on the conviction, shared by Burnett and Sully, that the child's thinking exceeds her language. Like Burnett's Small Person, Piaget's child-subject is not literally mute, but she is effectively so; and like those authors who, for Sully, could provide evidence of the child's mind because of their 'sympathetic insight', Piaget's interviewer must 'display a sense of respect' towards her subject, and show that she is 'deeply interested' in the child's mind.[51] Consequently, just as Burnett's task as a (remembering) adult is to interpret and articulate the Small Person's thoughts, the task of Piaget's (interviewing) adult is to interpret and (re)articulate the thoughts of her child-subject. In positioning certain, sufficiently sympathetic interviewers as authoritative interpreters of the child's limited 'verbalizations', Piaget's clinical method repeats the dynamic which characterizes Child Study, in which the articulate adult can both access and articulate the child's mind.

In such studies, the child's mind is imagined to be at a lesser stage in the progressive development of the human self. However, throughout the Victorian period at least, it is also imagined to elude the difficulties which the adult self encounters. Coe observes that, in autobiographies of childhood, 'the use of rational language . . . destroys the child's "intuitive" relationship with the world', particularly because it 'creates difference between the self and the object': language is the difference between the adult and the child, and between the divided and the coherent self.[52]

The child's mind contains an impression of a self which is coherent because it is undivided by language.

This idea that the content of the child-mind in some way transcends adult problems is clear in the conclusion to Taine's foundational essay in Child Study, which insists that 'all the shades of emotion, wonder, joy, wilfulness and sadness are expressed by differences of tone' in the child's 'twitter': 'in this she equals or even surpasses a grown up person'.[53] By suggesting that the child has superior emotional range, Taine evokes that idea of the child's purer receptiveness or sensitivity to impression which already had such a long history in nineteenth-century literature.[54] This marks a small but telling departure from Darwin. Both Darwin and Taine associate emotions with the early stages of racial or individual development. However, Taine implies that to identify with childish emotion imbues the adult with the child's intuitive insight. Darwin asserts that the human expression of emotion supports 'the conclusion that man is derived from some lower animal form'.[55] For Darwin, the human expression of emotion is evidence of an animal ancestry which many considered debasing. For Taine, the adult expression of emotion is evidence of a childhood which many saw as transcendent.

Thus, when Preyer insists that the child 'shows plainly . . . [that] long before . . . the first successful attempt to express himself in articulate words . . . he combines ideas in a logical manner—i. e., he *thinks*', he not only insists that the child is capable of thought before he is capable of speech but also makes this claim in a context in which *what* the child thinks is seen by many as in some way superior to what the adult thinks.

Neither Taine nor Preyer refers explicitly to the child's impression of the self. However, the interchange between Child Study and autobiography aligns the objective of the former with the self-making function which the latter self-evidently performs. As Lyubov G. Gurjeva argues, for psychologists 'the study of children was the study of the inception of the human mind'.[56] Scientists and authors study the same subject – the child-mind – in response to the same problem – the problem of the self in the era of evolution.

This is emphatically clear in 'Baby Linguistics', which concludes with an analysis of the relationship between the development of language and of self-consciousness. Sully focusses on a child called Clifford, to observe that the process of 'generalising', which has begun prior to language, is revealed by Clifford's misapplication of the word 'papa' (p. 116) to refer to all men. The correction of this error, in 'the act of distinguishing between his father and other men[,] followed rapidly . . . the first use of his own name' (p. 116). Thus, Clifford's eventual ability to use the word 'papa' correctly 'clearly involved a dim apprehension of the special relation of things to himself' (p. 116): 'the recognition of kindred grew out of self-reflection' (p. 117). The articulation of perception by the child studied in 'Baby Linguistics' is analyzed in terms which equate the development of the child's language with the development of adult selfhood.

The Adult Self as a Progressive Whole

Child Study defines the child in terms of both its '"intuitive" relationship with the world' and its developing language.[57] The same characteristics define the representative Small Person of *The One I Knew the Best of All*. Burnett's text clarifies how this 'child', reimagined in the emergence of scientific and autobiographical Child Study, invokes a coherent yet progressive adult self. The relationship between childhood and selfhood portrayed in *The One I Knew the Best of All* is one in which the adult simultaneously identifies with, and has progressed beyond, the child. Burnett can thus identify with the unified child-mind, and, by articulating that mind, establish her own authorial adult self as the end to the developmental process which the child embodies.

The identity of retrospective adult with insightful child is figured in the Small Person's precociously writerly sensitivity. Burnett wonders '[w]hether as impression-creating and mind-moulding influences, Literature or the Doll came first into [the Small Person's] life' (p. 44). Her answer is that:

> [i]t is not in the least likely she did not own dolls before she owned books, but it is certain that until literature assisted imagination and gave them character, they seemed only things stuffed with sawdust and made no special impression.
>
> (p. 44)

The Small Person is precociously responsive to story. This reveals that the author, Burnett, is latent within, and can therefore retrospectively identify with, that Small Person.

However, although Burnett claims that '[i]t was not until Literature in the form of story, romance, tragedy, and adventure had quickened her imagination that the figure of the Doll loomed up in the character of an absorbing interest' (p. 50), her phrase can be inverted in as far as it accounts solely for the Small Person's experience. That it is story, rather than literature or story-in-language, which Burnett identifies as the Small Person's primary interest, is clear when she recalls her frustrated bewilderment that her Nurse could 'learn a couple of verses of a song suggesting a story, and not only neglect to learn more, but neglect to inquire about the story itself' (p. 46). For the child, the language of the song is incidental to the story which it serves to communicate.

The Small Person is thus comparable with, but, crucially, a limited or – to use an evolutionary term – primitive form of the adult author. Jenny Bourne Taylor observes that *The One I Knew the Best of All* 'stress[es] the psychic and social role of play, above all, in the creation of *miniature* worlds'.[58] The miniature status of the Small Person's play, with dolls and with stories, connotes its limited, primitive status. The separation Burnett introduces between the writing 'I' and her diminutive Other self, the 'Small Person', likewise implies that the adult author has transcended the limitations inherent to the Small Person's miniaturized insight.

In writing about the Small Person, Burnett is therefore indulging in the same 'pleasures of miniaturisation' which, as Gillian Beer observes, were available to Victorian writers through the theory of recapitulation.[59] By playing a miniaturized version of adult activities, the Small Person in Burnett's autobiography, and the child in recapitulation theory generally, represents a primitive stage in an individuated (or miniaturized) version of progressive evolution. In other words, miniaturization, as depicted in the child's play in Burnett's and so many other autobiographical and scientific studies of childhood, implies both ontogenic and phylogenic progress towards the adult human as an end. Burnett's interest in her miniaturized childhood self is an interest in the miniaturized version of progressive evolution offered through recapitulation theory.

That Burnett is specifically interested in the *progressive* evolution of her self is clear in the moment when the Small Person comes to commit her first story to paper, to make the transition from story to story-in-language. This moment is imbued with significance. Burnett recalls that she:

> felt very still and happy, and as if she wanted to say or do something new, which would somehow be an expression of feeling and goodness and—and—she did not know at all what else . . . She turned slowly to the exercise-book again . . . A delightful, queer, and tremendously bold idea came to her. It was so daring that she smiled a little. 'I wonder if I could write—a piece of poetry'.
>
> (p. 194)

The significance of moment gestures towards the ultimate object of Burnett's 'record of the principal events which influenced the mental life of a Small Person' (p. 241), which is to narrate the development of the Small Person into language and, synonymously, into Frances Hodgson Burnett.

The chapter with which Burnett concludes her autobiography, 'The First One', is therefore, inevitably, the account of her first publication. The end of Burnett's story is her transition from remembered child into present author. After this transition, Burnett claims that the Small Person 'had crossed the delicate, impalpable dividing line. And after that, Life itself began, and memories of her lose the meaning which attaches itself to the memories of the Mind of a Child' (p. 325). The publication of a story in language represents the beginning of Burnett herself, and therefore the end of the story which led to that self. The story of the child's progression into language is the story of the development of the self.

On a species level, language acquisition has similarly profound implications. Darwin claims that '[w]hether primeval man . . . when his power of language was extremely imperfect, would have deserved to be called man, must depend on the definition we employ', and that it is therefore 'impossible to fix on any definite point when the term "man" ought to be used'.[60] Language is a sign, if not the defining characteristic, of humanity. Burnett's autobiography allows for no uncertainty on when language is acquired and, thus, on when the term 'adult' ought to be used. Since the Small Person not only represents any child but, through the theory of recapitulation, individuates her species, Burnett's evolutionism counteracts Darwin's. If the Small Person's growth is recapitulated in the development of the human species, it is entirely possible to fix on the point at which the process of evolution reaches its goal in 'man'.

Studies of language acquisition are therefore the spur for the invention of Child Study during the non-Darwinian revolution, because, as Burnett's autobiography makes clear, language acquisition is the ultimate sign not only of progress but also of end. Burnett's resolution to the opposition between the childhood self with whom she both identifies, and has progressed beyond, is a progressive story of the inarticulate child's development into an adult with language. The theory of recapitulation meant that this story is not only consonant with, but actually substantiates, progressive models of species evolution. *The One I Knew the Best of All* is a story of the progressive development of the human race.

The same story of progressive evolution is implicit in Child Study. At the start of 'Baby Linguistics', Sully observes that

> scientific fathers have been taking notes of the first utterances of their children, with as much care as if they might be expected to contain clear reminiscences of that exalted antenatal condition which some philosophers have ascribed to the soul.
>
> (p. 111)

The conclusion Sully draws from the connection between the child's ability to use his own name and his ability to distinguish his own father from other men shows that, once again, the significance Sully places on 'the babblings of infancy' is not as 'fanciful' (p. 111) as he first presents it to be. Biographical studies of children like Clifford have offered an insight into the relationship between 'that exalted antenatal condition' (p. 111) which, after Darwin, had to be attributed to the self, and the language which might be used to articulate that self.

As in Burnett's autobiography, however, that insight is qualified. If the child is defined by the absence of language, his insight is inarticulable. The development of Clifford's selfhood is aligned not with any insight into that selfhood which they have as inarticulate children, but with the acquisition of language which marks their entry into adulthood. This process is much more gradual than in Burnett's autobiography, but it is nevertheless a comparable model for selfhood. Like the Small Person, Clifford emblematizes the primitive selfhood contained within the child-mind. By articulating that mind, the adult can retain its unity and coherence, and register her own progress beyond its primitivism.

That language enables the adult's identification with and progress beyond the child is clear in Sully's analysis, in *Studies of Childhood*, of what he describes as the 'slow and irksome business' of acquiring 'pronominal forms'.[61] Sully suggests that the transition to the correct use of pronominal forms, and particularly to the use of first- rather than third-person pronouns in referring to the self,

> seems to be due in part . . . to a growing self-consciousness, to a clearer singling out of the *ego* or self as the centre of thought and activity, and the understanding of the other "persons" in relation to this centre.[62]

Note, he argues, that:

> self-consciousness *begins* with the use of 'I'. The child has no doubt a rudimentary self-consciousness when he talks about himself as about another object: yet the use of the forms 'I', 'me' may be taken to mark the greater precision of the idea of 'self' as not merely a bodily object and nameable thing just like other sensible things, but as something distinct from and opposed to all objects of sense, as what we call the 'subject' or *ego*.[63]

In this discussion of 'The Little Linguist' in general, Sully summarizes the premise of his own analyses of the individual child-mind in Clifford's biography, and the basis of Burnett's autobiography of childhood experience. Greater precision of the idea of the self is constituted through the expression of the child-mind by the articulate adult who identifies with that child.

This same idea is evident in the discussion of childhood, selfhood, and language offered in the most widely used textbook in psychology during the first decades of the twentieth century, Stout's *Manual of Psychology*.[64] Stout suggests that '[s]elf as a whole uniting present, past and future phases . . . [is an] ideal construction, built up gradually in the course of human development'.[65] However, this 'ideal construction of Self . . . is comparatively rudimentary in the lower races of mankind' (p. 226) because

> [i]n the case of the lower animals and young children, it is impossible, and in the case of savages it is difficult, to obtain verbal descriptions of their own mental states and processes . . . partly because

> they either do not use language, or use language inadequate to the purpose.
>
> (p. 21)

Language is essential for the 'ideational processes' through which moments of perception can 'unite to form a continuous system, such as is implied in the conception of a person' (p. 266). 'Lower races', and their individuated equivalent, children, are limited to what Stout calls 'the perceptual plane' (p. 266) as far as they are limited in the linguistic capacities which enable ideation.

Consequently, for the child 'there is no single continuous Self contrasted with a single continuous world', because, for as long as the child exists on a purely perceptual plane, the construction of Self has 'never begun' (p. 266). Stout thus offers the attainment of language as the end to the story (or 'ideational process' [p. 266], in his words) of the self. His theory of selfhood resolves the opposition between the identification with, and Otherness of, the child. The adult must both identify with the coherent self of the child-mind and have progressed beyond that child's primitive inability to use language. To resolve this contradiction in Victorian self-making by Burnett, Sully, and Stout, the child-mind is the primitive origin, and the adult's language is the end, to the progressive evolution of the self.

It is thus inevitable both that Piaget's model of cognitive development culminates in 'social reciprocity', and that that model is outlined through the analysis of children's speech.[66] Among adults,

> [o]ne's speech is a function of what the other speaker either ignores or already knows; we thus put ourselves in his place. . .with the firm purpose of influencing another. . .and knowing full well what is his frame of mind, so as to judge the effect produced.[67]

By contrast, 'when he soliloquizes in communion with the adult, the child does not differentiate between his own thought and his hearer's'.[68] Thus;

> [i]f egocentrism is an absorption of the ego in things and in persons, without differentiation of one's own point of view and other people's, this clearly shows that the child's use of speech, in what we call ego-centric language, is a particular case of this general phenomenon and may, in this respect, serve as a guide in analysing its evolution as a function of age.[69]

The child is 'egocentric', and it is this which defines her difference from the adult, whose social reciprocity, or sense of self in relation to others, is both emergent from and evinced by her speech.

This theoretical model is repeated in the clinical interview which Piaget pioneered. Piaget's interviewer must have sufficient sympathetic insight to identify with her subject. She must also have the ability to articulate what her subject cannot. Both are essential if the interviewer is to reliably articulate the subject's thinking, and together these seemingly contradictory qualities of identification and difference constitute the adult (interviewer) as the self towards which the child (subject) progresses.

The enduring impact of this idea of the progressive development of the child into a stable adult self is evident in studies in developmental psychology right up to the end of the twentieth century.[70] Thomas H. Ollendick and Michael W. Vasey, for example, critique the clinical effects of what Philip C. Kendall has called the 'developmental uniformity myth', whereby children of all ages are imagined to be alike: 'Quite obviously, a 4-year old's world and his or her interpretation of it is different from an 8-year old's and a 12- or 16-year old's'.[71] However, they are less attentive to their own version of the same myth. The assertion that 'Just as children differ from adults, so too do young children differ from older ones', treats all adults alike.[72] Although language is no longer necessarily its basis, there is still a difference between child and adult. Adulthood is imagined as the stable, homogenous end-point – selfhood – to the developmental process of childhood in developmental psychology, and clinical practice, throughout the twentieth century.

Conclusion

Darwin's contribution to natural history propagated a revolutionary debate about all of the scientific disciplines, as Lightman has pointed out (in Chapter 1), including the study of humanity. In the standard text for psychology students in the decades following the publication of *The Origin of Species*, language is the means by which a self-as-end can be constructed. The soul, refashioned in an era of evolutionism, is now the expression of the remembered insight of the Other, childhood self. In attributing to the child an inarticulate and therefore undivided perception of self, the Victorian origins of child psychology create a child who is a primitive yet unified ancestor to the adult. The child-mind might contain the undivided self, but it is, crucially, differentiated from – and a lower form of – that self. In other words, because of what Sully might call a 'gift of sympathetic insight' into the child's mind, certain adults can identify with the unified self as it existed in the mind of the child.[73] In the Victorian period, that gift is primarily the preserve of authors of children's literature like Burnett. By the early twentieth century, the same gift is claimed by child psychologists, to validate the method and findings of the clinical interview. By articulating that Other, child-self, the adult can progress beyond it, and can thereby attain Jameson's ideal: the self as a progressive whole.

Autobiography has been recognized as a distinct literary genre 'since the late eighteenth century'.[74] That late nineteenth-century revolution in the genre, which produced so many works devoted to the recollection and representation of childhood experience, is too inextricably associated with Child Study to be recognized in the same terms. Similarly, psychology became an established and autonomous discipline during the Victorian period, but the affiliated practice of Child Study owed, acknowledged, and even celebrated a debt to contemporary autobiographies of childhood experience (and, indeed, to a broad range of other accounts of childhood) which must preclude it from disciplinary categorization. Victorian Child Study and autobiography of childhood experience are not so much nascent branches of psychology and autobiography, respectively, as they are amalgams, or what might now be called interdisciplines, on the theme of childhood.

Autobiography of childhood experience and Child Study can thus be understood as symbiotic, interdisciplinary studies of the newly necessary idea of selfhood in the Victorian period. The link between autobiography and Child Study is only one example of how disciplines intersected in complicated ways. Connections can similarly be traced between classics and theology (Chapter 9), antiquarianism and archaeology (Chapter 7), literature and science (Chapter 11), or musicology and a number of other studies (Chapter 12). In the case of autobiography and Child Study, by formulating a specifically progressive model of ontogenic development, these discourses offer a self which replicates the most essential quality of the Christian soul, namely, the teleology with which it imbues the individual human life. For authors of autobiography, and for the psychologists with whom they were contemporary, the story of the self is a story of progress from inarticulate Other child to fully coherent adult. Since these disciplines studied the child as a miniaturized embodiment of the human species, they can be seen as responses to the revolutionary effect of *The Origin of Species*. Child Study is invented, and autobiography radically reimagined through childhood experience, in the late nineteenth century, to substantiate an emphatically non-Darwinian view of human evolution.

Several questions are raised by this discussion of the connections between autobiography, Child Study, and evolutionism in the Victorian period. First, Burnett was viewed as an expert on children because she wrote literature for children. Jessica Straley has shown that a study of children's literature can inform current understandings of both childhood and evolutionism in Victorian discourse, but she honours a long tradition in treating children's literature as a discrete genre.[75] If two such seemingly distinct discourses as autobiography and psychology are so demonstrably co-dependent when it comes to Victorian studies of childhood, the far more dubious boundaries between categories of fiction should perhaps be treated with less respect.

An analysis of literature for children in comparison with canonical and scientific literature about children would offer a more fully synthesized picture Victorian debates on both childhood and evolution, by eroding anachronistic boundaries between discourses. There are, for example, clear continuities between Burnett's fiction for children and the more literary fiction about children written by her contemporary and acquaintance Henry James, and between these disparate fictional works and contemporary psychological studies of the child-mind.[76] The long-respected divide between children's literature and other literature impedes a full analysis of these continuities and, indeed, of the validity of the divide itself.

Second, childhood was only one of many subjects through which ideas about evolution were explored and consolidated in the decades following the publication of *The Origin of Species*. Childhood was complexly interrelated with another subject – race – which was equally central to Victorian evolutionism: the equivalence Stout invokes, between the savage and the child, for example, is ubiquitous in the period.

This may be because it legitimizes a progressive view of the history of human life in which the white European adult is the pinnacle and endpoint. However, Barbara Larson has observed that, '[d]espite the significant and expanding literature on Empire and the colonies' – including several recent studies of the child in imperial discourse – 'no major study has been offered to date on the various strands of evolutionism and how this might complicate the representation of race during the Victorian period'.[77] Such a study could not be conducted without an analysis of the alignment between child and savage which was so central to Victorian ideas about race and about evolution.

This chapter has argued that the Victorian origins of child psychology are evident in the extent to which ideas about progressive evolution inform emergent scientific and autobiographical studies of the child-mind in the period. This invites a broader study of the function and significance of childhood and race as co-constructed ideologies in nineteenth-century scientific, literary, and anthropological discourses, and of the dialogue between these discourses and contemporaneous debates about the mechanisms for and implications of evolution.

Notes

1 Susan Jean Mayer, 'The Early Evolution of Jean Piaget's Clinical Method', *History of Psychology* 8/4 (2005), 362–382, at p. 362.
2 Mayer, 369. See also, for example, Michael J. Chandler, 'Piaget on Piaget', *British Journal of Psychology* 100/1 (2009), 225–228, esp. p. 225, on Piaget's influence.
3 Peter Bowler, *The Non-Darwinian Revolution: Reinterpreting a Historical Myth* (Baltimore, MD: Johns Hopkins University Press, 1988), 47.

4 Deborah J. Coon, 'Salvaging the Self in a World without Soul: William James's *The Principles of Psychology*', *History of Psychology* 3/2 (2000), 83–103, at p. 85.

5 Carolyn Steedman, *Strange Dislocations: Childhood and the Idea of Human Interiority, 1790–1930* (London: Virago, 1995), 5.

6 See Sally Shuttleworth, *The Mind of the Child: Child Development in Literature, Science, and Medicine, 1840–1900* (Oxford: Oxford University Press, 2010), for a detailed overview of Victorian Child Study, and Katharina Boehm, *Charles Dickens and the Sciences of Childhood: Popular Medicine, Child Health, and Victorian Culture* (Basingstoke: Palgrave Macmillan, 2013), for an analysis of the dialogue between the sciences of childhood and their counterparts in Dickens's work.

7 See, for example, the opening chapters of Charles Dickens's *David Copperfield* (1850) and *Great Expectations* (1867), and of George Eliot's *The Mill on the Floss* (1860). The earliest works in what is now known as the golden age of children's literature – Charles Kingsley's *The Water Babies* (1863), Lewis Carroll's *Alice in Wonderland* (1865), and George MacDonald's *At the Back of the North Wind* (1871), for example – were written in the same period.

8 Jonathan Loesberg, 'Self-Consciousness and Mediation in Victorian Autobiography', *University of Toronto Quarterly* 50/2 (1980/1981), 199–220, at p. 199.

9 Bowler's is the seminal work on the subject. See also Bernard Lightman, *Victorian Popularizers of Science: Designing Nature for New Audiences* (Chicago: University of Chicago Press, 2007), on the role of non-scientists in promoting theories about evolution in the same period.

10 Sally Shuttleworth, 'Inventing A Discipline: Autobiography and the Science of Child Study in the 1890s', *Comparative Critical Studies* 2/2 (2005), 143–163, at p. 144.

11 Loesberg, for example, focusses on Darwin and Carlyle. See also John Sturrock, *The Language of Autobiography: Studies in the First Person Singular* (New York: Cambridge University Press, 1993), and Deborah Epstein Nord, 'Victorian Autobiography: Sons and Fathers', in *The Cambridge Companion to Autobiography*, eds. Maria DiBattista and Emily O. Wittman (Cambridge: Cambridge University Press, 2014), 87–101. Andrew Taylor, *Henry James and the Father Question* (Cambridge: Cambridge University Press, 2002), discusses autobiography in the work of Henry James. This research substantiates Epstein Nord's claim that a 'psychic and philosophical battle between generations' is 'at the heart of' many Victorian autobiographies, but neither it nor Epstein Nord's essay discuss the extent to which the divide between generations was figured as a divide between adult and child (Epstein Nord, 87). Valerie Sanders discusses what she calls 'the minor women novelists', but none so minor that they wrote for children (Valerie Sanders, *The Private Lives of Victorian Women: Autobiography in Nineteenth-Century England* (New York: Harvester Wheatsheaf, 1989), 2).

12 Jenny Bavidge, 'Exhibiting Childhood: E. Nesbit and the Children's Welfare Exhibitions', in *Childhood in Edwardian Fiction: Worlds Enough and Time*, eds. Adrienne E. Gavin and Andrew F. Humphries (Basingstoke: Palgrave Macmillan, 2009), 125–142, at p. 139.

13 As Sanders has observed, childhood was one area in which women were permitted to have special expertise in the nineteenth century. See Penny Brown, *The Captured World: The Child and Childhood in Nineteenth-Century Women's Writing in England* (New York: Harvester Wheatsheaf, 1993), for a discussion of childhood in women's writing of the period.

14 See, for example, LuAnn Walther, 'The Invention of Childhood in Victorian Autobiography', in *Approaches to Victorian Autobiography*, ed. George P. Landow (Athens: Ohio University Press, 1979), 64–86, and the discussions of nineteenth-century autobiographies of childhood experience in Richard Coe, *When the Grass Was Taller: Autobiography and the Experience of Childhood* (New Haven: Yale University Press, 1984). See also Sanders, *Private Lives of Victorian Women*, 50–74, on the ideology of femininity in autobiographies of childhood experience. None of these works discuss autobiographies by the supposed experts on the subject of childhood – authors of children's literature. The discussion of Burnett's autobiography in Brown, 125–128, is a notable exception.

15 See L. M. Rutherford, 'Frances Hodgson Burnett (24 November 1846 – 29 October 1924)', in *Dictionary of Literary Biography, Vol. 141: British Children's Writers. 1880–1914*, ed. Laura M. Zaidman (Detroit: Gale, 1994), 59–78, for an overview of Burnett's work and its critical and commercial reception during her lifetime.

16 See Lyubov G. Gurjeva, 'James Sully and Scientific Psychology, 1870–1910', in *Psychology in Britain: Historical Essays and Personal Reflections*, eds. G. C. Bunn, A. D. Lovie and G. D. Richards (Leicester: BPS, 2001), 72–94, on Sully's role in the history of Child Study, and p. 77 for a useful summary of Sully's publications.

17 James Sully, *Studies of Childhood* (London: Longmans, 1919), 2. Gurjeva discusses Sully's acknowledged debt to women's expertise on children and childhood (pp. 88–91) but does not discuss the use he makes of their published work on the subject.

18 Sully, *Studies*, p. 16, n. 1. *The One I Knew the Best of All* was published two years before the first edition of *Studies of Childhood*, but the latter had in fact been written, and published in the form of essays in various periodicals, during the 1880s. See Gurjeva, 78–81.

19 Sully, *Studies*, 4.

20 Marylène Bennour and Jacques Vonèche, 'The Historical Context of Piaget's Ideas', in *The Cambridge Companion to Piaget*, eds. Ulrich Müller, Jeremy I. M. Carpendale and Leslie Smith (Cambridge: Cambridge University Press, 2009), 45–63, at p. 46.

21 Bennour and Vonèche, p. 46.

22 Lisa J. Cohen, 'Jean Piaget's Theory of Cognitive Development', in *Handy Answer: The Handy Psychology Answer Book*, 2nd edn. (Canton: Visible Ink Press, 2016), https://search.credoreference.com/content/entry/viphapsyc/jean_piaget_s_theory_of_cognitive_development/0, accessed February 12, 2019; Frank B. Murray, 'Piaget's Theory', in *The Concise Corsini Encyclopaedia of Psychology and Behavioural Science*, eds. W. Edward Craighead and Charles B. Nemeroff (Hoboken: Wiley, 2004), https://search.credoreference.com/content/entry/wileypsych/piaget_s_theory/0, accessed February 12, 2019; Jennifer Brubaker, 'Cognitive Development Theory', in *The Wiley Blackwell Encyclopaedia of Family Studies*, ed. Constance L. Shehan (Hoboken: Wiley, 2016), https://search.credoreference.com/content/entry/wileyfamily/cognitive_development_theory/0, accessed February 12, 2019 (emphases added). Brubaker's is the only entry to describe children's cognitive development both as growth (which is implicitly progressive) and as change (which is not). Recently, psychologists have challenged not only the hierarchy but also the idea that it is inevitably implied by Piaget's theory. See, for example, Thomas Kesselring, 'The Mind's Staircase Revised', in Ulrich Müller, Jeremy I. M. Carpendale and Leslie Smith, 371–399.

23 Herbert P. Ginsburg, *Entering the Child's Mind: The Clinical Interview in Psychological Research and Practice* (Cambridge: Cambridge University Press, 1997), 39–40.
24 Anna Jameson, 'A Revelation of Childhood', in *A Commonplace Book of Thoughts, Memories, and Fancies; Original and Selected*, 1854; 2nd edn. (London: Longmans, 1855), 117–146, at 121.
25 Coe, 76.
26 Ibid.
27 William James, *The Principles of Psychology* (Cambridge, MA: Harvard University Press, 1981), vol. 1, 614. Coon describes *The Principles of Psychology* as 'a shaper of the developing discipline' of psychology (Coon, 88).
28 See Stout, *A Manual of Psychology*, 1899; 4th edn. (London: University Tutorial Press, 1932), especially 525, and Wundt, *Principles of Physiological Psychology*, trans. Edward Bradford Titchener, 1874; 5th edn. (London: Swan Sonnenschein, 1904), especially p. 14. See Alan Collins, 'The Psychology of Memory', in *Psychology in Britain: Historical Essays and Personal Reflections*, eds. G. C. Bunn, A. D. Lovie and G. D. Richards (Leicester: BPS Books, 2001), 150–168, (p. 166), on Stout's role in early psychology. Wundt, meanwhile, founded the first psychology laboratory.
29 Shuttleworth, *The Mind of the Child*, 333.
30 See Howard Helsinger, 'Credence and Credibility: The Concern for Honesty in Victorian Autobiography', in Landow, 39–63.
31 Burnett, *The One I Knew the Best of All: A Memory of the Mind of a Child* (New York: Charles Scribner's, 1893), 7. Subsequent citations will be given in parentheses.
32 Sully, *Studies*, 16.
33 James Sully, 'The Story of a Child', *Longman's Magazine*, 19/110 (December 1891), 200–214, at p. 201. Subsequent citations will be given in parentheses.
34 Lightman notes that another Victorian popularizer of science, Lydia Becker, 'called on Darwin and Newton to help her make the point that anyone could make an important scientific discovery' (Lightman, 162). In his reference to Darwin, Sully may similarly have been attempting to legitimize both Loti's recollection and the inference – the scientific discovery – which he himself draws from it.
35 Coe, 41.
36 Loesberg, 199. See Sanders, 1–27, on the additional charges female autobiographers were susceptible to in the nineteenth century.
37 Shuttleworth, 'Inventing a Discipline', 159.
38 Ibid., 153.
39 Sully, 'George Sand's Childhood', *Longman's Magazine* 15/86 (1889), 149–164, at p. 149.
40 Sully, 'A Girl's Religion', *Longman's Magazine* 16/91 (May 1890), 89–99, at p. 90, and *Studies*, 507.
41 Sully, *Studies*, 513, emphasis added.
42 Ibid., 489.
43 James Sully, 'Baby Linguistics', *The English Illustrated Magazine* 14 (November 1884), 110–118, at p. 111. Subsequent page numbers will be given in parentheses.
44 Shuttleworth, 'Inventing a Discipline', 144. These essays initiated the wave of so-called baby biographies from which scientific Child Study emerged. See Wayne Dennis, 'A Bibliography of Baby Biographies', *Child Development* 7/1 (1936), 71–73.

45 William Preyer, *The Mind of the Child Part II: The Development of the Intellect* (New York: Appleton, 1895), 3.
46 Preyer, 3.
47 Ibid.
48 Sully, *Studies*, 160.
49 Herbert Spencer, *On Education*, ed. F. A. Cavenagh (Cambridge: Cambridge University Press, 1932), 82–83.
50 Bowler, 51.
51 Sully, 16; Ginsburg, 39.
52 Coe, 252.
53 Hippolyte Taine, 'On the Acquisition of Language by Children', *Mind* 2/6 (1877), 252–259, at 253.
54 See Peter Coveney, *The Image of Childhood: The Individual and Society: A Study of the Theme in English Literature*, 1957; 2nd edn. (Middlesex: Penguin, 1967), on this and other tropes in literary studies of childhood from the eighteenth to the twentieth century.
55 Charles Darwin, *The Expression of the Emotions in Man and Animals* (London: Watts, 1934), 171.
56 Gurjeva, 73.
57 Coe, 252.
58 Jenny Bourne Taylor, 'Between Atavism and Altruism: The Child on the Threshold in Victorian Psychology and Edwardian Children's Fiction', in *Children in Culture: Approaches to Culture*, ed. Karín Lesnick-Oberstein (Basingstoke: Macmillan, 1998), 89–121, at p. 103, emphasis added.
59 Gillian Beer, *Darwin's Plots: Evolutionary Narrative in Darwin, George Eliot and Nineteenth-Century Fiction*, 1983; 3rd edn. (Cambridge: Cambridge University Press, 2009), p. 99.
60 Charles Darwin, *The Descent of Man and Selection in Relation to Sex*, eds. James Moore and Adrian Desmond (London: Penguin, 2004), 209–210.
61 Sully, *Studies*, 181.
62 Ibid, 180.
63 Ibid.
64 Collins, 151.
65 Stout, *Manual*, 268. Subsequent page numbers will be given in parentheses.
66 Kesselring, 380.
67 Jean Piaget, *The Language and Thought of the Child*, 1926; 3rd edn. (London: Routledge and Kegan Paul, 1959, trans. Marjorie Gabain), 261.
68 Piaget, 262.
69 Ibid.
70 For Nira Granott, psychology is by then undergoing a paradigm shift away from Piagetian theory (Nira Granott, 'A Paradigm Shift in the Theory of Development', *Human Development* 41/5/6 (1998), 360–365).
71 Thomas H. Ollendick and Michael W. Vasey, 'Developmental Theory and the Practice of Clinical Child Psychology', *Journal of Clinical Child Psychology* 28–24 (1999), 457–466, at p. 461; Philip C. Kendall, 'Social Cognition and Problem Solving: A Developmental and Child-Clinical Interface', in *Applications of Cognitive-Developmental Theory*, eds. Barry Gholson and Ted L. Rosenthal (New York: Academic, 1984), 115–148.
72 Ollendick and Vasey, 461.
73 Sully, *Studies*, 16.
74 Linda Anderson, *Autobiography*, 2001; 2nd edn. (London: Routledge, 2011), 1.

75 Jessica Straley, *Evolution and Imagination in Victorian Children's Literature* (Cambridge: Cambridge University Press, 2016).

76 See Roisín Laing, 'Candid Lying and Precocious Storytelling in Victorian Literature and Psychology', *Journal of Victorian Culture* 21/4 (2016), 500–513, and Roisín Laing, '*What Maisie Knew*: Nineteenth-Century Selfhood in the Mind of the Child', *Henry James Review* 39/1 (Winter 2018), 96–109, on these connections.

77 Barbara Larson, 'Evolution and Victorian Art', in *Evolution and Victorian Culture*, eds. Bernard Lightman and Bennett Zon (Cambridge: Cambridge University Press, 2014), 121–148, at p. 143.

Section V

Disciplinary Boundaries

9 Disentangling Antiquity

Classics and Theology in the Nineteenth Century

Simon Goldhill

Introduction

Since its beginnings, Christianity has struggled – longingly and dismissively – to articulate its relationship with the lures of Hellenism and the power Rome represents. The study of late antiquity in recent decades, led by Peter Brown and his students, has repeatedly emphasized that, however much Christianity promoted itself not just as the Good News, but also as a new form of goodness, a new form of religiosity, a new way of life, nonetheless it remained profoundly imbricated with the institutions, schools of thought, patterns of social behaviour it came to destroy.[1] Christianity takes shape from the start in a double battle for self-identification. On the one hand, the 'great divide' from its foundational soil of Judaism leads to increasingly aggressive rhetoric – and behaviour – of separation from the institutions and practices of Judaism – for all that the Hebrew Bible, constituted precisely as an Old Testament by the language of supercessionism, and read largely in Greek or Latin, remained at the core of Christian narrative. The complexity of this narrative of origin and division still leads to intense analysis and heated disagreement.[2] On the other, Christianity's opposition to what it terms the polytheism of Greco-Roman paganism is distinctive, powerful, and expressed in the most bitterly committed language. Yet Christianity became the dominant religion of the Roman Empire; it became fully assimilated into the institutions of power, and adopted the language, dress, and authority of the very systems it set out to despise.[3]

The history of these competing trajectories of assimilation and division dominates the historiographical debate of the first six centuries of the common era – both during these centuries themselves and in subsequent re-tellings of the past: how Christianity and its thinking can be separated from Greco-Roman culture and its thinking is the means and matter of so much early Christian and late Greco-Roman writing, and these gestures of mutual antagonism and entanglements have been played out repeatedly over the centuries. At one level, the debate is one of socio-politics – when could Christianity be defined as more than a Jewish sect? How and with what impact did Christianity rise to a position of power across the Empire? How, for example, should religious violence in Africa be comprehended?[4] This question fuels not just academic debate but the novels, films, plays, and operas of modernity which have repeatedly staged the story of the clash between Christians and imperial authority – a cultural battle over the imagination of the West.[5] At another level, the argument is one of ideology and theology: to what degree is Christianity indebted to Stoic and Cynic philosophy for its asceticism?[6] To what degree is neo-Platonism integral to Christian theology?[7] How new – how pure and original – is the thinking that proclaims itself as the (good) news? Christianity, as a religion, is constantly re-telling the story of its origin – from the manger to the grave – and understanding this foundation story is foundational for religious self-understanding and self-representation. When Tertullian, with his characteristic over-emphatic rhetoric, demands 'what has Athens to do with Jerusalem?', he knows all too well that the answer to his question was multiform, complex, painful – and certainly not the clear and certain borderline he wanted to draw.

How, then, do the disciplines of classics and theology, as the study of Greco-Roman antiquity, on the one hand, and the study of the development of Christianity from antiquity, on the other hand, as an intellectual, moral, ritual, and social system of religious ideas and practices, find a place in this long-drawn out campaign of contested self-definition?[8]

There has been no point in the history of the West when the study of antiquity and the study of Christianity have not been in significant and often passionate interaction. Medieval philosophy was deeply indebted to Aristotle and found the problem of how therefore paganism was to be conceived and evaluated a continuing vexation.[9] The Renaissance was a rediscovery of the authority of classical antiquity, and it would be impossible to tell the story of the religious battles of the Reformation without taking account of the consequent re-evaluation of the Greek of the New Testament[10] – any more than the development of new sciences in the era could be separated from their theological framing, or theology could be appreciated without the new learning.[11] If the myth of the Enlightenment is instrumental in the later establishment of the disciplines as sciences, a myth for which a fundamental separation between theology and science is foundational, recent scholarship has underlined how such a myth misrepresents the continuing importance of divine explanation, theological practice, and religious thinking in academic argumentation.[12]

Yet there can be no doubt that the development of the disciplines in the nineteenth century *as* disciplines – that is, through institutionalization, professional training, and accreditation, leading to the increased enforcement of the boundaries of expertise – significantly redrew the map of interaction between classics and theology, especially in the context of the heightened religious conflicts of the century, fuelled as they were by the evangelical movement of the first decades of the century, the missionary movement in the expanding British Empire, and the intense self-reflection produced in response to critical history on the one hand and the new sciences, especially geology and evolutionary biology, on the other hand.[13] The aim of this chapter is first to trace how the nineteenth century produced a particular configuration of the long battle between classics and theology as approaches to antiquity, as systems of values, and as understandings of the world. And, second and much more briefly, to consider how this legacy still has an impact on today's conceptualization and practise of the disciplines. In particular, this chapter will demonstrate that the projection and promotion of increasingly firm boundaries of disciplinary knowledge, typical of the expansion and reorganization of the universities through the later nineteenth century, require and perform an increasing disavowal and misrecognition of the continuing entanglement of the two fields. Where so much of current criticism has focussed first on increasing secularization and professionalization of the disciplines, with a focussed (and especially self-serving) teleological narrative of the growth of the sciences, here we will see both the continuing importance of theology and classics throughout the nineteenth century, and, what is more, the continuing impact of the dynamic interrelations between theology and other disciplines.

In Britain in the nineteenth century, particularly for the educated elite – though certainly not solely for them – classics and religion provided the furniture of the mind. There was a remarkable dominance of the study of antiquity and the bible in the curriculum, even and particularly as it became more systematically institutionalized through the new policies and practices of state education. Classics, according to the Clarendon Report of 1864, in the average public school took up eleven of each week's twenty classes.[14] Sunday School classes were also introduced across the country, with the result that the topography of the Holy Land, it was claimed with delight or shock, was more familiar to young children who learned to sing its cities and towns, than their own country's geography.[15] Many children learned to read with the bible at their mother's knee – in the projected ideal if not always the reality of Victorian home-life.[16] Learning passages of the bible off by heart, and then, when older, the poems of Horace, say, in Latin, played a major role in the daily practice of education: the rhythms and language of the bible and ancient poetry were incorporated into the physical and emotional memory of the educated.

What's more, classics and theology – along with social change (classics and theology, providing, as it were, the history, philosophy, and morality for social change) – were perhaps the two subjects that excited most controversy and passion over the century. They provided the cultural resources through which society defined itself and its ideals. Matthew Arnold's celebrated opposition of Hellenism and Hebraism, as the two frameworks of comprehending modern European cultural identity, was so successfully influential because his book systematized and extended what was already a comprehensible model (and drew easily on less salubrious anti-Semitic prejudices too in its Philhellenism).[17] From Niebuhr's accounts of Roman history, through Grote's Greek history to Strauss's or Renan's life of Jesus – or one could take Marx's materialism starting with a PhD on Epicurus, or Marshall, the great theorist of economics, starting his study with the economics of ancient Greece, or Millman's *History of the Jews*[18]. . . – the books which convulsed Victorian debate turned back to religious and classical history to recalibrate modernity. Classics and the bible became a deeply contested arena for cultural self-expression and historical self-understanding.

For an iconic moment of this ineluctable self-definitional matrix of religious and classical history, we could recall that when the British Prime Minister William Gladstone wrote a lengthy pamphlet entitled 'The Place of Ancient Greece in the Providential Order of the World' (1865), which showed how Homer and the Bible both took a privileged place in God's historical ordering of things, it sold extraordinarily well – especially after Schliemann claimed to have discovered Troy, and Gladstone travelled introducing Schliemann's lectures across England.[19] Classics and theology, on this understanding, shared a project of setting man – Western civilization – in his proper place at the apex of history. The glories that were Greece and the wonders of Christianity grounded modern man's place in history. And the Prime Minister shared his take on this with an eager public. The religion of antiquity was fundamental in the contested self-expression of modernity – to such a degree that Gilbert Murray, a man who would go on to help found the League of Nations, could write in 1907:

> It is a bold statement, yet on reflection we are prepared to maintain it, that one of the greatest practical advances made by the human race in the last fifteen or twenty years has been in our improved understanding of ancient and especially of Greek religion.[20]

He knew about the wireless, airplanes, radium, but for him – and he knows he is being contentious – there was no *practical* advance more significant than the self-understanding provided by the study of antiquity's religion.

The story of the institutionalization of classics as the dominant discipline of the nineteenth-century universities and schools has been well explored from multiple perspectives. From the sociology of education, Christopher Stray has detailed the easy movement – of people and thought – between schools and university, as well as the increasingly conservative educational principles and practices invoked across the century.[21] Historians of the disciplines and the university itself have explored the functioning of institutionalization itself.[22] Intellectual historians have outlined the importance of classical history to politics, of philology to the professionalization of scholarship, and of the new scientific thinking to theology.[23] Historians of classical reception – a newly flourishing field – have outlined the multiform ways in which classical antiquity moulded the cultural output in art, fiction, opera, architecture, poetry.[24]

Consequently, this story needs rehearsing here only with the most lapidary of headlines. The institutionalization of the study of classical language and literature in the British universities is a crucial part of the story, just as the universities played a significant role in the establishment and maintenance of such disciplines as art history (Chapter 3), history (Chapter 4), and music (Chapter 12). The model of the German Humboldtian university, with its professionalized professors, with their seminars, increasingly committed to a paradigm of *Wissenschaft*, of science and scientific method, was adopted and adapted across Europe and America on different timescales and with different emphases. The role in England of Oxford and Cambridge, its tripos system with specific subjects for teaching, defined the parameters of the field – with the delimitation of a canon supported by an ideology of the classical age of Athens matched by the golden age of Latin artistry.[25] The burgeoning culture of reviews, along with increased university control, the importance of university exams and eventually further training, produced forms of regulation for the subject's practice. The new value of objectivity and empirical research helped the formation of the sub-discipline of archaeology – which was readily brought under the telling general heading of *Sachphilologie*, 'The Philology of Things' – and, under the guidance of August Boekh, professor at Berlin for fifty years, the ideal of a full understanding of classical culture as an integrated unity was promoted as the aim of true scholarship.[26] The connection between classics as a training of the mind and subsequent entrance to the civil service and the professions, maintained classics' privileged position in the hierarchy of disciplines.[27] The traffic between university research and teaching, the public schools, and the church, made the study of antiquity, especially through the language of Latin and Greek, part of the social glue of British elite society – just as a staggeringly high percentage of Oxbridge students who studied classics entered the church. It was often noted that the first attempt to get compulsory Greek removed from the Oxford curriculum was easily defeated by the massed ranks of the clergy who bussed in from the Home Counties to vote the measure down.[28] At the beginning of the century, Shelley's battle-cry for radicalism was 'We are all Greeks'; by the end of the century classics was the institutionalized route of establishment training. It offered another world of projected idealism for sexual liberation and religious renegades and aesthetic politics[29] – but by 1900 classics was deeply embedded in the structures of education and authority from schools, through universities, the church, the Empire.

So, the professionalization and disciplinarization of classics as the dominant institutional discipline in nineteenth-century Britain are well-known and paradigmatic for the new and less immediately institutionalized or culturally valued fields, such as geology or natural sciences, and, even more obviously, for the fledgling worlds of English literature or history. It might be thought, therefore, that the combination of this history, together with equivalent developments in the institutional scholarship of theology, would constitute a paradigm not simply for the separation of disciplines but also for scholarship's self-definition as a secular science which demands, after all, a rejection of confessional bias, religious commitment, and explanations through divine agency. And it would indeed not be difficult to collect a series of explicit methodological claims by scholars in favour of a principle of objectivity in *Wissenschaft* increasingly from across the century.[30] Yet in this chapter I want to look at how the intermixing – the infection – of classics and theology lasted right through and beyond the process of professional institutionalization and separation of disciplines, a story that is far less appreciated, not least because it stands against both the self-image of modern scholarship, and the current history of disciplines. Despite the Devonshire Commission of 1870–1875 and other projects to reform the university, not only did classics and theology maintain a significant role as the dominant disciplines for teaching and research, but also, more importantly, they continue to cross the increasingly rigid borders of disciplinarization in a dynamic if often disavowed cross-fertilization. I will look at this hybridity at three levels: first at the level of individual scholars, their careers, work, expectations; second, at the level of method – what techniques, resources, and intellectual approaches are shared and how do they interrelate? Third, at the level of argument and subject development: when Christianity takes shape in the Roman Empire and theology is formed in relation to Greek philosophy in particular, how do such contingencies of contact affect the construction of scholarly topics in either classics or theology?

The Heroes

Many of the most distinguished religious leaders of the nineteenth century had a classical education to an advanced degree, and moved to the church from university via school-teaching. Archbishop Edward White Benson, for example, the charismatic archbishop of Canterbury from 1883 to his death in 1896, took a first in classics at Cambridge and became a don at Trinity College.[31] He left to teach classics at Rugby, that icon of Victorian educational principle, where he was also ordained. He was asked by Prince Albert to become the headmaster of the Prince's new school, Wellington. He left the headmastership there to become chancellor of Lincoln Cathedral, before becoming bishop of the new see of Truro and then archbishop of Canterbury. His most important theological decision, whose impact is still felt in the Anglican church today, was the Lincoln Judgment (1889), which defined the acceptable forms of ritualism within the liturgical practice of the church, a judgment based on a long scholarly analysis of church history back into its earliest days. And Benson famously read the Gospels in Greek every day, while shaving. Such traffic between major institutions produced its own discourse, where the figure of 'the Greek play Bishop', a bishop appointed to office because of his skills as a classical philologist rather than any theological rigour, started as *ad hominem* accusations against Bishops Monk and Blomfield but eventually became almost a 'nostalgic fantasy' as the century progressed.[32]

My key example, however, reveals a different type of overlap from this stereotype. Benjamin Jowett (1817–1893) was appointed to the Regius Professorship of Greek at Oxford in 1855.[33] After many years of hoping and trying, he was appointed master of Balliol College in 1870. He is best known to classicists today – and more generally in the history of disciplines – as the man who translated Plato for the Victorians, and who introduced the Oxford tutorial system. His translation of Plato was a bestseller that defined the reception of Plato in English for a generation; he used Socratic dialogue as a model for this style of teaching, and through this personal educational involvement produced generations of connected students who were sent out as classically trained young men to run the Empire. As such, Jowett has played a significant role in the histories of the invention of the don, of the interconnections of Greek teaching and homosexuality, and of classics as a training for Empire.[34] Jowett epitomizes the potential authority and influence of the Victorian university educator in classics. His coffin was carried at his funeral by seven heads of Oxford colleges and the provost of Eton, all former students.

Yet Benjamin Jowett was perhaps best known to his contemporaries first as a contributor to the scandalous volume *Essays and Reviews*. This book, which was published in 1860, brought together seven authors – six of whom were ordained, including Jowett – each of whom offered a reflective engagement with German critical theory from a liberal, broad church perspective (or, as the preface puts it, 'theological subjects. . .freely handled in a becoming spirit').[35] It was a work of theological scholarship that was so shocking that it was brought before the ecclesiastical courts for its apparent heresies, and which produced an extraordinary outpouring of evangelical and conservative ire, including a condemnation for heresy by the Convocation of Canterbury, an act of redress not even attempted for three centuries. It was also – after a slow start, but on the back of such emotion – a bestseller, with eleven editions in the first year.

Jowett was close to Dean Stanley, the embodiment of the liberal, broad church establishment, and had already been involved with campaigns to reform the relation between the universities and religion. He had long been pondering the subject of his essay, and, at hundred pages long and the last in the volume, it certainly packed a punch. One sentence of Jowett's long piece became an icon of the controversy – his summary claim that the bible 'is to be interpreted like any other book'. He wished, that is, to treat scripture with the same critical spirit as he would a classical text or a modern historical argument: there was, wrote Jowett disingenuously, no wish in the volume 'to do anything rash or irritating to the public or University', but there was a desire to resist 'this abominable system of terrorism' of orthodox church thinking (language not evidently designed to disassociate himself from irritating the authorities).[36] There had already been at Oxford a successful and highly cantankerous public challenge to Jowett, which stopped him for several years from receiving the proper increase to his salary (from £40 to £500, a significant difference) because of high church opposition to his religious views, as expressed especially in his *Essay on Atonement and Satisfaction.*[37] Now Edward Pusey, Regius Professor of Hebrew, and one of the founders of the Oxford Movement, spearheaded a prosecution against Jowett on the charge of heresy. The prosecution failed because the authorities refused to hear it – but not before it had also become part of a national debate – which helped make *Essays and Reviews* 'the greatest religious storm of the century'.[38]

Jowett's claim that the bible is to be 'read' or 'interpreted like any other book', which might seem now to be unaggressively modest, was taken to be a strident challenge to the inspired, divine status of the scriptures. His position was carefully expressed, though it seemed to its readers designedly inflammatory: 'Scripture, like any other books, has one meaning, which is to be gathered from itself without reference to the adaptations of the Fathers or Divines; and without regard to *à priori* notions about its nature or origins'. That scripture has one meaning may echo Augustine's promise towards the end of the *Confessions* (12.32.43) 'to select one meaning only, one that is inspired by you as true, certain and good' (although Augustine's multiple interpretations of Genesis make such a promise of univocality seem unlikely); so, too, the assertion that this one meaning is to be 'gathered from itself' sounds like the paradigmatic Protestant commitment to *sola scriptura.* Yet Jowett's blanket dismissal of the Fathers and the Divines (for their 'adaptations' rather than their interpretations or their pursuit of truth), and, in particular, his refusal of any commitment to the bible's origin or nature – that is, its status as revelation and as thus divinely inspired and necessarily true, certain, and good – were an enraging provocation to those of conservative religious belief. (Jowett's father, it should be noted, was a fierce evangelical, and Jowett himself had become a liberal only at university.) His argument was seen – rightly enough as Jowett had been a keen reader of Hegel and Kant – to be influenced not just by German critical philosophy but more specifically by German theologians and biblical scholars, headed by David Strauss or F. C. Baur. Their critical historical methods had already turned a sharp light on the coherence and stability of the texts on which church history and dogma were founded. For conservative and evangelical Anglicans Jowett's essay continued the very worrying signs of his already published theological work; and, produced as they were by a professor and an ordained member of the Anglican church, such arguments were regarded as doubly threatening because of the authority with which they were delivered. Jowett, who eventually became such a dominating bastion of Oxford, never lost the sense of danger his theological writing imparted.

Both in his practice and as a principle of theory Jowett brought classical scholarship and theology together, linked as they are by claims of methodology, ethical engagement, and an enquiry into truth. Jowett epitomizes how the work of individual scholars transcended the drive towards institutional disciplinarization. He lived almost to the end of the century (d 1893), when in the eyes of most historians the process of disciplinarization had fully taken shape. For him to write about St Paul as well as Plato remained a necessary horizon of expectation. Classics and the bible together continued to form the framework in which the ethical, historically self-conscious subject was educated. Jowett's life was defined by his role as an educator, in the tutorial and in the development of university policy, and for him critical thought about theology and antiquity were together integral to the process of making a ruler of Empire.

The Struggle for Method

Jowett's principles of interpretation were to be applied, then, across the full range of texts, and theology and classics remained so intimately bound together because they shared certain questions, approaches, and solutions – focussed on the philological analysis of texts, along with the increasingly technical understanding of archaeology – and this shared methodology forms the second strand of my enquiry into the interface of theology and classics.

Philology has become trendy again in the contemporary academy, but in the nineteenth century it was a potentially revolutionary topic. It was through philology that critical history challenged the received authority of scripture and classical texts. The translation of Niebuhr's *History of Rome* (1828), translated by Julius Charles Hare and Connop Thirlwall, can stand as an icon of the battle-lines that were forming in British intellectual and religious circles in these years.[39] Niebuhr's account of Livy was a founding text of critical history, in the rhetoric of the day often set parallel to Wolf's analyses of Homer and Strauss's unpicking of biblical texts.[40] Not only did Niebuhr's critique show the level of myth and legend in Livy's history of early Rome, but it also suggested that the beginnings of mankind were complex enough to indicate that creation might have taken place in different places – and polygenism was incompatible with biblical narratives.[41] Hare and Thirlwall were liberal luminaries, closely connected to George Grote and the Prussian intellectual and diplomat, Baron Bunsen, and, through marriage, Hare was related to F. D. Maurice, teacher of Charles Kingsley and others in the Christian Socialist movement.[42] Bunsen was the subject of Rowland William's essay in *Essays and Reviews*. Niebuhr's history thus came trailing clouds of Liberal progressivism. He was in consequence virulently attacked by the conservative and orthodox as a 'pert, dull scoffer', whose work was 'pregnant with crude and dangerous speculations' which led 'ungovernable youths [to hold] democratic meetings'.[43] Both his supporters and his enemies, however, agreed that Niebuhr's history of Rome spoke to the contemporary politics of church and democracy.[44] Indeed, Alfred Lord Tennyson – as quoted approvingly by Jowett – declared that 'the true origin of biblical criticism was to be ascribed not to Strauss, but to Niebuhr'.[45] With Niebuhr, Strauss, and Wolf, there was a deeply held sense that the Germans were coming. In particular, the threat of so-called rationalist critiques of the texts of religion from antiquity was perceived as a major threat to the establishment of church and society alike.

This philological threat was felt throughout the century, though perhaps most fearfully in the early decades. Mrs Humphry Ward's novel *Robert Elsmere* (1888), possibly the century's most successful novel of religious faith in crisis – it sold over 200,000 copies in America, and possibly over a million copies in total – dramatized how a religious man's faith was shattered by the critical study of ancient history. Mrs Ward, who on an early visit to Oxford had been shown the windows of the rooms where the shocking Jowett lived, and later met Ernest Renan there, had herself undergone such a transformation. 'What convinced *me* finally and irrevocably', she wrote to a friend, 'was two years of close and constant occupation with materials of history in those centuries which lie near the birth of Christianity'.[46] Renan had said the same: 'My faith has been destroyed by historical criticism, not by scholasticism nor by philosophy'.[47] Mrs Ward concluded: it is '*the education of the historic sense* which is disintegrating faith'.[48] Philological criticism challenged the authoritative status of the texts of antiquity, both biblical and classical. Textual criticism, the most privileged technical accomplishment of the queen of disciplines, *Altertumswissenschaft*, was turned onto biblical texts. If Niebuhr and his associates questioned whether ancient historical texts told us what actually happened, under philology's remorseless eye, the Word of God was opened to scrutiny and doubt. So Constantine Tischendorf, a scholar who aimed to use philology otherwise, characterized the crisis of faith produced by biblical textual scholarship as a 'painful uncertainty as to what the Apostles had actually written'.[49]

Tischendorf caused an international sensation when he brought to Europe the Codex Sinaiticus, the oldest known manuscript of the bible, which he had extracted from St Catherine's monastery in Sinai (he published it in 1862). He was explicit that his discovery was designed, from the very moment when he planned his adventures in the Middle East, to be a significant contribution to polemics about the status of the Gospels. In line with the dictates of modern philology, he aimed to discover and work from the 'most ancient manuscripts' possible, and not merely the *textus receptus*. He had searched the European libraries with notable successes, but his trip to the East was explicitly to hunt down 'some precious manuscripts slumbering for ages in dust and darkness'.[50] His self-representation as an adventurous hunter of lost treasures, a stereotype of many a novel, is fully fleshed out in his self-starring story of discovery. What he promises the reader in an 'age in which attacks on Christianity are so common' is nothing less than 'a full and clear light as to what is the real text of God's word written, and to assist us in defending the truth by establishing its authentic form'.[51] The Codex Sinaiticus was immediately recognized as a fourth-century witness, still some centuries from the autograph, but with an unparalleled authority. This was a triumph of the new philology. Readers in their thousands bought the expensively produced facsimile of the manuscript to get as close as possible to the very words of the gospels.

Yet there were at least two major worries that Tischendorf could not quell. First, the manuscript itself contains some 23,000 corrections. The extent of corrections is unmatched in other ancient manuscripts. These changes are early, and are made mainly by six hands; they not only include routine overwriting of faded letters or corrections of spelling, but also insert omitted lines and words, change wording, and even delete material: in some cases phrases are deleted by one corrector and re-added by another. At the very least, Codex Sinaiticus demonstrates 'how early Christian groups and individuals read and altered the text'.[52] That is, it shows how already in the fourth century, the text was corrupt, alterable, altered, and subject to dissent. It is at least a step or two away from the authentic, real text. Our oldest manuscript cannot provide the pure waters of truth but already needs evaluation, collation, and correction.

Second, the Codex Sinaiticus ends the Gospel of Mark at chapter 16 verse 8 with the closing formula *euangelion kata Markon: The Gospel according to Mark*. As scholars itemized, the roughly contemporary Codex Vaticanus, the Codex Bobbianus, one hundred or more of the earliest Armenian manuscripts, and the earliest Georgian manuscripts also lack the final lines of the Gospel, as printed in the *textus receptus* and the King James Bible, and as used as a familiar part of the liturgy. For most of the major textual critics of the nineteenth century – followed by almost all scholars today – this absence, coupled with the significant evidence that major early fathers did not know this ending, was conclusive proof that the traditional concluding eleven verses of the Gospel of Mark (16 9–20) were a later addition – an early addition, but an addition nonetheless. That is, the traditional text of the Latin bible, hallowed by long usage and familiarity, declared authentic – representing the best traditions of the church – by the Council of Trent, was an interpolation. The history of textual transmission, for all that it sought to find the established and authorized word of God, could not but also challenge the desired stability of the texts of the gospel.

Classical scholars and biblical scholars worked with a shared philological model on technical concerns of manuscript transmission, on the evaluation of manuscript witnesses, and on the relation between such manuscripts and the history of antiquity. They shared a profound respect for the languages of Greek and Latin in which the authorities of antiquity and the holy scripture, as well as most of earlier theology, were passed down. Both fields recognized Hebrew, Aramaic, Syriac, and other eastern languages as fundamental for the full study of the ancient Mediterranean and adjacent lands. And through such philologically informed critical history, both fields shared anxieties about authority, about modernity's genealogical link with an idealized past, and about the connection between such textual evidence and the Realien of antiquity. Philology opened a route towards a national identity by uncovering the buried linguistic life of the nation, its epic past, its history.[53] For all the construction of a divided disciplinary space, classics and theology shared a self-defining conversation about methodology.

A similar pattern of overlapping technical research is evident in the case of biblical and classical archaeology (supported later by photography) – both fields gradually becoming fully fledged partners in the disciplines of theology and *Altertumswissenschaft* as the century progressed.[54] When critical history challenged the status of the stories of the bible or of classical history, archaeology sought for material evidence to prove the truth of scripture or of history. As geology had turned the physical nature of the earth into evidence that challenged the Bible's chronology and thus its authority, so biblical archaeology set out to rediscover the truth of the bible in the physical soil of the Holy Land – while classicists uncovered the real of antiquity not just through *Sachphilologie* in the study but also through the spade in the land itself. As one religiously motivated archaeologist declared: 'results. . .won by the spade are undeviatingly true, and carry universal conviction'.[55] Archaeology set out to trump critical doubt with the established facts of a physical reality, facts on and from the ground. The history of archaeology has been well-traced by scholars to indicate how the antiquarian search for exotic or valued works of art, together with a general disregard for preservation or recording of sites, changed over the (long) nineteenth century into a discipline which demanded standard methods of recording and evaluating the process as well as the results of digging; which collected many examples of undervalued objects and shards of objects in order to construct timescales and cultural shifts through the close analysis of items in series; and which constructed a paradigm of methodology based on stratigraphy as the prime determinant of chronology: from plunder to preservation.[56] These methods were shared by classical and biblical archaeologists alike.

The objectivity that archaeology claimed to embody in its scientific uncovering of material reality should not be thought, however, to occlude desire or a motivated perspective. James Fergusson, for example, an influential intellectual who was a leading light in the history of architecture and its display in Victorian London, writes with what today would be regarded as an unnervingly direct statement of his wish-laden project:

> There is scarcely a fact or an expression in the whole [bible] that is not made clearer by the knowledge we have already derived or hope hereafter to obtain, from the discoveries in this long-buried land; and they promise to supply us with exactly what we wanted to understand and realise what we there find written.[57]

Archaeology's aim is to produce clarifying knowledge of scripture, and its promise is to give us 'exactly what we wanted' – both what we lacked and desired – not just 'to understand', but also 'to *realise*' the words of God – to *make real* scripture. You dig to find, and you find what you wanted to find all along. This is the ideology that motivated the establishment of the Palestine Exploration Fund in 1865 (followed by the Egypt Exploration Fund in 1888) and the many expeditions following their lead.[58] Even Sir William Flinders Petrie (1853–1942), whose place as a founder of modern scientific archaeology is celebrated, not only delighted in his discovery of the first Egyptian stele to mention the name Israel, but also spent many years of excavation in Egypt and elsewhere searching for evidence to locate the tribes mentioned in the bible, because of his commitment to rather nasty eugenic theories which denigrated African descent in favour of northern origins.[59] Flinders Petrie's earnest engagement with racist science underlines the multiple anxieties, desires, and political positions that underlie any claim to have uncovered the reality of things.

In the same way, the public controversy over the acquisition of the so-called Elgin Marbles – were these really of inestimable aesthetic value? Were they the paradigms of excellence demanded by the commitments of classicism? Were they worth it?[60]; or, from a quite different angle, the growing Victorian fascination with Roman Britain, with its particular purchase on nationalism, racial hybridity, and the beginnings of Christianity;[61] or, for that matter, the German imperial archaeologists' wilful clearing of all later buildings from around the Parthenon in Athens[62]; are all examples that reveal a similar matrix of ideology, aesthetics, politics, and projected history at work in classical archaeology. In short, classics and theology shared in and through archaeology not just a methodology but also an ideologically laden practice that served to determine and discover a particular version of reality on the ground.

Photography – with its asserted purchase on the real – fully contributed to this trajectory.[63] The intellectual horizons of the Victorian educated elite were imaginatively formed by the new possibilities of the grand tour opened by the technology of the steam-ship as much as the power of empire, a route that included Rome, Greece, Egypt, the Holy Land, Syria, and Istanbul. They not only visited and saw the real world in which the familiar figures of antiquity and the scriptures had walked, and walked in their footsteps, but also they prepared for such trips imaginatively by reading the explosion of guidebooks to the regions, looking at the newly available photography and other images, and studied bibles that now included photographs and other archaeological evidences as part of its battery of commentary, proof, and faith. When the Prince of Wales, accompanied by Dean Stanley and the photographer, Francis Bedford, among the usual entourage, visited the Eastern Mediterranean in 1861, the public at home could get news of each stage of the journey through the newspapers, and subsequently read the sermons delivered,[64] view the same views photographically reproduced,[65] and, at the Great Exhibition in Kensington in 1862, view the new Queen's Bible, produced at the behest of Queen Victoria, the first bible to have illustrative photographs of holy sites. Classics and theology share in the new technologies of scientific scholarship – and in the new media for communicating their knowledge and commitments to the public.

So while classics and theology are developing disciplinary form and the seeds of their current division, through the nineteenth century they continue to share a methodology at multiple levels, from their foundation in philology to their adoption of the new technologies of photography and archaeology as the means of determining the real of the past. Through shared methodological resources and anxieties, classics and theology maintained a conversation across any disciplinary divides.

The Tragedy of Theology

For the third strand of analysis I want to look at one particular area where one might expect to see the disciplinary formation of classics develop without a significant interaction with theology. The Greek tragedies of Aeschylus, Sophocles, and Euripides have been regarded as the epitome of the golden age of classical Athens, since the fourth century BCE, and acted as a mainstay of the educational syllabus wherever classics have been taught. The surviving Greek tragedies were all produced in Athens in the fifth century BCE – half a millennium before Jesus.

These plays not only are concerned with the relation between men and gods within a polytheistic system but also freely stage and even, in the comedies performed at the same festival as the tragedies, mocked the gods: Aristophanes' *Birds*, which invented Cloudcuckooland, imagines humans starving the gods of their usual sustenance from sacrifices and using this humiliation to take control – a fantasy a very long way from the earnestness of Victorian evangelicalism. It would seem that Greek drama, and tragedy in particular, is the paradigm of paganism: here are plays staged at a festival of Dionysus that dramatize and even question the power of the multiform gods of the ancient pantheon.

Yet it turns out that the study of Greek tragedy was deeply intertwined with a theological view of the world. There are two crucial interlocking strands of this story. The first concerns German idealism. The philosophers who wrote in response largely to Kant – including the luminaries Hegel, the Schellings, Schlegel, along with the more renegade Schopenhauer, and, of course, Nietzsche – were obsessed with Greek tragedy. Tragedy became a model for philosophy; Oedipus, the searcher, became the figure of the philosopher; and the tragedies themselves were read through a philosophical lens.[66] Across Europe, German idealism became the dominant critical model for understanding tragedy, even, if more slowly, in England. Yet all of these philosophers, typically for the heated religious atmosphere of the nineteenth century, struggled with their relation to institutionalized religion, whether it is the engaged Protestantism of Hegel or the Catholicism of Schelling. Hegel, for example, is fully aware that Oedipus cannot be simply Christianized: 'Attempts have been made', he writes of the *Oedipus at Colonus*, 'to find a Christian tone here: the vision of a sinner whom God pardons and a fate endured in life but compensated with bliss in death'. He is clear that there is a difference between the Christian dispensation and the Greek: 'the transfiguration of Oedipus always remains the Greek transfer of consciousness from the strife of ethical powers, and the violations involved, into the unity and harmony of the entire ethical order itself'.[67] Yet Hegel also declares that Oedipus is 'like Adam'; that Adam represents 'the second Adam, namely, Christ'; and that Oedipus dies for us, his 'transfiguration in death is his own and our reconciliation'.[68] 'Reconciliation' is a term familiar from theological debates about atonement (where, it will be remembered, Jowett had first upset the orthodox), the end of estrangement between man and God. Hegel's thinking is rooted in a teleological movement towards a Christian and, specifically, a Protestant dispensation. Yet, in this thinking, the Greek ethical past is a crucial grounding. The suffering of the hero, on which so much German idealist thinking on tragedy focussed, is not merely understood *through* Christian notions of the passion and the necessary suffering of man and its possible transcendence, but is itself *part of* the growth of man's ethical understanding and an insight into the philosophy of suffering and estrangement from God which fully contributes to a Christian self-understanding of man's ethical place in the world.[69]

The second strand of the interaction between theology and Greek tragedy finds its roots in British liberal thinkers, who were, in turn, influenced by German theologians and, particularly through George Grote, had a significant reciprocal influence on German scholarship. Grote's *History of Greece* was, according to E. A. Freeman, the Regius Professor of Modern History at Oxford, 'one of the glories of our age and country',[70] and following laudatory reviews from John Stuart Mill, George Cornewall Lewis, and Dean Stanley, it was not only a bestseller but also hugely influential on liberal thinking about the role of democracy in particular through its politicized reading of the history of ancient Athens. Grote epitomized a critical and historical attitude to myth, but he sought not only to separate historical narrative from legends but also to outline a developmental model, in which myth was redrafted by Greek thinkers towards a higher conceptualization of ethical and spiritual matters. Greek thought was instrumental in freeing man from the shackles of myth and in introducing a scientific and enlightened rationality. This developmental model found a particular and privileged place for tragedy.

Evelyn Abbott, who collaborated with Lewis Campbell both on the biography of Jowett and on books about Greek tragedy, gives a clear expression of this developmental model:

> The Greeks did not allow the mythology which stood to them in the place of doctrine to restrain them from the endeavour to bring their conception of the Supreme Being into harmony with their conceptions of justice and law. Their religious conceptions became ethical at an early period, and continued to be so to the last, ever growing higher and higher as the conception of life and duty became more elevated.[71]

So, within this incremental model of ethical growth (highlighting that prime Victorian virtue of duty), the tragedian Sophocles played a special role. For Abbott – and others – Sophocles is crucial testimony of a Greek journey towards reconciling abstract principles of justice and law with a notion of a Supreme being (a monotheistic term more suited to Anglican Britain than ancient Athens). So Edward Plumptre, another moderately distinguished scholar and clergyman, argued that Sophocles aimed to turn the mythology of Homer 'as far as it could be turned, into an instrument of moral education, and to lead men upwards to the eternal laws of God, and the thought of His righteous order'[72] – again the Anglican tones of his critical language are strongly marked. Plumptre concluded, with a portentous turn into Greek, that Sophocles 'may have become, to those who followed his guidance rightly, a παιδαγωγὸς εἰς Χριστόν', a 'guide to Christ'.[73] Greek tragedy here has become a preparation for the

Christian message, fully part of the Christian teleology. When Victorian critics called Sophocles 'pious', it was precisely from within this overlap of theological and classical thinking that such an evaluation made sense. So Bishop Westcott, normally a severely sober scholar, makes the connection between the Anglican church and the institution of tragedy explicit in the most extraordinary terms. The tragedians, he declares, were 'national preachers' in a 'national temple', and the 'sermon' of the *Oresteia* is 'a natural testimony of the soul' to the reality of sin and punishment.[74] 'Natural testimony of the soul' is the standard phrase from the Fathers of the church for pagans who anticipated Christianity in their piety and goodness, and Aeschylus emerges like a bishop in national pulpit, not unlike Westcott himself. So, for Westcott – and this is a sentence that even in such a context remains startling –'we can then study in Euripides a distinct stage in the preparation of the world for Christianity'.[75] It would be hard to find a clearer statement of how deeply theology informed the criticism of Greek tragedy in the nineteenth century.

Greek tragedy, then, was a privileged subject within the institutionalization of the discipline of classics. It was studied at all levels from schools through to advanced scholarship. It was a sign of the glory of Greece, the greatest literature of the greatest period of the classical city of Athens. 'Tragic language' had a special role in philosophical as well as aesthetic thinking. Both philology and archaeology happily focussed on the words and the material culture of theatre. Yet despite the key place tragedy plays in the disciplinarization of classics, the criticism – the reception, the understanding – of tragedy is formed in a teleological narrative of a Christian dispensation, itself fully informed by theological thinking. It is hard indeed to separate the disciplines of classics and theology in the nineteenth century, just as it is difficult to hive off archaeology from antiquarianism (Chapter 7), literature from science in general (Chapter 11), and musicology from many other disciplines (Chapter 12).

There is a great deal more that could be done in this area. The relation between the German Idealists and religion is still underexplored – especially where it bears on their Philhellenism. The work of the Revised Version of the Bible (published 1881–1894) marks a high point of engagement with the Greek of the testaments, and the history of the production and reception of this volume is only now being undertaken with any sophistication.[76] The interface of classical imagery and Christian iconography in the burgeoning world of stained glass as much as in the art-works exhibited at the Royal Academy and elsewhere is beginning to be appreciated – but much remains to be analyzed.[77] The close interaction of philology and theology itself has many twists and turns which needs further care – and the very study of Greek religion itself, and how classics and theology still combine to make this an insistently polemic area needs greater attention.[78] The sheer complexity and scope of how philology and theology shadow each other in nineteenth-century culture, and the impact of such a disavowed but integral dance of the disciplines, make it a pressing and daunting subject for further research.

Conclusion

I want to conclude, however, with a glance at the contemporary academy. Twenty-first-century classics has become acutely self-conscious of the political, moral, sexual, and aesthetic biases of its scholarly ancestors, and, often with a rather unreflective self-satisfaction, has declared its separation from them. In disciplinary terms, the separation between classics and theology can now seem extreme.[79] St Paul is studied in barely any classics department, Euripides in barely any theology department. Few classicists are comfortable even with Augustine; few theologians read Plato as a matter of course. Even in the study of the late antique, where such separations would seem particularly crass, it is possible to find that Nonnus' *Dionysiaca* is recognized if not embraced by classicists, while, with equal and opposite blinkers, Nonnus' *Paraphrase of John* finds a place in theology departments. The curricula of classics and theology courses have starkly opposite trajectories, then – and so too do methodologies. While confessional study, dogmatics, Christology are still part of theology departments (with the history of religions, for example, as a self-consciously secular bed-fellow), classics has attempted to divorce itself from any such credal structures, and is acutely embarrassed by its religious past (in England possibly in part because so many classicists, it appears, had clergy for parents).

Yet the nineteenth-century inheritance is much harder to discard than classicists would like to believe. Take Michel Foucault's *History of Sexuality*. This is a highly influential work, central to modernity's engagement with antiquity, and a crucial element in understanding of how history helps us engage with contemporary discourses of gender and sexuality. Yet even in this sophisticated and post-modern guise, we can see a continuing commitment to the genealogical idealism fundamental to classicism. Foucault's project, as a longing for a lost stylistics of the self, can be appreciated as a rehearsal of a long history of finding in antiquity a constructed ideal to yearn for. The history of sexuality, which starts with Greco-Roman antiquity, remains overshadowed by the Christianity it is mobilized to dethrone. In a similar if far less sophisticated way, it is surprising, indeed in Robert Parker's now standard discussion of Greek religion, to come across chapters entitled 'Why believe without revelation?' and 'Religion without a church'. The Christian framing of his questions seems startlingly unaware, not just in the assumption of the categories of 'belief', 'revelation', and 'church', but even in the very notion of religion, a term which, as several scholars have outlined, is hard to use to make sense of Greek or Roman practice or conceptualization. Disentangling classics from theology as disciplines remains vexing, especially when the entanglement is systematically misrecognized or denied.[80]

A disciplinary history of the nineteenth century will inevitably make classics its prime case, because of classics' privileged role in the institutionalization, professionalization, and public awareness of scholarly and artistic activity – despite our contemporary self-serving teleological accounts of growing scientific dominance. Yet the very regulation of boundaries of expertise and accreditation, on which the disciplines depend, cannot be properly appreciated without understanding their continuing porousness, and in particular classics' continuing and vexed engagement with theology. A shared life, a shared set of methodologies, a shared framing of central topics enabled classics and theology together to continue to provide a formative and mutually implicative frame for understanding the subject as a historical, and historically educated being.

Notes

1 P. Brown, *Society and the Holy in Late Antiquity* (Berkeley and Los Angeles; London: University of California Press, 1982); *The Body and Society: Men, Women and Sexual Renunciation in Early Christianity* (New York: Columbia University Press, 1988); *Authority and the Sacred: Aspects of the Christianization of the Roman World* (Cambridge: Cambridge University Press, 1995); *Through the Eye of a Needle: Wealth, the Fall of Rome and the Making of Christianity in the West, 350–550 A.D.* (Princeton: Princeton University Press, 2013); and from a potentially huge bibliography, R. MacMullen, *Christianity and Paganism from the Fourth to the Eighth Centuries* (New Haven: Yale University Press, 1997); I. Sandwell, *Religious Identity in Late Antiquity: Greeks, Jews and Christians in Antioch* (Cambridge: Cambridge University Press, 2007); M. Salzman, *The Making of a Christian Aristocracy: Social and Religious Change in the Western Roman Empire* (Cambridge, MA: Harvard University Press, 2002); G. Clark, *Women in Late Antiquity: Pagan and Christian Life-Styles* (Oxford: Oxford University Press, 1993). This and all future bibliographical footnotes are exemplary rather than exhaustive.

2 See paradigmatically D. Boyarin, *A Radical Jew: Paul and the Politics of Identity* (Berkeley: University of California Press, 1994); *Dying for God: Martyrdom and the Making of Christianity and Judaism* (Stanford: Stanford University Press, 1999); *Border Lines: The Partition of Judaeo-Christianity* (Philadelphia: University of Pennsylvania Press, 2004); *The Jewish Gospels: The Story of the Jewish Christ* (New York: The New Press, 2012).

3 C. Kelly, *Ruling the Later Roman Empire* (Cambridge, MA: The Belknap Press of Harvard University Press, 2004); J. Harries, *Law and Empire in Late Antiquity* (Cambridge: Cambridge University Press, 1999); S. MacCormack, *Art and Ceremony in Late Antiquity* (Berkeley: University of California Press, 1981); C. Humfress, *Orthodoxy and the Courts in Late Antiquity* (Oxford: Oxford University Press, 2007); J. Elsner, *Art and the Roman Viewer: The Transformation of Art from the Pagan World to Christianity* (Cambridge: Cambridge University Press, 1995).

4 See B. Shaw, *Sacred Violence: African Christians and Sectarian Hatred in the Age of Augustine* (Cambridge: Cambridge University Press, 2011).

5 S. Goldhill, *Victorian Culture and Classical Antiquity: Art, Opera, Fiction and the Proclamation of Modernity* (Princeton: Princeton University Press, 2011); R. Rhodes, *The Lion and the Cross: Early Christianity in Victorian Novels* (Columbus: Ohio State University Press, 1995).

6 M. Schofield, *The Stoic City* (Cambridge: Cambridge University Press, 1991); F. G. Downing, *Cynics and Christian Origins* (Edinburgh: T. & T. Clark, 1992).

7 G. O'Daly, *Platonism Pagan and Christian: Studies in Plotinus and Augustine* (Aldershot: Ashgate, 2001); J. Rist, *Augustine: Ancient Thought Baptized* (Cambridge: Cambridge University Press, 1994).

8 In this paper I am concerned with the formal discipline of theology as taught in the Victorian university. The study of religion is also being constructed as a field, distinct from but related to theology, as is the study of comparative mythology, and eventually anthropology: see G. Stroumsa, *A New Science: The Discovery of Religion in the Age of Reason* (Cambridge, MA: Harvard University Press, 2010); C. Kidd, *The World of Mr Casaubon: Britain's Wars of Mythography 1700–1870* (Cambridge: Cambridge University Press, 2017); and for the continuing connection of 'religious studies' and 'classics', R. Gagné, 'The Battle for the Irrational: Greek Religion 1920–1950', in *E. R. Dodds*, eds. S. Harrison, C. Pelling and C. Stray (Oxford, forthcoming); on anthropology see G. Stocking, *Victorian Anthropology* (New York: The Free Press, 1987), and for the relation between anthropology and theology T. Larsen, *The Slain God: Anthropologists and the Christian Faith* (Oxford: Oxford University Press, 2014).

9 J. Marenbon, *Medieval Philosophy: An Historical and Philosophical Introduction* (London and New York: Routledge, 2007), and especially J. Marenbon, *Pagans and Philosophers: The Problem of Paganism from Augustine to Leibniz* (Princeton: Princeton University Press, 2015).

10 S. Goldhill, *Who Needs Greek? Contests in the Cultural History of Hellenism* (Cambridge: Cambridge University Press, 2002); A. Grafton and L. Jardine, *From Humanism to the Humanities: Education and the Liberal Arts in Fifteenth- and Sixteenth-Century England* (Cambridge, MA: Harvard University Press, 1986).

11 A. Grafton, *Joseph Scaliger: A Study in the History of Classical Scholarship. I: Textual Criticism and Exegesis* (Oxford: Oxford University Press, 1983); *Joseph Scaliger: A Study in the History of Classical Scholarship. II: Historical Chronology* (Oxford: Oxford University Press, 1993); D. Levitin, *Ancient Wisdom in the Age of the New Science, Histories of Philosophy in England, c1640–1700* (Cambridge: Cambridge University Press, 2015).

12 J. Sheehan, 'Thomas Hobbes D.D. Theology, Orthodoxy, History', *The Journal of Modern History* 88 (2016), 249–274; J. Sheehan and D. Wahrman, *Invisible Hands: Self-Organization and the Eighteenth Century* (Chicago: University of Chicago Press, 2016).

13 Evangelicals: B. Hilton, *The Age of Atonement: The Influence of Evangelicalism on Social and Economic Thought 1785–1865* (Oxford: Oxford University Press, 1986; D. Bebbington, *Evangelicism in Modern Britain: A History from the 1730s to the 1980s* (London: Unwin Hyman, 1989); missionaries: A. Porter, *Religion versus Empire? British Protestant Missionaries and Overseas Expansion 1700–1914* (Manchester: Manchester University Press, 2004); B. Stanley, *The Bible and the Flag: Protestant Missions and British Imperialism in the Nineteenth and Twentieth Centuries* (Leicester: Apollos, 1990); geology: A. Buckland, *Novel Science: Fiction and the Invention of Nineteenth-Century Geology* (Chicago: University of Chicago Press,

2013); M. Rudwick, *Sciences from Deep Time: Early Pictorial Representations of the Prehistoric World* (Chicago: University Chicago Press, 1992); *Bursting the Limits of Time: The Reconstruction of Geohistory in the Age of Revolution* (Chicago: University of Chicago Press, 2005); biology: J. Secord, *Victorian Sensation: The Extraordinary Publication of the Vestiges of the Natural History of Creation* (Chicago: University of Chicago Press, 2001).

14 C. Stray, *Classics Transformed: Schools, Universities and Society in England, 1830–1960* (Oxford: Clarendon Press, 1998).

15 E. Bar Yosef, *The Holy Land in English Culture 1799–1917* (Oxford: Clarendon Press, 1998).

16 M. Carpenter, *Imperial Bibles, Domestic Bodies: Women, Sexuality and Religion in the Victorian Market* (Athens: Ohio University Press, 2003), for Family Bibles.

17 M. Leonard, *Socrates and the Jews: Hellenism and Hebraism from Moses Mendelssohn to Sigmund Freud* (Chicago: University of Chicago Press, 2012); S. Collini, *Matthew Arnold: a Critical Portrait* (Oxford: Clarendon Press, 1994); L. Gossman, 'Philhellenism and Anti-Semitism: Matthew Arnold and His German Models', *Comparative Literature* 46 (1994), 1–39; R. Young, *Colonial Desire: Hybridity in Theory, Culture and Race* (London: Routledge, 1995); S. Goldhill, 'What Has Alexandria To Do with Jerusalem? Writing the History of the Jews in the Nineteenth Century', *The Historical Journal* 59 (2016), 125–151; and, with a different focus, J. Freedman, *The Temple of Culture: Assimilation and Anti-Semitism in Literary Anglo-America* (Oxford: Oxford University Press, 2000).

18 See Goldhill, 'What Has Alexandria to Do with Jerusalem?'.

19 See D. Gange, 'Odysseus in Eden: Gladstone's Homer and the Idea of a Universal Epic', *Journal of Victorian Studies* 14 (2009), 190–206; D. Bebbington, *The Mind of Gladstone: Religion, Homer, Politics* (Oxford: Oxford University Press, 2004); with J. Parry, *Democracy and Religion: Gladstone and the Liberal Party, 1867–1875* (Cambridge: Cambridge University Press, 1986).

20 G. Murray, 'Olympic Houses', *Albany Review* 2 (1907), 199.

21 Stray, *Classics Transformed.*

22 J. Baldick, *The Social Mission of English Criticism, 1848–1932* (Oxford: Oxford University Press, 1983); S. Rothblatt, *The Revolution of the Dons: Cambridge and Society in Victorian England* (London: Faber and Faber, 1968); *The Modern University and Its Discontents: The Fate of Newman's Legacies in Britain and America* (Cambridge: Cambridge University Press, 1997); S. Rothblatt and B. Wittrock, eds., *The European and American University since 1800: Historical and Sociological Essays* (Cambridge: Cambridge University Press, 1993).

23 F. Turner, *The Greek Heritage in Victorian Britain* (New Haven: Yale University Press, 1981); C. Guthenke, *Studying Antiquity in Nineteenth-Century Germany: Classical Scholarship and the Language of Attachment, 1790–1920* (Cambridge, forthcoming); J. Zachhuber, *Theology as Science in Nineteenth-Century Germany: from F.C. Baur to Ernst Troeltsch* (Oxford: Oxford University Press, 2013); J. Turner, *Philology: The Forgotten Origin of Modern Humanities* (Princeton: Princeton University Press, 2014).

24 Goldhill, *Victorian Culture and Classical Antiquity*; *Who Needs Greek?*; Y. Prins, *Victorian Sappho* (Princeton: Princeton University Press, 1999); J. Sachs, *Romantic Antiquity: Rome in the British Imagination, 1789–1832* (Oxford: Oxford University Press, 2010); N. Vance, *The Victorians and*

Ancient Rome (Oxford: Blackwell, 1997); S. Evangelista, *British Aestheticism and Ancient Greece: Hellenism, Reception, Gods in Exile* (Basingstoke: Palgrave Macmillan, 2009); C. Winterer, *The Culture of Classicism: Ancient Greece and Rome in American Intellectual Life, 1780–1910* (Baltimore and London: Johns Hopkins University Press, 2002); *The Mirror of Antiquity: American Women and the Classical Tradition, 1750–1900* (Ithaca, NY: Cornell University Press, 2007); I. Hurst, *Victorian Women Writers and the Classics: The Feminine of Homer* (Oxford: Oxford University Press, 2006).

25 C. Stray, ed., *Classics in 19th- and 20th-Century Cambridge: Curriculum, Culture and Community* (Cambridge: Cambridge Philological Society, 1999).

26 A. Horstmann, *Antike Theorie und moderne Wissenschaft: August Boeckhs Konzeption der Philologie* (Frankfurt: P. Lang, 1992).

27 P. Vasunia, *The Classics and Colonial India* (Oxford: Oxford University Press, 2013).

28 J. Raphaely, 'Nothing But Gibberish and Shibboleths? The Compulsory Greek Debates, 1870–1919', in *Classics in 19th- and 20th-Century Cambridge: Curriculum, Culture and Community*, ed. C. Stray (Cambridge: Cambridge University Press, 1999), 71–94.

29 S. Fiske, *Heretical Hellenism: Women Writers, Ancient Greece, and the Victorian Popular Imagination* (Athens: Ohio University Press, 2008); L. Dowling, *Hellenism and Homosexuality in Victorian Oxford* (Ithaca, NY: Cornell University Press, 1994); Evangelista, *British Aestheticism and Ancient Greece*; A. Owen, *The Place of Enchantment: British Occultism and the Culture of the Modern* (Chicago: University of Chicago Press, 2004); R. Hutton, *The Triumph of the Moon: A History of Modern Pagan Witchcraft* (Oxford: Oxford University Press, 1999).

30 L. Daston and P. Galison, *Objectivity* (New York: Zone Books, 2007).

31 For a fuller account see S. Goldhill, *A Very Queer Family Indeed: Sex, Religion and the Bensons in Victorian Britain* (Chicago: University of Chicago Press, 2016).

32 A. Burns and C. Stray, 'The Greek Play Bishop', *Historical Journal* 54 (2001): 1013–1038; E. Richardson, *Classical Victorians: Scholars, Scoundrels and Generals in Pursuit of Antiquity* (Cambridge: Cambridge University Press, 2013).

33 The following paragraphs are indebted particularly to G. Faber, *Jowett: A Portrait with Background* (London: Faber and Faber, 1957); P. Hinchcliff, *Benjamin Jowett and the Christian Religion* (New York: Oxford University Press, 1987).

34 D. Orrells, *Classical Culture and Modern Masculinity* (Oxford: Oxford University Press, 2011); Dowling, *Hellenism and Homosexuality*; Vasunia, *Classics and Colonial India.*

35 'Becoming spirit' was picked up and mocked even by Matthew Arnold and G. W. Russell, eds., *Letters of Matthew Arnold*, 2 vols (London: Macmillan & Co., 1853–1919), ii, 32. On *Essays and Reviews*, see J. Altholz, 'The Mind of Victorian Orthodoxy: Anglican Responses to "Essays and Reviews", 1860–1864', *Church History* 51 (1982), 186–197, and the magisterial edition of V. Shea and W. Whitla, *Essays and Reviews: The 1860 Text and Its Readings* (Charlottesville-London: University Press of Virginia, 2000).

36 E. Abbott and L. Campbell, *The Life and Letters of Benjamin Jowett, M.A., Master of Balliol College, Oxford*, 2 vols (London: John Murray, 1897), vol. 1, 275–276.

37 Crucial background in Hilton, *Age of Atonement.*

38 Faber, *Jowett*, 245.
39 Niebuhr's history (first published in 1811) is contextualized in Goldhill, *Victorian Culture and Classical Antiquity*, 171–176. On Thirlwall, see J. Thirlwall, *Connop Thirlwall: Historian and Theologian* (London: SPCK, 1936).
40 On Wolf, see A. Grafton, G. Most and J. Zetzel, 'Introduction', in F. Wolf *Prolegomena to Homer: 1795*, eds. A. Grafton, G. Most, and J. Zetzel (Princeton: University of Princeton Press, 1985), 3–35; on Strauss see H. Harris, *David Friedrich Strauss and His Theology* (Cambridge: Cambridge University Press, 1973); H. Frei, 'David Friedrich Strauss', in *Nineteenth-Century Religious Thought in the West*, eds. N. Smart et al. (Cambridge: Cambridge University Press, 1985), 215–260; T. Larsen, *Contested Christianity: the Political and Social Contexts of Victorian Theology* (Waco, TX: Baylor University Press, 2004), 43–58; D. Pals, *The Victorian "Lives" of Jesus* (San Antonio, TX: Trinity University Press, 1982), 19–58.
41 See C. Kidd, *The Forging of Races: Race and Scripture in the Protestant Atlantic World, 1600–2000* (Cambridge: Cambridge University Press, 2006); with the backstory in C. Kidd, *British Identities Before Nationalism: Ethnicity and Nationhood in the Atlantic World 1600–1800* (Cambridge: Cambridge University Press, 1999), 9–33; G. Stocking, *Race, Culture and Evolution: Essays in the History of Anthropology* (Chicago: University of Chicago Press, 1982); Stocking, *Victorian Anthropology*, 247–252; and for a basic introduction J. Jackson and N. Weidman, *Race, Racism and Science: Social Impact and Interaction* (New Brunswick, NJ: Rutgers University Press, 2006), 35–59.
42 On Maurice, see J. Morris, *F.D. Maurice and the Crisis of Christian Authority* (Oxford: Oxford University Press, 2005). On Grote see Turner, *Greek Heritage*; K. Demetriou, ed., *Brill's Companion to George Grote and the Classical Tradition* (Leiden: Brill, 2014).
43 Barrow, 'Review of Granville's *Travels*', *Quarterly Review* 39 (1829), 1–41, at p. 8.
44 Turner, *Greek Heritage.*
45 H. Tennyson, *Alfred Lord Tennyson: a Memoir*, 2 vols (London: Macmillan & Co., 1905), vol. II, 463.
46 W. Petersen, 'Mrs. Humphry Ward on "Robert Elsmere": Six New Letters', *Bulletin of the New York Public Library* 74 (1970), 587–597, at p. 591.
47 E. Renan, *Recollections of My Youth*, 3rd edn. (London: Chapman and Hall, 1897), 224.
48 Petersen, 'Mrs. Humphry Ward on "Robert Elsmere"', 592.
49 C. Tischendorf, *When Were Our Gospels Written?* (London: Religious Tract Society, 1867), 17.
50 Tischendorf, *Gospels*, 20.
51 Ibid., 36.
52 D. Parker, *Codex Sinaiticus: the Story of the World's Oldest Bible* (London: The British Library/Peabody, 2010), 3 – from whom the figures in this paragraph are gleaned.
53 D. Van Hulle and J. Leerssen, eds., *Editing the Nation's Memory: Textual Scholarship and Nation-Building in 19th-Century Europe* (Amsterdam and New York: Rodopi, 2008); with J. Leerssen, *National Thought in Europe: a Cultural History* (Amsterdam: Amsterdam University Press, 2006); S. Dentith, *Epic and Empire in Nineteenth-Century Britain* (Cambridge: Cambridge University Press, 2006); S. Marchand, *German Orientalism in the Age of Empire: Religion, Race and Scholarship* (Cambridge: Cambridge University Press, 2009); T. Koditschek, *Liberalism, Imperialism, and the*

Historical Imagination: Nineteenth-Century Visions of a Greater Britain (Cambridge: Cambridge University Press, 2011).

54 See P. Levine, *Amateur and Professional: Antiquarians, Historians and Archaeologists in Victorian England, 1838–1886* (Cambridge: Cambridge University Press, 1986); N. Silberman, *Digging for God and Country: Exploration, Archaeology and the Secret Struggle for the Holy Land* (New York: Knopf, 1982); W. Stiebing, *Uncovering the Past: A History of Archaeology* (New York: Oxford University Press, 1994); A. Schnapp, *The Discovery of the Past: The Origins of Archaeology* (London: British Museum Press, 1996); V. Hoselitz, *Imagining Roman Britain: Victorian Responses to a Roman Past* (Woodbridge, UK: Royal Historical Society, 2007); and in particular S. Marchand, *Down from Olympus: Archaeology and Philhellenism in Germany, 1750–1870* (Princeton: Princeton University Press, 1996).

55 J. W. Grover, 'Pre-Augustinian Christianity in Britain: As Indicated by the Discovery of Christian Symbols', *Journal of the British Archaeological Association* 23 (1867), 221–230, at p. 221.

56 A. Swenson and P. Mandler, eds., *From Plunder and Preservation: Britain and the Heritage of Empire, Proceedings of the British Academy* (Oxford: Oxford University Press, 2013), 187 and the works cited earlier n 54.

57 J. Fergusson, *The Palaces of Nineveh and Persepolis Restored: An Essay on Ancient Assyrian Art and Persian Architecture* (London: J. Murray, 1851), p. 9.

58 See R. Hallotte, *Bible, Map and Spade: The American Palestine Exploration Society, Frederick Jones Bliss and the Forgotten Story of Early American Biblical Archaeology* (Piscataway, NJ: Gorgias Press, 2006); Silberman, *Digging for God and Country.*

59 N. Silberman, 'Petrie's Head: Eugenics and Near Eastern Archaeology', in *Assembling the Past*, eds. A. Kehoe and M. B. Emmerichs (Albuquerque: University of New Mexico Press, 1999); and generally D. Gange, *Dialogues with the Dead: Egyptology in British Culture and Religion, 1822–1922* (Oxford: Oxford University Press, 2013); S. Quirke, *Hidden Hands: Egyptian Workforces in Petrie Excavation Archives, 1880–1924* (London: Duckworth, 2010) also points out how little Petrie knew about his own workforce.

60 W. St Clair, *Lord Elgin and the Marbles: the Controversial History of the Parthenon Sculptures*, 3rd edn. (Oxford: Oxford University Press, 1998).

61 R. Hingley, *Roman Officers and English Gentlemen: The Imperial Origins of Roman Archaeology* (London and New York: Routledge, 2000); *The Recovery of Roman Britain 1586–1906* (Oxford: Oxford University Press, 2008); Hoselitz, *Imagining Roman Britain.*

62 W. M. Beard, *The Parthenon* (London: Profile Books, 2002).

63 S. Goldhill, *The Buried Life of Things: How Objects Made History in Nineteenth-Century Britain* (Cambridge: Cambridge University Press, 2014); S. Edwards, *The Making of British Photography: Allegories* (University Park: Pennsylvania Press State University Press, 2006); F. Bohrer, *Orientalism and Visual Culture: Imagining Mesopotamia in Nineteenth-Century Europe* (Cambridge: Cambridge University Press, 2003); E. Downing, *After Images: Photography, Archaeology and Psychoanalysis, and the Tradition of Bildung* (Detroit: Wayne State University Press, 2006).

64 A. P. Stanley, *Sermons Preached before His Royal Highness the Prince of Wales, During His Tour in the East, in the Spring of 1862, with Notices of Some of the Localities Visited* (London: J. Murray, 1863).

65 F. Bedford, *Mr F. Bedford's Photographic Pictures Taken During the Tour in the East in Which, by Command, He Accompanied His Royal Highness, the Prince of Wales* (London: Alfred W. Bennett, 1863).

66 See D. Schmidt, *On Germans and Other Greeks: Tragedy and Ethical Life* (Bloomington: Indiana University Press, 2001); P. Szondi, *An Essay on the Tragic*, trans. P. Fleming (Stanford: Stanford University Press, 2002); J. Billings, *The Genealogy of the Tragic: Greek Tragedy and German Philosophy* (Princeton: Princeton University Press, 2014); M. Silk and P. Stern, *Nietzsche on Tragedy* (Cambridge: Cambridge University Press, 1981); S. Goldhill, *Sophocles and the Language of Tragedy* (Oxford: Oxford University Press, 2012).
67 G. Hegel, *Aesthetics: Lectures on Fine Art*, 2 vols, trans. B. Knox (Oxford: Clarendon Press, 1975), vol. II, 1219–1220.
68 Hegel, *Aesthetics*, I, 1219.
69 For a fuller version see S. Goldhill, 'The Ends of Tragedy', *PMLA* 129 (2014), 634–648.
70 E. A. Freeman, 'Grote's *History of Greece*', *North British Review* 25 (1856), 141–172, at p. 172.
71 E. Abbott, ed., *Hellenica: A Collection of Essays on Greek Poetry, Philosophy, History and Religion* (London: Rivingtons, 1880), 38.
72 E. Plumptre, *The Tragedies of Sophocles* (London: A. Strahan, 1865), lxxxix.
73 Ibid., xcviii.
74 B. F. Westcott, *Essays on Religious Thought in the West* (London and New York: Macmillan, 1891), 52, 94.
75 Westcott, *Essays*, 140.
76 The study by Alison Knight is eagerly awaited.
77 Goldhill, *Victorian Culture and Antiquity*; K. Nichols, *Greece and Rome at the Crystal Palace: Classical Sculpture and Modern Britain, 1854–1936* (Oxford: Oxford University Press, 2014); E. Prettejohn, *The Modernity of Ancient Sculpture: Greek Sculpture and Modern Art from Winckelmann to Picasso* (London: I. B. Tauris, 2012).
78 Gagné, 'The Battle for the Irrational' shows how fruitful such work will be.
79 D. Boin, 'Classicists Christian Problem', *Chronicle of Higher Education*, January 15, 2016.
80 This paragraph was composed in part with Tim Whitmarsh.

10 From Truth to Proof to Computer Problem

Of Mathematical Discipline and Epistemological Change

Joan L. Richards[1]

Mathematics might be seen as one of the oldest disciplines. It was an essential part of the curriculum of the medieval universities, and unlike music, for example, maintained that position into the modern world. But mathematics is a properly plural word and a many-splendored thing. In nineteenth-century England it lay at the centre of the liberal arts curriculum, served as an essential support for the study of astronomy, and was recognized as a part of physics throughout the century. It only began to be pursued as an autonomous entity in the second part of Victoria's reign. For the purposes of this paper, the creation of the London Mathematical Society (LMS) in 1865 may serve to mark the time that English mathematics began to be recognized as an independent discipline worthy of a place of its own.

Creating an independent social and institutional locus for the study of mathematics was a significant development. It coincided with a change that Jeremy Gray has described as a mathematical revolution 'characterized by a change in the ontological status of the basic objects of study'.[2] At the beginning of the century, among the English, the mark of a legitimate mathematical statement was that it was ***true***, in some way that could be directly grasped. By the end of the century, within the community that identified with the LMS, that same legitimacy meant that it could be ***proved*** within a well-defined framework of mathematical propositions. Gray sees this ontological change as the result of an essentially internal dynamic; it was 'brought about by a number of mathematicians working in a number of areas of mathematics, who came to feel that the resolution of many advanced questions required for their solution a redefinition of the foundations of their subject'.[3] He recognizes that resisters do remain in his modern mathematical world, but he brushes them aside with the observation that they are like 'small dissident parties' within a larger 'body politic, which democratically ignores them'.[4] Thus, for Gray, mathematics is essentially defined as the subject as it has been pursued by the majority of mathematicians since the nineteenth century. A necessary prerequisite for the coherence of this group is a disciplinary boundary that is strong enough to support them in their isolation. In other words, mathematics' disciplinary status defines the subject itself.

Gray's dismissive approach to those who transgress the boundaries that were erected in the process of defining mathematics as a discipline may be a good way to maintain disciplinary power, but that does not mean it is helpful for understanding mathematics as it has been practised in the past or as it may be practised in the future. Mathematics is a remarkably chameleon subject that has adjusted to its surroundings for millennia. When, in the English nineteenth century, it was embedded in areas like education or astronomy or physics, it conformed to the values of those fields. Like most disciplines in this period, such as history (Chapter 5), music (Chapter 12), or even the scientific disciplines in general (Chapter 1), mathematics evolved significantly over the course of the century. Approaching the subject in terms of the many kinds of truth mathematics might uncover allowed it to flourish in many different guises. The mathematics of proof that emerged as a discipline in the late nineteenth century was rigid, unyielding, and inflexible. Clearly defined disciplinary boundaries were a necessary prerequisite to support this kind of highly specialized study. Formal proofs appear in geometry courses, but are otherwise quite absent in pre-college mathematics courses, and are equally secondary for those who are using mathematics to track the position of stars or describe physical phenomena. Mathematics could not be defined by its proofs until it became a discipline of its own.

Recognizing the central role that discipline formation has played in supporting the modern proof-driven view of mathematics may be a first step towards reopening the richness of its pre-disciplinary past, but is not enough to free our understanding of the subject's development from the constraints that have been imposed by disciplinary thinking. On the contrary, privileging the formation of the discipline in this way may serve just to divide the history of mathematics between a muddled pre-disciplinary, pre-modern past and an enlightened modern present. For the purposes of this chapter, then, I propose embedding the idea of discipline within a larger idea of 'epistemic culture' suggested by Karen Knorr-Cetina. In *Epistemic Cultures: How the sciences make knowledge*, Knorr-Cetina describes epistemic cultures as the combination of social and natural arrangements that 'in a given field make up *how we know what we know*'.[5] Her notion of a culture that decides '*how we know what we know*' fits very well with the modern discipline that supports a mathematics of proof. At the same time, it has the advantage of a breadth that recognizes that before the disciplinary turn, different kinds of mathematics were supported by different epistemic cultures—of education, astronomy, physics, and philosophy. Equally important, thinking in terms of epistemic cultures opens up the expanse of possible futures that have, or may, unfold after the late nineteenth-century discipline was well established.

This chapter will use Knorr-Cetina's concept of epistemic cultures to explore the development of mathematical ontology, what Gray calls the understandings of 'the status of the basic objects of study', from the mathematics of truth through the mathematics of proof and beyond. It will begin with Augustus De Morgan as an exemplar for the truth-driven mathematics that defined the subject in the first half of the nineteenth century. By some definitions, because De Morgan was the first to earn a living by pursuing mathematics both as a teacher and as a researcher, he might be seen as England's first professional mathematician. At the same time, this very uniqueness means that he had no experience working in the kind of clearly delineated mathematical community that supported the development of a proof-driven view of the subject in the latter half of the century. Nonetheless De Morgan did work within a community that, to use a phrase Knorr-Cetina applied to epistemic communities, served to 'create and warrant' his mathematical investigations. He worked within the nascent community of English intellectuals who Jack Morrell and Arnold Thackray have aptly dubbed the 'gentlemen of science'.[6]

In the 1820s Morrell and Thackray's 'gentlemen of science' were to be found clustered together in the Geological Society, the Linnaean Society, and the Astronomical Society; the defining crucible for their identity was the formation of the British Association for the Advancement of Science (BAAS) in the early 1830s. The group included men like William Whewell, John Herschel, Charles Babbage, George Peacock, and George Biddel Airy. These men were for the most part 'cultured Anglicans', who followed a latitudinarian theology, and a politics of 'moderate reform'. They were all highly educated but none of them could claim to be gentlemen in the most traditional sense of the word. Their challenge was to create a social space for themselves in which scientific prowess guaranteed the privileges and respect traditionally accorded to gentlemen. In the 1833 meeting of the BAAS, William Whewell suggested that the men gathered there call themselves 'scientists', but they were far too culturally conservative to adopt such a new-fangled, faintly grubby term for themselves.[7] Samuel Taylor Coleridge coined the term 'clerisy' to designate the group, which he saw as 'a sort of national church of intellect', but its members were equally unwilling to accept the neo-religious overtones of this designation.[8] Morrell's and Thackray's designation of them as 'gentlemen of science' signals their determined resistance to being understood as a narrowly defined disciplinary group. Their understanding of '*how we know what we kno*w' was embedded in a gentlemanly intellectual world in which natural knowledge was just one part of a much larger pursuit of truth in whatever guise it could be found.

Augustus De Morgan was the major representative of this gentlemanly ideal in mathematics. His Cambridge education, membership in the Astronomical Society, and determination to devote himself to a life at the forefront of intellectual change clearly locate him among Morrell's and Thackray's gentlemen of science, but equally important factors marginalized him. The Professor of Mathematics at the 'godless' London University was not a liberal, latitudinarian Anglican but a rebel who had left the Anglican Church entirely; the young man who responded to the French Revolution of 1830 with dispatches hailing the power of the French *citoyens* was far beyond of the politics of 'moderate reform'; and the reasoned, mathematical thinker was never involved either in the founding of, nor in the subsequent meetings of, the BAAS. De Morgan does not merit a single mention in Morrell's and Thackray's *Gentlemen of Science* but he was just as determined to be granted the respect due to a gentleman as were those who did; the difference may be signalled by noting that as they were forging positions for themselves as gentlemen of science, De Morgan was creating a place for himself as a gentleman of reason. The mathematics he pursued was the epitome of what Gray has called the 'mathematics of truth'.

The first section of this chapter will lay out the view of mathematics that De Morgan set out in 1828, in an 'Introductory Lecture' delivered at the opening of the London University, which later became University College London. In this lecture, composed when he was just twenty-two years old, De Morgan laid out the basic parameters of the subject that he was to pursue for the rest of his life. The key characteristic of mathematics De Morgan taught to his students at UCL was his conviction that the proper exercise of reason could uncover transcendent truths of the world around us. For him, to think mathematically was to align one's thoughts with the thoughts of the God who had created the heavens and the earth. Practising mathematics was a profoundly personal exercise, whose essential value lay in the ways it could lead its practitioners to a deeper understanding of truth. Learning mathematics was more akin to studying theology than it was to modern science.

The second section will consider the functioning of De Morgan's epistemic culture by following his response to a new mathematical challenge—the proposition that four colours suffice to colour a geographical map. De Morgan first heard this claim from one of his students, and an evening of experimentation convinced him that it was true. He then shared it with other members of intellectual circle, as an example of a new mathematical truth. None of his colleagues were particularly interested in following through on this discovery, but none of them disputed its essential truth. In their epistemic culture that four colours could colour a map was an axiom that, once recognized, could not be disputed. It stood as the epitome of a mathematical truth that could be recognized immediately and personally.

The third section will follow De Morgan's axiom into a new generation, in which many were intrigued by the claim that four colours sufficed to colour a map. They were members of a new world in which mathematics was beginning to emerge as a free-standing professional discipline. The boundaries of that discipline were becoming clear enough for them to claim the supremacy of their mathematics of proof over the mathematics De Morgan had pursued, in which an immediate experience of truth was accessible to all. That four colours suffice to colour a map was profoundly changed in this transition. What in De Morgan's truth-defined world had been an 'axiom' became for them a 'problem', a 'conjecture', or a 'theorem', which required proof. However, proving De Morgan's axiom was profoundly problematic for these proof-seeking mathematicians. It remained the case, as De Morgan had claimed, that a couple of hours with maps and paints was enough to persuade most people that it was self-evident, but proving it confounded generations of modern proof-seeking mathematicians.

The way out of this impasse lay in allowing a computer to declare that De Morgan's axiom was true. This outcome was the result of a four-year collaboration between a mathematician and a computer scientist and more than a hundred hours of computer time. Accepting the result as a mathematical proof entails a radical redefinition of that term. A mathematics in which a computer can prove the four-colour problem is as far from the proof-driven mathematics Gray described as that mathematics is from De Morgan's truth-driven one. Allowing a computer to prove a mathematical theorem happened within a new epistemological culture in which a mathematician and a computer scientist moved beyond their disciplines into a new mathematics that was essentially entwined with the powers of a machine.

Inaugural Lecture

On November 5, 1828, De Morgan delivered an 'Inaugural Lecture' to the opening of the Mathematical Class in the University of London (see Figure 10.1). The defining feature of the fledgling University was its secular nature; much of the previous two years had been devoted to finding ways to define the parameters of a secular institution that could transcend the religious divisions that defined so much of nineteenth-century English society. Reason was key to this vision, and in a singularly rich passage at the beginning of this talk, De Morgan succinctly laid out the essential characteristics of the mathematics of reason that he was to develop over the course of a more than forty year career. Standing before an audience of educators and parents he explained:

> This novel system of writing, this compendious language (for such in fact it is) contains in its very formation the germ of the most valuable improvements which the mathematics have ever received, and has been from its peculiar structure, a never failing guide to new discoveries. . . .[T]he study of this language, without reference to any of its

Figure 10.1 '"De Morgan Teaching" as sketched in class by one of his students'. Special Collections, University College London. MSADD 7.

> applications, is instrumental in furnishing the mind with new ideas, and calling into exercise some of the powers which most peculiarly distinguish man from the brute creation.[9]

As here presented, the defining essence of mathematics was its status as a symbolic language. At first glance this may seem to be a neutral characterization, because linking mathematics with reason by equating it to with language is an approach that has survived the major mathematical ontological upheaval of the late nineteenth century. The persistence of this connection, even as the definition of mathematics has gone through such a fundamental change, signals the need to look more closely at what De Morgan had in mind when he used it.

De Morgan was helpfully clear about what he meant and neatly laid out three qualities that essentially defined the power of the language that for him defined mathematics: first, mathematics is a 'compendious language'; second, mathematics is 'instrumental in furnishing the mind with new ideas, and calling into exercise some of the powers which most peculiarly distinguish man from the brute creation'; and third, mathematics is a language that 'contains in its very formation the germ of the most valuable improvements which the mathematics have ever received, and has been from its peculiar structure, a never failing guide to new discoveries'. Taken together, these three qualities comprise the essence of the subject that De Morgan pursued throughout his life.

Mathematics as a 'compendious language'

The word 'compendious' is not yet classified as obsolete in the Oxford English Dictionary, but it is rare enough that it is worth remembering its meaning: 'Containing the substance within small compass, concise, succinct, summary; comprehensive though brief; esp. of literary works; also of their authors'. De Morgan was a meticulous, highly educated and literate man who chose his words very carefully. That mathematics is 'concise, succinct, summary', and 'comprehensive though brief' is precisely what he meant when he described it as 'compendious'. In his lecture, he first used Locke as way to compare the compendious precision of mathematical language to the less compendious exactitude of English. He began by turning to Locke's *Essay Concerning Human Understanding* (1690) as a model of the 'correct application of terms' in English. As an illustration of the ways terms are used in English he found an example in which Locke used 'the four following terms, all used to signify the same thing, solidity—resistance—hardness and impenetrability'. These four words, De Morgan continues, are

> so much alike in their meaning, that in ordinary conversation, they might be used indiscriminately one for the other. Yet there are no two of them which convey precisely the same idea, and the difference between them cannot be expressed in (simple) words.[10]

This kind of subtle difference of meaning marked English as a nuanced spoken language, but it had no place in the language that constituted De Morgan's mathematics. In the language that was mathematics the meanings for all words and symbols were absolutely crisp and precise. De Morgan again turned to Locke to make this point:

> The simple modes of numbers are of all others the most distinct; every the least variation, which is an unit, making each combination as clearly different from that which approacheth nearest to it, as the most remote; and the idea of two as distinct from the idea of three as the magnitude of the whole earth, is from that of a mite.[11]

Whenever De Morgan spoke of mathematics as 'exact', it was the precision made possible by this tight linkage between symbol and meaning that he meant. Mathematics was for him the essence of a meaningful language, a 'concise, succinct, [and] summary' language whose power lay in the precision with which it captured meaning. It was this exactitude of definition that made mathematics unique, and which supported the development of the mathematics of reason.

Mathematics as Reason

De Morgan was not alone in this view of mathematics. His Lockean description of mathematics as a compendious language was the essential justification for the mathematical curriculum he had studied at Cambridge, but it had a particular resonance for the London University that had just hired him as its Professor of Mathematics. Locke's view that the faculty of reason essentially defined the human was a central part of the enlightenment ideal that England's first secular university was reaching towards. The challenge for the new Professor of Mathematics was to establish the importance of mathematics for achieving the goal of educating enlightened men.

De Morgan's starting point was a Lockean human being, who was born with a wide open mind. But De Morgan's Locke recognized that that mind was not 'like a blank sheet of paper fit and ready to receive any impression and retain it for its own use'. Before it could learn anything useful it had to 'be prepared, its powers of arranging and combining what was presented to it were to be developed'.[12] These organizing powers were the powers of reason, and strengthening them was crucial to bringing students to their full human potential.

De Morgan recognized that reason was the foundation for all of human achievement, from understanding the physical world, to practising a trade, but he was not particularly interested in these things. In his 'Inaugural Lecture' he summarily dismissed the value judgements of those looking for practical utility in their studies, and respectfully left the challenge of understanding the physical world to physics, or natural philosophy. For mathematics he reserved a different mission, at once circumscribed and huge; the mission of a mathematical teacher was to bring students to their full humanity by enabling them to 'distinguish right from wrong'.[13] The key word in this phrase is 'distinguish'. In De Morgan's view, people made bad decisions not because they were evil but rather because they were insufficiently clear; as he puts it in a later publication, 'evil is often chosen in preference to good, not from any lack of desire to do what is right, but from a want of means to distinguish clearly; in difficult circumstances, where the proper course lies'. People do evil things because they misunderstand the rules that are laid out for guidance. They succumb to 'potentates' who rest secure in the conviction that 'the few who have been taught to think are no match for the many, high and low, who are incapable of any such exercise'.[14] An education in the compendious language that was mathematics was uniquely suited to addressing these problems. It could protect students from being misled by vague promises and teach them the processes of accurate reasoning that led to truth. As De Morgan's mathematical student focussed on the fine distinctions in the meanings of mathematical words, and carefully followed the trains of reasoning that led to new discoveries he was truly 'calling into exercise some of the powers which most peculiarly distinguish man from the brute creation'.[15] Every day in class De Morgan was saving his students from the lives of 'crime and misery' that would ensue if they could not 'see through the misapplication of a few words'.[16]

Progressive Mathematics

Progress was the third aspect of De Morgan's mathematical vision. He was just twenty-two years old in 1828, a brilliant and forward looking young man in a country poised to explode in prosperity and scope. The mathematics he embraced 'contains in its very formation the germ of the most valuable improvements which the mathematics have ever received, and has been from its peculiar structure, a never failing guide to new discoveries'.[17] The compendious language that was De Morgan's mathematics was a field whose progressive potential matched that of the country within which he lived.

De Morgan's characterization of his subject as progressive was not an easy position to maintain. From the time of the ancient Greeks geometry had been seen as the study of space, arithmetic as the study of number. To the extent that mathematics was defined as a compendious language that captured its subject matter exactly, there was no place for change. As De Morgan stood before his audience in 1828, there were two levels to the challenge that faced him in defending his claim for mathematical progress. The first was the relatively straightforward problem of defining what he meant by progress. The second was the considerably more complex problem of understanding how to organize and think about the nature of mathematical research to ensure that real progress could continue to take place in the future. In 1828, he could do the first but it took another seven years and considerable intellectual struggle before he could come up with the second.

De Morgan's favourite example of mathematical progress was the development of exponents from the sixteenth through the eighteenth centuries. In his reconstruction, that study emerged from the development of as a simple shorthand—from $\mathbf{a} \times \mathbf{a}$ to $\mathbf{aa}$ to $\mathbf{a}^2$ and hence to the entire development of exponents. Never in this story did mathematics go outside of its language; working totally with its symbols it managed to reveal relations and develop powers that were not known before. In the development of exponents, De Morgan had a wonderful example of a language that 'contains in its very formation the germ of the most valuable improvements which the mathematics have ever received, and has been from its peculiar structure, a never failing guide to new discoveries . . .'[18] The development of exponents provided De Morgan with an example of progress within a compendious mathematics, but it was an essentially limited one. Exponents and the logarithms that grew from them were powerful calculating tools, but they did not in any way alter the understanding of the essential concept of number that the compendious language of mathematics was so precisely describing. Finding a way to introduce real conceptual progress into De Morgan's mathematics was a significantly more difficult problem.

Negative numbers exemplified this fundamental challenge. At the time that he was delivering his lecture De Morgan was acutely aware that no clear definition of the negative numbers was to be found in the classical concept of number that provided the meanings for the symbols of algebra. This meant that from the point of view of the mathematics of truthful reason they were essentially illegitimate, and he carefully steered his students around them.[19] But De Morgan fundamentally modified his view of negative numbers in response to *A Treatise on Algebra*, which was written in 1830 by his friend and former teacher, George Peacock. In this work Peacock reinterpreted the relationship between algebra and arithmetic. Instead of defining algebra as a compendious language that took arithmetic as its subject, Peacock established algebra as a separate subject, in its own right. In his view, arithmetic equations like $(4^2\text{-}2^2) = (4\text{-}2)(4\text{+}2)$ pointed the way to symbolic forms like $(\mathbf{a}^2\text{-}\mathbf{b}^2) = (\mathbf{a}\text{-}\mathbf{b})(\mathbf{a}\text{+}\mathbf{b})$, but that was all. Arithmetic equations suggested algebraic forms, but did not define them. The algebra that emerged was an essentially separate study that focussed on the symbolic forms and their inter-relationships, looking for interpretations wherever they could be found. It was a compendious language in the making.

It took De Morgan several years to respond to Peacock's approach: 'At first it seemed to us something like symbols bewitched and running around the world in search of meaning'.[20] Slowly, however, he began to accept that the validating interpretations of formal systems might lie in unexpected areas. The turning point for him was recognizing that not only negative but also imaginary numbers could be interpreted as points on the complex plane. What De Morgan took from this development was an instance in which the true meaning of a set of algebraically generated terms had emerged gradually over time. This struck him with all the force of a conversion experience. Ever after he was convinced that all algebraic forms, however opaque their meanings might be, would ultimately always be interpretable. To those who suggested that sometimes, as in the case of divergent series, algebraic manipulations generated absurd results, De Morgan replied with the battle cry: 'remember $\sqrt{-1}$!'[21]

The realization that algebraic systems might have interpretations beyond the concept of number was profoundly liberating for De Morgan, and in the late 1830s and 1840s he eagerly plunged into investigating them. It is to this De Morgan that we owe the explicit recognition of the basic laws (he omitted only associativity) that structure field algebras. It can be tempting to see this De Morgan as a formal mathematician, but to do so is to lose sight of the essential definition of his mathematical program. Recognizing that a set of laws structure a system and viewing that system as defined by those laws are two essentially different approaches. The difference between them is precisely what separates the mathematics of truth that lay on one side of Gray's ontological revolution from the mathematics of proof that lies on the other, and De Morgan never made the switch. Successful though he was in finding the laws that described the relations of the system, he never took the step of stating that algebraic systems were grounded in these laws alone. On the contrary, he emphasized their essential triviality for real mathematical work. 'By itself, this method of operation, this algebra of rules without meaning, is no more of a science than the use of the well-known toy called the Chinese puzzle. . .'[22] De Morgan was never interested in pursuing this kind of empty mathematics. His focus was always trained on finding the transcendent truth that lay beyond the symbols of algebra.

Little separates the mathematics of truth that De Morgan described in his 'Inaugural Lecture' and pursued throughout his career, from the subject he had studied at Cambridge. His talk of 'crime and misery' may be read as a marker of the differences that divided the religiously diverse, urban students he was to be teaching from that gentlemanly group with whom he had learned mathematics at Cambridge. His emphasis on reason and Locke was certainly attractive to the radical audience of UCL, but he had learned it as part of his gentlemanly education. His talk of progress undoubtedly resonated with his audience but he learned of it from Peacock. However proudly he might insist on his position as a radical, the subject De Morgan pursued was always the mathematics of truth supported by the epistemic culture of the gentlemen of science.

The Four-Colour Axiom

The mathematics that De Morgan described in his 'Inaugural Lecture' formed the basis for his teaching, but that teaching comprised only a small part of his mathematical work. He taught during the day, but spent his evenings working tirelessly to contribute to the progress of mathematics. The locus for his research was the library in the middle of his home. Very few people were admitted to this inner sanctum, but De Morgan was not alone there; an enormous volume of letters flowed in and out of his study. Among his most constant correspondents were William Whewell, John Herschel, Sir William Rowan Hamilton, and George Boole. In the social and political terms of nineteenth-century England, this group is strikingly diverse: Whewell was the High Anglican Tory

Master of Trinity College, Cambridge; Herschel was an independently wealthy Astronomical celebrity; Hamilton was the well-established Catholic Andrews Professor of Astronomy of Trinity College, Dublin; Boole was the struggling Professor of Mathematics at Queen's College, Cork. The central tie that bound the members of this group in correspondence with the determinedly radical, Professor of Mathematics at University College London, was their common respect for the study he described as 'calling into exercise some of the powers which most peculiarly distinguish man from the brute creation'. De Morgan's correspondents constituted the core of the epistemic community that understood and warranted the knowledge he developed in his library.[23]

De Morgan's library was the locus of his investigations into the compendious mathematics of words. He was an avid bibliophile who haunted London's bookshops in search of the books that had advanced mathematics since the invention of the printing press. Whereas his books were his ties to the historical side of progressive mathematics, conversations with his students and his children were his ties to the often parallel, developmental side. De Morgan's letters to his friends were filled with delighted stories of children's and students' early encounters with mathematical ideas and challenges. The focus of De Morgan's interest in these stories was less on the specific mathematical ideas being developed or learned than it was on the ways that people understood and related to those ideas. He was fascinated by the ways that people come to the mathematical understanding that defines their rational essence.

De Morgan's fascination with the ways we come to know mathematics formed the basis of his response to one of the mathematical contributions for which he is still well known: the proposition that four colours are sufficient to colour a map. This proposition began its mathematical career in the fall of 1852, when one of De Morgan's students, Frederick Guthrie, asked whether he knew the 'fact': 'that the greatest necessary number of colours to be used in colouring a map so as to avoid identity of colour in lineally contiguous districts is four'.[24] When De Morgan first heard this claim it did not seem to merit consideration as something that could be known with mathematical precision. It seemed strange, even unlikely, and what is more, it was nowhere to be found in any of his books. Nonetheless, after an evening spent drawing little pictures in hopes of proving it wrong, and he was astonished to find that he instead emerged absolutely convinced.[25] Did you know, he asked Hamilton, 'that if a figure be any how divided and the compartments differently coloured so that figures with any portion of common boundary *line* are differently coloured--four colours may be wanted, but not more?'[26] Hamilton was not impressed. 'I am not likely to attempt your 'quaternion' of colours very soon',[27] but his disinterest did not leave De Morgan any less convinced about the truth of Guthrie's 'fact'.

When, a year later, Hamilton had still not found the time to corroborate De Morgan's observation, he turned to Whewell. Whewell was an excellent audience for De Morgan's interest in his new-found recognition. He was as convinced as De Morgan was that history showed science, including mathematics, to be progressing. In 1838, he explored the growth of scientific and mathematical ideas in a three volume *History of Science*, and when he published his magisterial *Philosophy of the Inductive Sciences* in 1844, it was '*founded upon their history*'.[28] In these works, Whewell approached scientific knowledge in essentially Kantian terms. He saw true knowledge of the external world to be exemplified by Newtonian cosmology in which inborn ideas of geometry correlate with the external reality of space to form an absolute understanding. Kant characterized this kind of knowledge as a priori synthetic, and understood it an absolute, ahistorical category. Whewell's challenge was to open this kind of understanding of knowledge to progress. His response was to create a new category, the 'Fundamental Idea', which was large enough to include not only the classical ideas of Space and Time that constituted Kant's a priori synthetic but also historically emergent ideas, like Newton's idea of Force.

Whewell's enlargement of Kant's vision to incorporate historically developing ideas had its detractors, however, and when De Morgan brought Guthrie's 'fact' to his attention in December of 1853, Whewell was deep in discussion with the Oxford theologian, Henry Longueville Mansel. Mansel was insisting that the unchanging ideas of Space and Time, which Kant had recognized to be a priori synthetic, were unique and uniquely important. Whewell was wrong to downplay the permanence that characterized these ideas by placing them with more recently developed ideas, like Newton's idea of 'force', under the single umbrella of the Fundamental Idea. Over the course of their intense discussion Whewell was forced to concede that historically emergent ideas were considerably more obscure than were the classical ideas of Space and Time that comprised Kant's synthetic a priori. In response he began to focus on their status as 'axioms' which could be known as certainly as were Space and Time, although grasping them clearly could require considerable time and education.

Whewell's definition of 'axiom' was a good fit for De Morgan's understanding of the proposition that four colours sufficed (see Figure 10.2). In his December letter, he introduced the subject with a definition of 'axiom' that stressed its psychological nature:

> By an axiom I mean a proposition which cannot be made dependent upon obviously more simple ones—so that it may be possible that A's axioms are not those of B. The axiomatic character is purely subjective—and consists in <u>seeing</u> the proposition as clearly as its ultimate bases.

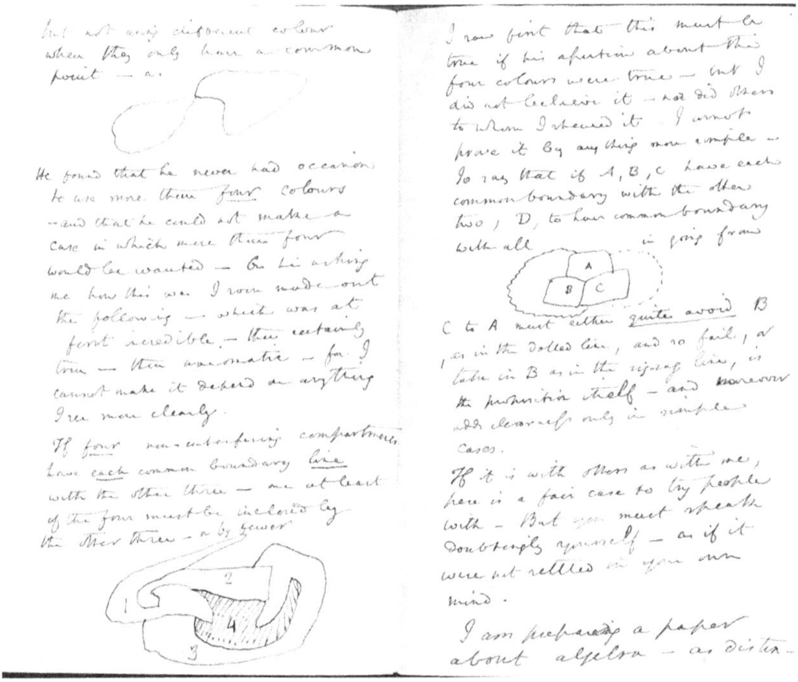
but not any different colour
when they only have a common
point — as

He found that he never had occasion
to use more than four colours
— and that he could not make a
case in which more than four
would be wanted — On his asking
me how this was I soon made out
the following — which was at
first incredible — then certainly
true — then axiomatic — for I
cannot make it depend on anything
I see more clearly.
If four non-interfering compartments
have each common boundary line
with the other three — one at least
of the four must be inclosed by
the other three — or by fewer

I now point that this must be
true if his assertion about the
four colours were true — but I
did not believe it — nor did others
to whom I showed it. I cannot
prove it by anything more simple —
To say that if A, B, C have each
common boundary with the other
two, D, to have common boundary
with all ... in going from

C to A must either quite avoid B
, as in the dotted line, and so fail, or
take in B as in the zig-zag line, is
the proposition itself — and moreover
adds clearness only in simple
cases.
If it is with others as with me,
here is a fair case to try people
with — But you must speak
doubtingly yourself — as if it
were not settled in your own
mind.
I am preparing a paper
about algebra — as distin-

Figure 10.2 'The letter of December 9, 1853, in which De Morgan presented the four-colour problem to Whewell'. Trinity College Library, ADD. ms.a 202.[125] By permission of Master and Fellows of Trinity College Cambridge.

He then devoted two pages to reproducing the little diagrams and approaches he had followed until 'I soon made out the following—which was at first incredible—then certainly true—then axiomatic—for I cannot made it depend on anything I see more clearly'. 'Having thus presented his own experience as exemplary, De Morgan tried to enlist Whewell's aid in confirming that his experience was a universal one. 'If it is with others as with me, here is a fair case to try people with—But you must speak doubtingly yourself—as if it were not settled in your own mind'.[29] De Morgan thus offered Guthrie's fact as a new example of an absolutely true insight that had emerged over time.[30]

There is no reason to believe that Whewell spent any time speaking doubtingly to Trinity Fellows and visitors about whether four colours sufficed to colour a map, but his silence did not rule out De Morgan's claim that Guthrie's observation was axiomatic. Certainly De Morgan was not discouraged, and six years later, in a review of Whewell's *Philosophy of Discovery*, he explicitly introduced Guthrie's observation as an example that showed 'knowledge of necessary truth may be *progressive*'.

> Now we believe that even in geometry, a fundamental and axiomatic position—meaning one which cannot be made to depend upon anything more simple and fundamental—may remain unknown and unthought of for century after century, though all the objects of thought employed in the proposition were familiar, and the proposition itself was actually leading to practical facilities. We believe this to be possible because we believe it has actually happened,[31]

he crowed.

Even as he wrote this, De Morgan recognized that it might seem strange to claim axiomatic status for an arcane observation that he himself had not suspected until he was well into his forties. But the man who had spent a lifetime teaching geometry to beginners was well aware that despite claims of self-evidence, actually coming to *see* the absolute truth of geometrical axioms may require considerable effort. 'That a geometrical axiom may be doubted, and even denied, by those who have not a clear conception of its terms, we know to be true', he explained, and gave the example of the slow process by which students came to accept the parallel postulate. Many students rebelled when they were first told that two lines could not enclose a space. He himself remembered drawing 'his two straight lines upon the ground, in thought' and following them further and further until 'he made them meet again at the antipodes, and inclose a gore of the sphere'.[32] But with education, all of these rebellions ended in insight and the acceptance of the truth of the parallel postulate. The same would happen to anyone who first doubted and then focussed on the four-colour axiom. It had not been recognized until the middle of the nineteenth century, but now its truth was becoming manifest with the same certainty that had attended the parallel postulate. For De Morgan this was marvellous evidence of the reality of mathematical progress. The four-colour axiom stood as wonderful evidence that true mathematical understanding was growing through time.

The Four-Colour Problem

Guthrie's observation that four colours suffice to colour a map did not last long as an axiom, because within a decade of De Morgan's publication, the epistemic culture of gentlemanly science that had supported De Morgan's progressively unfolding mathematics of truth collapsed. The breakdown can be seen clearly occurring on two fronts: the institutional world that supported his mathematical teaching, and the epistolary network that constituted his intellectual community of support. The founding of the LMS in 1865 marks the beginning of a new regime. De Morgan's son, George, was an important part of the impetus behind this organization and Augustus acted as a benign father figure to the group, but the LMS soon became an important site for a very different view of mathematics. The very creation of a society for mathematics alone separated the subject from all of the educational, philosophical, astronomical, and other contexts in which it had been pursued marked the creation of a new subject. The fast growing membership saw themselves as participants in a mathematical enterprise that stretched far beyond Cambridge or London or England itself. The LMS building still proudly bears the name 'De Morgan House', but the mathematics there pursued is far from that of its namesake.

It would be decades before the truth-seeking mathematics De Morgan had pursued vanished completely, but by the 1870s powerful forces for change were being ranged against it. The founding of the LMS coincided with the rise of a new group, the scientific naturalists, who rose to displace the gentleman of science as the voice of science in the second half of the nineteenth century. Led by pugnacious Darwinians like Thomas Henry Huxley and John Tyndall the scientific naturalists challenged the Anglican world of Whewell, Herschel, and Peacock. The term 'agnostic' that Huxley coined in 1869 signals their rejection of the claims of truth that were so central to the world view of the gentleman of science. Even as this younger generation was beginning to challenge their world view, De Morgan and his friends were being overtaken by mortality: Boole died in 1864, Hamilton in 1865, Whewell in 1866, and Herschel in 1871. De Morgan himself also died in 1871. The epistemic culture of their brand of gentlemanly science would die with them.

Both Thomas Archer Hirst and William Kingdon Clifford, who succeeded De Morgan as professors of mathematics in UCL, were vocal proponents of scientific naturalism. Hirst had learned his mathematics in Germany far from the epistemic community of England's gentlemen of science. He was infuriated by De Morgan's preoccupation with mathematical truth, and dismissed the older man's historically informed approach as the work of 'a dry dogmatic pedant'.[33] Clifford learned his mathematics at Cambridge, but he emerged fiercely opposed to the truth-driven approach he had learned there. De Morgan's story of mathematical awakening, in which a student moved from the erroneous belief that two lines could enclose a space to the wonderful recognition of the absolute truth of the parallel postulate, was for Clifford a tale of repression. Within months of graduation, he had shaken off the constraints of De Morgan's kind of geometrical truth, to plunge into the possibilities of non-Euclidean geometry. In the decade before his premature death at not-yet thirty-four, he led a new generation of Englishmen to question the validity of the Euclidean geometry that had served as defining example of mathematical truth since the age of the Greeks. Clifford may have lived his whole life in England, but there was no more room for De Morgan's truth based mathematics in his world than there was in Hirst's.[34]

One way to trace the collapse of the mathematics of truth is to follow the fortunes of De Morgan's four-colour axiom. Just seven years after De Morgan's death, Arthur Cayley considered the subject when he visited the LMS in 1878. But in his presentation, that four colours suffice to colour a map ceased to be an 'axiom' and became instead a 'statement' that required a 'solution'.[35] This choice of words signalled a significant change in the fortunes of Guthrie's observation. That four colours suffice was never again a 'fact' nor an 'axiom'; rather it was the 'four-colour problem' the 'four-colour conjecture', or the 'four-colour theorem'. These designations signal the destabilization of the truth that De Morgan had seen so clearly. It was no longer enough to spend a couple of hours experimenting with some coloured pencils to establish it as a fact. That four colours suffice to colour a map had become a problem that mathematicians needed to solve, a conjecture they needed to establish, a theorem they needed to prove.

Well into the twentieth century mathematicians continued in the effort to establish in their terms what De Morgan had seen so clearly in his. It is highly doubtful that De Morgan would have been particularly impressed that their efforts were effectively showing that his 'axiom' depended 'on anything I see more clearly', but the new group set little store by his form of insightful understanding. Within a decade of his death, his vision had evaporated so completely that his most successful mathematics student, J. J. Sylvester, could simply dismiss him with the comment: 'He did not write Mathematics, he wrote about Mathematics'.[36] Sylvester's comment presages Gray's view, in which mathematicians are a clearly defined group separate from the kinds of educational and philosophical concerns that supported De Morgan's mathematics. In this new disciplinary world, De Morgan's concerns with truth and meaning were essentially irrelevant. Mathematics had been freed of all of the human contingencies of language, reason, and personal insight that had previously encumbered it. Finally, it could stand pure and absolute.

Computing with Four Colours

Mathematics has, nonetheless, not been totally confined to this new disciplinary community. Some sense that the essence of rationality continues to undergird the mathematics we require of high school students; some form of De Morgan's vision flashes forth every time that anyone characterizes mathematics as a language. The persistence of such manifestations signals the continued role that mathematics plays in our understandings of concepts like reason, language, and truth. Our understandings of each of these may change over time, but those changes take place in tandem with one other.

Following the fortunes of De Morgan's four-colour axiom one step further may illustrate this dynamic. In the hundred years after Cayley had called for a 'solution' mathematicians followed the trail into topology, combinatorics, and graph theory. Their efforts began to generate clearer understandings of the various configurations of 'countries' for which four colours would have to suffice, but the number of configurations was so enormous that it seemed impossible that anyone could check each one independently. Obvious though it seemed, the four-colour problem stubbornly resisted proof.

The solution to this impasse lay in a moving beyond the proof definitions that for a century had defined mathematics as a discipline. In 1972, just one hundred years after De Morgan's death, a computer programmer, Kenneth Appel, suggested to the mathematician, Wolfgang Haken, that a computer might do what a human could not. For the next four years, Appel; Haken; and a graduate student, John Koch, together programmed a computer to check each of the possible configurations. In the first six months of 1976, they commandeered over a 1,200 hours of computer time at the University of Illinois to check all of the possible map configurations for the four-colour problem. Finally at the end of June, the computer seemed to have done the job that no human being could, and Appel wrote, 'Modulo careful checking, it appears that four colors suffice' on the bulletin board of the University of Illinois Mathematics Department.[37] Finally, it seemed that De Morgan's 'axiom' had ceased to be a 'problem'.

Or perhaps not. Notably lacking in Appel's announcement is any claim that he had 'proved' the four-colour 'theorem'. This was probably not an oversight. Appel was a computer scientist, but he posted his note in a mathematics department, where proof was a centrally important term with a very specific meaning. He worked in a different disciplinary world, but to claim he had 'proved' the Guthrie's observation in a mathematics department would be to change the meaning of proof dramatically. It was difficult to describe the demonstration his computer had produced as having been generated from a well-defined mathematical framework. Other mathematicians could not reproduce the work, by starting from the initial propositions and following it step by step. Gray's proof-driven, disciplinary mathematics may seem to have removed itself from the subjective confusions of human input, but the notion of human understanding remained implicit in that framework. Allowing mathematical proof to be defined by a machine constitutes a major challenge to the disciplinary mathematics that emerged at the end of the nineteenth century. Ever since Appel posted his quiet declaration, the question of whether a theorem could be considered proved if no human being could follow the steps of that proof has fuelled passionate discussion.[38] The computer proof of the four-colour theorem signals the birth of a new and burgeoning epistemic culture that lies at the intersection of mathematics and computer programming.

The history of the proposition that four-colours suffice to colour a map may be taken as an example of the central importance of epistemic cultures to our understanding of mathematics. As a practical fact,

Guthrie's fact was known by atlas makers for centuries before De Morgan identified it as a mathematical proposition. Its evolution from axiom to conjecture to computer problem in the subsequent century and a half is a valuable reminder of the ways that mathematics fundamentally changes over time. The creation of a mathematical discipline at the end of the nineteenth century had the profound effect of moving mathematics from the truth-driven world of De Morgan and his generation to the proof-driven world of mathematicians from Cauchy to Sylvester and the several generations who followed them. But Haken and Appel's work suggests that that approach may itself be shifting in response to the coming of computers in the twentieth century.

That the four-colour proposition was fundamentally reinterpreted in response to changing social, cultural, and technological factors is not an anomaly. The same could be said for ideas in any of the other fields that came together as disciplines in the late nineteenth century. In those fields, however, the changes are less hidden because reflected in language. Biology, Chemistry, Anthropology, Physics are terms that did not come into their own until they were solidified as disciplines and the term 'scientist' was not widely used until the early twentieth century. Mathematics and the mathematicians who pursued it, on the other hand, can be found from the Middle Ages to the present. But, behind this facade of permanence, mathematics has been as chamaeleon as any other subject since at least the time of the Greeks. Time and again its very essence has changed to fit the changing configuration of the epistemic cultures that 'create and warrant' the knowledge it encompasses.

Notes

1 An earlier version of this paper was delivered at the conference 'Cultures in Mathematics' sponsored by the Institute for the History and Philosophy of Science and Technology Studies at the University of Toronto from July 27–28, 2012.
2 Jeremy Gray, 'The Nineteenth Century Revolution in Mathematical Ontology', in *Revolutions in Mathematics*, ed. Donald Gillies (New York: Oxford University Press, 1992), 226.
3 Gray, 'Mathematical Revolution', 226.
4 Ibid., 242.
5 Karen Knorr Cetina, *Epistemic Cultures: How the Sciences Make Knowledge* (Cambridge, MA: Harvard University Press, 1999), 1.
6 Jack Morrell and Arnold Thackray, *Gentlemen of Science* (Oxford: Clarendon Press, 1981).
7 Sydney Ross, 'Scientist: The History of a Word', *Annals of Science* 18 (1962), 65–85.
8 Morrell and Thackray, *Gentlemen*, 19–20, 25–28. Steven Shapin, *A Social History of Truth: Civility and Science in Seventeenth-Century England* (Chicago: University of Chicago Press, 1994) found the definition of the gentleman to be central to the institutional shape of science as it arose in seventeenth-century England. For further reflections on the implications of

conceptions of gentility in the early nineteenth century, see 'The Paradoxes of Gentility' in James Secord, *Victorian Sensation: The Extraordinary Publication, Reception and Secret Authorship of Vestiges of the Natural History of Creation* (Chicago: University of Chicago Press, 2000), 403–436.

9 Ronald Anderson, 'Augustus De Morgan's Inaugural Lecture of 1828', *The Mathematical Intelligencer* 25/3 (2006), 19.

10 Anderson, 'Inaugural Lecture', 21–22.

11 Ibid., 23.

12 Ibid., 20.

13 Ibid.

14 Augustus De Morgan, 'Study of Natural Philosophy', *The Quarterly Journal of Education* III (January–April 1832), 60–61.

15 Anderson, 'Inaugural Lecture', 19.

16 De Morgan, 'Study of Natural Philosophy', 60–61.

17 Anderson, 'Inaugural Lecture', 19.

18 Ibid.

19 An example of De Morgan's effort to negotiate negative numbers can be found in his translation of a French textbook for his students: Louis Pierre Marie Bourdon, *Elements of Algebra: Translated from the First Three Chapter of the Algebra of M Bourdon*, trans. Augustus De Morgan (London: J. Taylor, 1828).

20 Augustus De Morgan, 'Review of George Peacock, *A Treatise on Algebra*', *Quarterly Journal of Education* 9 (1835), 311.

21 Joan Richards, 'Augustus De Morgan, the History of Mathematics, and the Foundations of Algebra', *Isis* 78 (1987), 28.

22 Augustus De Morgan, 'On the Foundations of Algebra, No. II', *Transactions of the Cambridge Philosophical Society* 7 (1842), 289.

23 Knorr Cetina, *Epistemic Cultures*, 1.

24 Robin Wilson, *Four Colors Suffice: How the Map Problem Was Solved* (Princeton: Princeton University Press, 2002), 19. This is a major source for the history of the four-color problem; another is Rudolf Fritsch and Gerda Fritsch, *The Four-Color Theorem: History, Topological Foundations, and Idea of Proof*, trans. Julie Peschke (New York: Springer, 1998).

25 The direct quotation from the letter De Morgan wrote to Hamilton is in first person and the present tense: 'the more I think of it, the more evident it seems'. Wilson, *Four Colors*, 18.

26 Wilson, *Four Colors*, 18.

27 Ibid., 23.

28 William Whewell, *Philosophy of the Inductive Sciences: Founded Upon Their History* (London: John W. Parker, 1847).

29 Augustus De Morgan [ADM] to William Whewell [WW], December 9, 1853. Trinity College Library. Add. Ms. a. 202[125].

30 For an overview of Mansel's views see Bernard Lightman, *The Origins of Agnosticism: Victorian Unbelief and the Limits of Knowledge* (Baltimore: Johns Hopkins University Press, 1987), 7–32. For a specific focus on the Whewell-Mansel debate see John Wettersten, *Whewell's Critics: Have They Prevented Him from Doing Good?* (New York: Rudopi, 2004), 77–84.

31 Augustus De Morgan, 'Philosophy of Discovery, Chapters Historical and Critical. By W. Whewell', *The Athenaeum* 1694 (April 14, 1860), 502.

32 De Morgan, 'Philosophy of Discovery', 501–502.

33 Thomas Hirst's diary, June 15, 1862. http://www-groups.dcs.st-and.ac.uk/~history/HistTopics/Hirst_comments.html (the remark about De Morgan is included in a list of Hirst's comments about other mathematicians).

34 Petrunic Josipa, 'Evolutionary Mathematics: William Kingdon Clifford's use of Spencerian Evolutionism', in *The Age of Scientific Naturalism: Tyndall and His Contemporaries*, ed. Michael Reidy and Bernard Lightman (Pittsburgh: University of Pittsburgh Press, 2016) 89–112.
35 Wilson, *Four Colors*, 62.
36 George Bruce Halstedt, 'De Morgan to Sylvester', *Monist* 10 (1900), 188.
37 Wilson, *Four Colors*, 204.
38 For an overview of these discussions see Wilson, *Four Colors*, 214–228.

Section VI

Interdisciplinarity

11 *Middlemarch* and the Limits of Interdisciplinarity

Renata Kobetts Miller

In the late 1880s, Thomas Henry Huxley and Mathew Arnold engaged in a debate that presaged the beginning of the 'Two Cultures' as defined by C. P. Snow and F. R. Leavis in the twentieth century.[1] Huxley argued that physical science is an essential part of a modern education, while Arnold cautioned that science must be tempered or mediated by the humanities. Huxley had already spent much of his career, in his own words, working 'to promote the increase of natural knowledge and to forward the application of scientific methods of investigation to all the problems of life'.[2] The 'application of scientific methods' required Huxley to argue for science as a discipline, and this meant demarcating the lines of what qualified as scientific method. In January 1854, his first column as a newly hired science writer for the *Westminster Review* began with a section titled 'Scientific Method', in which he criticized George Henry Lewes's book 'Comte's Philosophy of the Sciences', which incorporated essays that Lewes had previously published in the *Leader*. In his review, Huxley first defines the physical sciences as a distinct area of expertise. Moreover, he defines the physical sciences as a growth field undergoing rapid change. Referring to Harriet Martineau's condensed translation of Comte's 'Philosophie Positive', he notes that the portion of Comte's work that has to do with 'Social Physics' is its most valuable part because '[p]hysical science has made such progress since the "Philosophie Positive" was published, that a knowledge of its actual condition cannot be gained from M. Comte's work, as it has now been several years before the world'.[3] Moving on to Lewes, Huxley describes Lewes's work as 'more attractive to ordinary readers', approves of Lewes's representation of Comte, and praises its 'exposition' as 'clearness and lucidity itself', 'every now and then . . . ris[ing] into genuine eloquence'.[4] While casting Lewes's work as appropriately pitched and attractive for a non-specialized audience, Huxley strenuously objects to what Lewes described as his attempt to, '[bring] [Comte] to bear upon the *present* state of science', claiming familiarity with 'the very latest acts and ideas of 1853'.[5] Citing mistakes in Lewes, Huxley claims that they reveal 'how impossible it is for even so acute a thinker as Mr. Lewes to succeed in scientific speculations, without the discipline and knowledge which result from being a worker also'.[6] In other words, Huxley claims science as a field that requires not merely intellectual ability but the particular experience of a practitioner.

Lewes's ally in responding to Huxley was Marian Evans. At this time they were in the first couple of years of their relationship; the two would be partners until his death in 1878. Evans had not yet assumed her male pseudonym and had not yet become the eminent novelist George Eliot. But this episode would reverberate in the fictional and historical world that she would create in her 1871–1872 masterpiece *Middlemarch*. Evans – whom I will call Eliot for clarity and consistency – responded at the time of the criticism of Lewes by representing Huxley as a narrow specialist. Upon seeing proofs of Huxley's essay, Eliot wrote two letters to *Westminster Review* owner and editor John Chapman, in which she urged him to withhold Huxley's manuscript, and she defended Lewes's material.[7] In a letter to phrenologist George Combe, Eliot represented the work of a specialist as virtually incompatible with the broad understanding required of a critic: 'Mr. Huxley's is not the organization for a critic, but it is difficult to find a man who combines special scientific knowledge with that well-balanced development of the moral and intellectual faculties, which is essential to a profound and fair appreciation of other men's works'.[8]

Lewes, meanwhile, publicly asserted his own polymath abilities and commitments in the *Leader*, adopting Huxley's assertion about the need to practice science while, at the same time, asserting his own experience:

> Appearing in the pages where it is well known I am also a writer . . . this attack will have more than usual significance; and being founded on the natural but false assumption that, because Literature is my profession, therefore in Science I can only have 'book knowledge,' it will fall in with the all but universal tendency of not allowing any man to be heard on more than one subject. Once for all let me say, that it is 18 years since I first began to occupy myself—practically and theoretically—with Biology, and that it is only within the last 4 years I have ventured to publish any opinions on that subject.[9]

In identifying literature as his profession but arguing that he can nevertheless still claim authority as a scientist, Lewes resists both the professionalization of science and the increasing division between humanities and sciences. Historians Jeremiah Rankin and Ruth Barton have compared Lewes's career and writings as a science popularizer with those of the scientist John Tyndall's. Rankin and Barton argue that, although Lewes often could have legitimately made similar claims to authority through connections with eminent scientists and the use of specialized methodology and equipment, in contrast to Tyndall he aimed to make science appear open to lay practitioners and amateurs instead of establishing the specialized expertise of the scientist. Indeed, Huxley's assessment that Lewes is appropriate for a popular audience, but that he lacks the specialization of a true scientific practitioner, is consistent with Rankin and Barton's reading, except that what Huxley criticizes as Lewes's lack of qualifications, Rankin and Barton identify as an ideologically motivated rhetorical stance on Lewes's part.[10] Rankin and Barton hold that Lewes defied specialization even while developing scientific credentials: 'He continued to earn his living as a critic, editor and popularizer and, while developing his expertise and reputation as a physiologist and pursuing physiological psychology, he continued to write articles beyond his specialized fields'.[11] Where Rankin and Barton appreciate Lewes's 'participatory' emphasis—his 'inclusive and democratic vision'—in contrast with Tyndall's 'elitism', Huxley aligned with Tyndall's rhetoric that bolstered specialization and discipline-formation.[12] This chapter will demonstrate how the professionalization promoted by Huxley, rather than being elitist, expanded opportunities for the practice of science beyond that of Lewes's model of gentlemen-scientists pursuing observations or experiments in their leisure hours.

Following Eliot's and Lewes's own anti-specialization, scholarship on the couple inclines towards viewing their partnership as one of productive exchange between the sciences and literature, with each established in a particular discipline but drawing on the sensibilities of the other. For example, drawing on a quotation from Lewes's *Life of Goethe* (1855), Diana Postlethwait has argued that by 1858, '[Lewes] had proven himself a practicing scientist; [Eliot], a practicing novelist. There was a fundamental intellectual affinity between their endeavours: Lewes aspired to be a "poet in science"; Eliot, to be a "scientific poet"'.[13] Henry James even criticized Eliot's *Middlemarch* for going too far in the direction of science. In James's view, Eliot sought 'to recommend herself to a scientific audience', but he did not view this as successful or desirable, as he found the novel 'too often an echo of Messrs. Darwin and Huxley'.[14] With regard to Lewes, Beverley Park Rilett's recent article calls him 'the Real Man of Science Behind George Eliot's Fictional Pedants' in its title, and argues that Proteus Merman's name in Eliot's *Impressions of Theophrastus Such* (1879) alludes to 'the shape-shifting sea god' and the 'constant remaking of Lewes's professional identity. He was novelist, poet, biographer, theater and literature critic, philosopher, and would-be scientist'.[15] Rilett also cites Rosemary Ashton's argument, in her collection of Lewes's journalism, *Versatile Victorian*, that '"omnicompetence" was a strike against his reputation as a scientific theorist'.[16] Rilett examines Merman's transition from a balanced generalist to an 'obsessive' specialist.[17] Nancy Henry, meanwhile, has described 'Lewes's many publications in which he sought to popularize difficult and specialized forms of knowledge such as philosophy and science', noting, 'He was very successful in these efforts'.[18]

This contemporary critical emphasis on the interdisciplinary partnership of Eliot and Lewes is a biographical instantiation of scholarship by Gillian Beer, George Levine, Gowan Dawson, Adelene Buckland, and others that compellingly demonstrates the commonalities and cross-influences between literature and science in nineteenth-century culture.[19] One thread in this body of work is the view, voiced by Buckland, that '"scientific writing *was* literature" in the nineteenth century, read and consumed by the many rather than the few in a culture in which the specialized disciplines we live with today had not yet crystallized'.[20] Conversely, Buckland also holds that, 'If science *was* literature, . . . literature was science too. Writing was not simply a means of imagining or publicizing geology, but rather was a kind of scientific practice'.[21] This was an argument that was applied to Huxley himself, who spoke to a broad audience in accessible prose in both his speeches and published work, but was also a scientific specialist. In his 1932 Huxley Memorial lecture, 'T. H. Huxley as a Man of Letters', Aldous Huxley felt compelled to respond to G. K. Chesterton's characterization of his grandfather as 'much more a literary than a scientific man' by arguing: 'The records of Huxley's scientific achievements are there to prove the contrary. He was a man of science first of all—a man of science who also had . . . a literary gift'.[22] Taking issue with a trend of attempts to claim scientists as humanists, he paradoxically argues that scientists are remembered for their more humanistic work precisely because of the specialization of science, which leads their scientific work to speak only to a highly specialized audience in a particular time period:

> Those who have not had a scientific education are incapable of understanding the technicalities of any scientific paper. Those who have been educated in one branch of science are hardly better off than laymen, when it comes to understanding a paper in some other branch. And those who have been educated in the particular science under consideration have no need to refer to the original papers of their predecessors.[23]

Nevertheless, Aldous Huxley also claims that because science is 'communication' as well as 'investigation', 'In one of its aspects, then, science is a branch of literature'.[24] Bernard Lightman reveals a similar sentiment on the part of T. H. Huxley when he refers to an undated note by Huxley stating that the '"work of the popular expositor" was a dimension of scientific work that deserved to be seen as "literature"'.[25]

Although Rilett claims that 'Lewes becomes Huxley's scapegoat for all that is wrong with current scientific methodology', Lightman provides a context for understanding that Huxley's criticism of Lewes was a defence of ground that had been gained, in part through his own work, to establish science as a discipline, and to defend the place of that discipline in the public forum of the popular press.[26] Melinda Baldwin has pointed out that 'in the nineteenth century, the line between "layman" and "expert" was significantly blurrier than we consider it now'.[27] Yet Huxley was acutely aware of this distinction and strove to strengthen it. Lightman emphasizes Huxley's reluctance to devote time to popular writing at the expense of original scientific research and his career as a 'professional scientist', and it was on the basis of his research that Huxley claimed his own authority.[28] When Huxley started writing his column in the *Westminster Review*, he 'wanted to avoid being stigmatized as a crass journalist, as it could have damaged his chances of establishing a career in science'.[29] Huxley was attacking both Lewes's credentials as a scientist and, in turn, Lewes's credentials to represent science to a popular audience. As Lightman points out, given the ascendency of science in the second half of the nineteenth century: 'The stakes were quite high in the fight to be recognized as an intellectual who spoke on behalf of science'.[30]

The dispute among Huxley, Lewes, and Eliot points to how claims of interdisciplinarity are complicated by the disciplinary drives that are their pre-condition. The terms of this conflict, with Huxley arguing for specialized experience and Eliot and Lewes arguing for an intellectualism that crosses disciplines, echo the attack by scientists, including Huxley, on Robert Chambers's *Vestiges on the Natural History of Creation* (1844), and Chambers's 'reject[ion of] the authority of practitioners' in his *Explanations, A Sequel* (1845).[31] This conflict between scientific specialists and interdisciplinarians was the result of what Lightman has demonstrated as the rise of science and its rise as a subject in the popular press in the second half of the nineteenth century. Nancy Henry characterizes Lewes's turn towards trying to establish his scientific credentials in the years after Huxley's criticism as the result of 'becoming disillusioned with the tastes of the general reading public, and his late scientific work was aimed at an elite, educated audience'.[32] In Lightman's terms, however, even though Lewes was not a proponent of natural theology as many popularizers were, he was one of the popularizers who 'subvert[ed] the agenda of the would-be scientific professional' – as Barton and Rankin have illustrated.[33] Lightman points out that the battle Huxley was waging was precisely about the need for scientific practitioners to be the ones educating the public about science. It is for this reason that, while Huxley believed that scientific writing could be literature, he did not believe that the literary were qualified to speak for science.

Eliot's contrary position that critics must develop 'moral and intellectual faculties' in order to equitably judge the work of others, regardless of subject, is consistent with critical understandings of how Eliot's novels seek to cultivate the sympathetic faculties of readers. These are the sort of sympathetic faculties, based as they are in the intellect rather than in the communication of feeling, that Rae Greiner has explored.[34]

While *Middlemarch* is emblematic of Eliot's work in this regard, it also provides a view into what I will call Eliot's interdisciplinarity. Published in 1871–1872, *Middlemarch* is set in the years of 1829 to 1832, and this historical shift places the novel's action on the eve of the political enfranchisement of the First Reform Bill and at the beginning of the era of railroad building. Additionally, and of significance because of the centrality of Tertius Lydgate, who aspires to be both a provincial doctor and a path-breaking researcher, setting her novel forty years prior to its writing enables Eliot to explore interdisciplinarity in a time before the disciplines – or the two cultures – of sciences and humanities had crystallized. Rather than merely offering Eliot the freedom to explore alternatives to the ways in which scientific specialization developed, the temporal setting of *Middlemarch* allows Eliot to place her characters at a critical moment in the development of science as a discipline, and to engage in thoughtful consideration of both the drawbacks and benefits of specialization and interdisciplinarity.

Middlemarch is thus a useful voice to add to the modern debate about specialization and interdisciplinarity. Amanda Anderson and Joseph Valente have pointed out, 'What has often been lacking in our current disciplinary debates is a longer perspective that would enable us to understand better their historical conditions and developments', and Christopher Keep has called for 'a more sustained and vigorous attention to the history of the disciplines themselves and the various private and public institutions that support and encourage their activities'.[35] *Middlemarch*'s historical retrospection provides an elaboration of Robert Frodeman's view that 'disciplinarity is the precondition for interdisciplinarity' and that interdisciplinarity 'express[es] . . . dissatisfaction with current modes of knowledge production'.[36] An analysis of *Middlemarch* as set in a historical moment when the disciplines were in formation also accords with Joe Moran's claims that 'we cannot understand interdisciplinarity without first examining the existing disciplines, since interdisciplinary approaches are always an engagement with them, and the modes of knowledge that they exclude by virtue of their separation from each other'.[37] In the case of *Middlemarch*, we must examine the discipline of science as it developed between the 1830s and 1870s – indeed how it fragmented into a range of increasingly specialized disciplines that were yoked into unity through beliefs, theories, or methods, as Lightman's essay (Chapter 1) in this collection demonstrates. Although Frodeman holds that 'As a self-conscious movement interdisciplinarity only arose in the face of academic specialization that so markedly accelerated in the late nineteenth century', in this essay I demonstrate that the roots of interdisciplinarity are evident earlier in the nineteenth century.[38] Indeed, in their dispute with Huxley, Eliot and Lewes were aligned with Arnold in imagining the humanities as having what Frodeman calls 'the best claim and pedigree to being broad and incisive studies of the relation between knowledge and the good life' before they became specialized in the twentieth century.[39] Yet while Frodeman also writes, 'the bias for the deep rather than for the broad is rarely defended. It is in fact indefensible', in *Middlemarch* Eliot would ultimately temper her interdisciplinarity.[40]

The world that Eliot created in *Middlemarch* served as her own laboratory in which she could model various forms of interdisciplinarity, playing out simulations in a historically reconstructed world.[41] The notion of novel as laboratory is foregrounded in Eliot's first words in the Prelude to *Middlemarch*: 'Who that cares much to know the history of man, and how the mysterious mixture behaves under the varying experiments of Time, has not dwelt, at least briefly, on the life of Saint Theresa. . . ?'[42] Beer, exploring disciplinary crossings of the Victorians, demonstrates the 'common language' that scientists shared 'with other educated readers and writers of their time', and traces the 'two-way' 'traffic' of 'not only *ideas* but metaphors, myths, and narrative patterns . . . between scientists and non-scientists'.[43] Beer reads Eliot's scientific method, in *Middlemarch*, as part of a pattern of parallels between the imaginative 'enterprise' of the novelist and that of the scientist, and emphasizes 'the accord between scientific imagination, healer's imagination, and that of the novelist'.[44] I hold, however, that the scientific and healing aims of the character Tertius Lydgate, in contrast, in the end are not capable of mutually reinforcing co-existence, and that Eliot herself, ultimately and reluctantly, comes to see the benefits of specialization and disciplinarity.

Henry James called Lydgate 'the real hero of the story' of *Middlemarch*, suggesting that Ladislaw paled in comparison to 'the noble, almost sepulchral, relief of the neighboring figure of Lydgate'.[45] As if to answer Eliot's own query: 'But why always Dorothea?' (312), this essay takes as its focus Lydgate, but also, as complementary male intellectuals, Edward Casaubon and Camden Farebrother. I hold that Eliot's representation of these characters is informed by how science developed in the years between Eliot's writing of the novel and its setting.

Science is central to Eliot's characterization of Lydgate, yet she never uses the term 'scientist' to describe him. Eliot is scrupulously true to linguistic history: the word 'scientist' was first used in an exchange between Samuel Taylor Coleridge and William Whewell on June 24, 1833, at a meeting at Cambridge of the British Association for the Advancement of Science.[46] Indeed, many of the ways in which science developed as a discipline in the years between 1830 and 1870 are embodied in – and were driven by – the British Association (which continues today as the British Science Association). Peter Weingart argues that such 'Disciplinary associations . . . became the structuring principle of knowledge formation in the nineteenth and twentieth centuries'.[47] While the Royal Society was founded in 1660 and the Royal Institution was founded in 1799, the British Association for the Advancement of Science was founded in 1831, and it represented a newly emergent class of professional, and increasingly specialized, scientists.[48] Lightman's essay in this collection details how the seven sections of the British Association broke from earlier understandings of natural history and natural philosophy, and also how specialization was propounded by free-standing associations such as the Royal Astronomical Society and the Zoological Society. Eliot and Lewes were familiar with the British Association. After Huxley's attack Lewes undertook a study of marine life, going so far as to travel with Eliot to Tenby, where Huxley had been the year before, and his paper 'On the Spinal Chord as a Sensational and Volitional Centre' was delivered by Richard Owen to the Association's annual meeting in Leeds in 1858.[49] Moreover, Beer provides evidence of close textual echoes of both Huxley and John Tyndall in *Middlemarch*, and particularly of an address that Tyndall gave to the Association in 1870.[50] Tyndall would become president of the Association in 1874. Lightman has written that when Huxley became president of the Association in 1870 it 'was not only the crowning triumph of his early career, it also indicated how influential scientific naturalism had become within British science'.[51] At the time that Eliot was writing *Middlemarch*, the British Association embodied the major trends of scientific professionalism, and those trends were the very causes that Huxley had championed.

Although he does not represent the sort of purposeful interdisciplinarity that we will see in Lydgate, Mr Brooke's dilettantism and his wandering associations that range across disciplines represent the pre-disciplinary cultural condition of the time in which *Middlemarch* is set. They also provide a comic backdrop that underscores the benefits of specialization and foreshadows that Lydgate's interdisciplinary ambitions, noble as they appear, may not be without problems. In fact, Eliot foregrounds these disciplinary matters for the novel in the opening of Chapter 2, when Mr Brooke hosts Edward Casaubon, who, admitting that he does not have time to read outside of his field of research, stands at the other end of the spectrum as a specialist (39). Mr Brooke responds to James Chetham's news that he is reading Humphry Davy's *Agricultural Chemistry* by blithely describing how he once dined with Wordsworth and Davy. Davy, Mr Brooke says, 'was a poet too. Or as I may say, Wordsworth was poet one, and Davy was poet two. That was true in every sense, you know' (38). Moreover, Mr Brooke represents an amateur scientist who lacks rigor and focus: 'I went into science a great deal myself at one time; but I saw it would not do. It leads to everything; you can let nothing alone' (39). Brooke provides a caricature of the free interdisciplinarity that was possible around 1830. Laura Snyder provides a description of the conditions that allowed for a character such as Brooke, and that are critical to understanding Lydgate and Farebrother:

> At the start of the 1800s, the man of science was likely to be a country parson collecting beetles in his spare hours, or a wealthy gentleman performing experiments in his own privately funded laboratory,

> or a factotum of a wealthy patron; by the end of the century he was a "scientist"—a member of a professional class of (still mostly) men pursuing a common activity within a certain institutional framework: professional associations open to practicing members; research grants; university and laboratory training for younger professionals.[52]

Snyder also describes the crossings between poetry and science that Brooke's mention of Wordsworth reflects:

> When Coleridge, the most famous poet of the day, wrote his tract on scientific method in 1817 it was not considered an oddity; by 1833, the time of the third meeting of the British Association of the Advancement of Science, it was already remarkable, and in the years that followed it was almost inconceivable.[53]

Granting that Snyder's characterization may be influenced by *Middlemarch*, Farebrother is nevertheless representative of the country parson-naturalist. In this chapter, I hold that Lydgate represents the researcher who stands at the threshold of an enormous shift in the profession of science and its definition as a discipline in relation to other disciplines.

Lydgate earns his living as country physician, and his reforming tendencies – his determination to prescribe without dispensing drugs himself or accepting kick-backs from pharmacists – suggest that he is a harbinger of the professionalization of medicine. But in other ways, Lydgate's aspirations and practices in the year 1829 – as Eliot specifies – contrast with the ways in which science develops as a specialization and as a profession (177). Broadly educated, Lydgate views medicine as an interdisciplinary field, believing

> that the medical profession as it might be was the finest in the world; presenting the most perfect interchange between science and art; offering the most direct alliance between intellectual conquest and the social good. Lydgate's nature demanded this combination: he was an emotional creature, with a flesh-and-blood sense of fellowship which withstood all the abstractions of special study. He cared not only for "cases", but for John and Elizabeth, especially Elizabeth.
>
> (174)

That Lydgate's professional goals included both research aims and ambitions as a practitioner reveals his investment in what we now colloquially call 'real-world applications'.[54] Thus Eliot characterizes Lydgate's interest as being not only interdisciplinary but also what theorists have called 'transdisciplinary'. Julie Thompson Klein has described one of the 'trendlines' in late twentieth- and twenty-first-century transdisciplinarity (or TD), as 'trans-sector TD problem solving': 'The core premise of this trendline is that problems in the *Lebenswelt*—the life world—need to frame research questions and practices, not the disciplines'.[55] Lydgate is given to say that 'a man's mind must be continually shrinking and expanding between the whole human horizon and the horizon of an object-glass' (690). This allows us to see Lydgate's interests as more than a matter of the 'interconnected[ness]' of 'concrete particular and abstract generalization', 'organization and medium', as Postlethwait has argued, and rather as a figure for inter- and trans-disciplinary interests, whose research crosses the threshold of the laboratory, aims for real-world applications, and engages with the complexity of the human experience.[56]

In this way, Lydgate, whom we know was a devotee of the theatre in Paris, seems aligned more closely with the theatrical and, more broadly, cultural critic Lewes than with the scientist Huxley. He also bears a resemblance to Eliot's eponymous Romola, who, according to Susan David Bernstein, embodies two key elements of an interdisciplinarity that was Eliot's intellectual ideal: engagement with 'diverse subjects of mental and physical arts including poetry and medicine, commerce and music', and 'learning imbued with a broad and continuous experience through the currents of life'.[57] Moreover, Lydgate seeks not only to work as a doctor but also, as a 'spirited young adventurer', to engage in laboratory science. Eliot characterizes him as following up on the research of Bichat, thirty years earlier, and framing his work as inquiry-based. Lydgate

> longed to demonstrate the more intimate relations of living structure and help to define men's thought more accurately after the true order. The work had not yet been done, but only prepared for those who knew how to use the preparation. What was the primitive tissue? In that way Lydgate put the question—not quite in the way required by the awaiting answer; but such missing of the right word befalls many seekers.
>
> (178)

Representing Lydgate as ambitious to serve both his community and the world of knowledge, 'to do good small work for Middlemarch, and great work for the world', seems unmitigatedly positive (178). Indeed, Lydgate believes that these two aims can serve each other:

> There was fascination in the hope that the two purposes would illuminate each other: the careful observation and inference which was his daily work, the use of the lens to further his judgment in special cases, would further his thought as an instrument of larger inquiry. Was not this the typical pre-eminence of his profession? He would be a good Middlemarch doctor, and by that very means keep himself in the track of far-reaching investigation.
>
> (176)

When Dorothea is first enamoured with Edward Casaubon, she views him as pursuing a similar inter- and trans-disciplinarity as Lydgate. She

> was altogether captivated by the wide embrace of this conception. . . . [H]ere was a living Bossuier, whose work would reconcile complete knowledge with devoted piety; here was a modern Augustine who united the glories of doctor and saint.
>
> (47)

She views Casaubon as possessing broad understanding and being capable of both great thoughts and great deeds. On the surface, the thrusts of Lydgate's research and Casaubon's scholarship on a 'Key to all Mythologies' seem analogous as they are both engaged in epistemological inquiries in order to establish a unifying theory (87).[58] But as so many characters in *Middlemarch* misapprehend others, Dorothea is projecting on to Casaubon her own ideals. As the narrator observes: 'Dorothea's inferences may seem large; but really life could never have gone on at any period but for this liberal allowance of conclusion, which has facilitated marriage under the difficulties of civilization' (45). Dorothea is making assumptions without adequate evidence, violating the central principle of scientific method that Huxley propounded. Casaubon's own characterization of his research contrasts with Dorothea's view:

> I feed too much on the inward sources; I live too much with the dead. My mind is something like the ghost of an ancient, wandering about the world and trying to mentally construct it as it used to be, in spite of ruin and confusing changes.
>
> (40)

Where Lydgate is involved in the 'flesh-and-blood' living, Casaubon dwells with the 'dead'. Lydgate appreciates music and the arts; Casaubon finds music distracting and is personally uninterested in the artistic riches of Rome (90, 229). Lydgate insists on being outward looking; Casaubon is focussed on the 'inward'. The narrator later describes him as 'lost among small closets and winding stairs, and in an agitated dimness about the Cabeiri, or in an exposure of other mythologists' ill-considered parallels, easily lost sight of any purpose which had prompted him to these labours' (229). While Lydgate's work aligned him with inter- and trans-disciplinary goals of timeliness, relevance to the general population, and capability for grappling with complexity, Casaubon's work is mired in the past, of little interest to even his own wife, and incapable of allowing for change and complexity. In short, Casaubon is a specialist, and the sharp contrast between his work and Lydgate's throws into relief the limitations of specialization. Casaubon fails because of his narrow-mindedness. But, we must note, neither does Lydgate ultimately succeed.

Lydgate's ambitions seem to anticipate the 'holistic scientific inquiry' that, according to Daniel Sarewitz, 'strives for insight that embraces and explains context and complexity, that enhances comprehension of human and natural systems—the very systems that are being rendered more complex and incomprehensible due to the technological fruits of reductionist inquiry'.[59] Ultimately, however, Lydgate's fate seems to support, at least to a degree, Sarewitz's assertion: 'Disciplinary, reductionist science and its embodiment in technology are the most powerful sources of social transformation in the world today'.[60] Sarewitz's point that

> *[c]laims of holistic expertise are always political claims.* They are political claims because they reflect a choice process—about how to define the system, about what system functions and outcomes are important, about what is to be done to make things better, about what "better" means,[61]

is thematized in the conclusion of the novel, when Dorothea feels 'that there was always something better which she might have done, if she had only been better and known better' (893). Dorothea dramatizes that understanding where and in what way to intervene in the social world is no easy matter. While Lydgate hopes to be a researcher engaged in the real world, he ultimately finds himself too much of that world.

Lydgate's joint endeavours as medical practitioner and scientific researcher were quickly becoming supplanted by the professional division of these two fields as independent specializations. In 1832, just one year after the British Association for the Advancement of Science was founded, Charles Hastings founded the Provincial and Medical Surgical Association, which in 1855 became the British Medical Society. The fact that the British Association gradually modified how it defined the specializations represented by its seven sections reflects the organization's commitment to specialized fields, and a significant change during this period was that in 1842 Medical Science comprised one of its sections, but by 1858 this section had been eliminated entirely.[62] Snyder points out that the Association's 'divisions would be both a reflection of and a contribution to the greater specialization of the sciences'.[63] The Association also contributed to the development of peer review, insisting in a dispute over whether published material should be retracted that the matter must be adjudicated not by the board of the Association but by specialists in the field.

Even as the Association promulgated the division of science into specialized fields, its annual conference sought to encourage 'friendly intercourse among the cultivators of different departments of science'.[64] Moreover, it sought to do this on a national and even international scale, with 'those who cultivate Science in different parts of the British Empire with one another, and with foreign philosophers'.[65] The logo on an elaborate ticket for the Association's 1844 conference in York reveals its ambitions to be a national society (see Figure 11.1). In the shape of a wheel, itself representing mobility, it displays the locations and dates of its annual conference, in cities that range from Plymouth to Edinburgh, and York to Dublin, as well as the names of the presidents for each year. The hub of the wheel contains the botanical emblems of the rose for England, thistle for Scotland, and shamrock for Ireland. This formation of the modern academic conference is clearly dependent on the development of rail travel, which figures so prominently as an emerging technology for the town of Middlemarch. Significantly, however, Tertius maintains his provincialism, working in isolation from others. Indeed, even as Casaubon's scholarship is associated with the past and Lydgate's with reform and, by implication, with the future, like Casaubon, who lives 'too much with the dead', Lydgate connects himself to figures of the past – Edward Jenner, who died in 1823, and François Bichat, who died in 1802 – rather than to his own contemporaries (174, 177).

It is clear that one reason Lydgate fails as a scientist is that he marries, and he marries the wrong woman, and all the petty concerns about his household and his debt force him to focus on his income and prevent him from fulfilling his research ambitions. Henry James describes this as

Figure 11.1 British Association for the Advancement of Science, Entry card for H[enry] F[ox] Talbot, Esq., F.R.S., [1844], Talbot: Publications Concerning Societies and Associations, Add MS 88942/3/2/50, National Trust Accession 36816, British Library. © The British Library Board.

> a tragedy based on unpaid butcher's bills, and the urgent need for small economies. The author has desired to be strictly real and to adhere to the facts of the common lot, and she has given us a powerful version of that typical human drama, the struggles of an ambitious soul with sordid disappointments and vulgar embarrassments. As to her catastrophe we hesitate to pronounce (for Lydgate's ultimate assent to his wife's worldly programme is nothing less than a catastrophe).[66]

It is fair, therefore, to say that Lydgate's failure because he cannot support himself as a researcher and must work as a doctor argues in favour of specialization to advance scientific discovery. Paul White describes the historical shift of institutionalized scientific research:

> Research performed in a domestic setting, still relatively common at mid-century, was increasingly marginal and aggressively marginalized by the 1870s. As a consequence, the opportunities for practitioners outside of the institution-based sciences to make original contributions and critical interventions were greatly diminished.[67]

I propose that a different conception of cause and effect obtains in the case of Lydgate: instead of home researchers being forced out of science, it seems more plausible to infer that the shift to institution-based sciences occurred because the structures provided by institutions were more effective in yielding results or, as Jerry Jacobs puts it: 'Disciplines thrive because they create effective research communities'.[68] While Rankin and Barton read Lewes's emphasis, in his popular scientific writings, on the equipment for an amateur naturalist and on 'domestic spaces that were accessible to his readers', instead of 'specialized laboratory spaces', as part of his 'inclusive' and 'democratic' view, it is also important to recognize that the rise of science as a discipline allowed for the rise of professional researchers apart from those who had the wealth and leisure to excel in science as a hobby.[69] What Rankin and Barton characterize as Tyndall's 'elitist and meritocratic vision', in contrast with Lewes's democratic 'vision', created professional opportunities that freed men such as Lydgate from the material conflicts that James describes.[70] Read in isolation of its historical context, Lydgate's aim to perform his research as a provincial man of medicine seems valiant. Read in the context of the development of science as a profession, with its national and international networks, developing culture of peer review, and developing areas of specialization, it seems tragically naive and arrogant for Lydgate to believe that he could make a serious contribution to the world of scientific knowledge.

Lydgate's only sympathetic interlocutor for his scientific work is the Reverend Camden Farebrother, who represents a different form of interdisciplinarity. When Lydgate first visits him at home, we learn that

Farebrother has a study filled with an impressive collection of natural specimens that seems to represent his true passion. Farebrother longs to have conversations with Lydgate 'about all [his] new species' (204). By virtue of his ecclesiastical profession, Farebrother's enthusiasm as a naturalist stands at the intersection of what would become vastly divergent world views. It is more accurate to view him as a proto-professional scientist than as an amateur, as Snyder explains that, in the early nineteenth century, clergymen had

> the leisure to conduct experiments, collect fossils, study minerals. It was a tried-and-true career path for many men of science in those days when there was no graduate education in science, and no scientific careers to pursue, besides the few professorships that paid little, if anything.[71]

Postlethwaite describes how 'as befits a society on the cusp . . . of old and new worlds', *Middlemarch* 'portrays two typical—and dramatically contrasting—scientists of the early Victorian era': 'the gentlemanly, old-fashioned "natural history" of a Farebrother and the theoretical, professionalized "natural science" of a Lydgate'.[72] The gilded, damask-upholstered furnishings in Farebrother's parsonage, inherited from his father and grandfather, bespeak Farebrother's genteel background, as do his mother, aunt, and sister, who possess 'a faded but genuine respectability' (198). Farebrother avows that men of his 'profession' generally do not smoke, and his gambling is also held against him by censorious members of the community (202). Eliot presents Farebrother's smoking at the same time that he shares his collection with Lydgate and because she remains silent on the disposition of his naturalism and his religion – there is no indication that Farebrother is motivated by natural theology – this suggests that Farebrother's naturalism distracts from his profession. Indeed Farebrother himself speaks satirically about the contrived harmony between his profession and his hobby when he describes

> a learned treatise on the entomology of the Pentateuch, including all the insects not mentioned, but probably met with by the Israelites on their passage through the desert; with a monograph on the Ant, as treated by Solomon, showing the harmony of the Book of Proverbs with the results of modern research.
>
> (202)

Lydgate reflects on the

> implied meaning—that the Vicar felt himself not altogether in the right vocation. The neat fitting up of drawers and shelves, and the bookcase filled with expensive illustrated books on Natural History, made him think again of the winnings at cards and their destination.
>
> (202)

Lydgate explains to Farebrother: 'I have never had time to give myself much to natural history. I was early bitten with an interest in structure, and it is what lies most directly in my profession' (202). Yet I have demonstrated that even Lydgate's professional model was outdated for the time in which *Middlemarch* was written. If Lydgate represents a union of art and science as well as medicine and biological research that was unsustainable, Farebrother represents a union of science and religion that would be rent asunder over theories of evolution. Lightman notes that the science-minded clergy 'was one of the groups that would-be professionalizers like . . . Huxley were trying to push out of science', and he has detailed how, in his role as a 'practitioner-popularizer', Huxley aimed to 'lead readers away from a theology of nature'; he 'wanted to replace natural history with the study of biology, as this was more conducive to his vision of a professionalized and secularized science'.[73] Lightman describes a distinction that Huxley made that closely describes the differences between Farebrother and Lydgate: 'Huxley wanted science to be associated with expertise, laboratory research, and naturalism, and he wanted to break its connection with the Anglican clergy, amateurism, and natural theology'.[74] Weingart has pointed out that the formation of disciplinary communities does not only draw divisions between different specialists, but also 'between specialists and laypersons'.[75] As science became professionalized, those who did not specialize became 'laypersons'. To Lydgate, Farebrother's contemporary in the 1830s, Farebrother as a clergyman-naturalist was recognizable as a form of scientific practitioner. But by 1870, both Farebrother and Lydgate would stand in different relation to the scientific profession.

Farebrother can pursue his profession and his hobby because his collections represent a naturalism that has not yet displaced the timeline of creationism. By the time Joseph D. Hooker addressed the opposition of religion to science in his 1868 presidential address, the British Association for the Advancement of Science clearly had become well established. Looking back on his own thirty years of attendance at the conference, Hooker reflects on the traditions and expectations for the address and looks forward to future presidents.[76] Like Huxley, he also makes a claim for the need for specialization, as he argues that scientists, rather than boards of trustees of non-experts, should control collections such as the Natural History Collections of the British Museum, and that museums should be arranged in ways that allow them to serve a more educational purpose.[77] He spends most of his speech, however, discussing a 'dawning science, "the Early History of Mankind"', saying:

> this new science has proclaimed man himself to have inhabited this earth for, perhaps, many thousands of years before the historic period;—a result little expected less than thirty years ago, when the Rev. W. V. Harcourt, in his address to the Association at

> Birmingham, observed, that 'Geology points to the conclusion, that the time during which mankind has existed on the globe, cannot materially differ from that assigned by Scripture,' referring, I need not say, to the so-called Scripture chronology, which has no warrant in the Old Testament, and which gives 5874 as the age of the inhabited globe.[78]

In the time between the setting of *Middlemarch* and its publication date, the age of the world had changed, and Eliot's readers would have recognized that Farebrother's vocation and avocation would stand in contrast with each other. Yet while asserting that the geologic evidence is undeniable, Hooker nevertheless urges an interdisciplinary approach to its conclusions:

> Prehistoric Archaeology now offers to lead us where man has hitherto not ventured to tread; can we, whilst truthfully and fear-lessly pursuing this inquiry, separate its physical from its spiritual aspect? will be the uppermost thought in the minds of many here present. To separate them is, I believe, indeed impossible, but to search out common truths that underlie both is permitted to all. . . . And it should be emphatically so in the minds engaged in this search, where religion and science should speak peace to one another, if they are to walk hand in hand in this our day and generation.[79]

Describing how, earlier in his career, the clergy rarely spoke of science, and in contrast, 'Now, and of late years, science is more frequently named than ever, but too often with dislike or fear, rather than with trust and welcome', notably, according to Hooker, rural clergy are the most strongly opposed to science. Hooker ultimately argues for a sympathetic relationship between religion and science that sounds like something Eliot would write:

> In return, let each pursue the search for truth, the archaeologist into the physical, the religious teacher into the spiritual history and condition of mankind. It will be in vain that each regards the other's pursuit from afar, and turning the object glass of his mind's telescope to his eye, is content when he sees how small the other looks.[80]

According to Hooker, it is only through a wilful illusion of distance, created by the misuse of a scientific instrument, that one can disambiguate science and religion. In Farebrother, Eliot envisions such a sympathetic interdisciplinarity and, indeed, Farebrother is notable for his sympathetic acceptance of others.

Farebrother's collection of specimens, however, gestures towards the challenging world that is to come. Middlemarch and its inhabitants are persistently on the brink of worlds beyond their ken. Ian Duncan has called this 'the character of provincial life as a limit'.[81] Farebrother refers to Lydgate as 'a sort of circumnavigator come to settle among us, and will keep up my belief in the antipodes' (206). Dorothea confronts the history of ancient Rome. Ladislaw contemplates leaving Middlemarch for an unknown career on the continent. Rosamund wistfully longs to move away from the familiar. The town of Middlemarch itself faces an unknown future as it becomes part of a railway network. Indeed, Eliot's readers would have recognized both Farebrother's and Lydgate's interdisciplinarities as unsustainable in the years to come after the close of the novel. In both of these characters, Eliot seems to acknowledge reluctantly that despite her belief in theory for a balanced, multi-perspectived world view, in practice discovery requires at least some degree of specialization. The world that Eliot creates in the novel demonstrates that the exigencies of funding and the demands of vested interests are not to be dismissed, and discovery can only progress if protected from such forces. But more than this, understanding Lydgate and his failure in the context of how science developed in the mid-nineteenth century, as Eliot's readers would have, reveals that the emergence of scientific specializations and the intellectual communities that they enabled were not only defensive and pragmatic, but rather they also created new forums in the world of ideas that created the conditions for scientific discovery.

This chapter has examined how a particular novel engaged with the emergence of disciplines in the nineteenth century. It points to the interaction between disciplines similar to those found in the relationship between autobiography and evolutionary psychology (Chapter 8), classics and theology (Chapter 9), antiquarianism and archaeology (Chapter 7), and music and a number of other disciplines (Chapter 12). Although the influence of Victorian scientific developments on literary form has enjoyed significant critical attention, the ways in which literary genres and narrative forms were shaped by the rise of disciplines, and how literary genres and narrative forms contributed to how such disciplinary lines were both drawn and crossed, warrant more attention. Such literary interventions in the rise of both disciplinarity and interdisciplinarity provide historical perspectives and contribute useful voices in modern-day theorizing of disciplinarity and interdisciplinarity.

Notes

1 See Matthew Arnold, 'Literature and Science' [1883], electronic edition by Ian Lancashire, accessed May 2, 2017, homes.chass.utoronto.ca/~ian/arnold.htm; Thomas Henry Huxley, 'Science and Culture', 1880, *Internet Modern History Sourcebook*, 1998, accessed May 2, 2017, www.fordham.edu/halsall/mod/1880huxley-scicult.asp; C. P. Snow, *The Two Cultures and a Second Look* (New York: Mentor Books, 1964); and F. R. Leavis, *Two*

Cultures?: The Significance of C. P. Snow, ed. Stefan Collini (Cambridge: Cambridge University Press, 2013).

2 Walery and L. Engel, 'Professor Huxley', *Our Celebrities: A Portrait Gallery*, 11 (May 1899), 7.

3 Thomas Henry Huxley, 'Science', *Westminster Review*, American Edition, 61 (1854), 134.

4 Ibid., 134.

5 Ibid.

6 Ibid.

7 Gordon S. Haight (ed.), *The George Eliot Letters*, 9 vols. (New Haven: Yale University Press, 1954–1978), vol. II, 132–133.

8 Haight, *George Eliot Letters*, vol. VIII, 91.

9 George Henry Lewes, 'Literature', *Leader* 5 (January 14, 1854), 40.

10 Jeremiah Rankin and Ruth Barkin, 'Tyndall, Lewes and Popular Representations of Scientific Authority in Victorian Britain', in *The Age of Scientific Naturalism: Tyndall and His Contemporaries*, eds. Bernard Lightman and Michael S. Reidy (London: Pickering and Chatto, 2014), 51–70.

11 Rankin and Barkin, 'Tyndall, Lewes, and Popular Representations', 56.

12 Ibid., 53, 65.

13 Diana Postlethwaite, 'George Eliot and Science', in *The Cambridge Companion to George Eliot*, ed. George Levine (Cambridge: Cambridge University Press, 2001), 107.

14 Henry James, 'Literature', *Galaxy* 15 (March 1873), 428.

15 Beverley Park Rilett, 'George Henry Lewes, the Real Man of Science Behind George Eliot's Fictional Pedants', *George Eliot – George Henry Lewes Studies* 68 (2016), 4–24, 22, n. 20.

16 Rosemary Ashton, *Versatile Victorian: Selected Writings of George Henry Lewes* (London: Bristol Classical Press, 1992), 2, cited in Rilett, 'George Henry Lewes, the Real Man of Science', 22, n. 21.

17 Rilett, 'George Henry Lewes, the Real Man of Science', 14.

18 Nancy Henry, *The Life of George Eliot* (Chichester: John Wiley & Sons, 2012, 2015), 11.

19 Gillian Beer, *Darwin's Plots: Evolutionary Narrative in Darwin, George Eliot and Nineteenth-Century Fiction*, 1983 (London: ARK Paperbacks, 1985); George Levine, *One Culture: Essays in Science and Literature* (Madison: University of Wisconsin Press, 1987); Gowan Dawson, 'Literary Megatheriums and Loose Baggy Monsters: Paleontology and the Victorian Novel', *Victorian Studies* 53 (2011), 203–230; Adelene Buckland, *Novel Science: Fiction and the Invention of Nineteenth-Century Geology* (Chicago and London: University of Chicago Press, 2013).

20 Buckland, *Novel Science*, 14, quoting Ralph O'Connor, *Earth on Show: Fossils and the Poetics of Popular Science, 1802–1856* (Chicago: University of Chicago Press, 2007), 11.

21 Buckland, *Novel Science*, 15.

22 G. K. Chesterton, *The Victorian Age in Literature* [1913] (London: Oxford University Press, 1961), 26; Aldous Huxley, *Huxley Memorial Lecture 1932: T. H. Huxley as a Man of Letters* (London: Macmillan and Co., 1932), 1.

23 Aldous Huxley, *Huxley Memorial Lecture*, 2.

24 Ibid., 7.

25 Thomas Henry Huxley, n.d., 'On Literary Style', Imperial College, Huxley Collection, HO 49.55, quoted in Bernard Lightman, *Victorian Popularizers of Science: Designing Nature for New Audiences* (Chicago: University of

Chicago Press, 2007), 396, n. 126. I am indebted to Lightman for pointing out that John Tyndall, in his Belfast Address (1874), also claimed for science a 'command' of 'literary culture'. Citing the 'less technical writings of its leaders—of its Helmholz, its Huxley, and its Du Bois-Reymond', Tyndall argued: 'Where among modern writers can you find their superiors in clearness and vigour of literary style? Science desires not isolation, but freely combines with every effort towards the bettering of man's estate'. John Tyndall, 'The Belfast Address', *Fragments of Science*, 2 vols. (New York: D. Appleton and Company, 1898), vol. II, 199.

26 Rilett, 'George Henry Lewes, the Real Man of Science', 8.

27 Melinda Baldwin, *Making Nature: The History of a Scientific Journal* (Chicago and London: University of Chicago Press, 2015), 2.

28 Lightman, *Victorian Popularizers of Science*, 355–356.

29 Ibid., 359.

30 Ibid., 5.

31 See Ibid., 26.

32 Henry, *The Life of George Eliot*, 11.

33 Lightman, *Victorian Popularizers of Science*, xi.

34 Rae Greiner, *Sympathetic Realism in Nineteenth-Century British Fiction* (Baltimore: Johns Hopkins University Press, 2012), 17.

35 Amanda Anderson and Joseph Valente (eds.), *Disciplinarity at the Fin de Siècle* (Princeton: Princeton University Press, 2002), 1; Christopher Keep, 'Institutional Memory: History, Disciplinarity, and Victorian Studies', *Victorian Review* 33 (2007): 39.

36 Robert Frodeman (ed.), 'Introduction', in *The Oxford Handbook of Interdisciplinarity* (Oxford: Oxford University Press, 2010), xxxvi, xxxii.

37 Joe Moran, *Interdisciplinarity* (New York: Routledge, 2002), 2.

38 Frodeman, Introduction, xxxvi.

39 Ibid., xxxi.

40 Ibid., xxxiv.

41 Henry points out 'The scientific model for understanding' in *Middlemarch*,

> showing the cross-fertilization of her own and Lewes's work as he continued to research *Problems of Life and Mind*. The very word "study", rather than scene, romance, story, or even history, suggests distance and objectivity as a motivation and goal of examining provincial life.

Life of George Eliot, 192.

42 George Eliot, *Middlemarch* [1871–1872], W. J. Harvey (intro.) (London: Penguin Books, 1988), 25. Hereafter cited within the text.

43 Beer, *Darwin's Plots*, 6–7.

44 Ibid., 151, 165.

45 James, 'Literature', 426.

46 Baldwin details how in 1924 the term 'scientist' was still a source of controversy when physicist Norman Campbell advocated, in a letter to the editor of *Nature*, for its adoption in place of 'man of science' and 'scientific worker'. In fact, one of the arguments against it was that it failed to denote specialization in a particular scientific field. Baldwin, *Making Nature*, 4, 7. For an account of the meeting at which 'scientist' was coined, see Laura J. Snyder, *The Philosophical Breakfast Club* (New York: Broadway Books, 2011), 148.

47 Peter Weingart, 'A Short History of Knowledge Formations', in *The Oxford Handbook of Interdisciplinarity*, ed. Robert Frodeman (Oxford: Oxford University Press, 2010), 8.

48 For an account of the founding of the British Association for the Advancement of Science, see Snyder, *The Philosophical Breakfast Club*, 128–157.
49 Paul White, 'Cross-cultural Encounters: The Co-Production of Science and Literature in Mid-Victorian Periodicals', in *Transactions and Encounters: Science and Culture in the Nineteenth Century*, eds. Roger Luckhurst and Josephine McDonagh (Manchester: Manchester University Press, 2002), 75–98, 88–89.
50 Beer, *Darwin's Plots*, 152.
51 Lightman, *Victorian Popularizers of Science*, 364.
52 Snyder, *The Philosophical Breakfast Club*, 4.
53 Ibid.
54 My reading of Lydgate thus contrasts with Postlethwaite's characterization of him as standing for theoretical science which, in contrast with Farebrother's interest in natural history, is disconnected from the world in which he lives. 'George Eliot and Science', 105.
55 Julie Thompson Klein, 'A Taxonomy of Interdisciplinarity', in *The Oxford Handbook of Interdisciplinarity*, ed. Robert Frodeman (Oxford: Oxford University Press, 2010), 15–30, 25.
56 Postlethwaite, 'George Eliot and Science', 116.
57 Susan David Bernstein, *Roomscape: Women Writers in the British Museum from George Eliot to Virginia Woolf* (Edinburgh: Edinburgh University Press, 2013, 2014), 131–132.
58 According to Postlethwait, 'the novel overflows with failed monistic cosmologists', and Beer explores how Lydgate and Casaubon are both concerned with 'relations' and 'origins'. Postlethwaite, 'George Eliot and Science', 102–103; Beer, *Darwin's Plots*, 172.
59 Daniel Sarewitz, 'Against Holism', in *The Oxford Handbook of Interdisciplinarity*, ed. Robert Frodeman (Oxford: Oxford University Press, 2010), 68.
60 Sarewitz, 'Against Holism', 67.
61 Ibid., 73.
62 British Association for the Advancement of Science, Notice of the Twelfth Meeting of the Association, April 16, 1842, Talbot: Publications Concerning Societies and Associations, Add MS 88942/3/2/50, National Trust Accession 25265, British Library, 2.
63 Snyder, *The Philosophical Breakfast Club*, 145.
64 British Association for the Advancement of Science, Notice of the Twelfth Meeting, 1.
65 Ibid.
66 Henry James, 'Literature', 427.
67 Paul White, 'Cross-cultural Encounters', 89.
68 Jerry A. Jacobs, *In Defense of Disciplines: Interdisciplinarity and Specialization in the Research University* (Chicago: University of Chicago Press, 2013), 6.
69 Rankin and Barkin, 'Tyndall, Lewes, and Popular Representations', 67, 69, 65.
70 Ibid., 70.
71 Snyder, *The Philosophical Breakfast Club*, 50.
72 Postlethwait, 'George Eliot and Science', 99.
73 Lightman, *Victorian Popularizers of Science*, ix, 419–420.
74 Ibid., 12.
75 Weingart, 'A Short History of Knowledge Formations', 6.
76 Joseph D. Hooker, 'Address to the British Association for the Advancement of Science, Delivered by the President, Joseph D. Hooker' (Norwich: Fletcher and Son, Printers, 1868), Add MS 88942/3/2/50, item 35658, British Library, 3–5.

77 Hooker, 'Address to the British Association for the Advancement of Science', 8–9.
78 Ibid., 26.
79 Ibid., 26–27.
80 Ibid., 27–28.
81 Ian Duncan, 'George Eliot's Science Fiction', *Representations* 125 (2014), 18.

12 All Arts Constantly Aspire to the Condition of Musicology

Victorian Musicology as Interdiscipline

Bennett Zon

Introduction

Although not a Victorian term the word 'interdiscipline' has existed since 1930, when it was used in the eighteenth annual report of the Social Science Research Council: 'Concern with "co-operative research" or "inter-discipline problems" should not be allowed to hamper the first-rate mind, alert to the possibilities inherent in whatever problem enlists its energies'.[1] Subsequent usage continues to reflect this definition, not least in periodical titles ranging across an array of topics.[2] This chapter traces the idea of an interdiscipline to Walter Pater's famous adage 'All art constantly aspires to the condition of music'[3] and it uses Pater's idea to identify the origin of Victorian musicology not as a discipline, but as an interdiscipline. Pater, like many Victorian musicologists, makes his claim by using two interrelated, interdisciplinary concepts: ekphrasis and anderstreben. Broadly speaking, ekphrasis is a method of writing designed to embody literally the essential characteristics of another art; anderstreben explains how the arts seek one another as they progress towards perfection. Pater uses ekphrasis to describe a painting representing a concert, and in doing so reveals how literature seeks to embody painting in the same way painting seeks to embody music. According to the rules of anderstreben all art aspires to the condition of music because music is the only art that successfully collapses matter and form. In the construction of their interdiscipline Victorian musicologists, like Pater, would adopt ekphrasis as a methodological practice and anderstreben as a theoretical belief. Pater's structural preoccupation with matter and form provides a strong organizational framework for interrogating key issues underpinning the interdiscipline of Victorian musicology. An introduction explores the meaning of 'interdiscipline' today, followed by two main sections: under the section titled 'Matter' are two subsections on practice investigating the close symbiotic relationship between the Victorian musical object and the Victorian musicological subject; under 'Form' two subsections on theory illustrate how Pater's seemingly oppositional methodologies of ekphrasis and anderstreben combine to create the dynamic interdiscipline of Victorian musicology. A conclusion reiterates my thesis, summarizes main points and overarching principles, discusses limitations, and offers a projection towards further areas of research.

Interdisciplin(arity)

Good definitions of 'interdiscipline' are elusive. Wikipedia and the *OED* give the impression that they stem largely from interrelated sciences like biosemantics, forensic kinesiology, genetic toxicology, humour and translation, information science, public health, social science in agriculture, and sociolinguistics. According to J. Stycos demography, for example, is 'clearly a discipline' because as a field it contains

> its own body of interrelated concepts, techniques, journals, and professional associations . . . But by the nature of its subject matter and methods demography is just as clearly an 'interdiscipline', drawing heavily on biology and sociology for the study of fertility; on economics and geography for studies of migration; and on the health sciences for the study of mortality.[4]

Historically, definitions have tended to reflect a hard scientific or social scientific origin, even if they are widely applicable across the arts as well. Human communications theorist S. W. Littlejohn defines an *interdiscipline* as 'a field of scholars who identify with various disciplines but share a common interest in a theme that crosses traditional boundaries'.[5] Echoing Littlejohn humanities computing expert Willard McCarty claims that

> A true *interdiscipline* is, however, not easily understood, funded or managed in a world already divided along disciplinary lines, despite the standard pieties. Properly so called an interdiscipline is not just another administrative entity with its budget, chair and department members – difficult as this is to carve these days out of existing turf; it isn't an institutionally sa[n]ctioned (sic) kind of poaching. Rather it is an entity that exists in the interstices of the existing fields, dealing with some, many or all of them.[6]

An interdiscipline is

> constituted precisely by that unifying perspective on what happens at the intersection of two or more fields. This perspective gives the interdiscipline integrity and basis for its own research agenda,

> curriculum and publications. Nevertheless, as long as it remains an interdiscipline it depends on continuous activity in the intersecting fields. Preoccupation with what they share puts it in position to foster cross-fertilising exchange among them, as a merchant trader among mutually incomprehending cultures. Thus it serves them, not as a servant his master but collegially – which has radical implications for its institutionalisation.[7]

More recent theorists struggle to develop these definitions, emphasizing the fundamentally binaristic nature of disciplinary and interdisciplinary projects rather than the collective unity of an interdiscipline. Theorists today tend to focus on the constantly changing dynamics of disciplinary configuration, admitting that they produce inevitably 'fuzzy' interdisciplinary boundaries.[8] For them the very production of new research militates against disciplinary stability because disciplines are congenitally driven to change themselves from within. The notion that disciplines are inherently fluid is confirmed and explored in this volume in the fields of science (Chapter 1), mathematics (Chapter 10), and history (Chapter 5). Jerry Jacobs recognizes this condition as 'a form of social organization that generates new ideas and research findings, certifies this knowledge, and in turn teaches this subject matter to interested students'.[9] Predictably, the self-negating or self-fulfilling cycle of disciplinary configuration produces taxonomic implications. Julie Klein identifies a host of socio-institutional forces pressurizing disciplinary stability, including multidisciplinarity, interdisciplinarity, and transdisciplinarity. These range across a spectrum of methodologies from disciplinarity to interdisciplinarity; complementarity to hybridization; partial to full integrationism;[10] and even something as potentially extreme and intractable as 'deviant interdisciplinarity'[11] – an interdiscipline yearning for lost disciplinary unity. It must have been these same forces which pressured editors of the tantalizingly (yet in reality only modestly) subversive *In(ter) discipline: New Languages for Criticism* (2007) to bracket interdiscipline into indiscipline in the title of their otherwise profoundly interdisciplinary proceedings.[12] For Peter Szendy an interdiscipline 'has the disadvantage of presupposing the boundaries of the very disciplines it seeks to question'.[13] For today's ethnomusicologists, for example – long used to working across musicology and anthropology – an interdiscipline is porous; it is 'a discipline itself that has its roots in two older disciplines . . . rather than an interdisciplinary field'.[14] Wolfgang Krohn makes a not dissimilar point when he refers to interdisciplines as 'disciplines with interdisciplinary features'.[15] Like Joe Moran – who as it so happens omits 'interdiscipline' from *Interdisciplinarity* (2010) – Krohn encapsulates the fuzziness and conceptual recalcitrance of the term. As William McCarty says, not only does an interdiscipline defy definition but in the way it behaves interdisciplines are almost indistinguishable from disciplines themselves:

> an interdiscipline manoeuvres for power in the same way as a discipline. But rather than as a discipline, which seems to delimit and maintain its conceptual boundaries, an interdiscipline embraces other areas of thought. A discipline defends – an interdiscipline bridges.[16]

Matter

The Musical Object

We tend to think of the Victorians as great bridge-builders, architecturally and conceptually, but the origin of disciplines tells another story. Far from building bridges, many disciplines appear to burn their bridges in the unrelenting quest for specialization. Not the interdiscipline of musicology. Musicology built bridges spanning every conceivable discipline, including a wide array of increasingly professionalized disciplines in the arts and sciences such as zoology, anthropology, ethnology, pedagogy, biography, history, philosophy and theology, to name but a few. Victorian musicology owes its interdisciplinarity partly to the fact that no single discipline can speak definitively about an object; equally, Victorian musicology found its object particularly troublesome. For one thing Victorian musicologists struggled to understand and explain music's purpose without reference to other disciplines, and in some instances disciplines like anthropology and theology seemed to hold mutually contradictory opinions, even if voiced through the same musicologist.

Modern ethnomusicologist Chris Small famously contends that music's purpose is entirely social:

> There is no such thing as music. Music is not a thing at all, but an activity, something that people do. The apparent thing "music" is a figment, an abstraction of the action, whose reality vanishes as soon as we examine it at all closely.[17]

Small's contemporary Richard Blacking utilizes a similar anthropological approach: music, he claims, is 'humanly organized sound'.[18] In fact, Small and Blacking update a common Victorian trope first voiced by public intellectual, Victorian polemicist and musical theorist Herbert Spencer in 1857. Influenced by comprehensive reading across disciplines in the sciences and social sciences Spencer considered music to be intrinsically social because it arose from language as 'impassioned speech': 'The distinctive traits of song', he claims, 'are simply the traits of emotional speech intensified and systematized . . . all music, is an idealization of the natural language of passion'.[19] Spencer also believed that the emotional experience which prompts music into being also prompts an altruistic socio-evolutionary characteristic: sympathy. For Spencer musical feelings are 'the chief media of sympathy':

> In its bearings upon human happiness, this emotional language which musical culture develops and refines is only second in importance to the language of the intellect; perhaps not even second to it. For these modifications of voice produced by feelings are the means of exciting like feelings in others. Joined with gestures and expressions of face, they give life to the otherwise dead words in which the intellect utters its ideas, and so enable the hearer not only to *understand* the state of mind they accompany, but to *partake* of that state. In short they are the chief media of sympathy.[20]

Described by George S. Carr as 'the very apostle of Altruism'[21] Spencer reflects an increasingly long line of liberal social thinkers when he equates the musical object with musical emotion, musical emotion with sympathy, and sympathy with social progress. According to nineteenth-century philosopher and religious thinker John Fiske social progress 'is *the continuous weakening of selfishness and the continuous strengthening of sympathy*. Or—to use a more convenient and somewhat more accurate expression suggested by Comte—it is a gradual supplanting of egoism by altruism'.[22] For Spencer all altruistic feelings may be a mixture of enlightened self-interest and social sympathy[23] – 'sympathetic excitements of egoistic feelings',[24] he calls them – but music is chief amongst them because the musical object is intrinsically connected to the musical subject in the mutually contingent relationship of 'musicking'. In other words, music is only music because it is felt; it is only felt if it is musicked (to use Small's term); and it only musicked because it embodies favourable socio-evolutionary characteristics (sympathy and altruism). Even sympathy and altruism are selfish memes,[25] however, and according to Spencer music is chief amongst them; at least this is what many scientifically minded Victorians seemed to believe about the purpose of music.[26]

Yet Spencer's evolutionary anthropology is not entirely consistent from a purely disciplinary standpoint. Obsessed with the relation of unity and diversity from the 1860s Spencer embarked upon an embarrassingly retrograde transcendental odyssey eventually reprised in 'Religion: A Retrospect and Prospect' (1884) which would describe the 'an Infinite and Eternal Energy, from which all things proceed'.[27] Spencer attracted huge critical opprobrium when he dallied (unsuccessfully) with the idea of a transcendental Absolute – what he described as the Unknown Reality – because for some it compromised the integrity of his unremittingly materialistic philosophical project: 'Though Spirit and Matter [are antithetical conceptions] . . . the one is no less than the other to be regarded as but a sign of the Unknown Reality which underlies both'.[28] The Rev George Ladd tried to help but probably made matters worse by suggesting the Unknowable was effectively God in everything but name:

> the Unknowable is known to be a Power; and it must be a great Power, for the *Universe* – that is, all manifestations of power – is manifest to us. But power, inconceivably great – enough to accomplish all things done and even more – has been by Theists from time immemorial held to be an attribute of God. But Mr Spencer speaks of *the* Power; and as he nowhere uses the plural and doubtless holds to the unity of the Universe, having himself made and attempt to represent in philosophy this unity of the universe, he must believe in the unity also of the Power which the one universe manifests.[29]

Spencer believed in the relativity of all things – music included. Everything is interconnected by the unifying force of evolution, even thought itself: 'every thought expresses a relation – since thinking is relational'; 'every thought involves a whole system of thoughts and ceases to exist if severed from its various correlatives'.[30] With the admission of an Absolute Unknowable the idea that music was the idealized language of the emotions took on an undeniably transcendental hue. Suddenly musical sympathy began to look more and more theological and less and less anthropological. Even arch-agnostic Darwin failed to help. Writing about music's function as part of the rituals of sexual selection amongst birds Darwin claims that music conjures up a range of emotions of a long past age, the most importance of which is the most spiritually essentialized – love: 'Love', Darwin claims, 'is still the commonest themes of our own songs'.[31]

Spencer's disciplinary confusion over music's purpose mirrors contemporary philosophical confusion over the meaning of form and content in music. Is music 'absolute' and transcendental; or is it 'programmatic' and culturally contingent? Should content map onto pre-determined form like sonata or rondo; or should form structurally mirror the literary narrative (the programme) its content seeks to represent? Not unconnectedly, does the use of words diminish or increase the purity of compositional meaning? Yet again the musical object was a site of intense disciplinary contingency. If neither anthropology nor theology could explain its purpose maybe philosophy could, at the very least, explain its meaning. Easier said than done, as philosopher Roger Scruton proves: music, he avers,

> does not merely echo or imitate things which have an independent reality; the development of programme music is determined by the

> development of its theme. The music moves in time according to the logic of its subject and not [like absolute music] according to autonomous principles of its own.[32]

The fierceness of debate is captured in the diametrically opposing disciplinary perspectives of absolutist Eduard Hanslick and programmaticist Franz Liszt. Drawing upon metaphysical philosophies of German Idealism Hanslick considered the term music to exclude not only compositions with words, but even instrumental compositions with programmatic inscriptions: music's 'union with poetry', he opines, 'though enhancing the power of music, does not widen its limits'.[33] For Liszt, however, the most meaningful music is theological, and the most theological music is programmatic because art, like music, should reflect life in the way life reflects its divine Creator, even music which includes no literary programme at all[34]: 'In program music', he advises,

> the recurrence, variation, alteration, and modulation of motifs are determined by their relationship to a poetic idea. Here one theme no longer begets another . . . Though not ignored, all exclusively musical considerations are subordinated to the treatment of the subject at hand. Accordingly, the treatment and subject of this symphonic genre demand an engagement that goes beyond the technical treatment of the musical material. The vague impressions of the soul are elevated to definite impressions through an articulated plan, which is taken in by the ear in much the same manner in which a cycle of paintings is taken in by the eye. The artist who favors this kind of artwork enjoys the advantage of being able to connect with a poetic process all those affects which an orchestra can express with such great power.[35]

The Musicological Subject

Whether absolutist or programmaticist, Victorian musicologists made theology, anthropology, philosophy, and many other disciplines unwitting partners in the construction of their interdiscipline. They did that by defining *themselves* as much as they defined the musical object they studied. The Victorian musicological subject (the musicologist) defined himself or herself within a matrix of three intersecting areas of sociocultural development: professionalization, education, and popularization. If the founding of a professional organization signals the origin of a discipline, then Victorian musicology began in 1874 with the founding of the Musical (later Royal) Association. Unsurprisingly perhaps the Musical Association's manifesto is consummately interdisciplinary; according to one of its first Vice Presidents, William Spottiswoode,

> It has been suggested by several leading persons interested both in the theory and practice of Music, that the formation of a Society, similar in the main features of its organisation to existing Learned Societies, would be a great public benefit. Such a Musical Society might comprise among its members the foremost Musicians, theoretical as well as practical, of the day; the principal Patrons of Art; and also those Scientific men whose researches have been directed to the science of Acoustics, and to kindred inquiries. Its periodical meetings might be devoted partly to the reading of Papers upon the history, the principles, and the criticism of Music; partly to the illustration of such Papers by actual performance; and partly to the exhibition and discussion of experiments relating to the theory and construction of musical instruments, or to the principles and combination of musical sounds.[36]

Spottiswoode expresses a categorical interdisciplinary criterion when he emphasizes the need for parity between theory and practice, and models the association and its patronage upon similar professional societies. He also embraces experimental science (especially acoustics) at the same time as developing *intra*disciplinary methodologies in music history, criticism, analysis, and technology (organology). If an interdiscipline 'exists in the interstices of the existing fields'[37] and is a 'field of scholars who identify with various disciplines but share a common interest in a theme that crosses traditional boundaries'[38] – if 'a discipline defends and an interdiscipline bridges'[39] – Spottiswoode's interdisciplinary Victorian musicologist would be a wholehearted advocate. Indeed, Spottiswoode came with excellent interdisciplinary credentials. Amongst them he was a fellow of the Society of Antiquaries; treasurer of the British Association for the Advancement of Science (1861–1874); president of the Ethnological Society of London from 1864; treasurer of the Royal Institution (1865–1873); in 1865 president of the mathematical section, and in 1878 president of the British Association; president of the London Mathematical Society (1870–1872); and from 1853 fellow, from 1871 to 1878 treasurer, and in 1878 president of the Royal Society. In addition, he was a fully paid up member and later president in 1878 of the influential dining club for scientific naturalists the X-Club.[40]

In referring to the association's educational remit Spottiswoode also highlights the epistemic tension between discipline and interdiscipline by creating 'a form of social organization that generates new ideas and research findings, certifies this knowledge, and in turn teaches this subject matter to interested students'.[41] In fact the Musical Association effectively joined an educational programme already underway in universities like Edinburgh, Cambridge, Oxford, and London. Here, as in the cases of dance (Chapter 2), art history (Chapter 3), history (Chapter 4), theology (Chapter 9), and classics (Chapter 9), the role of the university could be crucial. Edinburgh created an undergraduate music curriculum in 1838. Cambridge taught acoustics from the 1830s and had developed a music curriculum by the 1870s. Oxford was slower off the mark in teaching acoustics, but along with Trinity College of Music (University of London) had caught up with Cambridge by the time they inaugurated their own curriculum in the 1870s. The Rev. Peter Maurice, Chaplain to New and All Souls colleges in Oxford, discussed the role disciplines played in this transitional process. In an incendiary letter to Earl Derby, then Chancellor of the university, Maurice complains vociferously about music's inferior status within the university; a lack of cohesion between music students and graduates to their colleges and institution; disadvantageous distinctions between doctors of music and other disciplines; and the denial of honours allowing them the privilege of voting in university elections and sitting in Convocation.[42] The topic of Oxford's historical DMus (Doctor of Music, always in Composition) degree says it all: 'A Doctor (or Inceptor) in Music must have studied and practices his art for a long time of years, though Oxford contributes not a mite towards his qualification, but exacts, without taking any steps to ensure the decent performance of those elaborate and finished compositions which a Doctor in Music must compose . . . The musical degrees, as far as Oxford is concerned, are an empty name, with no privilege whatever attached to them within its walls; even a seat among its Doctors in the House of Assembly is denied to the entire faculty. And, if this is the treatment which the representatives of the most liberal of all the Arts and Sciences meets with, in the most famous of all the Universities in the world, who can feel astonishment at the little respect paid to the faculty elsewhere!'[43] Two of Maurice's imperatives signal the origin of a Victorian musicological interdiscipline. First it is absolutely imperative that the university's self-perpetuating prejudice against music is abolished for only then can we prevent 'those very talents which nature may have lavished upon us' from being 'buried, or perhaps rusted away';[44] second, and contingent upon succeeding in abolishing prejudice, is the need to reformulate the university's understanding of music's historical position amongst the Arts and Sciences. This is more than a plea to reassert music's place within the medieval quadrivium but an interdisciplinary imperative to reinvigorate lost, lapsed relationships with Classics and Theology in particular: 'All classical literature', he opines, 'from its earliest era, has been invariably identified with Music'; 'What', moreover, 'has been done for Music ever since its divorcement from Theology?'[45]

Maurice's musicologist may be uncompromising in the interdisciplinary educational demands he places upon an unresponsive university – to rise to the highest class Music, he claims, must pay 'diligent and painful attention to all the disciplines of the Art and Science'[46] – but he is equally demanding upon the development of culture more popularly.

Popularization puts interdisciplinary musicological theory into cultural practice by triangulating professionalization and education, and it does so through an array of disciplines distributed across the arts and sciences. Bernard Lightman offers an assessment of scientific popularization; for him science

> became fashionable and respectable within a broader spectrum of the populace, not just within the circles of the well to do . . . Scientific knowledge seemed to offer the magical password – the "open sesame" – that unlocked the doors to exhilarating new works in the second half of the century.[47]

But as Lightman and I have aimed to prove science is nothing without the Arts;[48] indeed, by focussing on the interdisciplinary 'threshold' between the sciences and the arts (particularly as expressed by female popularizers), Lightman highlights the importance their cross-fertilization contributes to the creation of knowledgeable Victorian generalists.[49] Scientific popularizer Annie Carey may as well be speaking for musicology when she claims that 'Elementary knowledge – meaning by that phrase a knowledge of the facts that stand on the threshold of every department of Science and Art – needs most especially to be accurately presented and carefully instilled in early life'.[50] The same interdisciplinary concept of 'threshold' appears in Victorian musicology, culminating in the popularizing book *The Threshold of Music: An Inquiry Into the Development of the Musical Sense* (1908) by late Victorian music psychologist William Wallace. In his lugubriousness Wallace reads much like Maurice did some sixty years earlier despite all the advances in music over the years, but while Maurice represents the origin of an interdisciplinary initiative Wallace is already operating within an established – if slowly developing – interdisciplinary threshold: 'The scientific man is somewhat complacent', he maintains: 'All scientific men are not musicians, nor are many musicians versed in science'.[51]

Form

Ekphrasis and the Interdisciplinary Musical Object

If tested, the same could perhaps be said of literary figures – with one major exception: Walter Pater. Critic and philosopher Walter Pater is not generally interpreted in interdisciplinary contexts to my knowledge (he does not appear in *The Oxford Handbook of Interdisciplinarity*, for example) but his work provides a rare opportunity to theorize musicological interdisciplinarity from a contemporary Victorian standpoint. Pater's reference to music is famous as much for its clarity as its opaqueness:

> *All art constantly aspires towards the condition of music.* For while in all other kinds of art it is possible to distinguish the matter from the form, and the understanding can always make this distinction, yet it is the constant effort of art to obliterate it. That the mere matter of a poem, for instance, its subject, namely, its given incidents or situation –that the mere matter of a picture, the actual circumstances of an event, the actual topography of a landscape – should be nothing without the form, the spirit, of the handling, that this form, this mode of handling, should become an end in itself, should penetrate every part of the matter: this is what all art constantly strives after, and achieves in different degrees.[52]

The enigmatic meaning behind Pater's assertion has eluded scholars for years. More recently, and not unlike many literary historians, musicologist Mark Evan Bonds has tried explaining it as an extension of Hanslick's concept of absolute music. Having presumably read Hanslick's treatise, Pater, according to Bonds, hoped to apply to art the same kind of inseparability of form and content possible only in music[53]: 'It is the art of music', Pater avers,

> which most completely realizes this artistic ideal, this perfect identification of matter and form. In its consummate moments, the end is not distinct from the means, the subject from the expression; they inhere in and completely saturate each other; and to it, therefore, to the condition of its perfect moments, all the arts may be supposed constantly to aspire.[54]

Two interrelated concepts emerge from Pater's dalliance with music: ekphrasis and anderstreben. Music philosopher Lydia Gochr defines ekphrasis as producing 'images for the mind's eye by means of words'.[55] Pater comes in a long line of ekphrastic communicators, and uses the technique to describe Titian's *Concert* (1510–1512), praising 'the skill with which he caught the waves of wandering sound, and fixed them forever on the lips and hands' of the performers'.[56] But as Goehr claims, Victorian and ancient ekphrasis differ: Victorian ekphrasis focussed on the comparison of aesthetic objects like music, art, and poetry; ancient ekphrasis, on the act of conjuring up an image through spoken of written words.[57] Goehr distinguishes these by referring to '*aesthetic presence* when ekphrasis remains within the domain of the arts, and to *imaginative presence* when it extends beyond this domain'.[58] Aesthetic (modern) and imaginative (ancient) presence are not unlike the disciplines they draw upon to conjure up an image; all aesthetic presences aspire to condition of imaginative presence.

Ekphrasis plays an important role in the way the musical object is imagined and constructed by the Victorian interdisciplinary musicological subject. For Pater although as an aesthetic presence the musical object represents the perfect conflation of matter and form (presumably whether absolute or programme) it is paradoxically only through the imaginative presence that its properties come to life. This is roundly proved by Victorian musicology, which invests the musical object with inherent social properties, like Spencerian sympathy or Darwinian love, while through literary prose communicating those characteristics in ways which seek to mirror the very object they wish to study. Spencer is not renowned for the elegance of his prose, but when it comes to music he is unusually ekphrastic. In addition to describing non-vocal expression Spencer peppers 'The Origin and Function of Music' with short ekphrastic illuminations of spoken text. The 'Oh' of astonishment or delight exemplifies the middle voice; 'Beware!', the lower voice; 'Hallo! How came you here?', contrasting registers; calling for the maid 'Mary', an ascending interval of a third – the list is extensive. Fuller sentences extend this ekphrastic approach, and replicate the emotional tempo: 'The slowest movements, *largo* and *adagio*, are used where such depressing emotions as grief, or such unexciting emotions as reverence, are to be portrayed; while the more rapid movements, *andante*, *allegro*, *presto*, represent successively increasing degrees of mental vivacity'.[59] Darwin is noticeably similar, if more elegantly poetic, when writing about musical origins, as he conjures up the intangible sensations of musical experience in the words he uses to describe them: 'The sensations and ideas excited in us by music, or by the cadences of impassioned oratory, appear from their vagueness, yet depth, like mental reversions to the emotions and thoughts of a long-past age'.[60]

While Darwin's ekphrastic imagination is well known,[61] and Spencer's has probably never attracted attention, the influence of an ekphrastic imagination has never been placed in Victorian musicological contexts, even though examples of it are ubiquitous. It was 1896 before Victorian ornithological field books, for example, included illustrations of birdsong transcribed into musical notation[62] – before then field guides used mnemonics in lieu. But mnemonic books like *A Dictionary of Bird Notes* (1889) take ekphrastic techniques to an altogether higher zoomusicological level, producing a veritable Note-Bird/Bird-Note dictionary crammed not simply with mneumonics but ekphrastic glosses on onomatopoeic syllables. Thus, the Great Black-backed Gull produces a 'croak (harsh)'; the Ring Dove, 'coo-coo-co-co-coo (soft)'[63] in a way which aspires to the conflation of form and content heralded by Pater and Hanslick as absolute music. Earlier still, the same ekphrastic imagination occurs in pedagogical writing which for educational purposes tries to replicate the actual sound of musical objects, in reverse literary direction to programme music. 'The Butterfly' in Henry Keatley Moore's emphatically Froebelian *Child's Pianoforte Book* (1880?) makes this explicit:

> Now you know how the butterfly flutters its wings as it hovers over the flowers; and how frequently it rests, with wings quite still . . . Let us try to express both the fluttering and the resting in our music.[64]

For Keatley Moore, like all Froebelians, there is a tangible – one might say 'programmaticist' – relationship between concepts and reality and music exemplifies that more than any other art; according to Froebel music is 'representation through sound', and song 'life-giving word'.[65]

Keatley Moore was not alone in applying an ekphrastic imagination to an interdisciplinary musical object caught between its epistemic reality as music and its linguistic representation in words. Like Keatley Moore, co-educationist John Curwen, founder of Britain's most popular singing method Tonic Sol-Fa, also roots his teaching in an ekphrastic language combining all the ingredients of music – amongst them rhythm, tone, melody, phrase, timbre, accent and meter:

> Now, children, we are going to learn the art of singing in tune. What are we going to learn? First, then, you must remember that any musical sound is called a *note*. What is a musical sound called? This is a note.' (*I hear you singing to the sound* ah *any note you please.*)[66]

Heavily influenced by educationist Johann Heinrich Pestalozzi (Froebel's teacher), Curwen like Keatley Moore triangulates visual, musical, and textual ekphrasis in a kind of imagesoundtext, to expand W. J. T. Mitchell's concept of imagetext.[67] The image of the 'The Butterfly' (Figure 12.1), for example, not only harmonizes text and tune (Figure 12.2) by encapsulating two states of stillness and movement but also captures in perspective and position the rising opening figure of the music.

The more distant fluttering butterfly is the note G, which nears as it rises up to the note D (the dominant to G's tonic) on the third beat of the first bar where it stops briefly for honey. Whereas Keatley Moore uses ekphrasis to represent individual pieces of music; however, Curwen elevates it to a structural feature of a system in which emotions, hand signs, and pitches of the scale (Figure 12.3) combine in an imagesoundtext to form the very pedagogical basis of Tonic Sol-Fa (learning to read with do, re, mi, fah, sol, la, ti, do).

Hand signs indicating pitch are allocated 'mental effects' (emotions) in images representing an emotional spectrum from positive to negative, happy to sad, strong to weak. In some respects Keatley Moore

XV.

IN our other tune we represent THE BUTTERFLY. Now you know how the butterfly flutters its wings as it hovers over the flowers; and how frequently it rests, with wings quite still, while its long trunk (or proboscis) sucks out the honey. Let us try to express both the fluttering and the resting in our music. Beside these, we must have gaiety; for what is gayer than a butterfly? We will hope to find this expressed too in the music; but as for the honey, nothing but really eating it will do. Neither music nor anything else can make-believe the sweetness and delightful stickiness of honey.

Sometimes you may sing the words to THE BUTTERFLY, but more often you must count.

D.C. is short for Da Capo.

Da is Italian for *from*
Capo is Italian for *the beginning*
al is Italian for *to the*
fine is Italian for *end.*

So *D.C. al fine* means "From the beginning to the end;" and you will find the word *fine* just before the first double-bar, where it is put to show you that in the repeat you have to make that the end of the tune.

These double-bars are quite different from the usual bars; they have nothing to do with the counting; they only mark the place where a division of the tune comes, and such a division or musical *sentence* is just like a "stanza"* in poetry.

* Commonly and wrongly called a "verse," but the proper meaning of "verse" is a *line* of poetry, the *versus* or place where one turns over from one line to the next.

Figure 12.1 The Butterfly (image). H. Keatley Moore, *The Child's Pianoforte Book: Being a First Year's Course at the Pianoforte for the Home, The Kindergarten, and the School: With Upwards of Fifty Original Tunes and Songs*. London: W. Swan Sonnenschein & Co., 77.

and Curwen seem to express what Goehr calls an *aesthetic presence*, if by aesthetic presence we concentrate on the mutual representationality of occasionally unified images, sounds, and texts. But Curwen's more structural ekphrasis is also indicative of an *imaginative presence* in which language is systemically implicated in the representational essence of an interdisciplinary musical object. For Curwen that object is

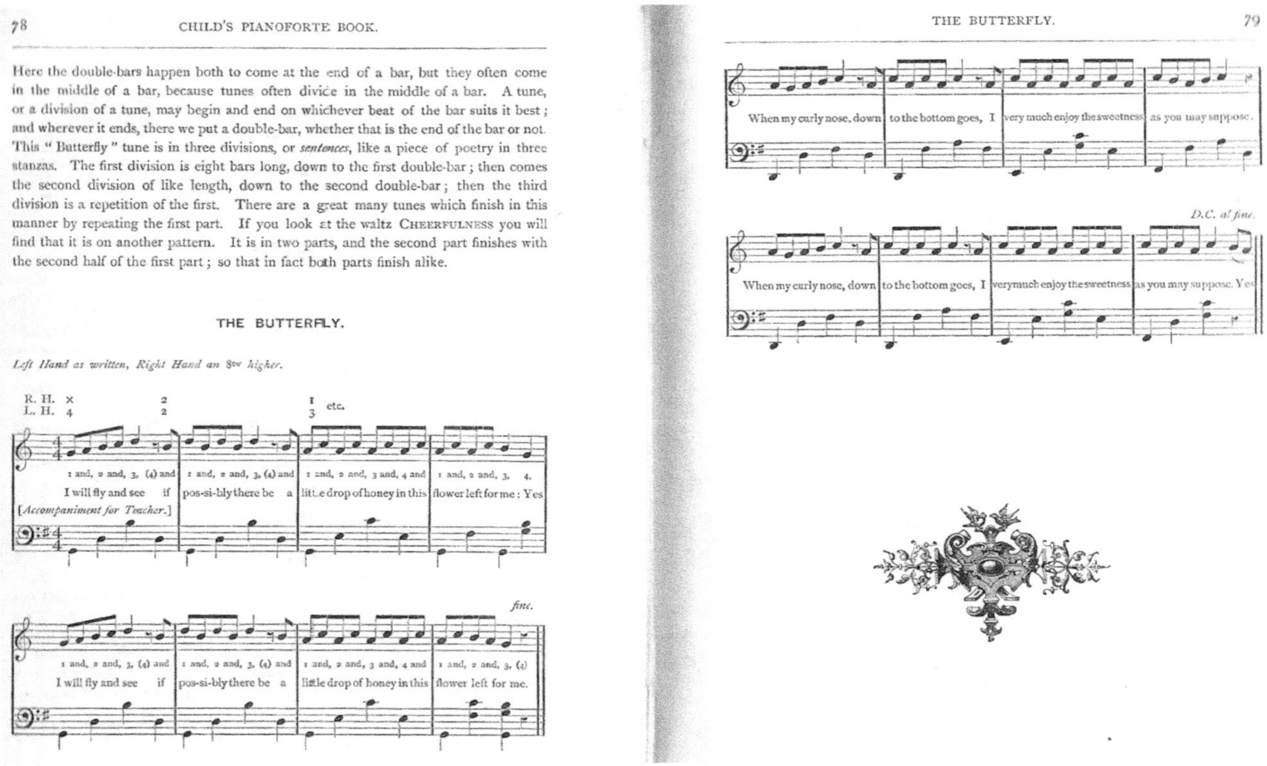

78 CHILD'S PIANOFORTE BOOK.

Here the double-bars happen both to come at the end of a bar, but they often come in the middle of a bar, because tunes often divide in the middle of a bar. A tune, or a division of a tune, may begin and end on whichever beat of the bar suits it best; and wherever it ends, there we put a double-bar, whether that is the end of the bar or not. This "Butterfly" tune is in three divisions, or *sentences*, like a piece of poetry in three stanzas. The first division is eight bars long, down to the first double-bar; then comes the second division of like length, down to the second double-bar; then the third division is a repetition of the first. There are a great many tunes which finish in this manner by repeating the first part. If you look at the waltz CHEERFULNESS you will find that it is on another pattern. It is in two parts, and the second part finishes with the second half of the first part; so that in fact both parts finish alike.

THE BUTTERFLY.

Left Hand as written, Right Hand an 8ve higher.

R. H. × 2 1 etc.
L. H. 4 2 3
1 and, 2 and, 3, (4) and
I will fly and see if
[*Accompaniment for Teacher.*]
1 and, 2 and, 3, (4) and
pos-si-bly there be a
1 and, 2 and, 3 and, 4 and
little drop of honey in this
1 and, 2 and, 3, 4.
flower left for me: Yes
fine.
1 and, 2 and, 3, (4) and
I will fly and see if
1 and, 2 and, 3, (4) and
pos-si-bly there be a
1 and, 2 and, 3 and, 4 and
little drop of honey in this
1 and, 2 and, 3, (4)
flower left for me.
THE BUTTERFLY. 79
When my curly nose, down
to the bottom goes, I
very much enjoy the sweetness
as you may suppose.
D.C. al fine.
When my curly nose, down
to the bottom goes, I
very much enjoy the sweetness
as you may suppose. Yes

Figure 12.2 The Butterfly (music). *The Child's Pianoforte Book: Being a First Year's Course at the Pianoforte for the Home, The Kindergarten, and the School: With Upwards of Fifty Original Tunes and Songs*, 78 and 79.

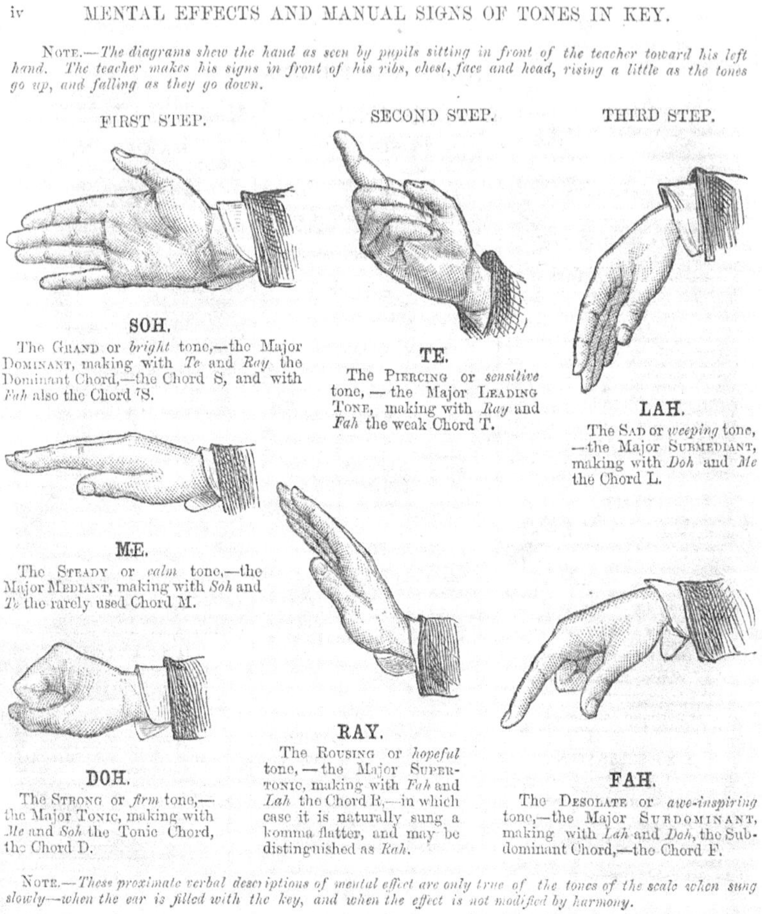
iv MENTAL EFFECTS AND MANUAL SIGNS OF TONES IN KEY.
NOTE.—*The diagrams shew the hand as seen by pupils sitting in front of the teacher toward his left hand. The teacher makes his signs in front of his ribs, chest, face and head, rising a little as the tones go up, and falling as they go down.*
FIRST STEP.
SECOND STEP.
THIRD STEP.
SOH.
The GRAND or *bright* tone,—the Major DOMINANT, making with *Te* and *Ray* the Dominant Chord,—the Chord S, and with *Fah* also the Chord ⁷S.
TE.
The PIERCING or *sensitive* tone, — the Major LEADING TONE, making with *Ray* and *Fah* the weak Chord T.
LAH.
The SAD or *weeping* tone, —the Major SUBMEDIANT, making with *Doh* and *Me* the Chord L.
ME.
The STEADY or *calm* tone,—the Major MEDIANT, making with *Soh* and *Te* the rarely used Chord M.
RAY.
The ROUSING or *hopeful* tone, — the Major SUPERTONIC, making with *Fah* and *Lah* the Chord R,—in which case it is naturally sung a komma flatter, and may be distinguished as *Rah*.
DOH.
The STRONG or *firm* tone,—the Major TONIC, making with *Me* and *Soh* the Tonic Chord, the Chord D.
FAH.
The DESOLATE or *awe-inspiring* tone,—the Major SUBDOMINANT, making with *Lah* and *Doh*, the Subdominant Chord,—the Chord F.
NOTE.—*These proximate verbal descriptions of mental effect are only true of the tones of the scale when sung slowly—when the ear is filled with the key, and when the effect is not modified by harmony.*

Figure 12.3 Tonic Sol-Fa hand signs, John Curwen, The *Standard Course of Lessons & Exercises in the Tonic Sol-fa Method of Teaching Music*. London: Tonic Sol-Fa Agency, 1876, iv.

centripetal, unifying, convergent. To paraphrase Solis it is an object that has its roots in at least two different objects; or McCarty, an object that exists in the interstices of existing objects.

Anderstreben and the Interdisciplinary Musicological Subject

Curwen's interdisciplinary musical object may be forged by an ekphrastic (*aesthetic* or *imaginative*) presence but like 'The Butterfly' it also represents the locus of considerable (disciplinary) movement. Whether or not as disciplines all arts aspire to the condition of musicology, the Victorian musicological subject is disciplinarily polygamous because the musical object represents an experiential fullness sentiently impossible in other disciplines. Walter Pater explains that fact by invoking the word 'anderstreben', literally anders-streben – other-seeking:

> what German critics term as *Anders-streben* – a partial alienation from its own limitations, through which the arts are able, not indeed to supply the place of each other, but reciprocally to lend each other new forces . . . Thus, again, sculpture aspires out of the hard limitation of pure form towards colour, or its equivalent; poetry also, in many ways, finding guidance from the other arts, the analogy between a Greek tragedy and a work of Greek sculpture, between a sonnet and a relief, of French poetry generally with the art of engraving, being more than mere figures of speech; and all the arts in common aspiring towards the principle of music; music being the typical, or ideally consummate art, the object of the great *Anders-streben* of all art, of all that is artistic, or partakes of artistic qualities.[68]

The Victorian musicological subject effectively proved anderstreben through a consistently self-empowering interdisciplinarity drawn from selective extra-disciplinary methodologies. When Herbert Spencer arrived at his theory of musical origins, for example, it represented the coalescence of a synthetic philosophy later systemized to include biology, psychology, sociology, and ethics, amongst other disciplines. Spencer's synthetic philosophy revolves around principles of evolutionary thought the same way that absolute music revolves around sonata form. Content is mapped onto form. That Spencer is a methodological absolutist is apparent in his positively contrapuntal disciplinary treatment of music. Music may have originated in the 'physiological deduction' of impassioned speech (biology); it may be effected by 'mental energy' (psychology) and manifest 'a product of civilization' (sociology); and it may indeed be 'the chief media of sympathy' (ethics),[69] but through the 'other-seeking' of anderstreben the musicological subject produces a musical object escaping its limitations by reciprocally lending itself and other disciplines new forces. At the same time it is indisputable that Spencer's anderstreben, combined with an ekphrastic predilection, partly anticipated and contributed to the creation of musicology as a Victorian interdiscipline – an interdiscipline that 'embraces other areas of thought'; an interdiscipline that bridges.[70] Spencer claims rather emphatically that music is a product of civilization, for example, but implicitly – if the tenets of musical sympathy are to be believed – that civilization is also a product of music. The point is that Spencer's intellectual traffic flows both ways across the disciplinary bridges.

In fact the disciplinary bridges flow in more than two ways because Victorian disciplines intersect prolifically, and especially, with musicology. Partly, Victorian musicology's 'other-seeking' is due to the fact that it in tandem with developments in university education (particularly in the science of acoustics) it was also informed by years of professionally regulated teaching in conservatoires. By the time the Musical Association was founded in 1874 the Royal Academy of Music was already over fifty years old. The intersection of theory and practice is obviated in Spottiswoode's repeated proclamation of parity between theory and practice. The society should include 'persons interested both in the theory and practice of Music . . . the foremost Musicians, theoretical as well as practical'. The convergence of theory and practice inscribed Victorian musicology with an interdisciplinary motivation to cross-purpose the musical object methodologically as a genuine site of universal relativity. Thus, the Victorian musicological subject sought disciplinary connections with systemic, not merely aesthetic, implications for the late Victorian musical object. A good example of this is *Style in Musical Art* (1911) by C. Hubert H. Parry, composer, musicologist, and ardent Spencerian. Parry cloaks the classical symphony in Spencerian evolutionary language:

> In such slow steps of development the same law of progress is found as elsewhere; simple combinations first, and the more complex combinations as, step by step, men mastered the methods upon which they could be dealt with. Progress is always towards the more decisive differentiation, and it is surely is nowhere more conspicuously shown than in the story of orchestral music; beginning with a simple group of a few instruments, which were but inadequately used in respect of obtaining from each their appropriate ministrations, and then proceeding by constant addition of instruments which enhanced the possibilities of expression and colour, and by finding out how to amalgamate their idiosyncrasies into a composite and convincing whole.[71]

Parry does more than synthesize Spencer synthesizing evolution, however; he brings scientific theory into the realm of musicological practice, and musicological practice into compositional theory. As a composer himself Parry is both theoretician and practitioner, embodying in music his evolutionary compositional theory in practice. Jeremy Dibble gives us a glimpse of the closeness of the relationship in a description of the trio movement of Parry's Piano Quartet (1879) anticipating his later evolutionary sentiments: 'Parry succeeds in fashioning protracted, self-developing thematic paragraphs together with a series of broad, cumulative climaxes, and these are further enhanced by the sense of continuity created by the avoidance of full closes'.[72]

As a musicological subject Parry's theorist-practitioner is a common feature of an interdiscipline 'unifying', as McCarty suggests, 'perspective on what happens at the intersection of two or more fields'. But musicology not only unifies disparate fields in the way anderstreben reciprocally lends each discipline new forces; uniquely amongst the arts it can also lend its musical object an ekphrasis converting disciplinary thought (evolution) into musical sound (composition). Ekphrastic anderstreben occurs across a range of compositional types inflected by disciplinary predispositions and predilections. It may seem self-evident that as interdisciplinary musical objects Victorian hymns, for example, often embody in musical composition the very same characteristics they represent in theology. In current musicology that concept is called Music Theology, and is typified by works that interrogate and problematize their disciplinary episteme.[73] But the Victorians got there first. 'Abide with me' (text, 1847; music, 1861), for example, is veritably programmatic in the way it portrays the transient nature of life through a series of falling and lengthening melodic motifs, but it also recapitulates dogmatic theological principles like the eternal immutability of God and the Incarnation of Jesus Christ: in hymns as in the theology they embody 'Christ himself was synonymous with a figuration or metaphor of "the Church"'.[74] Conversely, music can inform theology – even theology reflecting scientific concepts of design: 'The correlations of Music are so many and so perfect', John Harrington Edwards suggests, 'that that of themselves they prove a Supreme creative mind'.[75]

Edwards not only expresses what many musicologists felt, he does it in a manner Victorians would have recognized methodologically; by using music to express theology (and theology to express science) the musical object and the musicological subject become reciprocally augmented in a way which echoes and magnifies the truth of incarnational doctrine. As this suggests, whether connecting theology, science, or other disciplines to musicology the Victorian musicologist was acutely aware of the recapitulatory capability a critical hermeneutic like anderstreben produces for interdisciplinarity. Victorian music philosopher and evolutionary spokesperson Joseph Goddard exemplifies this awareness in *The Rise of Music* (1908) when as a scientist he claims that

> the present work is not a history of music in the ordinary sense, but rather a tracing of the organic unfolding of the musical art. At the same time it presents a perspective of both the history and constitutions of music, in which history is seen to elucidate theory, and theory, history.[76]

Whether or not it is history in the ordinary sense, as anderstreben *The Rise of Music* typifies Victorian disciplinary reciprocality. If [music] history can elucidate theory and theory [music] history, then musicology had come of age, and by definition had become a true interdiscipline existing in the interstices of the existing fields.

Conclusion

Pater and Goddard would have probably enjoyed one another's company, so similar are their interdisciplinary approaches. Using music as a model, both aim to collapse theory and practice by breaking down the relationship of matter and form. Goddard and many other Victorian musicologists, like C. Hubert H. Parry, William Wallace, and Peter Maurice; educationists like John Curwen and Henry Keatley Moore; and theorists like Herbert Spencer and Charles Darwin do this by using the same organic properties they observe in musical objects to inform their methodologies.[77] Pater does this by expressing anderstreben through the technique of ekphrasis. Using those techniques Victorian musicology became an interdiscipline by collapsing distinctions between the objects it studied (matter) and the structure it was given by subjects studying them (form). In so doing, Victorian musicology went beyond the more limited bridge-building between two disciplines illustrated by the classics and theology (Chapter 9), autobiography and evolutionary psychology (Chapter 8), and the novel and the sciences (Chapter 11).

This is not altogether different from what disciplines do today: disciplines seek other disciplines to answer questions about themselves, and the result is an interdiscipline which bridges disciplines. But is this result an intrinsic feature of disciplinary behaviour, or is it unique to Victorian musicology? If it is unique why did Victorian musicology interdisciplinarize when all other disciplines of the time seem to begin crystallizing into the academic disciplines we recognize now? And if today modern disciplines all gravitate ineluctably towards interdisciplinarity is it not unreasonable to describe Victorian musicology as the first modern discipline? Helen Small may provide an answer to these admittedly rhetorical questions, if only partially and implicitly: not all disciplines interdisciplinarize in the same way, for the same reason or to the same extent. The humanities, she says, 'study the meaning-making practices of human culture, past and present, focussing on interpretation and critical evaluation, primarily in terms of the individual response and with an ineliminable element of subjectivity'.[78] Small hits the nail on the head: subjectivity. The humanities are prey to subjectivity in a way unmatched in the sciences because every object they study – every work of art they study – is studied specifically for its individuality. There are, in other words, no repeatable 'experiments' in the humanities. Unless technologically replicated every object the humanities study (today or historically) is designed to produce a manifestly different object. Even if an experiment in the broadest sense the artistic object is by its nature a study in plenitude, and music, according to Pater, the most plenitudinous of all artistic objects. Does music represent an apogee as an art or discipline, therefore? Certainly Walter Pater believed it, because like so many other Victorians he believed in music's transcendental plenitude.[79] An interdiscipline is not unlike plenitude, of course; whether contemporary or modern the fullest interdiscipline will presumably strive ineluctably for the greatest interdisciplinarity. Sheila Jasanoff suggests this when she defines two types of interdiscipline: a new 'interdiscipline' as coming into being 'principally through exchanges amongst scholars already belonging to one or another established disciplinary community and trained in its forms or reasoning and research practices'; and an '*inter*discipline',

> an interdependent disciplinary formation situated among other disciplines. Such a field may come into being through topical exploration and theoretical or methodological innovation as well as through exchange, coalescing into an autonomous island of knowledge-making with its own native habits of production and trading.[80]

Whether or not they are genuinely different is a matter of philosophical debate, but one thing is certain, both interdisciplines (interdiscipline and *inter*discipline) receive inverted commas of subjectivity, and the inverted commas are an epistemic give-away. Like the idea of a specimen type in evolutionary thinking, the very concept of an interdiscipline is ontologically unstable, caught between theory and practice, matter and form, absolute and relative, unity and diversity, science and religion. The specimen type may be taxonomically fixed, but no natural object subject to the laws of evolution can be said to be truly 'fixed' in position. Like the specimen type, an interdiscipline is a conceptual convenience for something we do not fully understand and never will, because it exceeds our imagination's ability to grasp its plenitude. We can at least observe its manifestation and origins in Victorian musicological practice, for example, and perhaps this is where future research should concentrate its efforts – identifying where in Victorian culture we find it operating; how it functions and why it behaves the way it does. Perhaps that will help us bridge to the threshold of the present, where a true interdiscipline bridges both time and space, arts and sciences.

Notes

1 'Interdiscipline', *Oxford English Dictionary*, http://www.oed.com.ezphost.dur.ac.uk/view/Entry/243540?rskey=cqn4Se&result=1#eid12528631, accessed March 20, 2017.

2 The term has certainly appeared from 1964, as *Interdiscipline*, the title of the journal of the Gandhian Institute of Studies. See also Edward Quinn, *Interdiscipline: A Reader in Psychology, Sociology, and Literature* (New York: Free Press, 1972); Yogendra Pal Singh, Udai Narain Pareek and D. R. Arora, *Diffusion of an Interdiscipline: Social Sciences in Agricultural Education*

(Delhi: New Heights for Indian Society of Extension, 1974); J. Leeds Polytechnic (author), *Interdiscipline* (Leeds: The University Photography Service, [1970–1979]); Mayone Stycos, *Demography as an Interdiscipline* (Brunswick, PA: Transaction Publishers, 1987/1989); Mary Snell-Hornby, Franz Pöchhacker and Klaus Kaindl, eds., *Translation Studies: An Interdiscipline* (Amsterdam and Philadelphia, PA: J. Benjamins, 1994); see also https://en.wikipedia.org/wiki/Interdiscipline, accessed February 2, 2017.

3 Walter Pater, 'The School of Giorgione', in *The Renaissance: Studies in Art and Poetry*, ed. Adam Phillips (Oxford and New York: Oxford University Press, 1986), 86.

4 *J Mayone Stycos, ed.,* Demography as an Interdiscipline *(New Brunswick, NJ: Transactions Publishers, 1989), vii.*

5 S. W. Littlejohn, 'An Overview of Contributions to Human Communication Theory from Other Disciplines', in *Human Communication Theory: Comparative Essays*, ed. F. E. X. Dance (New York: Harper & Row, 1982), 246.

6 Willard McCarty, 'Humanities Computing as Interdiscipline', A Seminar in the Series, "Is Humanities Computing an Academic Discipline?", held under the auspices of the Institute for Advanced Technology in the Humanities (IATH), at the University of Virginia, Guy Fawkes Day 1999. (Ver. October 13, 1999; rev. October 14, October 15; October 22, 1999), http://www.iath.virginia.edu/hcs/mccarty.html, accessed January 22, 2016.

7 Willard McCarty, 'Looking Through an Unknown, Remembered Gate: Millennial Speculations on Humanities Computing', *Interdisciplinary Science Reviews* 26/3 (Autumn 2001), 173–182, http://www.mccarty.org.uk/essays/McCarty,%20Through%20an%20unknown%20remembered%20gate.pdf, accessed January 22, 2016.

8 Jerry A. Jacobs, *In Defence of Disciplines: Interdisciplinarity and Specialization in the Research University* (Chicago and London: University of Chicago Press, 2013), 6.

9 Jacobs, *In Defence of Disciplines*, 28.

10 Julie Thompson Klein, 'A Taxonomy of Interdisciplinarity', in *The Oxford Handbook of Interdisciplinarity*, eds. Robert Frodeman, Julie Thompson Klein and Carl Mitcham (Oxford: Oxford University Press, 2010), 15–30, on 16.

11 Steve Fuller, 'Deviant Interdisciplinarity', in *Oxford Handbook of Interdisciplinarity*, eds. Julie Thompson Klein and Carl Mitcham (Oxford: Oxford University Press, 2010), 50–64, on 50.

12 See Gillian Beer, Malcolm Bowie and Beate Perrey (eds.), *In(ter)discipline: New Languages for Criticism* (London: Legenda, 2007).

13 Peter Szendy, 'Echoing the 'Mortal Ear': Orfeo's Indiscipline', in *In(ter)discipline: New Languages for Criticism*, eds. Gillian Beer, Malcolm Bowie and Beate Perry (London: Legenda, 2007), 63–66, on 66.

14 Gabriel Solis, 'Thoughts on an Interdiscipline: Music Theory, Analysis, and Social Theory', *Ethnomusicology* 56/3 (Fall 2012), 530–554, on 551.

15 Wolfgang Krohn, 'Interdisciplinary Cases and Disciplinary Knowledge—Epistemic Challenges of Interdisciplinary Research', *Oxford Handbook of Interdisciplinarity*, eds. Robert Frodeman et al. (Oxford: Oxford University Press), 31–49, on 33.

16 McCarty, 'Looking Through an Unknown, Remembered Gate'.

17 Christopher Small, *Musicking: The Meanings of Performing and Listening* (Middletown, CT: Wesleyan University Press, 1998), 2.

18 John Blacking, *How Musical Is Man?* (Seattle and London: University of Washington Press, 1973/2000), 32.

19 Herbert Spencer, 'The Origin and Function of Music (1857)', in *Literary Style and Music*, ed. Herbert Spencer (New York: Philosophical Library, 1951), 60–61.
20 Spencer, 'The Origin and Function of Music', 73–74.
21 George Shoobridge Carr, *Social Evolution and the Evolution of Socialism: A Critical Essay* (London: W. Stewart & Co., 1895), 37.
22 John Fiske, *Outlines of Cosmic Philosophy, Based on the Doctrine of Evolution, with Criticism on the Positive Philosophy*, 2 vols. (London: Macmillan & Co., 1874), vol. 2, 201.
23 Thomas Dixon, *The Invention of Altruism: Making Moral Meanings in Victorian Britain* (Oxford: Oxford University Press, 2008), 196–197.
24 Herbert Spencer, *The Principles of Psychology*, 2nd edn., 2 vols. (New York: D. Appleton & Co., 1870/1873), vol. 2, 612.
25 See Kate Distin, *The Selfish Meme: A Critical Reassessment* (Cambridge: Cambridge University Press, 2005).
26 See Bennett Zon, 'Spencer, Sympathy and the Oxford School of Music Criticism', in *British Musical Criticism 1850–1950*, eds. Jeremy Dibble and Julian Horton (Woodbridge: Boydell and Brewer, 2018).
27 Herbert Spencer, 'Religion: A Retrospect and Prospect', *Nineteenth Century* 15 (January 1884), 12.
28 Herbert Spencer (*First Principles*), cited in F. Howard Collins, *An Epitome of the Synthetic Philosophy* (London and Edinburgh: Williams and Norgate, 1894), 63.
29 The Rev. George T. Ladd, *Lectures on the Unknown God of Herbert Spencer. And the Promise and Potency of Prof. Tyndall* (Milwaukee, NJ: I. L. Hauser, 1900), 24.
30 Herbert Spencer, *First Principles*, 6th edn. (London: Williams and Norgate, 1862/1908), 94; 106.
31 Charles Darwin, *The Descent of Man, and Selection in Relation to Sex*, 2 vols. (London: John Murray, 1871), vol. 2, 336.
32 Roger Scruton, 'Programme Music', *Oxford Music Online*, accessed November 25, 2016.
33 Eduard Hanslick and Gustav Cohen (trans.), *The Beautiful in Music: A Contribution the Revisal of Musical Aesthetics* (London: Novello and Co, Ltd., and New York: H. W. Gray Co., 1891), 45.
34 See for example Paul Barnes, 'Franz Liszt and the Sacramental Bridge: Music as Theology of Presence', http://www.paulbarnes.net/pdfs/lisztsacramentalbridge.pdf; and Paul Merrick, *Revolution and Religion in the Music of Liszt* (Cambridge: Cambridge University Press, 1987).
35 Franz Liszt, Berlioz und seine 'Harold-Symphonie' (1855), cited in Mark Evan Bonds, *Absolute Music: The History of an Idea* (New York: Oxford University Press, 2014), 211.
36 William Spottiswoode, 'Letter, Addressed by William Spottiswoode, Esq., M.A., F.R.S., to Some Leading Members of the Musical and Scientific World, Originated this Association (8 April 1874)', *Proceedings of the Musical Association* 1 (1874–1875), iii.
37 Willard McCarty, 'Humanities Computing as Interdiscipline'.
38 S. W. Littlejohn, 'An Overview of Contributions to Human Communication Theory from other Disciplines', 246.
39 McCarty, 'Looking Through an Unknown, Remembered Gate'.
40 See Ruth Barton, 'An Influential Set of Chaps': The X-Club and Royal Society Politics 1864–1885', *The British Journal for the History of Science* 23/1 (March 1990), 53–81.

41 Jacobs, *In Defense of Disciplines*, 28.
42 Rosemary Golding, *Music and Academia in Victorian Britain* (Farnham: Ashgate, 2013), 4. See also Jamie Kassler, 'The Royal Institution Music Lectures, 1800–1831': A Preliminary Study', *Royal Musical Association Research Chronicle Volume* 29 (1983–1985), 61.
43 Peter Maurice, *What Shall We Do with Music? A Letter to the Rt. H., The Earl Derby: Chancellor of the University of Oxford* (London: G. H. Davison, 1856), 12–13.
44 Maurice, *What Shall We Do with Music?*, 9.
45 Ibid., 16; 11.
46 Ibid., 14.
47 Bernard Lightman, *Victorian Popularizers of Science: Designing Nature for New Audiences* (Chicago and London: University of Chicago Press, 2007), 2–3.
48 See Bernard Lightman and Bennett Zon, *Evolution and Victorian Culture* (Cambridge: Cambridge University Press, 2014).
49 Lightman, *Victorian Popularizers of Science*, 125–126.
50 Annie Carrie, *The Wonders of Common Things*, n.d., cited in Lightman, *Victorian Popularizers of Science*, 125.
51 William Wallace, *The Threshold of Music: An Inquiry Into the Development of the Musical Sense* (London: Macmillan and Co., Ltd., 1908), 2; 1.
52 Pater, 'The School of Giorgione', 86.
53 Mark Evan Bonds, *Absolute Music: The History of an Idea* (Oxford: Oxford University Press, 2014), 273. See for example Patricia Herzog, 'The Condition to Which All Art Aspires: Reflections on Pater on Music', *British Journal of Aesthetics* 36/2 (April 1996), 125.
54 Pater, 'School of Giorgione', 88.
55 Lydia Goehr, 'How to Do More with Words: Two Views of (Musical) Ekphrasis', *British Journal of Aesthetics* 50/4 (October 2010), 389.
56 Pater, 'School of Giorgione', 71.
57 Goehr, 'How to Do More with Words', 14.
58 Ibid.
59 Spencer, 'The Origin and Function of Music', 59.
60 Charles Darwin, *The Descent of Man, and Selection in Relation to Sex*, 2 vols. (London: John Murray, 1871), vol. 2, 336.
61 Richard M. Doyle, *Darwin's Pharmacy: Sex, Plants, and the Evolution of the Noösphere* (Seattle, WA: University of Washington Press, 2011), 141.
62 Bennett Zon, *Evolution and Victorian Musical Culture* (Cambridge: Cambridge University Press, 2017).
63 Charles Louis Hett, *A Dictionary of Bird Notes, To Which Is Appended a Glossary of Popular Local and Old-Fashioned Synonyms of British Birds* (Brigg: Jackson's Marketplace, 1898), 17.
64 Henry Keatley Moore, *The Child's Pianoforte Book: Being a First Year's Course at the Pianoforte* (London: W. Swan Sonnenschein & Co., 1880?), 77.
65 Friedrich Froebel, *Froebel's Chief Writings on Education Rendered Into English*, trans. S. S. F. Fletcher and J. Welton (London: Edward Arnold, 1912), 153, 176.
66 John Curwen, *Independent Magazine* (1842), 23, cited in Bernarr Rainbow, *The Land Without Music: Musical Education in England 1800–1860 and Its Continental Antecedents* (London: Novello and Co., Ltd, 1967), 148.
67 W. J. T. Mitchell, *Picture Theory: Essays on Verbal and Visual Representation* (Chicago and London: University of Chicago Press, 1994), 5.
68 Pater, 'School of Giorgione', 85–86.

69 Spencer, 'Origin and Function of Music', 52, 59, 68, 74.
70 McCarty, 'Looking Through an Unknown, Remembered Gate'.
71 C. Hubert H. Parry, *Style in Musical Art* (London: Macmillan and Co., Ltd., 1911), 84.
72 Jeremy Dibble, *C. Hubert H. Parry: His Life and Music* (Oxford: Clarendon Press, 1992), 168.
73 See for example, Jon Michael Spencer, *Theological Music: Introduction to Theomusicology* (Westport, CT: Greenwood Press, 1991); Don Saliers, *Music and Theology* (Nashville, TN: Abingdon Press, 2007); or Maeve Louise Heaney VDMF, *Music as Theology: What Music Has to Say about the Word* (Eugene, OR: Pickwick Publications, 2012).
74 Joseph Harper, 'Towards an Understanding of Tractarian Hymnody: A Critical Appraisal of the Interaction between Theology, Poetry and Music in Anglican Hymnody between 1840 and 1900' (PhD diss., Durham University, 2010), 13.
75 John Harrington Edwards, *God and Music* (New York: The Baker & Taylor Co., 1903), 99.
76 Joseph Goddard, *The Rise of Music: Being a Careful Enquiry Into the Development of the Art from Its Primitive Puttings Forth in Egypt and Assyria to Its Triumphant Consummation in Modern Effect* (London: William Reeves, 1908), xv.
77 See for example Solie, Ruth, 'Melody and the Historiography of Music', *Journal of the History of Ideas* 43/2 (April–June 1982), 297–308.
78 Helen Small, *The Value of the Humanities* (Oxford: Oxford University Press, 2013), 23.
79 David Deutsch, *British Literature and Classical Music: Cultural Contexts 1870–1945* (London: Bloomsbury, 2015), 19.
80 Sheila Jasanoff, 'A Field of Its Own: The Emergence of Science and Technology Studies', in *Oxford Handbook of Interdisciplinarity*, eds. Robert Frodeman, Julie Thompson Klein and Carl Mitcham (Oxford: Oxford University Press, 2010), 192–193.

Conclusion

Metapatterns, Metadisciplines

Bernard Lightman and Bennett Zon

When Rens Bod invokes the term 'metapattern' to describe the culmination of disciplinary knowledge he might well have had the Victorians in mind.[1] Certainly they would have appreciated – or recognized – the quest for underlying, or first, principles. The Metaphysical Society, for example, that most Victorian of debating societies, was devoted to the search for first principles. Founded in 1869 at the instigation of James Knowles (editor of the *Contemporary Review* and then of the *Nineteenth Century*), the Society was a private club that met throughout the 1870s. Building on the tradition of the Cambridge Apostles, they elected talented members from all disciplines with diverse political and religious backgrounds: bishops, one cardinal, philosophers, men of science, literary figures, and politicians all joined. The Society included in its sixty-two members many of the leading intellectual figures of the period, such as T. H. Huxley, William Gladstone, Walter Bagehot, Henry Edward Manning, John Ruskin, and Alfred Lord Tennyson. Their shared goal, never realized, was to reach a consensus on the principles underlying the most important issues of the day, the logic of the physical and social sciences, the universality and personal identity of the soul, the existence and personality of God, the nature of conscience, and the grounds for belief in a system of morality.[2]

What the Metaphysical Society exemplified in practice Herbert Spencer exemplified in theory: 'this law of organic progress', Spencer opines,

> is the law of all progress. Whether it be in the development of the Earth, in the development of Life upon its surface, the development of Society, of Government, of Manufactures, of Commerce, or Language, Literature, Science, Art, this same evolution of the simple into the complex, through a process of continuous differentiation, holds throughout. From the earliest traceable cosmical changes down to the latest results of civilization, we shall find that the transformation of the homogeneous into the heterogeneous, is that in which all Progress essentially consists.[3]

When the founding father of metapatterns Gregory Bateson defines metapattern he merely updates Spencer: a metapattern is 'a pattern of patterns. It is that metapattern which defines the vast generalization that, indeed, *it is patterns which connect*'.[4] Bateson's student Tylor Volk is even more similar: a metapattern is 'a pattern so wide-flung that it appears throughout the spectrum of reality: in clouds, rivers, and planets; in cells, organisms, and ecosystems; in art, architecture, and politics'.[5] This is not to diminish Bateson or Volk's importance but to suggest that the very idea of a metapattern is a Victorian concept the Victorians applied to themselves and their world. At its worst the Victorian evolutionary metapattern is what George Eliot ventriloquizes in the mouth of Casaubon as a 'key to all mythologies';[6] at its best, arguably, what Scottish philosopher Alexander Bain calls 'the principle of Universal Relativity'.[7] This may prove that the quest to identify metapatterns may be 'a continuous tradition'[8] according to Bods, but *Victorian Culture and the Origin of Disciplines* espouses an alternative approach by focussing on characteristics affecting mechanisms of disciplinary change. Far from observing neatly organized metapatterns, we see history producing only Darwin's incontestably 'tangled bank'; the tangled bank is our metapattern, if in principle we subscribe to metapatterns at all.

The characteristics affecting mechanisms of disciplinary change are many and varied, but *Victorian Culture and the Origin of Disciplines* brings them into high relief by focussing on change created by 'disciplinary selection', if you will, rather than the implicitly hierarchical relativity produced by metapatterns, Victorian, or otherwise. Bateson himself provides the answer. When rationalizing asymmetry in the size of a crab's claws he describes them as 'embodying similar relations between parts. Never quantities, always shapes, forms, and relations. This was, indeed, something that characterized the crab as a member of *creatura*, a living thing'.[9] For Bateson these characteristics – shape, form, relation – *are* metapatterns, but critically for us they are also metapatterns of a *living thing*. For the contributors to *Victorian Culture and the Origin of Disciplines* a discipline is exactly that – a *creatura*, a living thing characterized by shape, form, and relation. By shape Bateson refers to a creature's proportions, and later what he calls its '*contextual shaping*' (i.e., grammar);[10] so too with disciplines, if by proportion we mean the particular attributes of its disciplinary shape and by grammar we signify the study of its language that deals with 'the relations of words in the sentence, and with the rules for employing these in accordance with established usage'.[11]

When, for example, eminent Victorian ornithologist Alfred Newton describes the avian forebrain as being 'subdivided into the thalamencephelon and into the cerebral hemispheres'[12] he adopts specialist disciplinary (biological) language but his reader may have been an educated amateur and the dictionary itself an agent of those characteristics of authorship, authority, and audience Bernard Lightman invokes to define the shape of Victorian popularization.[13] Seemingly antithetical, specialization, and popularization can, in other words, combine to form the same discipline's shape, broadly imagined. The popularization of archaeology in journals and newspapers, for instance, shaped the formation of it as a discipline (see Chapter 7). Tyndall, for one, is emphatic about it: 'It has been said by its opponents that science divorces itself from literature; but the statement, like so many others, arises from a lack of knowledge'.[14] Tyndall is a perfect example of how disciplines were shaped by both would-be professionals extolling specialization and by popularizers who interpreted the significance of contemporary scientific theories to a broad reading audience. The same can be said of his close friend Huxley, often seen as an aggressive proponent of specialization and influential advocate of the creation of 'biology' as a discipline, as well as one of the preeminent popularizers of the nineteenth century. As Lightman has argued, 'The development of "professional" and "popular" science in adjacent, and sometimes even overlapping spaces' led to important zones of mutual influence.[15] It is perhaps this complicated relationship between popularization and professionalization that contributed to the remarkable fluidity and transformation of disciplines in this period. Shaped and reshaped by the grammars of professionalization and popularization, the Victorian disciplines were anything but stable. Even the oldest and seemingly most secure disciplines, such as mathematics, were not exempt from radical renovation (see Chapter 10).

If Victorian disciplines acquire their shape through grammar, they also acquire it through the processes that give them form. Bateson remarks, for example, that 'Language is itself a *form* [author's italics] of communication. The structure of the input must somehow be reflected in the structure of the output'.[16] And so too with disciplines; their form is defined by the selective processes that led to them – processes initiated and influenced by the existence and creation of societies, journals, and universities. Whether it was the establishment of the Imperial Society of Dance Teachers in 1904 (see Chapter 2) or the founding of the British Association for the Advancement of Science in 1831 (see Chapter 1), societies gave disciplines a form around which their practitioners could organize. The *Magazine of Nature History* (see Chapter 5) provided a focal point for the growth of natural history while the scandal surrounding the *Anthropological Review* (see Chapter 6) was the catalyst for a new evolutionary direction for anthropology guided by T. H. Huxley and his friends. Finally, the role of the tripos system at Oxford and Cambridge in the development of the classics and theology (see Chapter 9), the establishment of art history chairs in universities (see Chapter 3), and the key contributions of the Manchester school of history to the formation of a new historical discipline based on specialization driven by research (see Chapter 4) all attest to the powerful impact of processes on the organization of knowledge.

But if shape and form are crucial, so is the significance of relation between disciplines, or what Bateson describes ubiquitously as the metapattern of relation, or the relation between parts. Victorian disciplines, neé interdisciplines, are congenitally and inveterately dialogic, even when dialogue appears fraught – in the case of religion and science, for example. The interpenetration of the literary genre of autobiography, Darwinian evolution, and child psychology moulded each other in significant ways (see Chapter 8). Not only did literature and scientific disciplines interact, novelists like George Eliot presented an interdisciplinary ideal in her work to critique the narrowness of scientific specialists like Huxley (see Chapter 11). Similarly, musicology provided an interdisciplinary model for all disciplines to emulate (see Chapter 12).

Implicitly, the structure of *Victorian Culture and the Origin of Disciplines*, and its emphasis on shape, form, and relation, raises an important epistemic question for disciplinarity more broadly than the Victorian version alone: is 'disciplinary selection' intrinsically deconstructive if it leads ineluctably to interdisciplinarity and the diffusion of specialized disciplinary identity? Can disciplines lead to metadisciplines in the same way patterns lead to metapatterns, and if so what exactly would a metadiscipline be? Is a metadiscipline the same as an interdiscipline? If 'disciplinary selection' is intrinsically deconstructive disciplinarily, it can only be 'deconstructive' in the same sense in which evolution through natural selection gradually changes the existential identity of *creatura*, to use Bateson's term. To this extent the evolution of disciplines is an inherently stochastic, random, and unpredictable process, as Bateson suggests of thought itself: 'thought resembles evolution in being a stochastic process'.[17] Victorian – and subsequent – disciplines would seem to confirm this to be true, but whether 'disciplinary selection' produces metadisciplines in the same way 'pattern selection' produces metapatterns is an altogether different taxonomical proposition. If there are such things as metadisciplines surely they are not even greater disciplines but in fact what we call today by the appellation university. John Henry Newman's definition is suggestive:

> A University, I should lay down, by its very name professes to teach universal knowledge: Theology is surely a branch of knowledge: how then is it possible for it to profess all branches of knowledge, and yet to exclude from the subjects of its teaching one which, to say the least, is as important and as large as any of them? I do not see that either premiss of this argument is open to exception. As to the range of University teaching, certainly the very name of University is inconsistent with restrictions of any kind.[18]

If then universities are metadisciplines by any other name, perhaps this – in the *creatura* of the university – is where we should begin searching for the origin of Victorian disciplines. But then, as Newman claims, universities are themselves merely disciplinary conduits to help us 'to prepare for the world',[19] and as our contributors roundly prove, universities are not alone in shaping the dynamic evolutionary metapattern of

Victorian disciplines. So many factors produce the tangled bank of disciplinary history – the 'endless forms most beautiful and most wonderful',[20] to quote Darwin – too many factors for any one set of authors to define through disciplines themselves in a constant state of disciplinary evolution.

Notes

1 Rens Bod, *A New History of the Humanities: The Search for Principles and Patterns from Antiquity to the Present* (Oxford: Oxford University Press, 2013), 6.
2 Metaphysical Society, Minute book: manuscript, 1869–1880. MS Eng 1061 (2 vols.), Houghton library, Harvard University, Cambridge, MA, vol. 1, p. 1. See also Catherine Marshall, Bernard Lightman, and Richard England (eds.), *The Papers of the Metaphysical Society 1869–1880. A Critical Edition*, 3 vols. (Oxford: Oxford University Press, 2015).
3 Herbert Spencer, 'Progress: Its Law and Cause', *Humboldt Library of Popular Science Literature* 17/1 (1882), 234.
4 Gregory Bateson, *Mind and Nature: A Necessary Unity* (New York: E. P. Dutton, 1979), 11.
5 Tylor Volk, *Metapatterns Across Space, Time, and Mind* (New York: Columbia University Press, 1995), 8.
6 Martin N. Raitiere, *The Complicity of Friends: How George Eliot, G. H. Lewes and John Hughlings-Jackson Encoded Herbert Spencer's Secret* (Lewisburg, PA: Bucknell University Press, 2012), 149.
7 Alexander Bain, (*Logic*, 2 vols., 1870), as cited in Christopher Herbert, *Victorian Relativity: Radical Thought and Scientific Discovery* (Chicago and London: University of Chicago Press, 2001), 45.
8 Bod, *New History of the Humanities*, 7.
9 Bateson, *Mind and Nature*, 9.
10 Ibid., 12, 17.
11 'Grammar', *Oxford English Dictionary*, http://www.oed.com.ezphost.dur.ac.uk/view/Entry/80574?rskey=qY1nqj&result=1#eid, accessed January 26, 2019.
12 Alfred Newton, *A Dictionary of Birds* (London: Adam and Charles Black, 1893–1896), 51.
13 Bernard Lightman, *Victorian Popularizers of Science: Designing Nature for New Audiences* (Chicago and London: University of Chicago Press, 2007), 10.
14 John Tyndall, 'The Belfast Address', *Fragments of Science*, 8th edn., 2 vols. (London: Longmans, Green, and Co., 1892), vol. 2, 198.
15 Lightman, *Victorian Popularizers of Science*, 495.
16 Bateson, *Mind and Nature*, 17.
17 Ibid., 19.
18 John Henry Newman, Discourse 2, 'Theology as a Branch of Knowledge', *The Idea of a University* (1852 and 1858) (London: Longmans, Green and Co., 1907), http://www.newmanreader.org/works/idea/discourse2.html, accessed February 1, 2019.
19 Newman, Discourse 9, *Idea of a University*.
20 Charles Darwin, *On the Origin of Species by Means of Natural Selection, Or the Preservation, of Favoured Races in the Struggle for Life* (London: John Murray, 1859), 490.

Select Bibliography of Scholarly Works on the Victorian Disciplines

Anderson, Amanda, and Joseph Valente, eds. *Disciplinarity at the Fin de Siècle*. Princeton, NJ: Princeton University Press, 2002.

Augstein, H. F. *James Cowles Prichard's Anthropology: Remaking the Science of Man in Early Nineteenth-Century Britain*. Amsterdam: Rodopi B.V., 1999.

Boehm, Katharina. *Charles Dickens and the Sciences of Childhood: Popular Medicine, Child Health, and Victorian Culture*. Basingstoke: Palgrave Macmillan, 2013.

Bremner, G. A., and Jonathan Conlin, eds. *Making History: Edward Augustus Freeman and Victorian Cultural Politics*. Oxford: Oxford University Press for the British Academy, 2015.

Briggs, Asa. 'History and the Social Sciences', in *A History of the University in Europe*, ed. Walter Rüegg. Cambridge: Cambridge University Press, 2004, vol. III, 459–492.

Buckland, Theresa Hill. 'Crompton's Campaign: The Professionalisation of Dance Pedagogy in Late Victorian England', *Dance Research* 25/1 (2007), 1–34.

Buckland, Theresa Jill. *Society Dancing: Fashionable Bodies in England, 1870–1920*. Basingstoke, Hampshire: Palgrave Macmillan, 2011.

Daunton, Martin, ed. *The Organisation of Knowledge in Victorian Britain*. Oxford: Oxford University Press, 2005.

Farber, Paul Lawrence. *Finding Order in Nature: The Naturalist Tradition from Linnaeus to E. O. Wilson*. Baltimore and London: Johns Hopkins University Press, 2000.

Golding, Rosemary. *Music and Academia in Victorian Britain*. Farnham, Surry: Ashgate, 2013.

Gray, Jeremy. 'The Nineteenth Century Revolution in Mathematical Ontology', in *Revolutions in Mathematics*, ed. Donald Gillies. New York: Oxford University Press, 1992, 226–248.

Helmreich, Anne. *Nature's Truth: Photography, Painting, and Science in Victorian Britain*. University Park, PA: Penn State University Press, 2016.

Heringman, Noah. *Sciences of Antiquity: Romantic Antiquarianism, Natural History, and Knowledge Work*. Oxford: Oxford University Press, 2013.

Hesketh, Ian. *The Science of History in Victorian Britain*. London: Pickering & Chatto, 2011.

Heyck, T. W. *The Transformation of Intellectual Life in Victorian England*. New York: St. Martin's Press, 1982.

Levine, Philippa. *The Amateur and the Professional: Antiquarians, Historians and Archaeologists in Victorian England 1838–1886*. Cambridge: Cambridge University Press, 1986.
Mansfield, Elizabeth, ed. *Art History and Its Institutions: Foundations of a Discipline*. New York and London: Routledge Press, 2002.
Morell, Jack, and Arnold Thackray. *Gentlemen of Science: Early Years of the British Association for the Advancement of Science*. Oxford: Clarendon Press, 1981.
Rehbock, P. F. *The Philosophical Naturalists: Themes in Early Nineteenth-Century British Biology*. Madison, WI: University of Wisconsin Press, 1983.
Richards, Joan L. *Mathematical Visions: The Pursuit of Geometry in Victorian England*. Boston/New York: Academic Press, Harcourt Brace Jovanovich, 1988.
Schnapp, A. *The Discovery of the Past: The Origins of Archaeology*. London: British Museum Press, 1996.
Sera-Shriar, E. *The Making of British Anthropology, 1813–1871*. London: Picking & Chatto, 2013.
Shuttleworth, Sally. 'Inventing A Discipline: Autobiography and the Science of Child Study in the 1890s', *Comparative Critical Studies* 2/2 (2005), 143–163.
Slee, Peter R. H. *Learning and a Liberal Education: The Study of Modern History in the Universities of Oxford, Cambridge and Manchester 1800–1914*. Manchester: Manchester University Press, 1986.
Soffer, Reba N. 'The Development of Disciplines in the Modern English University', *The Historical Journal* 31/4 (1988), 933–946.
Soffer, Reba N. *Discipline and Power: The University, History, and the Making of an English Elite, 1870–1939*. Stanford, CA: Stanford University Press, 1994.
Stocking, G. W. *Victorian Anthropology*. New York, NY: The Free Press, 1987.
Stray, C. *Classics Transformed: Schools, Universities and Society in England, 1830–1960*. Oxford: Clarendon Press, 1998.
Stroumsa, G. *A New Science: The Discovery of Religion in the Age of Reason*. Cambridge, MA: Harvard University Press, 2010.
Turner, J. *Philology: The Forgotten Origin of Modern Humanities*. Princeton, NJ: Princeton University Press, 2014.
Valenza, Robin. *Literature, Language, and the Rise of the Intellectual Disciplines in Britain*. Cambridge: Cambridge University Press, 2009.
Yeo, Richard. 'Reading Encyclopedias: Science and the Organization of Knowledge in British Dictionaries of Arts and Sciences, 1730–1850', *Isis* 82/1 (March 1991), 24–49.

Index

For Product Safety Concerns and Information please contact our EU representative GPSR@taylorandfrancis.com
Taylor & Francis Verlag GmbH, Kaufingerstraße 24, 80331 München, Germany

www.ingramcontent.com/pod-product-compliance
Lightning Source LLC
Chambersburg PA
CBHW071158100726
47908CB00002B/422
9781032240930